ELEMENTARY GERMAN

Third Edition

ELEMENTARY GERMAN

Third Edition

Fred L. Fehling
The University of Iowa

Wolfgang Paulsen

Sigrid Bauschinger

Albert M. Reh
University of Massachusetts

VAN NOSTRAND REINHOLD COMPANY

New York Cincinnati Toronto London Melbourne

Van Nostrand Reinhold Company Regional Offices:
Cincinnati   New York   Chicago   Millbrae   Dallas

Van Nostrand Reinhold Company International Offices:
London   Toronto   Melbourne

Published by Van Nostrand Reinhold Company
450 West 33rd Street, New York, N.Y.   10001

Published simultaneously in Canada by
Van Nostrand Reinhold, Ltd.

10   9   8   7   6   5   4   3   2   1

Preface

The Third Edition of *Elementary German* represents a thorough revision of the previous edition. We have reviewed and revised the basic presentation, replaced many of the lesson texts, and brought the whole up to date. Most of the exercises are either new or thoroughly revised. We have prepared a separate *Workbook/Laboratory Manual*, and a new tape program will also be available.

The original authors invited two younger colleagues to participate in this revision. Sigrid Bauschinger and Albert M. Reh brought to their task varied teaching experience and a fresh outlook. Their energy, intelligence, and enthusiasm contributed much to the new edition, which in a preliminary form was tested for one year at the University of Massachusetts at Amherst.

We have maintained the basic organization of the Second Edition, which proved eminently successful:

LESSON TEXTS

The reading material in the book has received perhaps the greatest attention, since we feel that it has always constituted its special strength. Many of the old texts have been replaced by more relevant new ones, emphasizing biographical and—through the biographical—cultural interest. All purely anecdotal material has been removed. Directly following each text, *Fragen* provide opportunity for comprehension testing. Wherever possible, additional reading material has been inserted as a first section of the exercises. New vocabulary necessary to these passages has been added as visible page notes. The use of these supplementary texts will depend on the amount of time available in the course.

VOCABULARY

The lesson vocabularies have been thoroughly integrated with the lesson materials, the reading texts, and the exercises. Many of the words are cognates; training the student to recognize them seems to us an important step toward the mastery of the language. In the first six lessons, cognates are listed separately in order to direct the student's attention to the close relationship between English and German words. From Aufgabe 7 on, the student is encouraged to infer meanings of easily recognized cognates on his own. In order to aid the student in acquiring a better understanding of the structure of some German words, especially compounds, brief sections on word formation and on distinctions between words have been added where these seemed appropriate. In order to promote the mastery of strong verbs, groups of such verbs appearing in the text follow each Wortschatz beginning with Aufgabe 12. We are convinced that learning the most important strong verbs in small doses is the most realistic way of acquiring a working knowledge of them.

GRAMMATICAL TERMS

We have retained the brief explanations of grammatical terms. Experience has shown that many students come to us with a minimum of training in grammatical thinking. This section has been carefully checked for accuracy, pertinence, and conciseness.

GRAMMAR

The sequence in which the grammatical material is presented has been retained essentially from the previous edition, but several chapters have been completely or partly rewritten. Most drastically changed was the presentation of nouns, modal auxiliaries, sentence structure, and the subjunctive. More modern techniques seemed called for here. In addition, we paired those cases (chiefly nominative and accusative) whose forms are most closely related.

A beginning book must deal with the problem of presenting the grammar systematically without impairing the natural flow of the language. Every text, no matter how simple, requires explanation for more than just one or two grammatical problems. We therefore concluded that it was preferable to introduce the student right away to a few grammatical points of high frequency that are to be more fully explained in later chapters. When the text was used in mimeographed form, the results seemed to bear out our contention.

Wherever possible, we have retained the "helpful hints" as an aid in emphasizing special points. Material that seemed useful but not of primary importance is again relegated to footnotes, but such additional information is kept to a minimum. Each instructor may decide how much of it is useful to him in his class work.

RECAPITULATION OF MAIN POINTS

The grammatical presentation in each lesson is again followed by a "Recapitulation of the Main Points." These summaries are intended less for class use than as a guide for the student in his own review work.

EXERCISES

Special care has been taken that each lesson contain enough exercise material to suit most needs. The material offered is divided into sections for

"Practice in Reading and Writing" and "Oral Exercises." We suggest that the instructor decide for himself what to use and what to omit. He may also adjust his use of exercises to the needs and abilities of particular students. Ideally, one lesson should be covered in one week. Additional oral drills are provided in the separate *Workbook/Laboratory Manual*, which is designed for class and home practice and for work in language laboratories. A tape program supplements the *Manual*.

REVIEW

At regular intervals, review sections are inserted for those who wish to make use of them. They should be especially useful to the student in checking up on his own achievements.

READING GERMAN—SPEAKING GERMAN

The long-simmering disagreement between advocates of reading ability and those who consider it more important to learn to speak a foreign language has lost a great deal of its controversial nature. It has become apparent that a middle course is the most desirable, and it is this middle course that *Elementary German, Third Edition* takes. Although we have provided much audio-lingual practice (both in the text and workbook) and a tape program, we frankly admit that our primary interest remains that of taking the student to as high a level of reading proficiency as is possible in a one-year course. In the last instance, it is up to the instructor and his students to decide how much time they wish to devote to acquiring an adequate ability to express themselves in the language. The successful acquisition of speaking ability depends, as experience has shown, on the imaginativeness with which the work in the language lab is devised. Language learning should be fun and entertaining, and above all, it should be stimulating. We hope that this new edition of a book that has had so much time to prove itself will serve this purpose.

Information about the tapes accompanying *Elementary German, Third Edition*, appears inside the front cover of this book.

Contents

ELEMENTARY GERMAN

Third Edition

Introduction

1 THE ALPHABET

GERMAN FORM		GERMAN NAME	ROMAN FORM	
a	𝔄	ah	a	A
b	𝔅	bay (bé)	b	B
c	ℭ	tsay (tsé)	c	C
d	𝔇	day (dé)	d	D
e	𝔈	ay (é)	e	E
f	𝔉	eff	f	F
g	𝔊	gay (gué)	g	G
h	ℌ	hah	h	H
i	ℑ	ee	i	I
j	𝔍	yott	j	J
k	𝔎	kah	k	K
l	𝔏	ell	l	L
m	𝔐	emm	m	M
n	𝔑	enn	n	N
o	𝔒	oh	o	O
p	𝔓	pay (pé)	p	P
q	𝔔	koo	q	Q
r	ℜ	err (trilled *r!*)	r	R
ſ, s	𝔖	ess	s	S
t	𝔗	tay (té)	t	T
u	𝔘	oo	u	U
v	𝔙	fow (*as in* fowl)	v	V
w	𝔚	vay (vé)	w	W
x	𝔛	icks	x	X
y	𝔜	üpsilon (*see ü, below*)	y	Y
z	ℨ	tset	z	Z

1

2 COMPOUND CONSONANTS

ch	tsay-hah	ch
ck	tsay-kah	ck
ß	ess-tset	ß
tz	tay-tset	tz

3 PRONUNCIATION

Modern language instruction stresses the importance of the spoken word. Read every word out loud and read every sentence clearly. Reading out loud is an important aid in learning.

German is rather easy to pronounce, once you have mastered the basic sounds.

Note the following:

a. Initial consonants begin a word or syllable; medial consonants stand between vowels; final consonants end a word or syllable.

b. Vowels are either long or short: long when followed by a single consonant, short when followed by two or more consonants. Double vowels have the same quality as single vowels. An **h** following a vowel is silent and tends to lengthen the vowel.

e. The voice stress generally falls on the first or stem syllable. In the Introduction and in the lesson and end vocabularies, variations will be indicated by a dot for short vowels and by a dash for long vowels and diphthongs.

d. Except for the lengthening **h,** there are no silent letters in German.

Vowels

a	(long, like *a* in *father*):	**Abraham, Abel, Adam, Baal, Baden-Baden**
a	(short; also pronounced *ah,* but very short, like *o* in *hot*):	**alt** *old*, **kalt** *cold*, **Mann** *man*, **Ball** *ball*, **Das** ist **alles.** *That is all*.
e	(long, like *a* in *mate*, but without the glide to *i* in English):	**Meter, Peter, Greta, Bremen**
e	(short, as in *bet*):	**Bett** *bed*, **nett** *nice*, **Emma. Emma** ist **nett**
e	(final, like *a* in *comma*):	**Lampe** *lamp*, **Dame** *lady*, **Katze** *cat*

i	(long, like *ee* in *bee*):	**Bibel** *bible*, **Tiger, Liter, Berlin, Kino** *movies*, **Mine** *mine*, **Titel** *title*
i	(short, like *i* in *bit*):	**bitter, bitte** *please*, **immer** *always*
o	(long, like *o* in *hole*, but without the glide to *u* in English):	**holen** *fetch*, **Boot** *boat*, **Robert, Brot** *bread*, **groß** *big*, **rot** *red*, **Moos** *moss*
o	(short, like *o* in *occur*):	**Bonn, offen** *open*, **Gott** *God*, **kommen** *come*
u	(long, like *oo* in *boot*):	**gut** *good*, **Blut** *blood*, **Mut** *courage*, **Flut** *flood*, **Lukas**
u	(short, like *oo* in *foot*):	**Futter** *fodder*, **Mutter** *mother*, **Butter, unter** *under*, **bunt** *colorful*

Diphthongs

ai	(like *y* in *my*):	**Mai** *May*, **Main** (*name of river*), **Maier, Kaiser** *emperor*
ay	(like *y* in *my*):	**Mayer, Bayer** *Bavarian*
au	(like *ou* in *house*):	**Haus** *house*, **Maus** *mouse*, **raus** *out*, **laut** *loud*, **Laus** *louse*
ei	(like *i* in *mine*):	**mein** *my*, **dein** *your*, **nein** *no*, **klein** *small*, **Klein aber mein.** *Small but mine.*
ie	(long *i*, like *ee* in *bee*):	**Bier** *beer*, **hier** *here*, **Tier** *animal*, **Lieder** *songs*

Note: you can easily remember the difference between **ie** and **ei** by taking only the second letter in the diphthong and pronouncing it as in English: **ei** is *i*, **ie** is *ee*.

-ie	(final, in a few words, is pronounced *ye*):	**Familie, Lilie** *lily*, **Linie** *line*, **Serie** *series*
eu	(like *oy* in *toy*):	**teuer** *expensive*, **treu** *faithful*, **neu** *new*, **Feuer** *fire*, **deutsch** *German*, **Europa** *Europe*

Umlaut

Umlaut is a term used to describe a change in the sound of the vowels **a, o, u, au,** as indicated by two dots over the letter: **ä, ö, ü, äu:**

ä	(long, like *a* in *care*):	**dänisch** *Danish*, **Bäder** *baths*, **Räder** *wheels*
ä	(short, like *e* in *hen*):	**Händel, Hände** *hands*, **Männer** *men*

ö	(long, like *a* in *ale*, but pronounced with rounded lips):	**Öl** *oil;* **schön** *beautiful* (try to pronounce "shane" with rounded lips). Now say: **Flöte** *flute*, **Töne** *tones*, **Römer** *Roman*
ö	(short, like *e* in *get* but pronounced with rounded lips):	**Götter** *gods* (try to pronounce "getter" with rounded lips). Now say: **Göttingen**, **Hölle** *hell*, **Köln** *Cologne*, **Röntgen**
ü	(long, like *ee*, but pronounced with rounded lips):	**kühl** *cool* (try to pronounce "keel" with rounded lips). Now pronounce: **Führer** *leader*, **fühlen** *feel*, **Tübingen**
ü	(short, like *i* in *hit*, but pronounced with rounded lips):	**Hütte** *hut*, **Mütter** *mothers*, **Küste** *coast*, **küssen** *kiss*
äu	(like *oy* in *boy*):	**Läuse** *lice*, **Häuser** *houses*, **Mäuse** *mice*, **Fräulein** *Miss*

Consonants

b	(like English in initial or medial position; when final in a word or syllable, like *p*):	**ab** *off*, **ob** *whether*, **Grab** *grave*, **Leib** *body*, **Liebling** *darling*
c	(before **a, o, u, au,** or consonant, like *k*):	**Café, Coburg, Creme**
	(before **ä, e, i,** like *ts*):	**Cäsar, Cicero, Celsius**
ch	(after—and in a few words before—e and i, after umlauted vowels, and after **l, n, r: ich**-sound. It is produced by saying "ick" but allowing the air to pass over the arched tongue:	**ich** *I*, **mich** *me*, **dich** *you*, **Milch** *milk*, **Chemie** *chemistry*, **China**, **Kelch** *chalice*, **manchmal** *sometimes*, **durch** *through*
	(after **a, o, u, au: ach**-sound):	**ach** *oh*, **Bach** *brook*, **hoch** *high*, **Buch** *book*, **auch** *also*
	(in some words of Greek origin, like *k*):	**Charakter, Chor** *chorus*, **Chlor** *chlorine*
	(in some words of French origin, like *sh*):	**Chef** *boss*, **Chauffeur**
chs	(like *ks*):	**Lachs** (*smoked*) *salmon*, **Sachsen** *Saxony*, **sechs** *six*
d	(like English *d* in initial or medial position; in final position like *t*):	**Hand** *hand*, **Land** *land, country*, **Bad** *bath*, **Bild** *picture*, **und** *and*

g	(initial or medial like in English *get*, but never as in *general;* in final position like *k*):	**Tag** *day*, **weg** *away*
	(in words of French origin, like the second *g* in *garage*):	**Gage** *wages*, **Garage**, **Page** *page boy*, **Gen<u>ie</u>** *genius*
-ig	(final, like **ich**):	**billig** *cheap*, **selig** *blessed*, **heilig** *holy*
	(if a vowel follows the suffix **-ig, g** is hardened to *g* as in *get*):	**heilige** Nacht *holy night*
h	(silent after a vowel, but lengthens it):	**Fehler** *mistake*
	(initial, like English *h*):	**Haushalt** *household*
j	(like *y* in *yes*):	**ja** *yes*, **Jahr** *year*, **Jacke** *jacket*, **jung** *young*, **Junge** *boy*
kn	(both **k** and **n** are pronounced):	**Knie** *knee*, **Knabe** *boy*, **Knopf** *button*
l	(like *l* in *eleven*):	**all, Ball, Milch** *milk*
ng	(as in *singer*, NEVER as in *finger*):	**Finger, Englisch, England**
pf	(both **p** and **f** are pronounced):	**Pfanne** *pan*, **Pferd** *horse*, **Pfeffer** *pepper*, **Pfennig** *penny*
ps	(both **p** and **s** are pronounced):	**Psychologie, Psalm, pseudo-**
qu	(like English *kv*):	**Quelle** *spring, source*, **Qual** *torment*, **Quatsch** *nonsense*, **quitt** *quits*, **Quittung** *receipt*
r	(either by trilling the tip of the tongue against the front palate or by vibrating the uvula):	**rennen** *run*, **rot** *red*, **Herr** *gentleman*, **her<u>ein</u>!** *come in!*, **raus!** *get out!*
s	(initial or medial, like *z* in *zero*):	**sehen** *see*, **lesen** *read*, **Saar, Siegfried**
sp	(initially, pronounced as *shp*):	**spielen** *play*, **springen** *jump*, **Spanisch, Spengler, Sport**
st	(initially, pronounced as *sht*):	**Stein** *stone*, **Einstein, Stock** *stick*, **Stil** *style*, **Stickstoff** *nitrogen*
s	(final, as in *this*):	**Hans, dies** *this*, **das** *that*, **Karlsbad, Bismarck**
ss	(as in *this*):	**besser** *better*, **Kissen** *pillow*, **küssen** *kiss*
ß	(stands for **ss** after long vowels and diphthongs and in final position):	**heißen** *to be called*, **heiß** *hot*, **Fuß** *foot*, **naß** *wet*

sch	(pronounced like English *sh*):	**scheinen** *appear, shine*, **Schuh** *shoe*, **Schule** *school*, **Fisch** *fish*
th	(like *t;* **h** remains silent):	**Thema** *theme, subject*, **Theorie** *theory*, **Thomas**, **Theater** *theatre*, **Thermometer**
-tion	(like *tsyon*):	**Nation, national, Portion, Ration**
tz	(like *ts*):	**Platz** *place, seat*, **sitzen** *sit*, **Katze** *cat*
v	(like *f*):	**Vater** *father*, **viel** *much*, **Vogel** *bird*, **von** *from*, **Viertel** *quarter*, **Volk** *people*
	(In words of non-German origin, like English *v*):	**November, Venus, Villa**
w	(like *v*):	**was** *what*, **wer** *who*, **wo** *where*, **wie** *how*, **Wein** *wine*, **Wien** *Vienna*, **Wienerwurst** *Vienna sausage*, **Wagen** *wagon, car*, **Volkswagen**
y	(pronounced like **ü**, see above):	**Mythe** *myth*, **psychisch** *psychic*, **physisch** *physical*, **Physik** *physics*

4 GLOTTAL CATCH

Words or syllables beginning with an accented vowel are kept from running together by what is known as the glottal catch. To imitate the glottal catch, be careful to enunciate each word separately:

> **Mein armer Onkel!** *My poor uncle!*
> **Das ist alles.** *That is all.*

The glottal catch is applied even when words are written together:

> **überall** *everywhere*
> **das Postamt** *post office*

5 ACCENT

a. The main stress in German words generally falls on the stem or the first syllable:

> **Jeden Morgen lesen wir die Zeitung.**
> *Every morning we read the newspaper.*

b. Some prefixes and suffixes may carry the word accent; these will be discussed in detail later on. Examples:

<u>auf</u>machen   *to open*
zur<u>ü</u>ckkommen   *to come back*

c. Words of non-German origin are generally accented on the last syllable: **die Nati<u>o</u>n, der Stud<u>e</u>nt, die Universit<u>ä</u>t, das Pap<u>ie</u>r.**

6 CAPITALIZATION

a. German capitalizes all nouns and words used as nouns, the pronoun **Sie** (*you*) and its derivatives, and, of course, proper names:

Haben **Sie Ihren** neuen **Wagen** schon?   Was gibts **Neues?**
Do you have your new car already?   *What's new?*

b. The pronoun **du** (*you*) and its derivatives are generally capitalized in letters only.
c. The pronoun **ich** is capitalized only at the beginning of a sentence.
d. Adjectives denoting nationality are not capitalized: **die amerikanische Jugend** *American youth.*

7 PUNCTUATION

Note the following differences between English and German punctuation:

In general, commas are more numerous than in English. The comma is used in German:

a. to set off all dependent clauses:

Ich wußte nicht, daß er krank war.
I didn't know that he was sick.
Das Zimmer, das er mieten will, ist zu teuer.
The room he wants to rent is too expensive.
Wir wissen nicht, was er will.
We don't know what he wants.

b. to set off infinitive phrases preceded by objects or modifiers:

Ich hoffe, ihn bald zu sehen.
I hope to see him soon.

The exclamation point is generally used after an imperative:

Kommen Sie mit!   *Come along.*

8   USEFUL EXPRESSIONS

Sprechen Sie Deutsch?	*Do you speak German?*
Ja, ein bißchen.	*Yes, a little.*
Nein, kein bißchen.	*No, not a bit.*
Guten Tag!	*Hello.*
Wie geht es Ihnen?	*How do you do?*
Sehr gut, danke.	*Very well, thanks.*
Guten Morgen!	*Good morning.*
Guten Abend!	*Good evening.*
Gute Nacht!	*Good night.*
Auf Wiedersehen!	*Good-by.*
Bitte.	*Please.*
Danke schön.	*Thanks.*
Bitte sehr.	*You're welcome.*
Entschuldigen Sie!	*Excuse me.*
Was ist das?	*What is that?*
Wieviel kostet das?	*How much is that?*
Wie heißen Sie?	*What is your name?*
Ich heiße. . . .	*My name is. . . .*
Herr, Frau, Fräulein . . .	*Mr., Mrs., Miss . . .*
mein Herr, meine Herren	*sir, gentlemen*
Was ist los?	*What is the matter?*
Ich weiß nicht.	*I don't know.*
Aufgabe, Fragen, Wortschatz, Übungen	*Lesson, questions, vocabulary, exercises*

eins, zwei, drei, vier, fünf, sechs, sieben,   *1–22*
acht, neun, zehn, elf, zwölf, dreizehn,
vierzehn, fünfzehn, sechzehn, siebzehn,
achtzehn, neunzehn, zwanzig, einundzwanzig, zweiundzwanzig

1

Basic Sentence Structure;

Present Tense; Imperative

Hans lernt etwas

Hans und Fritz sind Freunde und besuchen dieselbe Universität. Sie studieren nicht dasselbe, aber sie beide lernen Deutsch. Und man lernt manchmal mehr, als[1] man studiert!

Nach der Deutschstunde stehen sie noch eine Weile im[2] Korridor der[3] Universität und reden miteinander.[4] Eine Studentin kommt, und Fritz zwinkert 5 mit den Augen.

„Nett, hm?" sagt er zu Hans.

„Sehr nett", antwortet Hans. Gute[5] Freunde verstehen einander ohne viele Worte.

„Guten Tag!" sagt Hans zu dem Mädchen. Aber das Mädchen antwortet 10 nicht und geht weiter.[6]

„Hübsch", sagt Hans, „aber nicht sehr freundlich."

„Und du bist freundlich, aber nicht sehr intelligent", sagt Fritz. „Man macht das anders. Warte, ich zeige dir, wie man das macht."

Eine zweite Studentin kommt. Fritz macht jetzt den zweiten Versuch. 15

1. **als** (after comparative) *than.* 2. **im** (= **in dem,** contraction) *in the.* 3. **der** (genitive of **die**) *of the.* 4. **miteinander** *with one another.* 5. **gute** (adjectives modifying nouns have certain endings, which will be discussed later on; for the time being simply disregard these endings.). 6. **geht weiter** *walks on.*

„Entschuldigen Sie", sagt er zu dem Mädchen. „Ist das Ihr Bleistift? Ich glaube, Sie haben ihn[7] eben verloren."[8]

„Oh, danke schön", antwortet das Mädchen und lächelt freundlich. „Das ist sehr nett von Ihnen",[9] und geht weiter, aber sehr langsam.

20   „Donnerwetter!"[10] sagt Hans. „Wer ist das?"

„Keine Ahnung", antwortet Fritz, „ich kenne sie[11] nicht. Und das war mein Bleistift. So macht man das!"

„Das war dein Bleistift? Gute Idee! Jetzt verstehe ich alles. Also, auf Wiedersehen."

25   „Gehst du in die Bibliothek?"

„Sei nicht so dumm", antwortet Hans, „ich kaufe mir[12] ein Dutzend Bleistifte."

7. **ihn** (here:) *it*.   8. **Sie haben . . . verloren** *you lost*.   9. **von Ihnen** *of you*.   10. **Donnerwetter!** (exclamation of surprise) gosh!   11. **sie** (here:) *her*.   12. **mir** (*for*) *myself*.

FRAGEN

1. Was sind Hans und Fritz?   2. Was besuchen sie?   3. Studieren sie dasselbe?
4. Was lernen sie beide?   5. Wo stehen sie nach der Deutschstunde und reden miteinander?   6. Wer kommt?   7. Was tut (*does*) Fritz?   8. Was sagt Fritz zu Hans?   9. Was antwortet Hans?   10. Wie verstehen gute Freunde einander?   11. Was sagt Hans zu dem Mädchen?   12. Was tut das Mädchen?
13. Was sagt Hans jetzt?   14. Was antwortet Fritz?   15. Wer kommt jetzt?
16. Was macht Fritz?   17. Was sagt Fritz zu dem Mädchen?   18. Was antwortet das Mädchen?   19. Was tut das Mädchen?   20. Was sagt Hans jetzt?
21. Was antwortet Fritz?   22. Kennt Fritz das Mädchen?   23. Geht Hans in die Bibliothek?   24. Was kauft Hans?

WORTSCHATZ

COGNATES[1]

alles	"all," everything	**dumm**	"dumb," stupid
danke (schön)	thanks (very much)	das **Dutzend,** –e[2]	dozen

[1] Cognates are German words closely related to their English equivalents. Here and in the next six lessons, we shall list separately the obvious cognates which occur in the reading material. It is good practice to train yourself to recognize such cognates. Read them aloud a few times, and you will find that you do not even have to make an effort to commit them to memory.

[2] Endings given after nouns indicate the nominative plural. Thus, the plural of **der Freund** is **die Freunde,** of **das Mädchen, die Mädchen.**

	finden	to find
der	**Freund,** –e	friend
	freundlich	friendly, in a friendly manner
	gut	good
die	**Id**ee**,** –n	idea
	intelligent	intelligent
	kommen	to come
der	**Korridor,** –e	corridor, hallway
	lernen	to learn
	machen	to make; to do
	sagen	to say
	so	so, thus, like this
die	**Stud**ent**in,** –nen	(girl) student, co-ed
	studieren	to study

der	**Tag,** –e	day
	Guten Tag!	"hello" (good morning, good afternoon, *etc.*, *according to the time of day; also* "good day" *when parting*)
	und	and
die	**Universit**ät**,** –en	university
	er, sie, es war	he, she, it was (*past tense of* **sein**)
	eine Weile	(for) a while
das	**Wort,** –e	word
	zu	to

VOCABULARY

	aber (*conj.*)	but
die	**Ahnung,** –en	inkling
	keine Ahnung!	no idea!
	also, . . .	well then, . . .
	anders	different(ly)
	antworten	to answer
	auch	also, too
die	**Aufgabe,** –n	lesson
das	**Auge,** –n	eye
	beide	both
	besuchen	to visit
die	**Biblioth**ek**,** –en	library
der	**Bleistift,** –e	pencil
	dein (*poss. adj.*)	your
	derselbe, dieselbe, dasselbe (*according to gender*)	the same
(das)	**Deutsch**	German (language)
die	**Deutschstunde,** –n	German lesson
	dir (*dat.*)	you, to you
	eben	just now
	einander	one another
	eins	one
	entschuldigen	to excuse
	etwas	something
	gehen	to go (on foot); to walk
	glauben	to believe
	heißen	to be called
	Wie heißt das Mädchen	What's the girl's name?
	hübsch	pretty
	Ihnen (*dat.*)	you, to you
	Ihr	your

	jetzt	now
	kaufen	to buy
	kein (*masc. and neuter*), **keine** (*fem.*)	no, not a, none
	kennen	to know; to be acquainted with
das	**Kind,** –er	child
	lächeln	to smile
	langsam	slow(ly)
das	**Mädchen,** –	girl
	manchmal	sometimes
	mehr	more
	mein	my
	mit	with
	nach	after
	nett	nice
	nicht	not
	noch	still
	nur	only
	ohne	without
	reden	to talk
	sehr	very
	sie	her
	stehen	to stand
	verstehen	to understand
der	**Versuch,** –e	attempt, experiment
	viele	many
	warten	to wait
	wer?	who?
	wie (?)	how (?)
	auf Wiedersehen!	good-by
	wo?	where?
	zeigen	to show
	zweite	second
	zwinkern	to wink

DISTINGUISH BETWEEN

wo? where?
wer? who?

GRAMMATICAL TERMS

1. A *verb* is a word which expresses action or a state of being: we *work;* he *is* rich; they *slept.*

2. The *tense* of a verb indicates the time of action:

Present tense:	he drives, is driving, does drive
Past tense:	he drove, was driving, did drive
Future tense:	he will drive, will be driving
Present perfect tense:	he has driven, has been driving
Past perfect tense:	he had driven, had been driving
Future perfect tense:	he will have driven, will have been driving

3. *Auxiliary verbs* are verbs which help to form the compound tenses (the future, present perfect, past perfect, future perfect) in the active and the passive voice: he *will* go, he *has* gone, he *was* killed, etc.

4. To *conjugate* a verb is to give the personal forms of a tense in order. Thus, the verb *to work* is conjugated in the present tense as follows:

SINGULAR		PLURAL	
1st person:	I work	*1st person:*	we work
2nd person:	you work	*2nd person:*	you work
3rd person:	he (she, it) works	*3rd person:*	they work

An ending added to a verb stem (he work*s*) is called a personal (or inflectional) ending.

5. Pronouns are words used in place of nouns:

the man—he	my wife—she
the book—it	the new car—it

The words *I, you, he, she, it, we, they* are called personal pronouns.

6. The infinitive is the unconjugated form of the verb, the "verb at rest." In dictionaries and vocabularies, the English infinitive is commonly identified by *to*, as in: *to work* (*to* is not, strictly speaking, a part of the infinitive).

7. The imperative is used when telling someone to do something or when giving a command: *Come! Go! Tell me!*

PRELIMINARY REMARK

When forming even simple sentences in another language, grammatical forms are likely to occur which cannot be discussed all at once. For our purpose now it is sufficient to call attention to the following:

der, die, das, den, etc. are various forms of the definite article; they all mean *the.*

BASIC SENTENCE CONSTRUCTION IN GERMAN

1. Word Order in Main Clauses

The positions of the various parts of a German main clause are not as rigid as in English.

In contrast to English, only the inflected verb has a fixed position, while most other parts of the main clause that are usually placed after the inflected verb may sometimes be placed in front of it.

The effect that such changes of position have will be discussed later. For the time being, you need only know that the inflected verb always takes the second position (II) and that—instead of the subject—an adverb, a prepositional phrase, or an object may precede the inflected verb. The subject then follows the inflected verb, usually directly after the verb.

Er		(II)		jetzt das Mädchen.	*He understands the girl now.*
Jetzt	}	**versteht**	{	er das Mädchen.	*Now he understands the girl.*
Das Mädchen				er jetzt.	*It is the girl whom he understands now.*

Note that "second position" does not mean that the inflected verb is the second word:

(II)

Nach der Deutschstunde **stehen** sie noch eine Weile im Korridor.

The coordinating conjunctions **und** (*and*), **aber** (*but*), **sondern** (*but*, after negative sentences), **oder** (*or*), **denn** (*for, because*) do not affect word order:

Denn er		(II)		jetzt das Mädchen.
Und jetzt	}	**versteht**	{	er das Mädchen.
Aber das Mädchen				er jetzt.

2. Word Order in Questions

In a question with an interrogative (**wer?, wie?, wo?,** etc.), the interrogative comes first, then the inflected verb, then usually the subject:

(II)

Wer **ist** dieses Mädchen?   *Who is this girl?*
Wie **macht** man das?   *How do you do that?*

In a question without an interrogative (when the answer is yes or no), the inflected verb comes first, and the subject usually follows immediately after it:

Gehst du in die Bibliothek?   *Are you going (in)to the library?*
Ist das dein Bleistift?   *Is that your pencil?*

3. Word Order in Commands

In commands the inflected verb comes first:

Antworte mir, Fritz!   *Answer me, Fritz!*

4. Word Order in Dependent Clauses

In contrast to English, the inflected verb stands last in dependent clauses:

Ich zeige dir, wie man das   **macht.**   *I will show you how to do that.*
Er sagt, daß sie sehr hübsch   **ist.**   *He says that she is very pretty.*

PRESENT TENSE

1. The German infinitive ends in **-en**, sometimes in **-n.**[1] By dropping this infinitive ending, the stem of the verb is obtained:

INFINITIVE		STEM
gehen	*to go*	**geh-**
glauben	*to believe*	**glaub-**

2. The personal pronouns in German are:

SINGULAR		PLURAL	
ich	*I*	**wir**	*we*
du	*you*	**ihr**	*you*
er	*he*	**sie**	*they*
sie	*she*		
es	*it*		
man	one, you (impersonal)		

---

[1] When the stem ends in **l** or **r: lächeln** *to smile,* **zwinkern** *to wink;* also **sein** *to be* and **tun** *to do.*

Sie is the pronoun used in conventional forms of address, singular and plural (see paragraph 5, below).

3. To form the present tense of a verb, add the present tense endings to the stem:

	SINGULAR			PLURAL
1st person	ich	glaube		wir	glauben
2nd person	du	glaubst	Sie glauben	ihr	glaubt
3rd person	er		(singular or plural)	sie	glauben
	sie	glaubt		
	es			
	man			

4. **Ich studiere** may mean: *I study, I am studying,* or *I do study.* German does not have progressive or emphatic verb forms. *They are studying* (or *do study*) *the same thing* is simply: **Sie studieren dasselbe.**

In translating from the German use the appropriate English verb form. The sentence context will indicate which form fits best:

Fritz redet jeden Tag mit dem Mädchen.	*Fritz talks to the girl every day.*
Fritz redet jetzt mit dem Mädchen.	*Fritz is talking to the girl now.*
Fritz redet mit dem Mädchen, aber nicht oft.	*Fritz does talk to the girl, but not often.*

5. German has two forms of address, the conventional form (singular and plural: **Sie,** always capitalized) and the familiar forms (singular: **du;** plural: **ihr**), which are generally used only when speaking to close friends, relatives, children, or animals. In case of doubt, use the **Sie**-form.

EXAMPLES

FAMILIAR	**Verstehst du** das, Fritz?	*Do you understand that, Fritz?*
	Versteht ihr das, Kinder?	*Do you understand that, children?*
CONVENTIONAL	**Verstehen Sie** das, Herr Schmidt?	*Do you understand that, Mr. Schmidt?*
	Verstehen Sie das, Herr Schmidt und Herr Braun?	*Do you understand that, Mr. Schmidt and Mr. Braun?*

6. If the stem of a verb ends in **d** or **t,** or when a succession of consanonts makes it difficult to pronounce the conjugated form (as it would be in: **du öffnst**), an **e** is inserted between the stem of the verb and the **st** or **t** of the ending:

EXAMPLES

	finden *to find* (stem ends in **d**)	**antworten** *to answer* (stem ends in **t**)	**öffnen** *to open* (stem ends in a succession of consonants)
ich	find**e**	antwort**e**	öffn**e**
du	find**est**	antwort**est**	öffn**est**
er (sie, es, man)	find**et**	antwort**et**	öffn**et**
wir	find**en**	antwort**en**	öffn**en**
ihr	find**et**	antwort**et**	öffn**et**
sie	find**en**	antwort**en**	öffn**en**
Sie	find**en**	antwort**en**	öffn**en**

7. If the stem of a verb ends in **s, ß, tz,** or **z** (sibilants or s-sounds), the second person singular drops the **s** of the ending **st,** leaving the forms of the second and third persons singular identical.

EXAMPLES

sitzen *to sit*	**heißen** *to be called*
ich sitze	ich heiße
du **sitzt**	du **heißt**
er **sitzt**[1]	er **heißt**

The **e** of the plural (and of the infinitive) ending **-en** is dropped if the stem of the verb ends in **l** or **r**. This change also applies to the verb **tun:**

EXAMPLES

lächeln *to smile*	**zwinkern** *to wink*	**tun** *to do*
wir **lächeln**	wir **zwinkern**	wir **tun**
sie **lächeln**	sie **zwinkern**	sie **tun**

8. The present tense of the auxiliary verbs **haben** (*to have*), **sein** (*to be*), and **werden** (*will*)[2] is slightly irregular:

	sein	**haben**	**werden**
ich	**bin**	**habe**	**werde**
du	**bist**	**hast**	**wirst**
er	**ist**	**hat**	**wird**
wir	**sind**	**haben**	**werden**
ihr	**seid**	**habt**	**werdet**
sie	**sind**	**haben**	**werden**
Sie	**sind**	**haben**	**werden**

[1] From here on, only the **er**-form will be given for the third person singular.
[2] **Werden** can also serve as independent verb meaning *to become, to get,* as in: **es wird warm** *it is getting warm.*

IMPERATIVE

1. If a command is addressed to a person to whom one would speak in the **du**-form, the singular familiar imperative is used. It is formed by adding the ending **-e** to the stem:

> **Sage** das nicht, Hans! *Don't say that Hans.*
> **Antworte** mir Fritz! *Answer me, Fritz.*

2. If a command is addressed to persons to whom one would speak in the **ihr**-form, the plural familiar imperative is used. It is formed by adding the ending **-t** (or **-et**) to the verb stem:

> **Sagt** das nicht, Kinder! *Don't say that children.*
> **Antwortet** mir, Kinder! *Answer me, children.*

3. If a command is addressed to a person or to persons to whom one would speak in the **Sie**-form, the conventional imperative is used. It is formed by adding the ending **-en** to the stem and by placing **Sie** after the verb, both in the singular and plural:

> **Sagen Sie** das nicht, Herr Schmidt!   *Don't say that, Mr. Schmidt.*
> **Sagen Sie** das nicht, Herr Braun und *Don't say that, Mr. Braun and Mr.*
>   Herr Schmidt!   *Schmidt.*

Note that the pronoun **Sie** in the conventional imperative has normally no equivalent in English.

4. A command in the first person plural is, strictly speaking, an admonition directed to a group of which the speaker is a part. It is formed by placing the pronoun **wir** after the appropriate verb form. English uses the phrase "let's":

> **Glauben wir** ihm! *Let's believe him.*
> **Gehen wir** in die Bibliothek! *Let's go to the library.*

5. The imperative of **sein** (*to be*) is irregular: **sei!, seid!, seien Sie!**

> FAMILIAR: **Sei** so gut Fritz, und **tu** das nicht!
>   *Please* (lit.: be so good) *Fritz,* (and) *don't do that!*
>   **Seid** so gut, Kinder, und **tut** das nicht!
>   *Please* (lit.: be so good) *children,* (and) *don't do that!*
>
> CONVENTIONAL: **Seien Sie** so gut, Herr Schmidt, und **tun Sie** das nicht!
>   *Please* (lit.: be so good) *Mr. Schmidt,* (and) *don't do that!*

FORMING QUESTIONS

1. To form a question, begin with the verb and place the subject after it:

Verstehst du das, Fritz?
Verstehen Sie das, Herr Schmidt?

2. As in English, interrogatives come first, and are followed immediately by the verb:

Was ist das?   *What is that?*
Wo bist du?   *Where are you?*

3. German questions are never formed with an auxiliary verb (such as *do* or *does* in English):

Kennen Sie sie?   *Do you know her?*
Studiert er Deutsch?   *Does he study German?*

RECAPITULATION OF MAIN POINTS

1. To form the present tense of a verb, drop the **-en** of the infinitive and add the personal endings to the stem:

ich . . . . e		wir . . . . en
du . . . . st	Sie . . . . en	ihr . . . . t
er	(singular or plural)	sie . . . . en
sie } . . . . t		
es		

2. German has neither progressive nor emphatic forms. **Ich gehe** may mean: *I go, I am going,* or *I do go.*

3. English *you* is rendered by **du, ihr,** or **Sie**: in familiar address, use **du** for the singular and **ihr** for the plural; in conventional address, singular and plural, use **Sie** (always capitalized).

4. Note that **sie** (not capitalized) may mean *she* or *they*, depending on the ending of the verb:

sie geht   *she goes*
sie gehen   *they go*

5. The German imperative is formed as follows:

In the singular familiar, add **e** to the stem: **sage!**
In the plural familiar, add **t** (sometimes **et**) to the stem: **sagt!**
In the conventional imperative, singular and plural, add **en** to the stem
   and follow the verb form with the pronoun **Sie: sagen Sie!**

The imperative in the first person plural is equivalent to "let's": **gehen wir**
let's go!

6. Simple questions which do not require an interrogative pronoun are
formed by placing the verb before the subject: **Gehst du?** An auxiliary
(such as English *do* or *does*) is never used in German: *Do you go?* **Gehst du?**
Geht ihr? Gehen Sie?

ÜBUNGEN

Practice in Reading and Writing

These and the following exercises are based on the vocabulary in each lesson.
Additional words used are immediately recognizable as cognates and are
listed in the end vocabulary.

A. *Read aloud and translate:*

1. Hans hat ein Dutzend Bleistifte. 2. Eine Studentin kommt. 3. „Entschuldigen Sie", sagt Hans, „hier ist Ihr Bleistift." 4. Aber das Mädchen
antwortet nicht. 5. Das Mädchen geht weiter, und Hans sagt: „Hübsch,
aber nicht sehr freundlich." 6. Eine zweite Studentin kommt. 7. „Entschuldigen Sie", sagt Fritz, „ist das Ihr Bleistift?" 8. „Danke schön", antwortet das Mädchen, „das ist sehr nett von Ihnen." 9. „Wer ist das?" sagt
Hans. 10. „Keine Ahnung", antwortet Fritz, „ich kenne sie nicht." 11. Das
Mädchen sagt: „Was studieren Sie?" 12. „Ich studiere Deutsch", antwortet
Hans. 13. „Sie studieren Deutsch? 14. Ich glaube, Sie haben ein Problem.
15. Was machen wir jetzt?" 16. Das Mädchen lächelt freundlich. 17. Dann
sagt sie: „Also, machen wir einen Versuch! 18. Ich heiße Elisabeth. 19. Und
wie heißen Sie?" 20. „Die Mädchen verstehen alles!" lacht Hans. „Gehen
Sie auch in die Bibliothek?"

B. *Translate and identify the verb forms:*

1. Gehen Sie in die Bibliothek? 2. Was hast du? 3. Was sagen Sie? 4. Was
sagen sie? 5. Was sagt sie? 6. Sie lächelt freundlich. 7. Kennen Sie sie?

8. Kennt sie Sie?   9. Es wird warm.   10. Gehst du in die Bibliothek?   11. Geht ihr manchmal in die Bibliothek?   12. Wir fragen sie sehr freundlich.   13. Lächeln Sie manchmal?   14. Er kauft ein Dutzend Bleistifte.   15. Was machst du in der Bibliothek?   16. Was antwortet ihr jetzt?   17. Wir gehen in die Universität.   18. Entschuldigen Sie, Herr Schmidt, kennen Sie die Studentin?   19. Was kauft ihr jetzt?   20. Seid ihr Freunde?   21. Lächelt er manchmal dumm?   22. Kennen Sie New York nicht?   23. Wartest du auf das Mädchen?   24. Wer macht den Versuch?   25. Ist sie intelligent?   26. Wir haben keine Ahnung.   27. Was sagst du zu der Idee?

C. *Translate and identify the imperative forms:*

1. Antwortet, Kinder!   2. Sei freundlich Hans!   3. Gehen Sie und kaufen Sie ein Dutzend Bleistifte!   4. Warten wir noch eine Weile!   5. Sag(e) das nicht!   6. Sagen Sie das nicht!   7. Antwortet nicht!   8. Seien Sie so gut und sagen Sie etwas!   9. Studiert Deutsch!   10. Sagen wir jetzt etwas!

D. *Distinguish between* sie *(she or they) and* Sie *(you):*

1. Was sagen sie da?   2. Was sagt sie da?   3. Was sagen Sie da?   4. Was antworten Sie?   5. Was antworten sie?   6. Was antwortet sie?   7. Wo kauft sie das?   8. Sie antworten nicht.   9. Wer sind sie?   10. Wer sind Sie?   11. Wer ist sie?   12. Was hat sie?   13. Was haben Sie?   14. Studieren sie Deutsch?   15. Sie gehen langsam.

E. *Translate:*

1. Where are you, Hans?   2. She is studying German.   3. They are walking very slowly.   4. It is getting warm.   5. Do they have pencils?   6. They ask, but I do not answer.   7. Are you coming, children?   8. Excuse me, I do not understand you.   9. Wait, children!   10. Wait, Mr. Schmidt!   11. What is she doing now?   12. Are they going now?   13. The girl doesn't understand Hans.   14. The girl smiles and says "Thank you!"   15. Where are the pencils?   16. Do you understand German, children?   17. We don't believe that.   18. What don't you believe?

Oral Exercises

F. *Change the sentences by putting the expressions in italics into the first position:*

EXAMPLE: Hans geht *nach der Deutschstunde in die Bibliothek.*
Nach der Deutschstunde geht Hans in die Bibliothek.
In die Bibliothek geht Hans nach der Deutschstunde.

1. Man macht *das so*.   2. Beide verstehen *jetzt das Problem*.   3. Hans wartet *eine Weile*.   4. Gute Freunde verstehen einander *ohne viele Worte*.   5. Fritz macht *jetzt den zweiten Versuch*.   6. Hans und Fritz stehen *eine Weile im Korridor der Universität*.

G. *Give the conventional imperative for the familiar forms listed on the left:*

1. Lache nicht!   Lachen Sie nicht!
2. Sei freundlich!
3. Kauft das nicht!
4. Entschuldige mich!
5. Entschuldigt mich!
6. Antworte, bitte!

H. *Change the conventional imperative on the left to familiar forms:*

1. Sagen Sie das nicht, Fritz!   Sage das nicht, Fritz!
2. Seien Sie nett, Anna!
3. Lächeln Sie bitte freundlich, Anna!
4. Entschuldigen Sie mich, Fritz!

I. *Begin the following sentences with* **Ich glaube, daß . . .**, *changing the word order:*

EXAMPLE: Hans und Fritz sind Freunde.
        Ich glaube, daß Hans und Fritz Freunde sind.

1. Sie besuchen dieselbe Universität.   2. Das Mädchen lächelt freundlich. 3. Das ist Ihr Bleistift.   4. Fritz kennt das Mädchen nicht.   5. Er versteht jetzt alles.   6. Er kauft ein Dutzend Bleistifte.   7. Er ist nicht so dumm. 8. Gute Freunde verstehen einander ohne viele Worte.

J. *Add the correct ending to the following verb forms:*

EXAMPLE: du versteh– = du verstehst

1. wir lächel– 2. du sag– 3. sie hab– 4. ich komm– 5. Anna studier– 6. Geh– Sie, Herr Schmidt? 7. Hans und Fritz antwort– 8. ihr glaub– 9. Anna sag– 10. Was sag– Sie? 11. er antwort– 12. ihr antwort– 13. Wo wart– sie? 14. Was ha– du? 15. Was öffn– er da? 16. Kenn– ihr sie? 17. Ich studier– Deutsch. 18. Wir kauf– etwas. 19. Komm– sie? 20. Lächel– das Mädchen?

K. *Change the following statements to questions:*

1. Du bist da. 2. Es wird warm.   3. Hans kennt Fritz.   4. Das Mädchen ist sehr nett.   5. Du hast etwas (*change* etwas *to* was?).   6. Ihr kommt nach Berlin.   7. Hans kennt das Mädchen sehr gut.

L. *Change the following pattern sentences by using the subjects given in the right-hand column. Follow the examples. Repeat the exercises until you can do them without hesitating.*

PATTERN	CUE
Du kennst das Mädchen. Ich kenne das Mädchen.	ich
Wir finden den Bleistift. Er findet den Bleistift.	er
1. Die Freunde besuchen die Universität.	ihr
2. Wir studieren dasselbe.	du
3. Die Studentin lernt Deutsch.	wir
4. Ich stehe im Korridor.	Hans und Fritz
5. Du sagst „Guten Tag".	er
6. Ihr antwortet nicht.	er
7. Wir reden jetzt.	du
8. Er sitzt in der Deutschstunde.	wir
9. Hans und Fritz gehen in die Bibliothek.	ich
10. Ich warte manchmal.	er
11. Wir entschuldigen Hans.	du
12. Hans und Fritz lächeln dumm.	er
13. Ich heiße Fritz.	du

M. *Continue in the same manner:*

PATTERN	CUE
1. Hans hat einen Bleistift.	wir
2. Die Studentin ist nett.	du

3. Ich habe eine Idee.   wir

4. Der Student wird freundlich.   ihr

5. Ich habe eine Idee.   Fritz und Hans

6. Die Studenten sind nett.   du

7. Fritz ist in der Bibliothek.   ich

8. Ich werde Student.   Hans

9. Die Studentin hat eine Deutschstunde.   wir

N. *Respond to the question using the correct pronoun and verb form.*

EXAMPLES:

Lernen Sie Deutsch?   Studiere ich dasselbe?
Ja ich lerne Deutsch.   Ja, Sie studieren dasselbe.
Und Hans?   Und Hans und Fritz?
Hans lernt auch Deutsch.   Hans und Fritz studieren auch dasselbe.

1. Verstehen Sie alles?   6. Mache ich das anders?
   Und die Studentin?   Und Hans?
2. Kaufe ich Bleistifte?   7. Kommen Sie jetzt?
   Und die Mädchen?   Und Hans und Fritz?
3. Sind Sie freundlich?   8. Gehe ich in die Bibliothek?
   Und Fritz?   Und die Studentin?
4. Lächele ich freundlich?   9. Warten Sie manchmal?
   Und Anna?   Und die Mädchen?
5. Lächeln Sie manchmal?   10. Kenne ich Fritz?
   Und die Studentinnen?   Und Hans?

2

Definite Article and Der-Words

Die Damen

Zwei Damen fahren mit der Eisenbahn nach Berlin. Die eine[1] Dame ist sehr dick, die andere ist sehr dünn. Der dicken Dame ist es sehr heiß, und der dünnen Dame ist es kalt. In der Ecke des Abteils sitzt ein Mann und raucht eine Zigarre, denn das Abteil ist ein Abteil für Raucher.

5   Alle drei sitzen und schweigen. Plötzlich schreit die dicke Dame: „Diese Hitze ist ja[2] furchtbar! Und dann der Rauch dieser Zigarre!" Sie öffnet das Fenster.

    Kalte Luft strömt ins[3] Abteil. Die dünne Dame zittert und ruft: „Ich friere furchtbar!" und schließt das Fenster wieder.

10   Jetzt ist die dicke Dame böse. „Kein Mensch erträgt[4] das!" ruft sie empört. „Ich ersticke hier." Und sie öffnet das Fenster wieder.

    Aber die dünne Dame jammert jetzt laut: „Ich hole mir[5] hier noch den Tod, o Gott!" Und sie schließt schnell das Fenster. Der Mann in der Ecke raucht ruhig seine Zigarre.

15   In diesem Augenblick kommt der Schaffner. „Was wünschen Sie, meine Damen?" fragt er freundlich.

1. **die eine** (*the*) *one*.   2. **ja** (in the middle of a sentence lends emphasis; equivalent to *isn't it* or *you know*).   3. **ins** (contraction for **in das**) *into the*.   4. **erträgt** (here:) *can stand*. 5. **mir** (lit., *for myself*).

„Ach,[6] Herr[7] Schaffner", sagt die dicke Dame, „helfen Sie mir. Ich ersticke in diesem Abteil. Diese Leute schließen immer wieder das Fenster."

„Und ich sterbe in der Kälte!" erklärt die dünne Dame.

Der Schaffner betrachtet ratlos das Fenster, dann die dicke Dame und schließlich die dünne Dame. Endlich fragt er den Mann in der Ecke: „Was tun wir denn[8] nun?"

„Ganz einfach", antwortet dieser. „Wir öffnen das Fenster weit, dann stirbt die eine Dame. Dann schließen wir das Fenster wieder, und die andere Dame erstickt. Und dann haben wir endlich Ruhe."

20

25

6. **Ach** (exclamation of distress) *Oh!*   7. **Herr** (lit., *Mr.;* in addressing a male person, German places **Herr** before another title).   8. **denn** (for emphasis in the middle of a question).

FRAGEN

1. Wohin (*where to*) fahren die Damen?   2. Wie ist die eine Dame?   3. Wie ist die andere Dame?   4. Wie ist es der dicken Dame?   5. Wie ist es der dünnen Dame?   6. Wer sitzt in der Ecke?   7. Was tut der Mann?   8. Was tun alle drei?   9. Was schreit die dicke Dame plötzlich?   10. Was tut sie? 11. Was tut die dünne Dame nun?   12. Wie wird die dicke Dame?   13. Was sagt sie empört?   14. Was tut sie?   15. Was tut jetzt die dünne Dame? 16. Was tut der Mann in der Ecke?   17. Wer kommt in diesem Augenblick? 18. Was fragt der Schaffner?   19. Wie fragt der Schaffner das?   20. Was antwortet die dicke Dame?   21. Und was antwortet die dünne Dame? 22. Was tut der Schaffner?   23. Was fragt der Schaffner den Mann in der Ecke?   24. Was antwortet der Mann?   25. Was haben wir schließlich?

WORTSCHATZ

COGNATES

die **Dame, –n**	lady	**hier**	here
Meine Damen!	Ladies!	**kalt**	cold
dann	then	die **Kälte**	cold (*low tempera-*
dick	thick, fat		*ture*)
drei	three	**laut**	loud
dünn	thin	der **Mann, ⸗er**	man
endlich	in the end, finally	**nun**	now
für (*w. acc.*)	for	**öffnen**	to open
der **Gott, ⸗er**	god	**sitzen**	to sit
helfen	to help	**strömen**	to stream

der **Tod**	death		die **Zigarre, –n**	cigar
weit	wide			

Note how frequently an English *th* corresponds to a **d** in the German cognate: **dann**—then, **dick**—thick, **dünn**—thin, **Tod**—death.

VOCABULARY

das **Abteil, –e**	compartment		der **Mensch, –en**	human being
ander	other, else		**kein Mensch**	nobody
der **Augenblick, –e**	moment		**mir** (*dat. of pers.*	me, to me
betrachten	to look at, watch		*pronoun* **ich**)	
böse	angry		**nach** (*referring*	to
denn	for, because		*to geogr.*)	
die **Ecke, –n**	corner		**noch**	yet
einfach	simple		**plötzlich**	suddenly
die **Eisenbahn, –en**	railroad		**ratlos**	perplexed
empört	outraged		der **Rauch**	smoke
erklären	to declare		**rauchen**	to smoke
ersticken	to suffocate		der **Raucher, –**	smoker
fahren	to travel		**rufen**	to call
das **Fenster, –**	window		die **Ruhe**	quiet, peace
fragen	to ask (*a question*)		**ruhig**	quiet(ly)
frieren	to freeze		der **Schaffner, –**	conductor
furchtbar	terrible, terribly		**schließen**	to close
ganz	quite		**schließlich**	finally
heiß	hot		**schnell**	quick(ly), fast
die **Hitze**	heat		**schreien**	to scream
holen	to fetch, get		**schweigen**	to be silent
immer	always		**sterben (vor)**	to die (of)
immer wieder	again and again		**er, sie, es**	he, she, it dies
jammern	to wail, complain		**stirbt**	
die **Leute** (*plural*)	people		**wieder**	again
			wünschen	to wish
die **Luft, ⸗e**	air		**zittern**	to tremble
			zwei	two

DISTINGUISH BETWEEN

dann (*then*) and **denn** (*for*); **dann** is an adverb, **denn** a conjunction.

endlich (*in the end, finally*) and **schließlich** (*finally*); **endlich** usually expresses a degree of impatience: **endlich kommt er** *finally* (*thank goodness!*) *he is coming.*

der Mensch (*human being, man*) and **der Mann** (*man*); **der Mensch** is a generic term and includes women!

GRAMMATICAL TERMS

1. The definite article in English is *the: the* man, *the* men.

2. In English, the article is not declined, that is, its forms do not change according to *case* (nominative, accusative, dative, genitive) or number (singular, plural). Instead, prepositions are used to indicate case relationships: the title *of* the book; he gave it *to* the boy.

3. Cases have the following basic functions in a sentence:

a. The *nominative* denotes the subject or a predicate noun (or pronoun) (used after verbs like *to be, to become, to remain*):

> *The man* gave the child a dime.
> *He* is *the teacher.*

To identify the subject (nominative) ask *who?* or *what?: Who* gave the child a dime? Answer: *The man* (subject).

b. The *accusative* denotes the direct object, that is, the noun (or pronoun) receiving the "direct" action of the verb:

> The man gave the child *a dime.*

To identify the direct object (accusative), ask *whom?* (or *what?*): *What* did he give the child? Answer: *a dime* (direct object, accusative).

c. The dative denotes the indirect object, that is, *to* or *for whom* something is done:

> The man gave *the child* a dime. He gave a dime *to the child.*

To identify the indirect object (dative) ask *to* (or *for*) *whom?: To whom* did he give a dime? Answer: *to the child* (indirect object, dative). The dative may also be the sole object after certain verbs. In German a sole dative occurs after certain verbs and with certain adjectives:

Er antwortet dem Schaffner.	*He answers the conductor.*
Wir glauben dem Kind.	*We believe the child.*
Sie hilft der Frau.	*She helps the woman.*
Der Dame ist es kalt.	*The lady is cold.*

d. The genitive most commonly denotes possession:

> *The child's* face brightened.

To identify the possessive (or genitive) case, ask *whose?: Whose* face brightened? Answer: *The child's* (possessive; genitive).

In English, the genitive (or possessive) may also be indicated by the preposition *of:* the face *of the child.*

The genitive can also be used as an object:

> The discussion *of the book* (objective genitive).

DEFINITE ARTICLE AND DER-WORDS

1. In German, the definite article varies in form according to gender (masculine, feminine, neuter), number, and case, depending on the noun with which it is used. In the plural the forms of the article in a given case are the same for all three genders:[1]

		SINGULAR		PLURAL		
	Masc.	Fem.	Neuter	(all genders)		
NOM.	der	die	das	die		the
ACC.	den	die	das	die		the
DAT.	dem	der	dem	den		to the
GEN.	des	der	des	der		of the

2. Whether a masculine, feminine, or neuter form of the article is used depends on the gender of the noun. Since this gender cannot generally be derived from the noun itself, the article is the simplest way of clearly identifying the gender. Therefore: Always learn a German noun together with its article: **der Professor, die Frage, das Leben.** You must know the gender of a noun before you can use it in context.

3. The following words are commonly called "**der**-words" because they are declined like the definite article:

dieser   *this, that*   **mancher**   (sing.) *many a,* (plural) *some*
jeder   (sing.) *each, every*   **solcher**[2]   (sing.) *such a,* (plural) *such*
        (plural) **alle** *all, all the*   **welcher**   *which, what*
jener   *that*

The declension of **dieser** is:

		SINGULAR		PLURAL
	Masculine	Feminine	Neuter	(all genders)
NOM.	dieser	diese	dieses (or dies)	diese
ACC.	diesen	diese	dieses (or dies)	diese
DAT.	diesem	dieser	diesem	diesen
GEN.	dieses[3]	dieser	dieses[3]	dieser

---

[1] In general, the article is used in German as in English. In a few situations, however, German uses it where English does not, as with the names of meals, metals, seasons, months, days of the week, and with abstract and generalized nouns: **Das Leben** ist kurz. *Life is short.* **Das Frühstück** ist auf dem Tisch. *Breakfast is on the table.* Occasionally, the article is used colloquially with proper names: **der Hans, die Grete; der Goethe.**

[2] **Solcher** is not used much in modern German in the singular.

[3] These genitive forms can never be shortened to **dies.**

DECLENSION OF NOUNS (PRELIMINARY REMARKS)

Nouns, like articles, vary in form according to case and number. Many nouns add certain endings to indicate particular case forms.

1. Most masculine and neuter nouns require the ending **-s** (or **-es**) in the genitive singular; **-es** is normally added when the noun consists of only one syllable (monosyllable).

In the following table, **der Onkel** (*uncle*) and **das Mädchen** (*girl*) have more than one syllable and hence add the ending **-s** in the genitive, while **der Mann** (*man*) and **das Kind** (*child*) are monosyllables and hence add **-es**. Masculine and neuter nouns of one syllable may add the ending **-e** in the dative singular:

	MASCULINE SINGULAR		NEUTER SINGULAR	
NOM.	der Onkel	der Mann	das Mädchen	das Kind
ACC.	den Onkel	den Mann	das Mädchen	das Kind
DAT.	dem Onkel	dem Mann(e)	dem Mädchen	dem Kind(e)
GEN.	des Onkels	des Mannes	des Mädchens	des Kindes

2. Feminine nouns never have case endings in the singular. Thus, the singular of **die Mutter** (*mother*) and **die Frau** (*woman*) is:

NOM.	die Mutter	die Frau
ACC.	die Mutter	die Frau
DAT.	der Mutter	der Frau
GEN.	der Mutter	der Frau

3. The formation of the plural of nouns will be discussed systematically in Aufgabe 5. At this point, note only that the genitive and accusative plurals are always identical in form with the nominative plural; in the dative plural, **-n** is added unless the nominative plural already ends in **-n**. Make sure that the article used with the noun is in the correct case.

EXAMPLES: Plurals of **der Mann, ⸚er; das Mädchen, -; die Frau, -en:**

NOM.	die Männer	die Mädchen	die Frauen
ACC.	die Männer	die Mädchen	die Frauen
DAT.	den Männern	den Mädchen	den Frauen
GEN.	der Männer	der Mädchen	der Frauen

RECAPITULATION OF MAIN POINTS

1. German has three nominative forms for the singular definite article, depending on the gender of the noun with which the article is used:

Masculine:	**der**
Feminine:	**die**
Neuter:	**das**

In the plural, the article is **die** for all three genders. The article also varies in form according to case.

2. The **der**-words are:

dieser	mancher
jeder (pl. **alle** *all* [*the*])	solcher
jener	welcher

Der-words are declined like **dieser** (see table on page 28). Be careful to distinguish between **jeder** (*each, every*) and **jener** (*that*).

3. Most masculine and neuter nouns have the ending **-s** or **-es** (monosyllables) in the genitive singular.

4. Feminine nouns have no case endings in the singular.

5. The principal parts of a noun consist of the nominative singular, genitive singular, and nominative plural. From these principal parts all other case forms are derived.

6. In the dative plural all nouns end in **-n.**

ÜBUNGEN

Practice in Reading and Writing

A. *Read aloud and translate:*

1. Das Abteil ist für Raucher. 2. Der dicken Dame ist es heiß. 3. Diese Hitze ist ja furchtbar. 4. Solche Hitze haben wir nicht. 5. Was kaufst du dem Mann? 6. Ich kaufe den Männern Zigarren. 7. Jeder Student sagt das. 8. Was antwortet die Dame dem Mann? 9. Welchem Mann antwortet sie das? 10. Der Rauch dieser Zigarre ist furchtbar. 11. Diesen Schaffner fragt manche Dame freundlich: „Ist das Ihre Idee?" 12. Der Rauch solcher

Zigarren ist furchtbar.   13. Solche Mädchen frieren immer.   14. Manche Studentinnen sind nicht nett.   15. Die Studenten machen manche Versuche.   16. Kennst du den Freund dieses Mannes?   17. Er besucht diese Universität.   18. Diese Universität ist gut.   19. Die Studentin ist hübsch.   20. Manche Studentinnen sind hübsch.   21. Er hat den Bleistift der Studentin.   22. Nicht alle Studenten sind intelligent.   23. Solche Studenten haben wir nicht.   24. Die Bibliothek dieser Universität ist gut.   25. Zeigen Sie mir die Universität!   26. Wer öffnet die Fenster des Abteils?

B. *The following exercises work with cognates. Try to arrive at their meanings on the basis of English. If necessary, consult the end vocabulary. Give the number (singular or plural), case, and gender of the words in italics:*

1. *Jede Hand* hat fünf *Finger*.   2. Nicht *jedes Haus* hat einen Garten.   3. Die Mutter schenkt *dem Kind den Ball*.   4. Kennst du *diese Familie?*   5. Er kennt *den Autor dieses Buches* persönlich.   6. Ich kaufe *jedes Buch dieses Autors*.   7. *Die Armeen mancher Nationen* sind nicht sehr stark.   8. *Das Produkt dieser Firma* ist sehr gut.   9. Geben Sie mir *den Preis* für *diese Maschine*.   10. Wir geben *der Kuh das Futter*, und sie gibt (*gives*) uns (*us*) *die Milch* und *die Butter*.   11. Haben Sie *die Telefonnummer des Direktors?*   12. *Jede Katze*, sagt man, hat neun Leben.   13. Wir geben *der Katze* warme Milch.   14. *Die Spezialität dieses Restaurants* sind Austern.   15. *Die Kinder* gehen morgen in die Schule.

C. *Identify the case of each noun:*

1. Manche Mädchen sind sehr dumm.   2. Das Abteil dieser Damen ist kalt.   3. Er kauft allen Studentinnen Bleistifte.   4. Ich kenne solche Studenten nicht.   5. Solchen Studenten antworte ich nicht.   6. Der Schaffner kennt die Dame nicht.   7. Solche Damen frieren immer.   8. Welche Studenten dieser Universität kennen Sie?   9. Er antwortet diesen Mädchen.   10. Welchen Mädchen antwortet er?

D. *Translate:*

1. This man knows these students.   2. Who is opening the window?   3. I am suffocating in this air (use **in** with the dative).   4. What is the conductor closing in (use **in** w. dat.) the compartment?   5. The conductor closes the window again.   6. Many a man smokes only cigars.   7. What do you say to these ladies?   8. The man in the corner is getting angry.   9. The children don't believe that.   10. Which girl is called Marie?   11. At (**in** w. dat.) which moment does the conductor come?   12. What does he do with (**mit** w. dative) the window?   13. He opens every window.   14. Which child is screaming now?   15. These children do not always scream.   16. She is visiting the library of the University.   17. Which library are you visiting?   18. Does he

always smoke these cigars?   19. The students open the windows.   20. Which windows do they open?

Oral Exercises

E. *Decline in the singular and plural:*

1. welcher Schaffner?   2. diese Dame   3. jedes Abteil   4. manche Studentin
5. dieser Bleistift   6. die Frau   7. der Mann   8. manches Buch   9. welche Eisenbahn   10. jede Zigarre

F. *Give the nominative of the words in parentheses:*

1. (*every*) Kind   2. (*which*) Studenten?   3. (*this*) Dame   4. (*every*) Mann
5. (*that*) Zigarre   6. (*many a*) Mädchen   7. (*these*) Männer   8. (*this*) und
(*that*) Ecke   9. (*all*) Männer   10. (*the*) Mädchen

G. *Give the correct case form of the words in parentheses:*

1. Er holt (*every*) Kind einen Ball.   2. Das ist (*the*) Rauch (*of this*) Zigarre.
3. Das antwortet er (*every*) Studentin.   4. Wie heißt (*this*) Mädchen?   5. Nicht (*every*) Schaffner ist freundlich.   6. (*The*) Damen in (*this*, dat.) Abteil rauchen nicht.   7. Wer raucht (*such*) Zigarren?   8. Was antworten Sie (*the*) Studentin?   9. Ich kenne (*such*) Hitze nicht.   10. Kennen Sie (*the*) Studenten persönlich?

H. *Change the nouns to singular:*

1. Er betrachtet die Damen.
2. Er kennt jene Männer.
3. Er versteht manche Raucher.
4. Er schließt alle Abteile.
5. Er kennt jene Mädchen.
6. Er macht die Aufgaben.
7. Er öffnet diese Fenster.
8. Er schließt die Augen.
9. Er macht manche Versuche.
10. Er ruft die Freunde.
11. Er betrachtet jene Ecken.
12. Er fragt die Schaffner.

I. *Follow the example. Use* **antworten** *in each sentence below:*

EXAMPLE: Wir fragen das Kind.
       Wir fragen das Kind und wir antworten dem Kind.

1. Wir verstehen diese Frau.
2. Wir kennen jenen Schaffner.
3. Wir fragen jede Studentin.
4. Wir verstehen diese Dame.
5. Wir kennen den Freund.
6. Wir fragen jenen Mann.
7. Wir fragen manches Kind.
8. Wir fragen jedes Mädchen.
9. Wir kennen diese Mutter.

J. *Change the nouns to plural:*

EXAMPLE: Sie ruft jetzt *den Schaffner.*
          Sie ruft jetzt *die Schaffner.*

1. Sie öffnet immer wieder das Fenster.   2. Sie betrachtet ratlos den Raucher.
3. Sie schließt schnell das Abteil.   4. Sie versteht plötzlich jenen Mann.
5. Sie holt nun jeden Freund.   6. Sie macht ruhig diesen Versuch.   7. Sie
betrachtet ratlos die Dame.   8. Sie fragt schließlich jenes Mädchen.   9. Sie
macht nun manche Aufgabe.   10. Sie öffnet einfach jedes Abteil.

K. *Follow the example:*

EXAMPLE: Die Kinder fragen den Mann.
          Die Kinder fragen den Mann, und der Mann antwortet den
          Kindern.

1. Die Frauen fragen den Mann.
2. Die Mädchen fragen den Mann.
3. Die Schaffner fragen den Mann.
4. Die Raucher fragen den Mann.
5. Die Damen fragen den Mann.
6. Diese Kinder fragen den Mann.
7. Alle Studentinnen fragen den Mann.
8. Alle Freunde fragen den Mann.
9. Diese Raucher fragen den Mann.

L. *Progressive substitution. Replace the verb phrase* (**wir fragen, wir antworten,**
etc.) *and the noun object* (**. . . der Schaffner, . . . der Raucher,** *etc.*) *alternatively
as indicated. Follow the patterns:*

	PATTERN	CUE
1.	Wir fragen den Schaffner.	wir antworten
2.	Wir antworten dem Schaffner.	der Raucher
3.	Wir antworten dem Raucher.	wir kennen
4.	Wir kennen den Raucher.	die Dame
5.	. . . .	wir glauben
6.	. . . .	das Mädchen
7.	. . . .	wir rufen
8.	. . . .	das Kind
9.	. . . .	wir helfen
10.	. . . .	diese Frau
11.	. . . .	wir verstehen
12.	. . . .	jener Mann
13.	. . . .	wir antworten
14.	. . . .	jeder Freund
15.	. . . .	wir besuchen
16.	. . . .	dieses Mädchen
17.	. . . .	wir glauben
18.	. . . .	jede Mutter
19.	. . . .	wir fragen

3

Indefinite Article and Ein-Words

Ein Besuch beim Psychiater

Eine junge Dame besucht ihren Psychiater. Sie ist hübsch, elegant und kommt aus[1] einer guten Familie. Die Sekretärin des Psychiaters öffnet die Tür und stellt ihr einige Fragen: „Ihr Name? Ihre Adresse? Ihr Alter?"

Die junge Dame ist erstaunt. „Mein Alter?" fragt sie. „Was für eine
5 Frage! Ich bin nicht verheiratet."

Nun lacht die Sekretärin. „Ihr Alter, meine ich, nicht Ihren Alten. Bitte, nehmen Sie Platz, der Herr Doktor kommt gleich."

Nach einer Weile kommt der Arzt wirklich und bittet die junge Dame in sein Zimmer. Auch er hat manche Frage. „Haben Sie Angst vor Gewitter?
10 Was sind Ihre Interessen? Tanzen Sie gern? Sind Sie verliebt? Seit wann? In wen?[2] Warum?"

Die junge Dame beantwortet seine Fragen kurz und klar. „Nun",[3] sagt der Psychiater schließlich, „Sie sind ja wunderbar gesund und ganz normal. Aber warum sind Sie eigentlich hier?"
15 Die junge Dame hat auch jetzt eine Antwort. „Das war der Wunsch meiner Eltern. Meine Eltern behaupten, Pfannkuchen sind ungesund. Und ich weiß genau, das ist nicht wahr."

1. **aus** here: *from.* 2. **wen?** (acc. of **wer?**) *whom.* 3. **Nun** (exclamation followed by a comma) *well.*

34

„Was sagen Sie?" fragt der Arzt, „Ich verstehe Sie nicht ganz. Pfannkuchen sind ungesund? Ich esse auch gerne Pfannkuchen."

„Wirklich?" ruft die junge Dame erfreut. „Dann kommen Sie nur einmal 20 in unser Haus. In meinem Zimmer sind viele Pfannkuchen. Ganze Koffer voll."

FRAGEN

1. Wen besucht die junge Dame? 2. Wie ist die junge Dame? 3. Was tut die Sekretärin? 4. Was fragt die Sekretärin die junge Dame? 5. Warum ist die junge Dame erstaunt? 6. Was meint die Sekretärin? 7. Was meint die Sekretärin nicht? 8. Wer kommt nach einer Weile? 9. Was hat der Arzt auch? 10. Was für Fragen stellt der Arzt? 11. Wie beantwortet die junge Dame diese Fragen? 12. Was sagt der Arzt schließlich? 13. Was für eine Antwort hat die junge Dame jetzt? 14. Was behaupten die Eltern der jungen Dame? 15. Was antwortet der Psychiater? 16. Was sagt die junge Dame? 17. Was hat die junge Dame in ihrem Zimmer? 18. Wo hat die junge Dame die Pfannkuchen? 19. Wie viele Pfannkuchen hat sie in ihrem Zimmer? 20. Ist die junge Dame ganz normal?

WORTSCHATZ

COGNATES

die **Adresse, –n**	address	der **Pfannkuchen, –**	pancake
elegant	elegant	der **Platz, ⸗e**	place, seat
die **Familie, –n**	family	**Platz nehmen**	to sit down
das **Haus, ⸗er**	house	der **Psychiater, –**	psychiatrist
das **Interesse, –n**	interest	die **Sekretärin, –nen**	(woman) secretary
jung	young	**tanzen**	to dance
klar	clear	die **Tür, –en**	door
meinen	to mean	**voll**	full (of)
der **Name, –n**	name	**wann**	when
normal	normal	**wunderbar**	wonderful

VOCABULARY

der **Alte, –n**	the old man	der **Arzt, ⸗e**	doctor, physician
ein Alter	an old man	**beantworten**	to answer
das **Alter**	age	*(used only*	
die **Angst, ⸗e**	fear	*when a dir. ob-*	
Angst haben	to be afraid of	*ject follows,*	
vor *(w. dat.)*		*otherwise*	
die **Antwort, –en**	answer	**antworten)**	

	behaupten	to claim (*in the sense of assert*)		*another verb expresses liking*) **gern**
der	**Besuch, –e**	visit		
	bitte!	please!		**tanzen**	to like to dance
	bitten	to ask (*a favor*)		**gesund**	healthy, well
	eigentlich	anyway, really, properly speaking	das	**Gewitter, –**	(thunder)storm
	einige	a few		**gleich** (*adv.*)	in a minute, presently
	einmal	once	der	**Koffer, –**	suitcase
die	**Eltern**	parents		**kurz**	brief(ly)
	erfreut	pleased		**lachen**	to laugh
	erstaunt	surprised		**seit** (*w. dat.*)	since
	essen	to eat		**ungesund**	unhealthy
die	**Frage, –n**	question		**verheiratet**	married
	eine Frage stellen	to ask a question		**verliebt sein**	to be in love
	ganz (*adj.*)	whole		**wahr**	true
	genau	exact(ly)		**warum?**	why?
	gern(e)	gladly		**ich, er, sie weiß**	I, he, she know(s)
	(*in combination with*			**wirklich**	really
			der	**Wunsch, ⸗e**	wish
			das	**Zimmer, –**	room

DISTINGUISH BETWEEN

eigentlich *really, anyway* (*actually, but not necessarily*)
wirklich *really* (*in reality, factually*)

> EXAMPLE: **Ich habe wirklich keine Zeit.**   **Ich habe eigentlich keine Zeit, aber . . . .**
> *I really have no time.*   *I actually have no time, but . . . .*

bitten *to ask* (*a favor*) and **fragen** *to ask* (*a question*)

lachen *to laugh* and **lächeln** *to smile*

Note also that the prefix **un-** (which always carries the word stress) makes an adjective negative: **gesund—ungesund.**

GRAMMATICAL TERMS

1. The indefinite article in English is *a* or *an*.

2. The possessive adjectives are *my, your, his, her, its, our, their*. They are called adjectives because they modify nouns: *my house, your wife, his money,* etc., and possessive because they indicate possession (ownership).

INDEFINITE ARTICLE AND EIN-WORDS

1. The indefinite article in German is **ein.** It has the same case endings as the **der**-words, except in three cases: nominative masculine, nominative neuter, and accusative neuter, where **ein** has no ending:

	MASCULINE	FEMININE	NEUTER
NOM.	ein Mann	eine Frau	ein Kind
ACC.	einen Mann	eine Frau	ein Kind
DAT.	einem Mann(e)	einer Frau	einem Kind(e)
GEN.	eines Mannes	einer Frau	eines Kindes

A noun has the same form after a definite and indefinite article.

2. The expressions **manch ein** (*many a*), **solch ein** (or **so ein**), **ein solcher** (*such a*, *what a*) and **welch ein** (*what a*) may take the place of the corresponding **der**-words **mancher, solcher,**[1] **welcher** in the singular; **ein** then takes the case endings. In the plural, **der**-word forms must be used: **manche, solche, welche:**

> SINGULAR: **manch ein** (or **mancher**) **Mann**   *many a man*
> PLURAL: **manche Männer**   *some men*

Similarly constructed is the expression **was für ein** (*what kind of, what a*), which may be used in a question or in an exclamation. In the singular, **ein** has case endings; in the plural **was für** is used without article:

> **Was für eine Idee!**   *What an idea!*
> **Was für Ideen?**   *What kind of ideas?*

3. Words declined like **ein** are called **ein**-words. These **ein**-words (in the nominative masculine singular) are:

> **kein**   *no, not any, not a*

> Example: **kein Mann, keine Frau, kein Kind**

and the possessive adjectives:

mein	*my*			**unser**	*our*
dein	*your*	**Ihr** (sing. and plural)	*your*	**euer**	*your*
sein	*his*			**ihr**[2]	*their*
ihr[2]	*her*				
sein	*it*				

---

[1] **Der**-word forms of **solcher** are rather clumsy and, therefore, hardly used. More common is a construction in which **ein** is placed before **solcher; ein solcher, einen solchen, einem solchen, eines solchen.**

[2] Note that **ihr** may mean *her* or *their*. The context determines which is meant. Capitalized **Ihr** always means *your* (conventional address).

Distinguish also between the personal pronoun **ihr** and the possessive adjective **ihr:** Before a verb, **ihr** is a personal pronoun (**ihr habt** *you have*); before a noun, **ihr** is the possessive adjective (**ihr Freund** *her* or *their friend*).

4. Ein obviously has no plural forms, but all other **ein**-words have. The plural endings are the same as for the **der**-words:

NOM.	keine Männer (Frauen, Kinder)	meine (deine, etc.) Onkel
ACC.	keine Männer (Frauen, Kinder)	meine (deine, etc.) Onkel
DAT.	keinen Männern (Frauen, Kindern)	meinen (deinen, etc.) Onkeln
GEN.	keiner Männer (Frauen, Kinder)	meiner (deiner, etc.) Onkel

5. Kein is an old contraction of **nicht** and **ein** and must be used for English *no, not a, not any;* **nicht** and **ein** may remain separate only if **ein** is emphasized and has the meaning of "one":

Ich habe **keine Angst.**	*I have no fear.*
Keine Tür ist offen.	*Not a door is open.*
Haben Sie **keine Pfannkuchen?**	*Don't you have any pancakes?*

But: **Nicht eine Frage** war gut. *Not one question was good.*

6. Do not mistake the **ein**-words **unser** (*our*) and **euer** (*your*, plural), for **der**-words. To decline these two possessive adjectives, the case endings are added to the final **-er.** Compare the declension of the **der**-word **dieser** in the masculine singular with that of the **ein**-word **unser:**

NOM.	dieser	unser
ACC.	diesen	uns(e)ren
DAT.	diesem	uns(e)rem
GEN.	dieses	uns(e)res

7. To determine possessive adjectives in German, proceed as follows:

EXAMPLE: I know their father.

a. Determine the correct possessive adjective: *their* = **ihr.**

b. Determine the number and gender of the noun: **der Vater,** masculine, singular: **ihr Vater.**

c. Determine the case relationship: direct object = accusative.

d. Add the proper ending to the possessive adjective: **-en** = **ihren Vater.**

e. The completed statement becomes: **Ich kenne ihren Vater.**

8. The three possessive adjectives **dein, euer, Ihr** mean *your.* **Dein** and **euer** are the familiar forms, **Ihr** is for conventional address (singular and plural). Use **dein** if you address a person as **du; euer** (plural) if you address more than one person as **ihr;** and **Ihr** if you address a person or persons as **Sie:**

du—dein:	Du hast einen Wagen; es ist **dein Wagen.**	*You have a car;*
ihr—euer:	Ihr habt einen Wagen; es ist **euer Wagen.**	*it's your car.*
Sie—Ihr:	Sie haben einen Wagen; es ist **Ihr Wagen.**	

9. In referring to parts of the body or to clothing, German prefers to use the definite article instead of the possessive adjective if the possessor is the same person as the subject and no ambiguity is suggested:

> Was hast du **in der Hand?**
> *What do you have in your hand?*
> Er hat **die Hand in der Tasche.**
> *He has his hand in his pocket.*
> But: Er hat **seine Hand in meiner Tasche.**
> *He has his hand in my pocket.*

10. Contrary to English, the indefinite article **ein** is omitted with nouns indicating professions, nationality, or religion if the verb in the sentence is **sein, werden,** or **bleiben:**

> **Er wird sicher Lehrer.**
> *He'll certainly be a teacher.*
> **Er ist Künstler (Engländer, Katholik).**
> *He is an artist (an Englishman, a Catholic).*

On the other hand, the article **ein** is used with such nouns if they are modified by an adjective or a relative clause:

> **Er ist ein richtiger Engländer.**
> *He is a real Englishman.*
> **Er ist ein Fischer, der nie etwas fängt.**
> *He is a fisherman who never catches anything.*

RECAPITULATION OF MAIN POINTS

1. The indefinite article is **ein** (masculine), **eine** (feminine), **ein** (neuter).

2. **Ein** differs in its declension in only three forms from **der**-words, and in these three forms it has no endings:

	MASCULINE	NEUTER
NOM. ACC.	ein (Mann)	ein (Kind) ein (Kind)

3. The **ein**-words are: **kein** (*no, not any*) and the possessive adjectives:

mein	*my*		**unser**	*our*
dein	*your*	**Ihr** *your* (conventional)	**euer**	*your*
sein	*his*		**ihr**	*their*
ihr	*her*			
sein	*it*			

4. Do not confuse **unser** and **euer** with **der**-words: case endings are added to the full word: uns(e)res, uns(e)rem, eu(e)rer, eu(e)res, and so on.

5. Dein, euer, Ihr mean *your:*

> With **du** use **dein: Du** hast **deinen Freund.**
> With **ihr** use **euer: Ihr** habt **eu(e)ren Freund.**
> With **Sie** use **Ihr: Sie** haben **Ihren Freund.**

6. Kein is used for English *no, not a, not any.*

ÜBUNGEN

Practice in Reading and Writing

A. *Read aloud and translate:*

1. Kennen Sie meine Eltern?   2. Seine Eltern sind nicht hier.   3. Wir essen gerne Pfannkuchen.   4. Er raucht gerne Zigarren.   5. Rauchen Sie auch gerne Zigarren?   6. Der Koffer ist in seinem Zimmer.   7. Verstehen Sie meine Frage?   8. Verstehen Sie meine Fragen?   9. Was für eine dumme Frage!   10. Was für eine Frage verstehen Sie nicht?   11. Eine solche Luft ist ungesund.   12. Ich sterbe in solcher Luft.   13. Solch einen Menschen kenne ich nicht.   14. Hier haben wir unsere Ruhe.   15. Kennen Sie unseren Arzt?   16. Die Studenten in unserer Universität sind wirklich sehr gut.   17. Kein Mensch kauft das.   18. Ich kenne hier keinen Menschen.   19. Er redet mit keinem Menschen.   20. Was haben Sie da in der Hand?   21. Wie sage ich es meinem Kinde?   22. Wie sage ich es meinen Kindern?   23. Eure Kinder verstehen kein Wort.   24. Ich kenne eure Kinder nicht.   25. Ihre Kinder sitzen im Kinderzimmer.

B. *Translate and give case and number of the words in italics:*

1. Wer ist der Präsident *unserer* Universität?   2. Kennt ihr *euren* Professor nicht?   3. Der Professor kennt *seine* Studenten manchmal nicht.   4. Das ist *Ihre* und nicht *meine* Idee.   5. Du kennst Marie, aber kennst du auch *ihre* Mutter?   6. Kennt ihr *ihr* Haus?   7. Ist *Ihr* Freund auch Student?   8. Sie holt *ihrem* Vater einen Bleistift.   9. Wo ist die Bibliothek *eurer* Universität?   10. Sie schweigt *keinen* Augenblick.

C. *Complete the following sentences by inserting the correct form of the German word for the English word in parentheses:*

EXAMPLE: *(no)* Ich habe . . . . Bleistift.
> Ich habe keinen Bleistift.

1. (*my*) Wo hast du . . . . Bleistift?
2. (*our*) Wir essen heute in . . . . Zimmer.
3. (*her*) Ich verstehe . . . . Antwort nicht.
4. (*no*) Hast du . . . . Wunsch?
5. (*your*, fam. sing.) Warum sind . . . . Antworten immer so kurz?
6. (*a*) Was für . . . . Sekretärin hat der Mann?
7. (*a*) Was für . . . . Mann hat die Sekretärin?
8. (*their*) . . . . Haus ist sehr elegant.
9. (*our*) Kennst du . . . . Haus?
10. (*our*) . . . . Studenten sind noch sehr jung.
11. (*your*) Kennst du . . . . Professor gut?
12. (*my*) Meinen Sie . . . . Mann (*husband*)?
13. (*my*) . . . . Mann meint das nicht.

D. *Translate:*

1. What a man! 2. What a family! 3. Do you know my parents? 4. What does she have in her hand? 5. Nobody (not a human being) smokes such a cigar. 6. Do you like to eat pancakes, Mr. Schmidt? 7. They are sitting in our compartment. 8. She is opening her window and closing it again. 9. They have a house but no children. 10. The heat in your house is terrible, Mr. Schmidt. 11. She is talking with (**mit,** w. dat.) her parents. 12. Her pancakes are really wonderful! 13. Why are you buying his house? 14. Please answer my question, Fritz! 15. He asks the man for (**nach,** w. dat.) his address. 16. He is surprised at (**über,** w. acc.) her answer. 17. The mother is calling her children. 18. Do you know the names of her children? 19. She likes to answer his questions (use **gern**). 20. I really have no wish.

Oral Exercises

E. *Replace the* **der-***word by the indefinite article:*

EXAMPLE: Er weiß die Antwort.
　　　　　Er weiß eine Antwort.

1. Hier ist das Zimmer. 2. Wir antworten dieser Dame. 3. Du besuchst den Psychiater. 4. Du glaubst dem Psychiater. 5. Das ist der Platz. 6. Sie öffnet jedes Fenster. 7. Ihr fragt dieses Kind. 8. Sie öffnet den Koffer voll Pfannkuchen. 9. Sie essen den Pfannkuchen. 10. Wir helfen jeder Familie. 11. Er stellt die Frage.

F. *Complete each sentence using the possessive adjective corresponding to the pronoun subject:*

EXAMPLE: Ich glaube meinem Arzt, und du . . . .
　　　　　Ich glaube meinem Arzt, und du glaubst deinem Arzt.

1. Du rauchst deine Zigarre, und er . . . .
2. Er besucht seinen Freund, und sie (*she*) . . . .
3. Sie antwortet ihrem Psychiater, und wir . . . .
4. Wir haben unsere Idee, und ihr . . . .
5. Ihr fragt eure Familie, und sie (*they*) . . . .
6. Sie antworten ihrem Freund, und ich . . . .
7. Ich glaube meinen Kindern, und du . . . .
8. Du rauchst deine Zigarren, und er . . . .
9. Er fragt seine Eltern, und sie (*she*) . . . .
10. Sie hat ihre Ideen, und wir . . . .
11. Wir essen unsere Pfannkuchen, und ihr . . . .
12. Ihr habt eure Koffer, und sie (*they*) . . . .

G. *Change the sentences according to the example:*

EXAMPLE: Mein Zimmer hat eine Tür.
   Das ist die Tür meines Zimmers.

1. Deine Sekretärin hat einen Bleistift.   2. Sein Psychiater hat ein Haus.
3. Ihr Freund hat einen Koffer.   4. Unsere Studentin hat eine Frage.   5. Euer
Freund hat eine Zigarre.   6. Ihr Zimmer hat eine Tür.   7. Meine Eltern
haben ein Haus.   8. Deine Freunde haben eine Frage.   9. Seine Kinder
haben einen Arzt.   10. Ihre Eltern haben einen Psychiater.   11. Unsere
Kinder haben einen Freund.   12. Eure Universitäten haben eine Bibliothek.
13. Ihre Eltern haben eine Idee.

4

Der- and Ein-Words

as Pronouns

Der Kaufmann und der Tod

Nürnberg ist schon im Mittelalter eine Reichsstadt,[1] eine Stadt des Handels und des Gewerbes,[2] aber auch der Kunst. Es ist ebenso reich an[3] Geschichte wie an Sage. Von keiner anderen erzählt man in Deutschland so viele Geschichten. Eine solche ist die vom Kaufmann und dem Tod.

Die Kaufleute in Nürnberg führen alle ein gutes Leben, aber einer ist 5 besonders reich, und seine junge Frau besonders schön. Sie leben wie im Paradies. Junge Leute tun das nämlich. Der Kaufmann hat viel Erfolg, denn er ist schlau, und manchmal sogar ein wenig zu schlau, wie wir sehen werden.[4] Viele in der Stadt sind seine Freunde, und keiner ist wirklich sein Feind. So hat er keine Sorgen, bis auf[5] eine: er lebt in Angst vor dem Tod. 10

Eines Tages nun muß er[6] nach Rothenburg. Da packt ihn wieder die Angst: Was wartet auf ihn in Rothenburg? Er ist diesmal ganz sicher: der Tod kommt! Vielleicht steht er schon vor der Tür. Der Kaufmann ruft in der Angst seinen Diener: „Schnell", sagt er zu diesem, „hole mir mein Pferd. Der Tod kommt. Ich reite nach Rothenburg. Da habe ich viele Freunde, und 15

---

1. **Reichsstadt** (lit., *imperial city*) *free city.*   2. **des Handels und des Gewerbes** *of commerce and trade.*   3. **an** (here:) *in.*   4. **sehen werden** *will see.*   5. **bis auf** *except for.*   6. **muß er** (supply: **gehen**) *he has to go.*

die helfen mir sicher. Wenn der Tod kommt, sage ihm, ich bin in München. Da findet er mich nicht. Grüße meine Frau und sage ihr, ich bin bald wieder zurück." Dann besteigt er sein Pferd und reitet fort.[7]

Wenig später kommt der Tod wirklich. Er klopft an die Tür wie jeder
20 andere und der Diener ruft: „Herein!" Der Tod öffnet die Tür und sieht nur den Diener.

„Suchen Sie meinen Herrn?" fragt der Diener. „Er ist nicht hier. Er ist gerade auf dem Weg nach München."

„Nein", antwortet jener. „Ich suche heute einen anderen, den kranken
25 Bürgermeister. Sage mir, wo der wohnt!"

Der Diener zeigt dem Tod das Haus des Bürgermeisters. Der Tod dankt und meint:[8] „Gut. Das ist also[9] der eine, und morgen hole ich mir dann den anderen. Aber warum sagst du: mein Herr ist in München? Das verstehe ich nicht. Ich treffe ihn nämlich morgen in Rothenburg."

7. **reitet fort** *rides away, takes off.*   8. **meinen** is frequently used as synonym for **sagen** *to say.*   9. **also** (within a sentence) *then.*

FRAGEN

1. Was ist Nürnberg?   2. Was erzählt man von keiner anderen Stadt in Deutschland?   3. Wer lebt in Nürnberg?   4. Wie lebt man in Nürnberg? 5. Was ist der junge Kaufmann und was hat er?   6. Wie ist seine junge Frau? 7. Wie leben junge Leute?   8. Warum hat der Kaufmann viel Erfolg? 9. Sind die Leute in der Stadt seine Feinde?   10. Was für eine Sorge hat er? 11. Wohin (*where, where to*) muß der Kaufmann eines Tages?   12. Was packt ihn da?   13. Was sagt er zu seinem Diener?   14. Wohin reitet er wirklich? 15. Was tut der Tod?   16. Was sagt der Diener zu dem Tod?   17. Was antwortet der Tod?   18. Was tut der Diener?   19. Was antwortet der Tod?

WORTSCHATZ

COGNATES

da	there	nämlich	namely, for
danken	to thank	das **Paradies**, –e	paradise
der Feind, –e	("fiend"), enemy	reich (an)	rich (in)
grüßen	to greet, to send re- gards to	reiten	to ride (on horse- back)
leben	to live	schlau	"sly," clever, smart
das Leben	life	tun	to do
morgen	tomorrow	der Weg, –e	way
(das) **München**	Munich	auf dem Weg	on the way

VOCABULARY

bald	soon	das **Mittelalter**	Middle Ages
besonders	especially	**nein**	no (*in an answer, not an adjective!*)
besteigen	to climb on, to mount	**packen**	to seize; to pack (*a suitcase*)
der **Bürgermeister, –**	mayor		
(das) **Deutschland**	Germany	das **Pferd, –e**	horse
der **Diener, –**	servant	die **Sage, –n**	legend
diesmal	this time	**schon**	already
ebenso . . . wie	just as . . . as	**schön**	beautiful
der **Erfolg, -e**	success	**sicher**	certainly; (*as adj.:*) sure
erreichen	to reach		
erzählen	to tell	**er sieht**	he sees
die **Frau, -en**	wife, woman	**sogar**	even
führen	to lead	die **Sorge, –n**	worry
gerade	just now	**später**	later
die **Geschichte, -n**	history; story	die **Stadt, ⸗e**	city
herein!	come in!	**suchen nach** (*w. dat.*)	to look for
der **Herr, -en**	master; gentleman, (*in address:*) Mr.	**eines Tages**	one day
heute	today	**treffen**	to meet
ihm (*dat. of* **er**)	him, to him, for him	**viel**	much, a lot
ihn (*acc. of* **er**)	him	**vielleicht**	perhaps
der **Kaufmann** (*plural:* **die Kaufleute**)	merchant	**vor**	in front of
		wenig	little (in quantity)
klopfen (an) (*w. acc.*)	to knock (on)	**ein wenig**	a little
		wie	like, as
krank	sick, ill	**wohnen**	to live
die **Kunst, ⸗e**	art	**zurück**	back

DISTINGUISH BETWEEN

tun and **machen** both mean *to do; to make;* in general, **tun** is used in the sense of "to engage in," **machen** in that of "to produce," although in idiomatic usage the line cannot always be finely drawn.

schon *already* and **schön** *beautiful.*

wohnen and **leben** both mean *to live;* **wohnen** in the sense of "to reside"; **leben** describes a more permanent condition.

die Geschichte means *history* and *story;* the context decides; the plural is always *stories.*

GRAMMATICAL TERMS

1. *Demonstrative pronouns* point out a person or a thing without naming it: *this one, that one.* English often uses a personal pronoun instead of a demonstrative pronoun and gives it special stress: I know *him.*

2. *Possessive pronouns* are: *mine, yours, his, hers, ours, theirs.* In the sentence "It is my idea, not yours," *my* is a possessive adjective, *yours* is a possessive pronoun.

3. *Relative pronouns* (*who, whose, whom, which, that*) refer to somebody or something previously mentioned (their antecedent):

> This is the man *to whom* we owe everything.
> The situation *that* now prevails is serious.

DER-WORDS USED AS PRONOUNS

1. Der, die, das, when used with a noun, are articles and mean *the.* When standing alone they have the quality of demonstrative pronouns and function as emphatic substitutes for personal pronouns (meaning *he, she, it, they, that* [*one*], or [*to*] *him,* [*to*] *her,* etc.). When so used, they tend to be in first position. Compare:

Sie ist dumm.	Wir kennen **ihn.**	Ich weiß **es.**
She is dumb.	*We know him.*	*I know it.*
Die ist (aber) dumm!	**Den** kennen wir!	**Das** weiß ich.
Is she dumb!	*We know him!*	*That I know.*

2. Der, die, das, used as demonstrative pronouns, have the same forms as the definite article, except in the genitive singular and the genitive and dative plurals:

	SINGULAR			PLURAL
	Masculine	Feminine	Neute	(all genders)
NOM.	**der**	**die**	**das**	**die**
	(*he, it*)	(*she, it*)	(*it, that one*)	(*they, these*)
ACC.	**den**	**die**	**das**	**die**
	(*him*)	(*her*)	(*it, that one*)	(*them, these*)
DAT.	**dem**	**der**	**dem**	**denen**
	(*to him, him*)	(*to her, her*)	(*to it, it*)	(*to them, them*)
GEN.	**dessen**[1]	**deren**[1]	**dessen**	**deren**[1] or **derer**[2]
	(*his, its*)	(*her, its*)	(*its, of it*)	(*their*) (*of those*)

[1] **Dessen** and **deren** are generally used in place of the possessive adjective **sein, ihr, ihre** to avoid ambiguity, and are then often equivalent to "the latter": Hans, **sein** Freund und **dessen** Frau. *Hans, his friend and the latter's wife.*
[2] **Derer** is most frequently used when a relative clause follows it: Das Geld **derer, die nicht rauchen.** *The money of those who do not smoke.*

3. Der, die, das may also function as relative pronouns; they will be discussed as such in Aufgabe 19. At this point, it is only necessary to realize that relative pronouns introduce relative clauses, which have their verbs at the end, while the demonstrative pronoun is immediately followed by the verb. Compare:

DEMONSTRATIVE: Es war einmal ein König, **der hatte** eine Tochter.
There was once a king; he had a daughter.

RELATIVE: Es war einmal ein König, **der** eine Tochter **hatte.**
There was once a king who had a daughter.

4. All **der**-words (see Aufgabe 2, page 28) may be used as pronouns and have the same case endings as **der**-words which precede nouns:

SINGULAR		PLURAL	
dieser	*this one, that one*	**diese**	*these, those*
jeder	*each one, every one*	**alle**	*all (of them)*
jener	*that one*	**jene**	*those*
mancher	*many a one*	**manche**	*some*
solcher	*such a one*	**solche**	*such (ones)*
welcher	*which one*	**welche**	*which (ones)*

EXAMPLES: **Dieser**[1] ist es nicht.   *It isn't this one.*
Manche rauchen viel.   *Some smoke a lot.*
Das sagt **jeder**.   *Everyone says that.*

5. German constructions for pointing out things are similar to English:

Dies ist meine Pfeife.   *This is my pipe.*
Das ist sein Paket.   *That is his parcel.*

For the plural, however, German differs from English. The German verb (like English) changes to the plural, but the pronouns **dies** and **das** remain in the singular:[2]

Dies sind meine Pfeifen.   *These are my pipes.*
Das sind seine Pakete.   *Those are his packages.*

The same is true of the **es ist** construction, except that it does not have demonstrative quality:

Es ist meine Pfeife.   *It is my pipe.*
Es sind meine Pfeifen.   *They are my pipes.*

[1] **Dieser** and **jener** used as pronouns in the same sentence may be equivalent to *the latter* (**dieser**) and *the former* (**jener**):

Jene haben eine demokratische Tradition, **diese** oft nicht.
Those (the former) have a democratic tradition, these (the latter) often (do) not.

[2] Similarly with **welches?**:

Welches ist deine Pfeife?   *Which is your pipe?*
Welches sind deine Pfeifen?   *Which are your pipes?*

EIN-WORDS USED AS PRONOUNS

1. **Ein**-words used as pronouns have the endings of **der**-words in all cases and agree in gender, number, and case with the noun for which they stand. Thus, **ein**-word pronouns differ from **ein**-word adjectives in three case forms, all singular:

	ADJECTIVE		PRONOUN	
	Masculine	Neuter	Masculine	Neuter
NOM.	ein	ein	einer	eines (or eins)
ACC.		ein		eines (or eins)

2. The **ein**-word pronouns are:

> **einer (einen, einem, eines)**   *one, someone*
> **keiner (keinen, keinem, keines)**   *none, no one*

and the possessive pronouns (masculine singular):

meiner	*mine*	**unserer**[1]	*ours*
deiner	*yours*	**euerer**[1]	*yours*
seiner	*his (its)*	**ihrer**	*theirs*
ihrer	*hers*	**Ihrer**	*yours*

3. Here are some examples of the use of **ein**-words as pronouns compared with **ein**-words as adjectives:

a. The three cases in which pronouns differ in form from adjectives:

ADJECTIVES   PRONOUNS

Nominative Masculine Singular

Ein Wagen ist besser als **kein Wagen.**   **Einer** ist besser als **keiner.**
One car is better than no car.   *One is better than none.*

Nominative Neuter Singular

Dein Kind ist älter als **mein Kind.**   **Deins** ist älter als **meins.**
Your child is older than my child.   *Yours is older than mine.*

[1] **Unser** and **euer,** both adjective and pronoun, may be shortened when an ending is added; for example:

> unsere ⟶ unsre
> unserer ⟶ unsrer
> euerem ⟶ eurem

Accusative Neuter Singular

Ich habe **ein Buch.**	Hast du auch **eins?**
I have a book.	*Do you have one, too?*

b. Some of the cases in which pronouns and adjectives have the same
endings:

ADJECTIVES   PRONOUNS

Dative Masculine Singular

Ich gebe **meinem Freund** ein Buch.	Was gibst du **deinem?**
I am giving my friend a book.	*What are you giving yours?*

Accusative Masculine Singular

Ich habe **deinen Bleistift** und.......	du hast **meinen.**
I have your pencil and............	*you have mine.*

Dative Feminine Singular

Ich gebe **meiner Freundin** ein Buch.	Was gibst du **deiner?**
I am giving my girl friend a book.	*What are you giving yours?*

Nominative Plural

Hier sind **deine Bücher,** aber.......	wo sind **meine?**
Here are your books but..........	*where are mine?*

RECAPITULATION OF MAIN POINTS

1. **Der, die, das,** when not followed by a noun, are pronouns and are usually
equivalent to *he, she, it, they, that* (*one*), or (*to*) *him,* (*to*) *her.* They have
the same form as the definite article, except in the genitive singular masculine **(dessen),** feminine **(deren),** neuter **(dessen),** and in the dative and
genitive plurals (dative: **denen;** genitive: **deren).**

2. In **dies ist, das ist** and **es ist** constructions, the pronoun is invariable,
but the verb changes to plural if the predicate subject is in the plural:

dies ist	*this is*	**dies sind**	*these are*
das ist	*that is*	**das sind**	*those are*
es ist	*it is*	**es sind**	*they are*

3. **Ein**-words used as pronouns have the same endings as **der**-words in all
forms.

ÜBUNGEN

Practice in Reading and Writing

A. *Read aloud and translate:*

1. Der weiß das. 2. Die ist sehr gesund. 3. Den kenne ich. 4. Meinst du dieses Mädchen? Die kenne ich nicht. 5. Dem sage ich das nicht, und der glaube ich kein Wort. 6. Mit denen tanze ich nicht gerne. 7. Die sind aber schlau! 8. Das ist die Geschichte von dem Kaufmann und dessen Diener. 9. Die Herren und deren Diener. 10. Das weiß nicht jeder. 11. Das weiß keiner. 12. Manche rauchen zu viel. 13. Ich kenne diesen und jenen. 14. Der kennt jeden. 15. Den kennt jeder. 16. Wir haben unsere Zimmer und sie haben ihre. 17. Hier ist dein Zimmer, aber wo ist meins? 18. Er hat keins. 19. Hat Marie ihrs? 20. Er ist ganz normal; dessen bin ich sicher. 21. Kennen Sie diese Geschichten und welche kennen Sie nicht? 22. In was für einer Stadt lebt ihr? Unsere ist sehr schön. 23. Ich habe einen Platz; was für einen hast du? 24. Ich kenne die Frau.—Welche? —Die da! 25. Das ist die Sorge meines Mannes. 26. Das sind die Sorgen meines Mannes. 27. Hat er Erfolg oder hat er keinen? 28. Sie haben einen guten Bürgermeister; einen solchen haben wir nicht. 29. Die Mädchen sitzen da im Zimmer; kennst du die? 30. Welche kennst du nicht?

B. *Replace the **der**-words and nouns by **der**-word pronouns:*

EXAMPLE: *Jeder Mann* weiß das.
          Jeder weiß das.

1. Mancher Kaufmann hat keinen Erfolg. 2. Kennen Sie diesen Weg? 3. Was packen wir in diese Koffer? 4. Der Bürgermeister hat keine Sorgen. 5. Ich öffne dieses Fenster.

C. *Replace the **ein**-words and nouns by **ein**-word pronouns:*

EXAMPLE: Er hat keine Frau.
          Er hat keine.

1. Meine Frau ist heute in München. 2. Wo ist Ihre Frau? 3. Ich mache einen Versuch. 4. Er versteht keinen Menschen. 5. Kein Mensch versteht ihn.

D. *Translate:*

1. Nobody understands his story. 2. I am packing my suitcase; are you packing yours (**Sie**-form)? 3. Do they know him (use demonstr. pronoun)?

4. He (use demonstr. pronoun) tells many stories.   5. She knows my friends, but I don't know hers.   6. Here is my pencil, but where is hers?   7. One thing I know: this compartment is for smokers.   8. Is this one also for smokers?   9. He tells the story to everyone.   10. I like to smoke cigars. 11. Which one do you smoke today?   12. She does not like to tell that. 13. These are my father's cigars.   14. I'll get (present tense) the conductor; he'll know (present tense) that.   15. I have a seat, but he has none.   16. Do you have one?   17. Both girls are pretty, but one is not very nice.   18. Which one do you mean?   19. My room is as good as hers.

Oral Exercises

E. *Supply the proper form of the pronoun for the words in parentheses. Use the demonstrative forms of* **der, die, das** *where applicable:*

1. (Him) . . . . kennen wir gut.   2. (She) . . . . ist nicht hier.   3. (That) . . . . weiß ich auch.   4. (He) . . . . kommt nicht.   5. Er ist furchtbar dumm, (of that) . . . . bin ich sicher.   6. (Them) . . . . gebe ich etwas zu essen.   7. (Him) . . . . sage ich das nicht.   8. (Them) . . . . kenne ich gut.   9. (no one) . . . . ist hier.   10. (Everyone) . . . . kauft Bleistifte.   11. Ich kaufe sein Haus und er kauft (mine) . . . .   12. Hier ist dein Bleistift, aber wo ist (mine) . . . . ?   13. Er hat viele Freunde und ich habe (none) . . . .   14. Ich sitze in meiner Ecke und du sitzt in (yours) . . . .

F. *Complete the sentences by finding the correct equivalent for the English in parentheses.* (*Before doing so, review paragraph 5 on page 47*):

1. (That is) . . . . seine zweite Frau.   2. (Those are) . . . . seine Freunde. 3. (This is) . . . . eine dumme Frage.   4. (Those are) . . . . dumme Fragen. 5. (Are those) . . . . Studenten?   6. (Is it) . . . . eine unserer Studentinnen? 7. (Those are) . . . . Ihre Kinder?   8. (These are) . . . . meine Kinder und (those are) . . . . ihre.

G. *Answer in the affirmative replacing the subject noun or the object noun by a demonstrative pronoun:*

EXAMPLES: Kennen Sie unsere Studenten?   Ja, die kenne ich.
          Ist Rothenburg eine Stadt?   Ja, das ist eine Stadt.

1. Leben diese Leute wie im Paradies?   2. Ist dieser Kaufmann besonders reich?   3. Ist Nürnberg eine Reichsstadt?   4. Sagt er es seiner Frau?   5. Sagt er es seinen Kindern?   6. Hat er Erfolg?   7. Hat er Sorgen?   8. Glauben Sie unserm Bürgermeister?   9. Glauben Sie diesen Frauen?   10. Zeigt er es seinen Studenten?   11. Kennen Sie diese Geschichte?   12. Helfen Sie diesen Leuten?   13. Ist sein Diener auf dem Weg nach Rothenburg?

H. *Respond to the statements by using the appropriate* **ein-***word pronouns:*

EXAMPLES: Das ist ein Abteil.   Dies ist auch eins.
Das ist kein Korridor.   Dies ist auch keiner.

1. Das ist kein Weg.
2. Das ist eine Bibliothek.
3. Das ist ein Bleistift.
4. Das ist kein Zimmer.
5. Das ist ein Bürgermeister.
6. Das ist keine Geschichte.
7. Das ist kein Erfolg.
8. Das ist ein Versuch.
9. Das ist keine Sekretärin.
10. Das ist ein Koffer.

I. *Complete the sentences:*

EXAMPLE: Ich hole meine Kinder, und du . . .
Ich hole meine Kinder, und du holst deine.

1. Du öffnest dein Fenster, und er . . .
2. Er versteht sein Problem, und sie (*she*) . . .
3. Sie sagt es ihren Kindern, und wir . . .
4. Wir glauben unserm Freund, und ihr . . .
5. Ihr kommt mit eurer Familie und sie (*they*) . . .
6. Sie essen ihre Pfannkuchen, und ich . . .
7. Er macht seinen Versuch, und wir . . .

5

The Noun

Der ehrliche Mann und sein Hemd

In einem fernen[1], fernen Land lebt ein König. Er hat nur eine Tochter.
Sie ist wunderschön[2] und er liebt sie mehr als[3] sein Land und alle seine
Schätze. Er erfüllt ihr jeden ihrer Wünsche und lebt nur für sie. So vergeht
manches Jahr in Glück und Frieden. Aber plötzlich wird das Mädchen
krank. Sie redet kein Wort, spielt nicht mit ihren Puppen und ihren Freundin- 5
nen, hat keine Wünsche und weint viel. Die Feste im Schloß ihres Vaters,
Kleider und Speisen machen auf sie keinen Eindruck. Der König schickt
in seiner Verzweiflung nach[4] allen Ärzten seines Reiches, aber deren Weisheit ist bald am Ende. Die Krankheit bleibt ein Rätsel. Da ruft der König
die Weisen seines Landes in den Palast und sagt zu ihnen: „Meine Tochter 10
ist sehr krank. Sagt mir, wie findet sie ihre Gesundheit wieder?"

Die Weisen überlegen eine lange Zeit. Sie sitzen da im Kreise und denken.
Schließlich finden sie die Antwort: „Deine Tochter bekommt ihre Gesundheit wieder, o König, wenn sie das Hemd eines ehrlichen Mannes trägt."[5]

Nun schickt der König seine Boten in das Land mit dem Befehl, einen 15
ehrlichen Mann zu suchen.[6] Diesem verspricht[7] er Gold, Silber und alle

1. **fernen** *distant.* 2. **wunderschön** *very, very beautiful.* 3. **als** (after a comparative) *than.*
4. **nach** (here:) *for.* 5. **trägt** *wears.* 6. **zu suchen** translate infinitive first. 7. **verspricht**
promises.

Ehren seines Landes. Die Boten wandern viele Jahre über Berg und Tal, von Stadt zu Stadt und von Dorf zu Dorf. Endlich kehren sie zum König zurück.[8]

Der merkt sofort, daß sie kein Hemd in der Hand haben und fragt: „Ist
20 denn[9] in meinem ganzen Land kein einziger ehrlicher Mann?"

„Doch, Majestät", antworten die Boten. „Ganz am Ende[10] deines Reiches, in einem kleinen Dorf, lebt ein ehrlicher Mann. Aber er ist leider so arm, daß er kein Hemd hat."

8. **kehren . . . zurück** return.   9. **denn** (in the middle of a question expresses emphasis; translate by beginning with "But . . .").   10. **ganz am Ende** *at the very end.*

FRAGEN

1. Wo lebt der König unserer Geschichte?   2. Wie ist seine Tochter?   3. Wie sehr liebt er sie?   4. Was tut er für sie?   5. Wie vergeht manches Jahr?   6. Was tut das Mädchen in seiner Krankheit nicht mehr?   7. Was macht auf sie keinen Eindruck?   8. Was tut der König?   9. Was ist am Ende?   10. Was bleibt die Krankheit?   11. Wen ruft der König nun in seinen Palast?   12. Was sagt der König zu ihnen?   13. Was tun die Weisen?   14. Welche Antwort finden sie?   15. Was tut der König nun?   16. Was verspricht er dem ehrlichen Mann?   17. Was tun die Boten?   18. Wie kommen die Boten zu dem König zurück?   19. Was merkt der König sofort?   20. Wo lebt der ehrliche Mann?   21. Warum hat er kein Hemd?

WORTSCHATZ[1]

COGNATES

der **Affe,** –n, –n	ape, monkey	das **Jahr,** –e	year
daß (*conjunction*)	that	der **Junge,** –n, –n	"the young one,"
denken	to think		boy, son
der **Diamant,** –en,	diamond	das **Land,** ⸗er	land, country
–en		**lang(e)**	long
das **Ende,** –n	end	**lieben**	to love
das **Fest,** –e	festival, celebration,	die **Majestät,** –en	majesty
	party	der **Neffe,** –n, –n	nephew
die **Freundin,** –nen	(girl) friend	der **Ochse,** –n, –n	ox
das **Fräulein,** –	young lady, miss	der **Palast,** ⸗e	palace
das **Gold**	gold	das **Silber**	silver
die **Hand,** ⸗e	hand	der **Soldat,** –en, –en	soldier
das **Herz,** –ens, –en	heart	das **Tal,** ⸗er	("dale"), valley

1 From this chapter on, nouns and their endings will be given as follows: plural endings if the singular is regular (**-s** or **-es** for genitive masculines and neuters, no endings for feminines); genitive singular and plural endings if singular genitives end in **-n** or **-en(s).**

die **Tochter,** ⸗	daughter	**wandern**	to wander
über	over, across	der **Weise, –n, –n**	wise man
der **Vater,** ⸗	father	die **Weisheit, –en**	wisdom

VOCABULARY

arm	poor	das **Kleid, –er**	dress
der **Befehl, –e**	command, order	**klein**	small, little
bekommen	to get, receive	der **König, –e**	king
der **Berg, –e**	mountain	die **Krankheit, –en**	illness, disease
bleiben	to remain	der **Kreis, –e**	circle
der **Bote, –n, –n**	messenger	**küssen**	to kiss
doch (*after a*	yes, indeed	**leider**	unfortunately
negative ques-		**merken**	to notice, perceive
tion)		die **Puppe, –n**	doll
das **Dorf,** ⸗**er**	village	das **Rätsel, –**	puzzle, riddle
die **Ehre, –n**	honor	das **Reich, –e**	realm, empire
ehrlich	honest	der **Schatz,** ⸗**e**	treasure; sweetheart
der **Eindruck,** ⸗**e**	impression	**schicken**	to send
nicht einmal	not even	das **Schloß, Schlösser**	castle
einzig	single	**sofort**	immediately
erfüllen	to fulfill	die **Speise, –n**	food
der **Friede(n)**	peace	die **Speisekarte, –n**	menu
das **Geheimnis, –se**	secret	**spielen**	to play
die **Gesundheit**	health	**überlegen**	to reflect, ponder
das **Glück**	happiness	**vergehen**	to pass, elapse
das **Hemd, –en**	shirt	die **Verzweiflung**	despair
ihnen (dat. plural	them	**weinen**	to cry
of **sie**)		die **Zeit, -en**	time

GRAMMATICAL TERMS

A *suffix* is an ending added to a word to indicate inflection (to hate: hat*ed*) or derivation (stupid: stupid*ity*; soul: soul*less*).

THE NOUN

1. The cases. So far we have seen that:

   a. Both in the singular and the plural, the German noun has four cases: nominative, accusative, dative, and genitive.

   b. Most masculine and neuter nouns take the ending **-s** in the genitive singular (**-es** if the noun is monosyllabic): **der Vater, des Vaters; der Mann, des Mannes.** (Nouns with genitive endings **-s** or **-es** are called *strong nouns*.)

c. Strong monosyllabic masculine and neuter nouns may take the ending -e in the dative singular: **dem Mann** or **dem Manne; dem Kind** or **dem Kinde.**
d. Feminine nouns remain unchanged in the singular.
e. All nouns end in **-n** in the dative plural unless the nominative plural already ends in **-n: die Onkel** (nom.), **den Onkeln** (dat.); but **die Frauen** (nom.), **den Frauen** (dat.). Exceptions are a few nouns with plurals in **-s.**

2. The plurals. The general rule for the formation of English plurals is: add *-s* and learn the exceptions. Except for a few nouns taken from other languages in modern times, no *s*-plurals exist in German. The ending **-s** added to a German noun almost invariably indicates a genitive singular and *not* a plural. A German noun may either remain unchanged in the plural or take the ending **-e, -er,** or **-n (-en),** depending on the class to which it belongs.

3. German plurals are best learned by committing to memory the principal parts of a noun as you learn it. Dictionaries and vocabularies ordinarily list the principal parts of a noun, that is, those basic endings from which all other case forms are derived. These principal parts are: the *nominative singular*, the *genitive singular*, and the *nominative plural*. Most dictionaries list nouns in the nominative with case endings for the two other principal parts: **der Mann, -es, ⸗er; die Frau, -, -en,** etc. The genitive singular, however, follows such simple and clear-cut rules that its forms are—with a few exceptions—quite predictable and are needed only for the exceptions. We will, therefore, give the principal parts as follows: **der Mann, ⸗er; die Frau, -en,** but: **der Herr, -n, -en; das Herz, -ens, -en.**

4. Historically, German nouns fall into a certain number of classes depending on how they form their plurals. For practical purposes, however, this time-honored system of classification is of little help. At best, it may provide supplementary information; those who can derive some benefit from it will find it in the tables in Appendix 2, pages 343 to 345.

5. To be able to handle the German noun correctly in the singular and in the plural, all you need to know is that there are four different ways for forming plurals:

SINGULAR	PLURAL	ENDING
a. **das Mädchen**	**die Mädchen**	–
der Vater	**die Väter**	⸗ (with umlaut)
die Mutter	**die Mütter**	⸗ (with umlaut)

SINGULAR	PLURAL	ENDING
b. das Jahr die Wand	die Jahre die Wände	–e =e (with umlaut)
c. das Kind der Mann	die Kinder die Männer	–er =er (with umlaut)
d. die Frau die Tafel der Student	die Frauen die Tafeln die Studenten	–en –n –en

a. A noun may have the same form in the plural as in the singular (**das Mädchen—die Mädchen**), except that the plural may require an umlaut[1] (**der Vater—die Väter**). Such nouns are listed in vocabularies as follows: **das Mädchen, -; der Vater, =.**

b. A noun may add the ending **-e** in the plural, sometimes with and sometimes without umlaut: **das Jahr** (*year*)—**die Jahre, die Wand** (*wall*)—**die Wände.** The designation is: **das Jahr, -e; die Wand, =e.**

c. The plural ending may be **-er,** always with umlaut where possible (that is, if the stem vowel is **a, o, u, au**): **der Mann—die Männer; das Kind—die Kinder.** Designation: **der Mann, =er; das Kind, -er.**

d. The plural ending may be **-en** or **-n: die Frau—die Frauen, die Tafel** (*blackboard*)—**die Tafeln.** These nouns never take an umlaut. The majority of them are feminine. Their full declension:

NOM.	die Frau	die Frauen
ACC.	die Frau	die Frauen
DAT.	der Frau	den Frauen
GEN.	der Frau	der Frauen

There is, however, a small number of masculine nouns that also take the ending **-en** or **-n** in the plural. Most of these masculine nouns form all endings with **-en** or **-n,** except in the nominative singular. Their full declension is:

NOM.	der Student	die Studenten
ACC.	den Studenten	die Studenten
DAT.	dem Studenten	den Studenten
GEN.	des Studenten	der Studenten

[1] There are no hard and fast rules according to which a noun does or does not take the umlaut in the plural, except for the nouns with plurals in **-er** and **-(e)n** (see c and d). Since the umlaut may be the only distinguishing mark between a singular and a plural, it is important to distinguish its uses.

Pay special attention to the declension of **der Herr** (*master, mister*), which adds **-n** in the accusative, dative, and genitive singular, but **-en** in all plural forms:

NOM.	**der Herr**	**die Herren**
ACC.	**den Herrn**	**die Herren**
DAT.	**dem Herrn**	**den Herren**
GEN.	**des Herrn**	**der Herren**

Note that **Herr** together with a name **(Herr Meier)** is always declined according to its function in the sentence:

Kennen Sie Herrn Meier?   *Do you know Mr. Meier?*

A few masculine nouns with the plural ending **-n** take an additional **s** in the genitive singular:

NOM.	**der Name**	**die Namen**
ACC.	**den Namen**	**die Namen**
DAT.	**dem Namen**	**den Namen**
GEN.	**des Namens**	**der Namen**

Similarly: **der Friede** (*peace*), **der Gedanke** (*thought, idea*), **der Glaube** (*belief*), **der Wille** (*will*).

Note also that the neuter noun **das Herz** (*heart*) follows a similar pattern:

NOM.	**das Herz**	**die Herzen**
ACC.	**das Herz**	**die Herzen**
DAT.	**dem Herzen**	**den Herzen**
GEN.	**des Herzens**	**der Herzen**

6. A number of useful observations will help in the mastery of the German noun:

a. Diminutives are formed by adding the suffix **-chen** or **-lein** to a noun. A noun can usually take either one of the two diminutive endings without change of meaning; in a few cases, one combination will be more common than the other, and in some instances, special meanings have been attached to a given form **(das Mädchen** *girl;* **das Fräulein** *miss*). Diminutives are always neuter no matter what the gender of the noun from which they are derived. They normally take the umlaut, but no ending:

der Vater (*father*) — **das Väterchen, die Väterchen** (*dear old daddy*)
die Frau (*woman*) — **das Frauchen, die Frauchen** (*little old lady*)
          but: **das Fräulein, die Fräulein** (*miss*)

In some words, the noun suffix is dropped when a diminutive ending is added:

der Affe (*monkey*) — das Äffchen
der Garten (*garden*) — das Gärtchen
der Spiegel (*mirror*)—das Spiegelchen; but: das Spieglein

Be aware of such possibilities in order to recognize the noun from which the diminutive is derived.

b. Feminine nouns in **-in** (always referring to people) and all nouns in **-nis** double the final consonant before plural endings. For neuter nouns in **-nis** (**das Geheimnis** [*secret*]) this also applies to the genitive:

die Freundin — die Freundinnen
das Geheimnis — des Geheimnisses, die Geheimnisse

7. Irregularities.

a. A few masculine and neuter (but no feminine) nouns take the ending **-(e)s** in the singular and **-(e)n** in the plural; they never have an umlaut; example: **das Auge** (*eye*):

NOM.	das Auge	die Augen
ACC.	das Auge	die Augen
DAT.	dem Auge	den Augen
GEN.	des Auges	der Augen

Similarly: **das Bett** (*bed*), **das Hemd** (*shirt*), **das Ohr** (*ear*), **der Staat** (*state*), and all masculine nouns in **-or**, like **der Pastor, der Direktor, der Professor,** and others, usually stressed on the stem in the singular (**der Pạstor** or **der Pastọr, der Professọr**), but always on the suffix **-or** in the plural (**die Pastọren, die Professọren**).

b. The nouns **der Bauer** (*farmer, peasant*) and **der Nachbar** (*neighbor*) may end in **-s** or **-n** in the singular, but the forms in **-n** are preferred: **den Bauer** or **Bauern, dem Bauer** or **Bauern, des Bauers** or **Bauern.** The plurals always end in **-n: die Bauern, die Nachbarn.**

c. As previously mentioned, a few nouns that have come into German from other languages in the recent past, form plurals in **-s: das Auto, die Autos; das Hotel, die Hotels; das Kino, die Kinos** (*movie theater, movies*); **das Restaurant, die Restaurants,** etc. Such nouns are declined:

NOM.	das Auto	die Autos
ACC.	das Auto	die Autos
DAT.	dem Auto	den Autos
GEN.	des Autos	der Autos

d. Nouns of Latin origin in **-um** form plurals in **-en:**

NOM.	das Museum	die Museen
ACC.	das Museum	die Museen
DAT.	dem Museum	den Museen
GEN.	des Museums	der Museen

8. The compound noun is characteristic of German. It is commonly made up of two or more nouns but may also include adjectives, verb stems, adverbs, or prepositions. The final element determines the gender of the compound:

das Öl (*oil*), **die Farbe** (*paint*) = **die Ölfarbe**

schnell (*fast*), **der Zug** (*train*) = **der Schnellzug**

wohnen (*to live*), **das Zimmer** (*room*) = **das Wohnzimmer**

A connective **s** is frequently inserted between the two components of a compound noun:

die Liebe (*love*), **der Schmerz** (*pain*) = **der Liebesschmerz**

Many compounds, freely formed by writers, are not listed in dictionaries: their meaning must then be determined from their components. **Der Abendanzug = der Abend** (*evening*), **der Anzug** (*suit*): *evening suit;* in such cases, English and German construct their noun combinations the same way, except that in German the nouns become one word. In other instances, especially if the nouns are abstract, English cannot form such combinations. It is then better to begin the translation with the last part of the combination: **die Relativitätstheorie = die Theorie** (*theory*), **die Relativität** (*relativity*): *theory of relativity;* **die Wärmetheorie = die Theorie** (*theory*), **die Wärme** (*warmth, heat*): *theory of heat.*

RECAPITULATION OF MAIN POINTS

1. Most masculine and all neuter nouns end in **-s** in the genitive singular, **-es** if monosyllabic. They may add **-e** in the dative singular.

2. A small number of masculine nouns with plural ending **-en** or **-n** form all endings with **-en** or **-n,** except in the nominative singular.

3. Feminine nouns always remain unchanged in the singular.

4. All nouns end in **-n** in the dative plural, except a few with plural endings in **-s.**

5. Except for a few nouns of non-German origin, German nouns do not generally form their plurals in **-s.** The ending **-s** is essentially a genitive singular ending.

6. There are four ways of forming plurals:

a. **-** or **⸚** (no special plural ending)	c. **-e** or **⸚er**
b. **-e** or **⸚e**	d. **-en** or **-n**

ÜBUNGEN

Practice in Reading and Writing

A. *Read aloud and translate:*

1. Wo kauft man solche Kleider? 2. Mit solchen Kindern spielen wir nicht.
3. Was für eine Krankheit ist das? 4. Dieser Eindruck vergeht bald. 5. Solche Geschichten erzählt man Kindern nicht. 6. Manche Mädchen spielen mit Puppen, andere nicht. 7. Die Logik der Frau ist dem Manne ein Rätsel.
8. Die Schlösser am Rhein sind sehr romantisch. 9. Der Hudson ist sehr schön, aber er hat leider keine Schlösser. 10. Kennen Sie die Namen dieser Mädchen? 11. Er ist der Kandidat der Demokraten und nicht der Republikaner. 12. Mein Schatz, der hat einen Rosenmund (der Mund = *mouth*), und wer den küßt, der wird gesund. 13. Die Krankheit des Vaters macht der Familie Sorgen. 14. Sie sitzen im Kreise und diskutieren die Probleme der Zeit. 15. Seine Verzweiflung geht mir wirklich sehr zu Herzen. 16. Viele unserer Studenten sind Veteranen. 17. Wir lesen etwas von (*by*) diesem großen Philosophen. 18. Schopenhauer und Schleiermacher waren deutsche Philosophen. 19. Viele Leute kennen nicht einmal ihre Nachbarn. 20. Unsere Nachbarn sind Bauern. 21. Die Namen dieser Leute kenne ich nicht.
22. Ein Mann dieses Namens wohnt in dem Haus um (*around*) die Ecke.
23. Ich glaube, sie ist nur in seinen Namen verliebt. 24. In diesen Dörfern finden Sie kein einziges Hotel. 25. Fräulein, geben Sie mir bitte die Speisekarte!

B. *Translate and identify the phrases in italics as to case and number:*

1. die Weisheit *des Alten* 2. die Weisheit *der Alten* 3. die Puppen *dieses* Mädchens 4. die Puppen *dieser Mädchen* 5. die Fenster *ihrer Zimmer*
6. Ich kenne *diesen Menschen.* 7. Kennen Sie *diese Menschen?* 8. *Diesen Menschen* hole ich etwas zu essen. 9. die Idee *des Kandidaten* 10. Die Gedanken *mancher Professoren* 11. die Worte *des zweiten Paragraphen*
12. das Zimmer *meiner Freundin* 13. Kennen Sie *diese Rätsel?* 14. Kennen Sie *dieses Rätsel?* 15. die Schätze *in diesen Palästen* 16. *Herrn* Joseph Schmidt. 17. Kennen Sie *diese Herren?* 18. Die Adressen *dieser Herren* kenne ich nicht. 19. *Die Speisen* in diesem Restaurant 20. Die Sagen *der Deutschen* stammen aus (*date from*) dem Mittelalter.

C. *With the aid of the end vocabulary, translate the following compounds:*

1. der Kunstgegenstand 2. das Inhaltsverzeichnis 3. der Atomzertrümmerungsversuch 4. das Liebesabenteuer 5. die Universitätsbibliothek
6. das Einkommensteueramt 7. die Millionärswitwe 8. der Entwicklungsroman 9. die Gestaltpsychologie 10. das Landesregierungsgebäude.

D. *Translate:*

1. Do you know these girls?   2. Who lives in these castles today?   3. My landlady's rooms are very small.   4. He is studying the art of the Middle Ages.   5. She plays with her dolls in (w. dat.) the living room.   6. His room has a door and two windows.   7. They are wandering from village to village and do not find a wise man.   8. They have eyes and see not, and ears and hear not.   9. Do you see her dress? All her dresses are very short.   10. Which impression do you have of his daughter?   11. All his girl friends have cars.   12. The problem of our time is the preservation **(die Erhaltung)** of peace.   13. I believe these merchants are honest.   14. He knocks on **(an,** w. acc.) all the doors but nobody opens.   15. Our hotel has many beds.   16. These impressions are not new.   17. The way leads through **(durch,** w. acc.) a valley to **(zu,** w. dat.) a village.   18. Many villages lie at the (at the, **am)** end of these valleys.   19. He tells the children many stories.   20. The soldiers have the order to remain in (w. dat.) the villages.

Oral Exercises

E. *Supply the missing nouns in their correct case forms:*

EXAMPLE: (of the student) Die Gesundheit . . . . ist nicht gut.
　　　　　Die Gesundheit des Studenten ist nicht gut.

1. (of my friend) Die Tochter . . . . heißt Lotte.   2. (to the people) Er zeigt . . . . das Schloß.   3. (to the gentleman) Ich gebe . . . . die Adresse.   4. (These gentlemen) . . . . kennen unsere Adresse.   5. (of his daughters) Die Kleider . . . . sind ein wenig kurz!   6. (of his daughter) Das Kleid . . . . ist ein wenig lang.   7. (to the man) Geben Sie . . . . etwas zu essen!   8. (of this name) Kennen Sie einen Studenten . . . ?   9. (his secrets) Jeder hat . . . . .   10. (shirts) Sie schicken ihm zwei . . . . .   11. (shirts) Mit zwei . . . . habe ich genug (enough).   12. (palaces, museums) Die . . . . sind jetzt alle . . . . .   13. (the students) Die Mädchen tanzen mit (w. dat.) . . . . .   14. (the girls) Die Studenten tanzen mit . . . . .   15. (the country) Sie kennen . . . . genau.   16. (all these countries) . . . . sind Republiken.   17. (in forests) Die Affen leben in (w. dat.) . . . . .   18. (all his girl friends) Ich kenne . . . . .   19. (all his children) Er kommt mit . . . . .   20. (all his children) . . . . sind krank.

F. *Change the noun to plural:*

EXAMPLES: Sie suchen ihr Kind.　　　　Sie suchen ihre Kinder.
　　　　　　Sie erzählt es ihrer Tochter.　Sie erzählt es ihren Töchtern.

1. Du fragst deinenFreund.
2. Ich antworte jenem Mann.
3. Wir verstehen diesen Kandidaten.
4. Wir helfen diesem Fräulein.

5. Ihr besucht unser Museum.
6. Er kommt mit seiner Freundin.
7. Sie machen ihren Versuch.
8. Er erklärt es seinem Psychiater.
9. Wir kennen diesen Herrn.
10. Du erklärst es deinem Arzt.
11. Sie finden endlich ihr Auto.
12. Ihr helft jener Familie.
13. Ich grüße diesen Kaufmann.
14. Sie kaufen dieses Haus.
15. Wir kommen mit unserem Vater.
16. Wir geben es seinem Kind.

G. *Change the noun objects to singular:*

EXAMPLES: Wir glauben unseren Jungen.   Wir glauben unserem Jungen.
Er versteht diese Philosophen.   Er versteht diesen Philosophen.

1. Wir fragen keine Menschen.
2. Sie reden mit jenen Herren.
3. Ihr fragt euere Boten.
4. Ich helfe diesen Studenten.
5. Er kommt mit seinen Affen.
6. Wir glauben diesen Soldaten.

H. *Change the noun objects to singular:*

EXAMPLES: Sie ruft ihre Kinder.   Sie ruft ihr Kind.
Sie ruft ihre Jungen.   Sie ruft ihren Jungen.

1. Ich kenne diese Professoren.
2. Ich kenne diese Studenten.
3. Er kommt mit seinen Töchtern.
4. Er kommt mit seinen Kandidaten.
5. Sie helfen manchen Menschen.
6. Sie helfen manchen Frauen.
7. Ich frage unsere Kaufleute.
8. Ich frage unsere Soldaten.
9. Ich komme mit meinen Geheimnissen.
10. Er kommt mit seinen Affen.
11. Sie holt ihre Freunde.
12. Er holt seine Ochsen.
13. Er tanzt gern mit diesen Mädchen.
14. Sie tanzt gern mit diesen Studenten.

I. *Change the plural nouns in the genitive to singular:*

EXAMPLES: Der Geist dieser Zeiten.   Der Geist dieser Zeit.
Der Geist dieser Philosophen.   Der Geist dieses Philosophen.

1. Die Mutter dieser Töchter.
2. Die Mutter dieser Studenten.
3. Die Antwort jener Kandidaten.
4. Die Antwort unserer Sekretärinnen.
5. Die Angst jener Herren.
6. Die Angst dieser Damen.
7. Der Rauch seiner Zigarren.
8. Das Geheimnis mancher Künstler.
9. Der Laden jener Kaufleute.
10. Die Idee jener Philosophen.
11. Der Name seiner Autos.
12. Das Alter dieser Museen.

Review 1

Lessons One through Five

1 Use of the Present Tense and the Imperative

Remember the following basic rules about the use of the present tense and of the imperative:

A. German has no progressive or emphatic verb form. **Ich rede** may mean: *I talk, I am talking, I do talk*, depending on the context in which the verb occurs.

EXAMPLES:

Ich rede jeden Tag mit ihr.	*I talk to her every day.*
Ich rede eben mit ihr.	*I am just now talking to her.*
Ja, ich rede mit ihr, aber nicht oft.	*Yes, I do talk to her, but not often.*

Be sure that your translation is in idiomatic English.

B. The imperative form depends on the relationship of the speaker to the person he is addressing. If this relationship is of a personal or intimate nature, the ending of the verb is **-e** (in the singular) or **-(e)t** (in the plural); if it is conventional, impersonal, or formal, the verb ending is **-en** and the personal pronoun **Sie** must be placed after the verb:

EXAMPLES:

Personal, intimate: **Sage das nicht! Sagt das nicht!** ⎱ *Don't say that!*
Conventional: **Sagen Sie das nicht!**   ⎰

C. The imperative in the first person plural is rendered by the English phrase:
Let's . . .

EXAMPLE:

Gehen wir! *Let's go!*

D. *Translate and account for each verb form used:*

1. Wir gehen jetzt. 2. Gehen wir jetzt? 3. Gehen wir jetzt! 4. Sie antwortet nicht. 5. Antworten sie nicht? 6. Antworten Sie nicht? 7. Wer redet da? 8. Wo seid ihr? 9. Sei so gut und zeige dem Mann das Haus! 10. Er sagt das, aber sie antwortet nicht. 11. Warum antwortest du nicht? 12. Die Studentin glaubt das nicht. 13. Was habt ihr da? 14. Sprechen wir Deutsch? 15. Sprechen Sie Deutsch? 16. Es ist warm. 17. Es wird warm. 18. Sie hat Zeit, aber Sie haben keine Zeit. 19. Warum kaufen Sie das? 20. Fragen wir den Arzt!

2 Der- and Ein-Words

A. Recall the forms of the definite and indefinite articles. An unfaltering knowledge of these forms is basic for all sentence construction and other grammatical points coming up later on:

	SINGULAR			PLURAL	SINGULAR (only)		
NOM.	der	die	das	die	ein	eine	ein
ACC.	den	die	das	die	einen	eine	ein
DAT.	dem	der	dem	den	einem	einer	einem
GEN.	des	der	des	der	eines	einer	eines

B. Remember that:

des is always a genitive singular: **des Mädchens**

dem is always a dative singular: **dem Mann(e), dem Mädchen**

den is either masculine accusative singular (**den Mann**) or dative plural (**den Männern, den Frauen, den Mädchen**), in which case the noun also ends in **-n.**

A noun preceded by the article **des, dem,** or **den** can *never* be the subject of a sentence.

C. Der, die, das when used as pronouns (that is, without a noun) usually mean *he, she, it,* or *they.* They are then demonstratives and have the following genitive forms: **dessen, deren, dessen** in the singular, and **deren** in the plural. These genitive forms are generally equivalent to *his, her, its, theirs, the latter's.*

D. The dative plural of these pronouns is **denen.**

E. As a possessive adjective, **ihr** means *her* or *their;* **Ihr** (capitalized) always means *your.*

F. Ein-words used as pronouns have the same endings as **der**-words. Translate **einer** as *someone, one;* **keiner** as *no one;* **keins** as *none.*

G. Was für ein and **welch ein** mean *what a;* **solch ein** means *such a.*

H. *Translate; identify the cases of the words in italics:*

1. das Fenster *dieses Abteils.*   2. die Fenster *dieses Abteils.*   3. der Rauch *seiner Zigarre.*   4. der Rauch *jeder Zigarre.*   5. der Tod *jedes Menschen.* 6. der Tod *aller Menschen.*   7. Ich glaube *diesen Menschen* nicht.   8. Glauben Sie *einem solchen Menschen?*   9. Er betrachtet *jedes Zimmer* genau.   10. *Der* kennt das nicht.   11. *Was für ein Mädchen!*   12. *Denen* glaube ich nicht. 13. Haben Sie *Ihren Koffer?*   14. *Wer* kommt?—*Meine Freunde, ihre Tochter* und *deren Kinder.*   15. Kennen Sie *unseren Arzt?*   16. Was sagen Sie *Ihrem Arzt?*   17. *Mancher* weiß das nicht.   18. *Manchen* kennt er nicht.   19. Fragt *eure Eltern!*   20. Er fragt *jedes Mädchen.*   21. Er fragt *alle Mädchen.* 22. Das ist *mein Koffer,* nicht *deiner.*   23. *Keiner* ist hier.   24. Kommt *einer?* 25. Kennst du hier *keinen?*

3 Declension of Nouns; Plural

A. To determine the case forms of a given noun you need to know only the ending for the nominative plural (which can be looked up in any dictionary or word list).

B. All other forms can be derived from the basic forms (principal parts), provided some general rules are observed:

For the singular:

a. Feminine nouns never take an ending.
b. Most masculine and neuter nouns take **-s** (monosyllables usually **-es**) in the genitive.

c. Monosyllabic masculines and neuters with genitives in **-es** may have the ending **-e** in the dative.

d. Masculine nouns that take **-(e)n** in the plural take the same ending in the singular accusative, dative, and genitive.

e. There are some exceptions to these rules (see page 58), which should be carefully reviewed.

For the plural:

a. All dative plurals end in **-n.**

b. If a noun ends in **-n** in the nominative plural **(der Affe—die Affen),** no further ending is used throughout the plural; otherwise, **-n** must be added in the dative.

c. A few nouns of non-German origin add **-s (das Restaurant—die Restaurants).**

C. *Give the genitive singular and dative plural forms of the following nouns:*

1. der Freund, -e   2. der Mann, ⸗er   3. die Freundin, -nen   4. das Haus, ⸗er
5. die Frau, -en   6. die Stadt, ⸗e   7. das Mädchen, -   8. das Land, ⸗er
9. der Affe, -n   10. das Rätsel, -

D. *Explain the phrases in italics:*

1. Das ist *manchen Studenten* zuviel.   2. Das ist *manchem Studenten* zuviel.
3. Das ist *manchen Studentinnen* zuviel.   4. *Diesen Menschen* kenne ich nicht.
5. *Diese Menschen* kenne ich nicht.   6. *Diesen Menschen* gebe ich etwas.
7. *Die Mädchen* fragt er nicht.   8. Kennst du die Kinder *dieser Frauen?*
9. Die Hemden *dieses Alten* sind sicher neu (*new*).   10. Wir geben dem Alten *unsere Hemden.*   11. Welchem Alten geben Sie *das Hemd?*   12. Geben Sie *dem Herrn* Ihre Adresse!   13. Haben Sie *Herrn Schmidts* Adresse?   14. *Die Herren* haben Ihre Adressen.   15. Kennen Sie *ihre Töchter?*   16. Kennen Sie *ihre Tochter?*   17. Kennen Sie die Namen *ihrer Töchter?*   18. Kennen Sie den Namen *ihrer Tochter?*   19. Ich kenne den Namen *Ihrer Tochter.*
20. Ich sage das *ihren Töchtern.*

6

Weak Verbs

Bertolt Brecht

In vielen Theatern aller Länder spielt man heute die Dramen von Bertolt Brecht. Das Publikum schätzt besonders die „Dreigroschenoper",[1] schon wegen[2] der Musik von Kurt Weill, und dann vor allem die Geschichtsdramen, wie „Leben des Galilei" und „Mutter Courage". In allen seinen Stücken ist
5 Brecht Dichter, selbst dort, wo er den Lehrer spielt—und er spielt gern den Lehrer. Einige dieser Stücke heißen daher „Lehrstücke".[3]

Auch im Privatleben war Brecht gern Erzieher. So hatte einmal einer seiner Freunde im Ersten Weltkrieg den Gedanken, freiwillig[4] Soldat zu werden. Brecht war gegen den Krieg und reagierte daher auf seine Weise:
10 „Gut", sagte er zu ihm, „du wirst Soldat. Aber im Falle deines Heldentodes komme ich nicht zum[5] Begräbnis." Eine Woche später änderte er seine Meinung. „Ich komme doch zu deinem Begräbnis", erklärte er nun. Da änderte auch der Freund die seine: er verzichtete auf den Heldentod und wurde[6] nicht Soldat.
15 Immer wieder haben Freunde und Bekannte Brecht um seinen Rat gefragt.

1. **Dreigroschenoper** *Threepenny Opera.* 2. **wegen** (w. gen.) *because of.* 3. **Lehrstücke** *didactic plays.* 4. **freiwillig Soldat zu werden** (lit., *to become a soldier voluntarily:*) *to volunteer for the army.* 5. **zum** (contraction for **zu dem**) *to the.* 6. **wurde** *became, did become.*

Der eine beabsichtigte, Literaturwissenschaft[7] zu studieren, ein anderer eine
Schauspielerin zu heiraten. Was hatte Brecht dazu[8] zu sagen? Dem Liebhaber
der Literatur antwortete er: „Literaturwissenschaft? Was für eine Wissen-
schaft ist das? Nur die exakten Wissenschaften sind Wissenschaften. Ein
Pfund[9] Eisen ist ein Pfund Eisen. Aber was ist ein Pfund Meinung?" Dem 20
Liebhaber der Frauen: „Sie wollen heiraten? Warum fragen Sie mich, ob[10]
Sie schwimmen können, wenn Sie ins[11] Wasser springen?"

Aber Brecht war gar nicht gegen das Heiraten und noch weniger gegen
die Frauen. Er hat sogar mehr als[12] einmal geheiratet. Schon der junge
Brecht hatte Freundinnen in vielen Städten—oder, wie man sagt, in allen 25
Häfen. Und was verspricht man Freundinnen nicht alles?[13] Zum Beispiel
die Ehe. Zwei solche Freundinnen hörten voneinander.[14] Die eine besuchte
die andere, und sie diskutierten den Fall auf ihre Weise. Jede behauptete:
Brecht ist mein Bräutigam! Aber das war vielleicht auch wieder nur eine
Meinung. Sie fragten daher Brecht selbst nach[15] seiner exakten Meinung: 30
„Wen beabsichtigst du nun zu heiraten?" Brecht zögerte keinen Augenblick
und sagte: „Beide!"

Schüler imitieren oft ihre Lehrer. Auch Brechts Schüler imitierten ihn:
seinen Stil, seine Technik, seine Kleidung, seine Frisur—und das tat[16] auch
der Komponist Paul Dessau. Brecht merkte das und meinte: „Dessau ist so 35
gesund, der überlebt mich[17] sicher. Aber ich frage mich: wozu[18]?"

7. **Wissenschaft** *science;* **Literaturwissenschaft** *literary history.* 8. **dazu** *to that.* 9. **ein
Pfund** *a pound of.* 10. **ob** *whether.* 11. **ins** (contraction for **in das**) *into the.* 12. **mehr
als** *more than.* 13. **was . . . nicht alles** *how many things, how much, what . . . not.* 14. **voneinander** *of one another.* 15. **nach** (here:) *about.* 16. **tat** *did.* 17. **überlebt mich** (lit.,
outlives me:) lives longer than I. 18. **wozu?** (*lit., what for:*) *what's the good of it?*

FRAGEN

1. Wo spielt man heute die Dramen Brechts? 2. Was schätzt das Publikum
besonders? 3. Was ist Brecht in allen seinen Stücken? 4. Was tut er auch
dort, wo er Dichter ist? 5. Welchen Gedanken hatte einer der Freunde
Brechts im Ersten Weltkrieg? 6. War Brecht für den Krieg? 7. Was sagte
er daher zu dem Freund? 8. Wann änderte er seine Meinung? 9. Wurde
der Freund Soldat? 10. Was beabsichtigte einer der Freunde Brechts?
11. Was beabsichtigte der andere? 12. Was ist ein Liebhaber? 13. Ist die
Literaturwissenschaft eine exakte Wissenschaft? 14. Was antwortete er
dem anderen Freund? 15. Wo hatte Brecht Freundinnen? 16. Was taten
(*did*) die beiden Freundinnen? 17. Wen fragten sie um seine Meinung?
18. Was antwortete Brecht? 19. Was imitierten Brechts Schüler? 20. Was
sagte Brecht über (*about*) Paul Dessau?

WORTSCHATZ

COGNATES

diskut**ie**ren	to discuss	die **Mus**_i_**k (von)**	music (by)
dort	there	die **Mutter,** =	mother
dort wo	where	**oft**	often
das **Drama, die**	drama, play	das **Priv**_a_**tleben**	private life
Dramen		das **Publikum**	public, audience
das **Eisen**	iron	re**ag**_ie_**ren**	to react
ex**a**kt	exact	der **Stil, –e**	style
der **Hafen,** =	harbor, port	die **Technik**	technique
hören	to hear	das **The**_a_**ter, –**	theater
imit**ie**ren	to imitate	das **Wasser**	water
der **Kompon**_i_**st, –en,**	composer		
–en			

VOCABULARY

ändern	to change	der **Rat,**	
beabsichtigen	to intend	die **Ratschläge**	advice
das **Begräbnis, –se**	funeral	**um Rat fragen**	to ask (someone's) advice
das **Beispiel, –e**	example	**schätzen**	to value
zum Beispiel	for example	die **Schauspielerin,**	actress
der **Bekannte, –n, –n**	acquaintance	**–nen**	
der **Bräutigam, –e**	bridegroom	der **Schüler, –**	pupil, student
dah_e_**r**	therefore	**selbst**	even; (with names
der **Dichter, –**	poet		or pronouns:) **(er)**
doch (*in response*	after all		**selbst** (he) himself
to negative)		**springen**	to jump
die **Ehe, –n**	marriage	das **Stück, –e**	play, piece
erst	first	**versprechen**	to promise
der **Erzieher, –**	educator, pedagogue	**er verspricht**	he promises
der **Fall,** =**e**	case	**verzichten (auf,**	to renounce (some-
die **Fris**_u_**r, en**	haircut	*w. acc.*)	thing); to do with-
gar nicht	not at all		out
der **Gedanke, –ns, –n**	thought	**vor allem**	above all, especially
gegen (*w. acc.*)	against	die **Weise, –n**	manner
heiraten	to marry	**auf seine (ihre)**	in his (their) man-
das **Heiraten**	marrying	**Weise**	ner
der **Held, –en, –en**	hero	der **Weltkrieg, –e**	world war
der **Heldentod**	hero's death	**wenn**	if
die **Kleidung**	clothing	die **Wissenschaft,**	(natural) science
können	to be able to	**–en**	
Sie können	you can	die **Woche, –n**	week
der **Krieg, –e**	war	**wollen**	to want to
der **Lehrer, –**	teacher	**er will**	he wants to
der **Liebhaber, –**	lover, connoisseur	**zögern**	to hesitate
die **Meinung, –en**	opinion, mind		
oder	or		

GRAMMATICAL TERMS

1. English has *regular* and *irregular* verbs. Regular verbs form their past tense and their past participle by adding *-d* or *-ed* to the infinitive, irregular verbs by a variation of the stem vowel:

	INFINITIVE	PAST	PAST PARTICIPLE
REGULAR:	live	lived	lived (in: I have lived)
IRREGULAR:	give	gave	given (in: I have given)

2. The *infinitive*, *past tense*, and *past participle* are called the *principal parts* of a verb; from them it is possible to derive all other tenses and forms.

3. The tenses are:

PRESENT:	I live (am living, do live)
PAST:	I lived (was living, did live)
PRESENT PERFECT:	I have lived (have been living)
PAST PERFECT:	I had lived (had been living)
FUTURE:	I shall (will) live (be living)
FUTURE PERFECT:	I shall (will) have lived (been living)

4. Simple tenses are those consisting of the verb itself (the present and the past); compound tenses are those formed with the help of auxiliary verbs (present perfect, etc.).

5. The *finite verb* is the (inflected) verb form limited as to person, number, and tense. In simple tenses, the finite verb is the main verb of the clause; in compound tenses, the finite verb is the auxiliary:

> He *lived* with us for two weeks.
> He *will* live with us for two weeks.

6. The *present participle* in English ends in *-ing;* this ending is added to the stem of the verb: clos*ing*, do*ing:*

> Softly *closing* the door, she left the room.

7. The *past participle* is the form of the verb used in combination with auxiliaries to form the *present perfect, past perfect, future perfect,* and the *passive:*

> He *has bought* a book.
> He *had divided* the cake.
> You *were told* about it.

"WEAK" OR REGULAR VERBS

1. In German, we refer to the regular verb as weak and, generally, to the irregular verb as strong. Most German verbs are weak.

While it is necessary to know (and to memorize) the three principal parts of a strong verb in order to arrive at the various tenses, the tenses and forms of a weak verb can easily be derived from the infinitive. Thus, if we know the infinitive **leben** (*to live*), we can form the present and past tenses, as well as the past participle, by adding the appropriate endings and prefix to the stem **leb-:**

PRESENT·	ich lebe
PAST:	ich lebte
PAST PARTICIPLE:	gelebt

2. If the stem of a verb ends in **-d** or **-t,** or if a succession of consonants makes it difficult to pronounce an added **-st** or **-t** (as it would be in **öffnte**) an **e** is inserted between the stem and the **-st** or **-t** of the ending. The following forms are affected:

	PRESENT	PAST	PAST PARTICIPLE
antworten (*to answer*)	du antwortest er antwortet ihr antwortet	ich antwortete (and throughout the past)	geantwortet
öffnen (*to open*)	du öffnest er öffnet ihr öffnet	ich öffnete (and throughout the past)	geöffnet

3. The past participle, in addition to the ending **-t,** has the prefix **ge-,** except in verbs which:

a. end in **-ieren** (which always have the word accent on **-ier-**); the stems of these verbs are mostly of non-German origin and therefore easily recognized: **studieren, fotografieren, telefonieren,** and many others. The principal parts are, for example: **studieren, studierte, studiert.**

b. begin with one of the inseparable prefixes: **be-, emp-, ent-, er-, ge-, hinter-, miß-, ver-, zer-.** Examples:

INFINITIVE	PAST	PAST PARTICIPLE
besuchen (*to visit*)	**besuchte**	**besucht**
erzählen (*to tell*)	**erzählte**	**erzählt**

4. On the basis of these general observations, we can form the various tenses of a weak verb.[1] Examples: **leben** *to live*, **öffnen** *to open*.

---

[1] Since the function of the various tenses is different in German and English, the forms in the following tables are given without meanings. For the uses of the tenses, see the later sections of this Aufgabe.

PRESENT

ich lebe	ich öffne
du lebst	du öffnest
er lebt	er öffnet
wir leben	wir öffnen
ihr lebt	ihr öffnet
sie leben	sie öffnen
Sie leben	Sie öffnen

PAST

ich lebte	ich öffnete
du lebtest	du öffnetest
er lebte	er öffnete
wir lebten	wir öffneten
ihr lebtet	ihr öffnetet
sie lebten	sie öffneten
Sie lebten	Sie öffneten

The past tense of **haben** is slightly irregular:

ich **hatte** *I had*, etc.	wir **hatten**
du **hattest**	ihr **hattet**
er **hatte**	sie **hatten**

---

5. To form the present and past perfect, combine the appropriate forms of **haben** with the past participle, as in English:

PRESENT PERFECT   PAST PERFECT

[handwritten: OR SEIN FOR EVERY WORD OF MOTION —]

ich **habe gelebt (geöffnet)**	ich **hatte gelebt (geöffnet)**
du **hast gelebt (geöffnet)**	du **hattest gelebt (geöffnet)**
er **hat gelebt (geöffnet)**	er **hatte gelebt (geöffnet)**
wir **haben gelebt (geöffnet)**	wir **hatten gelebt (geöffnet)**
ihr **habt gelebt (geöffnet)**	ihr **hattet gelebt (geöffnet)**
sie **haben gelebt (geöffnet)**	sie **hatten gelebt (geöffnet)**
Sie **haben gelebt (geöffnet)**	Sie **hatten gelebt (geöffnet)**

6. For the future tenses, combine the appropriate forms of **werden** with the infinitive for the future, and with the past infinitive for the future perfect;[1] the only difference from English is the sequence of verb forms in the future perfect; example: **leben:**

FUTURE   FUTURE PERFECT

ich **werde leben**	ich **werde gelebt haben**
du **wirst leben**	du **wirst gelebt haben**
er **wird leben**	er **wird gelebt haben**

---

[1] The past infinitive consists of the past participle of the main verb combined with the infinitive of the auxiliary: **gelebt haben** *to have lived.* The future perfect is as rare in German as in English.

wir **werden leben**	wir **werden gelebt haben**
ihr **werdet leben**	ihr **werdet gelebt haben**
sie **werden leben**	sie **werden gelebt haben**
Sie **werden leben**	Sie **werden gelebt haben**

7. In compound tenses, infinitives and past participles are placed at the end of a main clause:

> Er **hat** den Bleistift erst gestern **gekauft.**
> *He bought the pencil only yesterday.*
> Er **wird** den Bleistift morgen **kaufen.**
> *He will buy the pencil tomorrow.*

In subordinate clauses the inflected verb form takes the last position:

> Ich weiß, daß er den Bleistift gestern **gekauft hat.**
> Ich weiß, daß er den Bleistift morgen **kaufen wird.**

8. The present participle is formed by adding **-d** to the infinitive:

> **spielen** (*to play*)   **spielend** (*playing*)

It is used primarily as an adjective:

> die **folgende** Geschichte   *the following story*
> die **kommende** Woche   *the coming week*

Never use a German present participle to form a progressive tense. Remember that German has no progressive tense forms: *I am living* **ich lebe;** *I was living* **ich lebte.**

USES OF THE TENSES IN GERMAN

1. Present and Present Perfect

a. The present:

In general, the present tense has the same function in German as in English, except that it may also express the future, especially when an adverb (or adverbial phrase) of time clearly points to the future:[1]

> Ich **sage** es ihm **morgen.**   *I'll tell him tomorrow.*

[1] The present tense is also used (a) as historical present in vivid accounts of events where English would use the past: Und dann **kommt** er da gestern wirklich und **verlangt** sein Geld! *And then he really came yesterday and asked for his money!;* (b) to express an action that began in the past and continues into the present, provided the clause contains a prepositional phrase with **(schon) seit** (*since, for*) or an adverbial phrase like **schon lange** (*a long time* [*already*]) or **wie lange (schon)?** (*how long* [*already*])*?.* English employs the present perfect in such constructions:

> **Ich bin (schon) seit zehn Jahren hier.**   *I have been here for* (*the last*) *ten years.*
> **Wie lange bist du (schon) hier?**   *How long have you been here?*

b. The present perfect:

The present perfect is used in conversational German where English usually requires the past tense:

Er **hat** sich gestern ein Auto **gekauft.**
He bought himself a car yesterday.
Sie **haben** meinen Wagen sofort **repariert.**
They immediately repaired my car.

However, with the auxiliaries **sein, haben, werden** and the modal auxiliaries **(dürfen, können, mögen, müssen, sollen, wollen),** the past and the present perfect are optional in conversation:

Ich **hatte** gerade kein Geld.
Ich **habe** gerade kein Geld **gehabt.**
I just didn't have any money.

Er **wollte** nicht kommen.
Er **hat** nicht **kommen wollen.**
He didn't want to come.

The present perfect also relates important single events, often of a historical nature:

Kolumbus **hat** Amerika **entdeckt.**   *Columbus discovered America.*

2. Past and Past Perfect

a. The past:

German uses the past tense primarily for description, reports, and (literary) narration; in this respect, German usage corresponds closely to English:

Das Kind **spielte** im Garten.
The child was playing in the garden.
Es **war** einmal ein König, der **hatte** eine junge Frau.
Once upon a time there was a king; he had a young wife.

b. The past perfect:

The past perfect is used in German as in English, that is, to report on a past action that had taken place prior to another past action:

Er **hatte** schon **gegessen,** als er nach Hause kam.
He had already eaten when he came home.

3. Future

The future, too, is used generally as in English, except that German prefers to use the present tense if an adverb, like **morgen** (*tomorrow*), clearly indicates futurity (see paragraph 1, page 74).

In addition the German future may express probability in the present, especially when used in combination with the adverb **schon** or **wohl** (or **wohl schon**) meaning *probably:*

> **Er wird es wohl (schon) wissen.**   *He probably knows it.*

Of course, English may sometimes use the future in the same way: *He'll probably know.*

4. Future Perfect.

The future perfect is used as rarely in German as in English, as the cumbersome sequence in the following example may illustrate:

> Es **wird** bis morgen mit ihr darüber **geredet haben.**
> *He will have talked with her about it by tomorrow.*

The future perfect is more common in expressing probability in the past, paralleling the use of the future, especially when used in combination with **wohl** or **schon:**

> **Er wird ihr (wohl** or **schon) nichts davon gesagt haben.**
> *He probably didn't say anything to her about it.*

RECAPITULATION OF MAIN POINTS

1. Weak verbs follow the pattern of **leben, lebte, gelebt.** All tense forms can be derived from the infinitive.

2. The prefix **ge-** of the past participle is dropped in verbs
   a. ending in **-ieren (fotografieren);**
   b. beginning with an inseparable prefix **(be-, emp-, ent-, er-, ge-, hinter-, miß-, ver-, zer-: besucht).**

3. Past participles and infinitives are placed at the end of a main clause.

4. The conversational past tense in German is the present perfect: Ich **habe** dich gestern **gesehen.** *I saw you yesterday.*

5. The German past tense is used for reports, descriptions, and literary narration.

6. The present participle is formed by adding **-d** to the infinitive: **lebend.**

ÜBUNGEN

Practice in Reading and Writing

A. *Read aloud and translate; try to get the meaning of obvious cognates from the context:*

Noch einmal (*once more*) der ehrliche Mann und sein Hemd

1. Es war einmal ein König, der hatte einen guten Finanzminister. 2. Dieser Minister holte Geld (*money*) aus den Leuten wie kein anderer. 3. Er machte nicht nur den König reich, sondern (*but*) auch sich selbst und alle seine Freunde. 4. Alle auf dem Schloß hatten, was sie wünschten. 5. Nur das Volk hatte nichts (*nothing*). 6. Eines Tages nun wurde die Tochter des Königs krank. 7. Der König rief (*called*) alle Ärzte des Landes auf sein Schloß, aber diese merkten nicht, was der armen Prinzessin fehlte (fehlen, w. dat. *to ail*). 8. Sie lebte allein in ihren vielen Zimmern, redete mit keinem, lächelte nicht und wurde immer blasser (*paler and paler*). 9. Nur wenn der schöne Page sie besuchte oder sie im Park freundlich grüßte, lächelte sie ein wenig. 10. Schließlich holte der König alle Weisen seines Landes auf das Schloß und fragte sie um Rat. 11. Diese erklärten endlich: „Deine Tochter wird gesund werden, o König, wenn sie das Hemd eines ehrlichen Mannes trägt (*wears*)." 12. Der König rief also seinen guten Freund, den Finanzminister, und sagte zu ihm: „Schenke (schenken, *to give as a present*) mir dein Hemd für meine Tochter." 13. Der Finanzminister aber lächelte sehr fein und antwortete: „Gerne schenke ich dir alles, was ich habe, oh König; ich glaube aber, die Weisen haben gesagt: das Hemd eines ehrlichen Mannes. 14. Ich aber bin leider nur dein Finanzminister." „Ach ja", meinte der König und schickte dann Boten in das Land, das Hemd eines wirklich ehrlichen Mannes zu finden. 15. Die Boten suchten viele Jahre lang einen solchen Mann, und sie fanden (*found*) auch einen. 16. „Wir haben einen ehrlichen Mann gefunden (haben gefunden *found*), Majestät", erklärten sie dem König, „aber leider hatte er sein Hemd schon verkauft (*sold*), denn er hatte dem Finanzminister die Steuern (*taxes*) zu bezahlen (*to pay*)."

B. *Read aloud and translate:*

1. Was hat er gesagt? 2. Er hatte das schon oft gesagt. 3. „Er hat nicht einmal telefoniert", sagte sie weinend. 4. Ich gehe morgen ins Theater. 5. Haben Sie ihn um seinen Rat gefragt? 6. Er wird ihn schon um seinen Rat gefragt haben. 7. „Du wirst sicher Lehrer", sagte er lachend, „denn du hast schon jetzt dein Pfund Meinung." 8. Die Menschen haben noch nicht viel gelernt. 9. Sie lernen das auch nicht bis (*until*) morgen. 10. Aber sie werden es schon lernen. 11. In einem Jahr werden sie es schon gelernt

haben. 12. Brecht hat das moderne Theater revolutioniert. 13. Er spielte gern den Lehrer. 14. Brecht wird die beiden Freundinnen nicht geheiratet haben. 15. Er hat sie sicher nicht geheiratet. 16. Er beabsichtigte gar nicht, sie zu heiraten. 17. Mein Freund und ich haben philosophiert. 18. Ich habe erklärt: „Das Leben wird immer schöner (*more and more beautiful*)." 19. Mein Freund meinte: „Es wird immer schlechter (*worse and worse*)." 20. Mein Freund hat immer eine andere Meinung! 21. Meinungen sind aber nur eine Frage des Temperaments. 22. Schließlich haben wir uns geeinigt (*we agreed*): er ist ein Pessimist und ich bin ein Optimist. 23. Wir sehen dasselbe, wir sehen es nur anders. 24. Das ist immer so mit den Optimisten und den Pessimisten. 25. Zum Beispiel: sie haben beide (*both*) ihr Glas Bier in der Hand. 26. Der Optimist jubelt (*rejoices*): „Mein Glas ist halb voll!" 27. Und der Pessimist klagt (*complains*): „Mein Glas ist halb leer (*empty*)." 28. Es ist aber dasselbe Glas Bier.

C. *Translate:*

1. weinende Kinder 2. lebende Philosophen 3. Sie sagte das halb weinend, halb lachend. 4. die folgende Geschichte 5. Sie wanderten singend durch das Dorf. 6. Man nennt (*calls*) Demokritos den lachenden und Heraklit den weinenden Philosophen.

D. *Translate:*

1. They have played Brecht in all theaters. 2. Some people value especially Weill's music. 3. He often discussed his technique with his friends. 4. They like to play Brecht, but they don't play him well. 5. They changed their minds and did not get married. 6. She telephoned today. 7. They first photographed the castle. 8. She always liked to play with dolls. 9. Where did you buy that shirt? 10. The king sent many messengers into the country. 11. She probably lives in Berlin now. 12. The girls did not talk to (**mit**) the man today. 13. The man knocked on the door, but we did not open. 14. I explained these words to the student, and now she has learned them. 15. Do you understand these examples? 16. He intended to (**zu**) marry her, but changed his mind. 17. The friends of the two girls visited him sometimes. 18. They were living in our house, but they did not smoke. 19. Many have imitated Brecht, and he always said, "What for?" 20. He always asked the same question.

Oral Exercises

D. *Change the sentences to present perfect:*

EXAMPLE: Du reagierst immer auf deine Weise.
            Du hast immer auf deine Weise reagiert.

1. Das Publikum schätzt besonders die Dreigroschenoper. 2. Die Leute ändern oft ihre Meinung. 3. Er heiratet eine Schauspielerin. 4. Die beiden Freunde hören voneinander. 5. Viele Schüler imitieren ihre Lehrer. 6. Brecht revolutioniert das moderne Theater. 7. Er antwortet seinen Freundinnen sofort. 8. Er beantwortet immer alle Fragen. 9. Sie bezahlen dem Mann das Haus. 10. Der Mann lächelt ein wenig. 11. Er überlebt die Leute sicher.

E. *Change the following sentences and questions to past tense:*

EXAMPLE: Wir diskutieren ein Drama von Bertolt Brecht.
     Wir diskutierten ein Drama von Bertolt Brecht.

1. Wie reagiert das Publikum heute?   6. Das höre ich auch.
2. Sie ändern immer ihre Meinung.   7. Wir schätzen immer seinen Rat.
3. Verzichtet ihr oft darauf?   8. Er imitiert seine Lehrer.
4. Warum zögert er immer?   9. Die Damen öffnen das Fenster.
5. Sie heiraten endlich in Berlin.

F. *Change the sentences to future. Omit the time adverb* **bald:**

EXAMPLE: Ich ändere bald meine Meinung.
     Ich werde meine Meinung ändern.

1. Wir besuchen euch bald in München.   5. Wir haben bald viel Zeit.
2. Sie hören bald voneinander.   6. Sie heiratet bald ihren Freund.
3. Wir diskutieren bald dieses Drama.   7. Er bezahlt bald sein Auto.
4. Dein Vater wird bald gesund.

G. *Change the following sentences and questions to present:*

EXAMPLE: Hat diese Straße nach Nürnberg geführt?
     Führt diese Straße nach Nürnberg?

1. Wir haben in München gewohnt. 2. Der Tod hat an die Tür geklopft. 3. Ihr hattet über ihr Privatleben geredet. 4. Wird sie unsere Freunde um Rat fragen? 5. Werden Sie den Schaffner holen? 6. Hat er das immer behauptet? 7. Sie wird ihn sicher nicht heiraten.

7

Strong Verbs

Friedrich Nietzsche (1844–1900)

Goethe[1] hat einmal gesagt: „Genie ist Fleiß." Genie ist vielleicht nicht nur
Fleiß, aber es ist sicher auch Fleiß. Nehmen wir Friedrich Nietzsche, den
Philosophen des „Übermenschen",[2] als Beispiel: Schon als Kind war er
wirklich fleißig, nicht nur in der Schule, auch zu Hause. Seine Interessen
5 gingen in viele Richtungen. Bereits im[3] Alter von zehn Jahren schrieb er
eine Motette[4] und fünfzig Gedichte, vier Jahre später seine erste Autobiographie. Da liest man den Satz: „Überhaupt war es stets mein Vorhaben[5],
ein kleines Buch zu schreiben und es selbst zu lesen. Diese kleine Eitelkeit
habe ich immer noch."
10   Sein Vater, ein Pastor, starb früh, und das Kind lebte seitdem mit fünf
Frauen: der Mutter, der Großmutter, zwei Tanten und der Schwester. Diese
Schwester spielte später überhaupt die Rolle der Frau in seinem Leben—
einer sehr unweiblichen Frau allerdings. Nach seinem Tode veröffentlichte
sie seine Schriften, aber sie unterdrückte alles, was ihr nicht gefiel, und ihr
15 gefiel vieles nicht: vor allem nicht sein Radikalismus. Außer[6] dieser Schwester

1. **Johann Wolfgang von Goethe,** 1749–1832, German poet.   2. **Übermensch** *superman* (a
distant ancestor of the American version).   3. **im** (here:) *at the.*   4. **Motette** *motet* (musical
composition).   5. **Vorhaben** *intention.*   6. **außer** (w. gen.) *besides.*

gab es[7] nur noch eine andere Frau in seinem Leben: die Russin Lou Andreas Salomé, Tochter eines russischen Generals und später Frau eines deutschen Professors. Sie wurde dann auch die Freundin des Dichters Rilke,[8] und später arbeitete sie mit Sigmund Freud. Die Eifersucht der Schwester zerstörte sehr bald ihre Freundschaft mit Nietzsche.   20

Nietzsche hatte als Philologe begonnen. Aber auch Geschichte interessierte ihn, sowie die Naturwissenschaften und die Philosophie, und in der Philosophie besonders die des großen Pessimisten Schopenhauer[9]. Bekannt sind die Worte Nietzsches: „Gott ist tot"—aber nicht so bekannt ist das Ende dieses Zitats: „Gott bleibt tot! Und wir haben ihn getötet! Wie trösten[10] wir 25 uns, die Mörder aller Mörder?"

Auch die Künste beschäftigten ihn sein Leben lang, die Literatur und vor allem die Musik. Nietzsche wurde einer der großen Meister der deutschen Sprache und in der Musik für einige Jahre ein Verehrer Richard Wagners.[11]

Das junge Genie war schon im Alter von 24 Jahren Professor an[12] der 30 Universität Basel. Da schrieb er nun nicht nur kleine, sondern viele große Bücher. Auch seine Eitelkeit verlor er nicht. Er vergaß nie, wer er war: „der erste Geist des Zeitalters". Aus Marienbad[13] schrieb er einmal: „Seit Goethe hier war, hat niemand hier so viel gedacht."[14]

Aber Nietzsches Gesundheit war immer schon schwach, und mit 34 Jahren 35 verließ er die Universität wieder. Er reiste seitdem viel, besonders in der Schweiz und in Italien. Überall suchte er einen Ort mit gutem Klima. Die Krankheit ergriff nicht nur seinen Körper, sondern auch seinen Geist. Im Jahre 1889[15], elf Jahre vor seinem Tode, kam die unheilbare[16] Geisteskrankheit. Kurz vorher las er noch einmal seine Bücher. Diese „kleine Eitelkeit" 40 hatte er immer noch. „Ich verstehe seit vier Wochen meine eigenen Schriften", sagte er, „mehr noch, ich schätze sie."

7. **es gab** *there was*   8. **Rainer Maria Rilke**, 1875–1926, modern lyrical poet.   9. **Arthur Schopenhauer**, 1788–1860.   10. **Wie trösten wir uns** *how do we comfort ourselves.*   11. **Richard Wagner**, 1813–1883, German opera composer.   12. **an** (here:) *at.*   13. **Marienbad** spa in Czechoslovakia, which Goethe visited often.   14. **hat . . . gedacht** *has thought.*   15. (read) **achtzehnhundertneunundachtzig.**   16. **unheilbare** *incurable.*

FRAGEN

1. Was hat Goethe einmal gesagt?   2. Wer war Friedrich Nietzsche?   3. Was schrieb er bereits im Alter von zehn Jahren?   4. Was schrieb er vier Jahre später?   5. Was war Nietzsches Vater?   6. Mit wem lebte er seit dem Tode des Vaters?   7. Welche Rolle spielte die Schwester in seinem Leben?   8. Was tat sie nach Nietzsches Tod?   9. Aber was unterdrückte sie?   10. Was

gefiel ihr nicht?   11. Gab es noch eine andere Frau in Nietzsches Leben?
12. Wen hat Lou Andreas Salomé später geheiratet?   13. Was zerstörte ihre
Freundschaft mit Nietzsche?   14. Was interessierte Nietzsche?   15. Welche
Philosophie interessierte ihn besonders?   16. Welche Worte Nietzsches sind
sehr bekannt?   17. Wie ist das Ende dieses Zitats?   18. Was beschäftigte
ihn sein Leben lang?   19. Was wurde Nietzsche?   20. Was war er schon mit
vierundzwanzig Jahren?   21. Warum verließ er mit vierunddreißig Jahren
die Universität?   22. Was tat er seitdem?   23. Was kam elf Jahre vor
seinem Tode?   24. Was sagte er noch kurz vorher?

WORTSCHATZ

COGNATES

die **Autobiographie**, –n	autobiography		der **Philologe**, –n, –n	philologist
das **Buch**, ⸗er	book		der **Philosoph**, –en, –en	philosopher
elf	eleven		die **Philosophie**, –n	philosophy
die **Freundschaft**, –en	friendship		der **Professor**, die **Professoren**	professor
fünfzig	fifty			
der **General**, ⸗e	general		die **Psychoanalyse**, –n	psychoanalysis
das **Genie**, –s	genius			
groß	great		der **Radikalismus**	radicalism
die **Großmutter**, ⸗	grandmother		die **Rolle**, –n	role
interessieren	to interest		der **Russe**, –n, –n	Russian (man)
(das) **Italien**	Italy		die **Russin**, –nen	Russian (woman)
das **Klima**, –s	climate			
die **Literatur**, –en	literature		**russisch**	Russian
der **Meister**, –	master		die **Schule**, –n	school
der **Mörder**, –	murderer		die **Schweiz**	Switzerland
die **Naturwissenschaft**, –en	(natural) science		**in der Schweiz**	in Switzerland
			die **Schwester**, –n	sister
der **Pastor**, die **Pastoren**	pastor		**sieben**	seven
			tot	dead
der **Pessimist**, –en, –en	pessimist		**vier**	four
			zehn	ten

VOCABULARY

allerdings	to be sure		die **Eitelkeit**, –en	vanity
als (*preposition*)	as (a)		der **Fleiß**	diligence, industriousness
arbeiten	to work			
bekannt	well-known		**fleißig**	diligent, industrious
bereits	already		**früh**	early
beschäftigen	to occupy (one's time)		das **Gedicht**, –e	poem
			der **Geist**, –er	mind, spirit, intellect
die **Eifersucht**	jealousy		die **Geisteskrankheit**, –en	mental illness
eigen	own (*adj.*)			

der **Geschmack, ⸗er**	taste	**sondern** (*conj.* *after negative clause*)	but, but rather
zu Hause	at home		
der **Hund, –e**	dog	**sowie**	as well as
immer noch	still	die **Sprache, –n**	language
der **Körper, –**	body	**stets**	always
nicht mehr	no longer	die **Tante, –n**	aunt
niemand	nobody	**töten**	to kill
noch ein	another, one more	**überall**	everywhere
		überhaupt	altogether, anyway
noch einmal	once more	**unterdrücken**	to suppress
der **Ort, –e**	place	der **Verehrer, –**	admirer
reisen	to travel	**veröffentlichen**	to publish
die **Richtung, –en**	direction	**vorher** (adv.)	before
der **Satz, ⸗e**	sentence	**weiblich**	feminine
die **Schrift, –en**	writing	**unweiblich**	unfeminine
schwach	weak	das **Zeitalter, –**	era, age
seit (*conjunction*)	since, for	**zerstören**	to destroy
seitdem (*adv.*)	since then	das **Zitat, –e**	quote, quotation

STRONG VERBS

(Beginning with this lesson, each Wortschatz will include a selected group of strong verbs that occur in the reading material. Since familiarity with the strong verbs is essential, they should be carefully memorized.)

INFINITIVE		PRESENT	PAST	PAST PARTICIPLE
beginnen	to begin	**beginnt**	**begann**	**begonnen**
bekommen	to get	**bekommt**	**bekam**	**bekommen**
bleiben[1]	to remain	**bleibt**	**blieb**	ist **geblieben**
brechen	to break	**bricht**	**brach**	**gebrochen**
ergreifen	to seize	**ergreift**	**ergriff**	**ergriffen**
geben	to give	**gibt**[2]	**gab**	**gegeben**
gefallen[3]	to please	**gefällt**	**gefiel**	**gefallen**
gehen[1]	to go	**geht**	**ging**	ist **gegangen**
halten	to hold	**hält**	**hielt**	**gehalten**
kommen[1]	to come	**kommt**	**kam**	ist **gekommen**
lesen	to read	**liest**	**las**	**gelesen**
nehmen	to take	**nimmt**	**nahm**	**genommen**
schreiben	to write	**schreibt**	**schrieb**	**geschrieben**
sterben[1]	to die	**stirbt**	**starb**	ist **gestorben**
vergessen	to forget	**vergißt**	**vergaß**	**vergessen**
verlassen	to leave (*something*)	**verläßt**	**verließ**	**verlassen**
verlieren	to lose	**verliert**	**verlor**	**verloren**
verstehen	to understand	**versteht**	**verstand**	**verstanden**

[1] **bleiben, gehen, kommen,** and **sterben** are conjugated with **sein** in the compound tenses.
[2] **es gibt** *there is, there are;* **es gab** *there was, there were.*
[3] **gefallen** is an impersonal verb.

DISTINGUISH BETWEEN

werden *to become* and **bekommen** *to get*

noch **ein** and **ein anderer** both mean *another:* noch **ein** in the sense of "one more"; **ein anderer** in that of "one in place of another."

nach Hause and **zu Hause; nach Hause** is *home* in the sense of "to the house," "homeward"; **zu Hause** is *at home.*

STRONG VERBS

1. German strong verbs change their stem vowel in the past and past participle (similar to the stem changes of irregular verbs in English: *sing, sang, sung*); this change is called "Ablaut":

singen	**sang**	**gesungen**	*to sing*
heben	**hob**	**gehoben**	*to lift, raise*

These stem changes cannot be deduced from a given infinitive; nor does the infinitive as such indicate whether a verb is weak or strong. The best way to learn the strong verbs is to memorize them as you come to them.[1]

2. Most strong verbs may be divided into seven classes on the basis of "Ablaut." An alphabetical listing is included in Appendix 2. The following table shows how the stem vowels change from class to class, illustrating each with one example:

CLASS	Stem Vowels			Examples			
	INF.	PAST	PAST PART.	INF.	PAST	PAST PART.	
I	ei	i, ie	i, ie	schneiden	schnitt	geschnitten	to cut
II	e, ie[2]	o	o	frieren	fror	gefroren	to freeze
III	i	a	o, u	singen	sang	gesungen	to sing
IV	e	a	o	sprechen	sprach	gesprochen	to speak
V	e, i, ie	a	e	geben	gab	gegeben	to give
VI	a	u	a	schlagen	schlug	geschlagen	to hit, strike
VII	a[3]	i, ie	(as inf.)	schlafen	schlief	geschlafen	to sleep

[1] Dictionaries and vocabularies usually indicate the principal parts of strong verbs by adding the "Ablaut"-series to the infinitive:

singen (a, u) = singen, sang, gesungen

Remember: You must determine the infinitive before you look up a verb in a dictionary. If you do not recognize a verb form or cannot determine its infinitive, consult the alphabetical list of strong verbs in a dictionary (or in Appendix 2 of this book) by going down the appropriate column until you come to the form wanted: then locate the infinitive.

[2] Also stems in **a, i, ä, ö, ü, au.**

[3] Also stems in **o, u, au, ei.**

3. Present Tense of Strong Verbs

Most strong verbs form their present tense like weak verbs. However, there are two important differences:

a. With a few exceptions, all strong verbs with the stem vowel **a** or **au** in the infinitive take an umlaut in the second and third persons singular:

tragen *to wear, to carry*		**laufen** *to run*	
ich **trage**	wir **tragen**	ich **laufe**	wir **laufen**
du **trägst**	ihr **tragt**	du **läufst**	ihr **lauft**
er **trägt**	sie **tragen**	er **läuft**	sie **laufen**

Similarly, **o** changes to **ö** in **stoßen** (*to push*): ich **stoße,** du **stößt,** er **stößt,** etc.

b. Most strong verbs with the stem vowel **e** in the infinitive change **e** to (short) **i** or (long) **ie** in the second and third persons singular and in the familiar imperative (where the ending **-e** is dropped):

sprechen *to speak*		**lesen** *to read*	
ich **spreche**	wir **sprechen**	ich **lese**	wir **lesen**
du **sprichst**	ihr **sprecht**	du **liest**	ihr **lest**
er **spricht**	sie **sprechen**	er **liest**	sie **lesen**

In general, short **e** changes to (short) **i,** long **e** to (long) **ie:**

> **essen** (*to eat*): du **ißt,** er **ißt**
> **stehlen** (*to steal*): du **stiehlst,** er **stiehlt**

but there are exceptions: **nehmen** (*to take*): du **nimmst,** er **nimmt; treten** (*to step*): du **trittst,** er **tritt.**

c. In the familiar imperative, note the following forms:

> **essen: iß!** **nehmen: nimm!** (note spelling!)
> **geben: gib!** **sehen: sieh!**
> **helfen: hilf!** **sprechen: sprich!**
> **lesen: lies!** **treten: tritt!** (note spelling!)

and others.

The imperative of **werden** (*to become*) is: **werde!, werdet!, werden Sie!**

Strong verbs with regular imperatives also frequently drop the final **-e** in the singular familiar form:

> **gehen: geh(e)! geht! gehen Sie!**

4. Past Tense of Strong Verbs

Strong verbs form their past tense by adding to the past-tense stem the following endings:

–	–en
–st	–t
–	–en

EXAMPLE: ich **sang**   wir **sangen**
                        du **sangst**   Sie **sangen**   ihr **sangt**
                        er **sang**   sie **sangen**

Note this characteristic of strong verbs in the past tense: they have no endings in the first and third persons singular.

The past tense of **werden** is irregular:

ich **wurde** (old form: **ward**)[1]   wir **wurden**
du **wurdest** (old form: **wardst**)   ihr **wurdet**
er **wurde** (old form: **ward**)   sie **wurden**

5. Past Participle and Perfect Tenses

a. Past participles of strong verbs consist of: (1) the prefix **ge-**, (2) the past participle stem, and (3) the ending **-en: ge sung en.**

b. The perfect tenses of most strong verbs are formed like those of weak verbs:

PRES. PERFECT: ich **habe gesungen**
PAST PERFECT: ich **hatte gesungen**
FUTURE PERFECT: ich **werde gesungen haben**

c. Strong verbs (like weak verbs) which have an inseparable prefix **(be-, emp-, ent-, er-, ge-, hinter-, miß-, ver-, zer-)** drop the prefix **ge-** of the past participle:

bekommen   *to get*   **bekam**   **bekommen**

6. Future and Present Participle

The future and the present participle of strong verbs are formed like those of weak verbs:

FUTURE: ich **werde essen**   *I shall eat*
PRESENT PARTICIPLE: **essend**   *eating*

[1] These old forms are still encountered in print.

RECAPITULATION OF MAIN POINTS

1. There are seven classes of strong verbs based on the "Ablaut"-series (the sequence of stem vowels in the infinitive, past tense, and past participle). Not all strong verbs, however, fit into these classes.

2. Most strong verbs

    a. with the stem vowel **a** or **au** in the infinitive take an Umlaut in the second and third persons singular of the present tense: du **trägst,** er **trägt.**

    b. with the stem vowel **e** in the infinitive change **e** to (short) **i** or (long) **ie** in the second and third persons singular of the present tense and in the singular of the familiar imperative (where they also omit the ending **-e**): du **sprichst,** er **spricht; sprich!;** du **liest,** er **liest; lies!**

3. Strong verbs have no endings in the first and third persons singular of the past tense: ich **sang,** er **sang.**

4. The past participle of strong verbs ends in **-en,** which is added to the past-participle stem of the verb; otherwise past participles and perfect tenses of strong verbs are formed like those of weak verbs.

ÜBUNGEN

Practice in Reading and Writing

A. Read aloud and translate; where needed, refer to the list of strong verbs in Appendix 2:

1. Schopenhauer, der Philosoph des Pessimismus, ging eines Tages in ein Restaurant. 2. Ein Philosoph denkt viel, aber er ißt auch. 3. Manche essen sogar sehr gut und sehr viel. 4. Schopenhauer hatte schon oft in diesem Restaurant gegessen. 5. Er saß immer an demselben Tisch (*table*). 6. An einem anderen Tisch aßen einige Engländer. 7. Diese Engländer sprachen immer nur über Frauen, Pferde und Hunde. 8. Nun verstand Schopenhauer sehr gut Englisch. 9. Er tat daher folgendes: 10. Vor dem Essen legte er Geld (*money*) auf den Tisch, und nach dem Essen steckte (*put*) er es wieder in die Tasche (*pocket*). 11. Ein Gast sah eines Tages, was Schopenhauer tat, und fragte ihn, warum er das tat. 12. Schopenhauer antwortete: Ich mache mit mir selbst eine kleine Wette (*bet*). 13. Wenn nur einer von diesen Engländern einmal über etwas anderes spricht als (*than*) über

Frauen, Pferde und Hunde, habe ich verloren.   14. Bis (*until*) jetzt habe ich noch immer gewonnen.

B. *With the help of the list of strong verbs in Appendix 2, determine the infinitive forms of the verbs used:*

1. Wer spricht Deutsch?   2. Du vergißt alles.   3. Hast du seine Schriften gelesen?   4. Es schlägt eins.   5. Wer sieht den Ort?   6. Das Kind läuft zu seiner Tante.   7. Warum schläft er immer in der Klasse?   8. Er hat zuviel getrunken!   9. Iß nicht so schnell!   10. Nimm meine Hand!   11. Haben Sie mich verstanden?   12. Er ging in dieser Richtung.   13. Sie hat mich um (*for*) die Adresse gebeten.   14. Wer hat das Brot (*bread*) geschnitten?   15. Hieß er wirklich Emil?   16. Sie betrog ihn die ganze Zeit.   17. Es schien gefroren zu haben.   18. Ich rief ihn, aber er kam nicht.   19. Sie hat sehr schön gesungen.   20. Gib mir die Hand und komm!   21. Wenn du nicht ißt, stirbst du.   22. Wovon (*about what*) haben Sie mit ihm gesprochen?

C. *Translate. Watch the tenses and determine the equivalent tense forms in English:*

1. Sie saßen da und tranken den ganzen Abend.   2. Sie kam ins Zimmer und bat ihn um (*for*) das Buch.   3. Er hat die Wette immer gewonnen.   4. Sie werden das sicher eines Tages verstehen.   5. Er schien sehr intelligent zu sein.   6. Die Sonne scheint. Das heißt, es wird schön werden.   7. Sie schlief den ganzen Tag, und am Abend ging sie ins Theater.   8. Ich habe ihm versprochen, früh zu kommen.   9. Sie haben in ihrem ganzen Leben so etwas nicht getan.   10. Ich habe ihr heute einen Brief geschrieben.   11. Hast du heute schon deine Medizin genommen?   12. Wann starb er?   13. Das Buch gefiel ihm nicht.   14. Hat dir das Buch gefallen?   15. Sie hat ihn wieder verlassen.   16. Wann hat er seine Eltern verloren?   17. Wie lange blieb er hier?   18. Er hat sein Wort gebrochen.   19. Er hat mir sein Wort gegeben.   20. Glück (*happiness*) und Glas—wie leicht bricht das!

D. *Translate:*

1. She came to (**nach**) Berlin and stayed there (for) a year.   2. Did you find his book, and did you read it?   3. He did what everybody does.   4. He speaks German, but they did not understand him.   5. They are sitting in the living room and are talking about (**über** w. acc.) the weather.   6. He likes to read from (**aus** w. dat.) his books.   7. Be nice and come with me, Fritz.   8. She came crying into (**in** w. acc.) the room.   9. How often have you eaten in this restaurant?   10. She is nice, but she speaks too much.   11. What did you do in (**auf** w. dat.) the country?   12. He cut the cake into two parts.   13. He got the letter and read it.   14. Don't forget your book, Fritz!   15. His aunt always forgets his birthday.   16. Why didn't you do anything?   17. His

business is growing and thriving.   18. I saw him, but he was talking to
(**mit** w. dat.) his landlady.   19. It is getting cold; I am freezing.   20. Why
do you run so fast, Fritz?

Oral Exercises

E. *Give the correct form in the present tense of the verbs in parentheses:*

1. Er (sitzen) da mit einem Buch in der Hand.   2. Er (lesen) Nietzsches *Also
sprach Zarathustra* mit seinen Studenten.   3. Männer (sterben) früher als
Frauen.   4. Wer (sprechen) davon?   5. (Sehen) du heute deine Tante?
6. Was (halten) er in der Hand?   7. (Vergessen) mich nicht!   8. (Nehmen)
dieses interessante Buch und (lesen) es, Fritz!   9. Meine Frau (bleiben) den
ganzen Tag zu Hause.   10. Wer (sterben) gerne jung?   11. Dieser Satz (gefallen) mir.   12. Er (brechen) sein Wort.   13. Warum (bleiben) du zu Hause?
14. (Verlieren) das Buch nicht, Herr Schmidt!   15. Ich glaube, er (schlafen)
den ganzen Tag.

F. *Change the subject of the sentence as indicated:*

EXAMPLE: Die Studenten nehmen die Bücher. (Du)
        Du nimmst die Bücher.

1. Wir helfen euch immer. (Er)
2. Die Kinder essen zu viel. (Die junge Dame)
3. Wir lesen seine Autobiographie. (Du)
4. Sie vergessen wirklich nichts. (Er)
5. Wir treffen ihn heute in München. (Du)
6. Alle laufen in die Schule. (Er)
7. Sie verlassen heute Italien. (Du)

G. *Change the conventional imperatives to familiar forms:*

EXAMPLE: Essen Sie den Pfannkuchen!
        Iß den Pfannkuchen!

1. Helfen Sie den Kindern!
2. Vergessen Sie diesen Satz nicht!
3. Nehmen Sie dieses Buch!
4. Sprechen Sie bitte laut!
5. Versprechen Sie ihr nichts!
6. Lesen Sie dieses Gedicht!

H. *Change the sentences to present perfect:*

EXAMPLE: Er schreibt viele Gedichte.
        Er hat viele Gedichte geschrieben.

1. Wir lesen dieses Zitat immer wieder.   2. Du findest dein Geld nicht.   3. Er

schläft den ganzen Tag.   4. Der Optimist gewinnt immer.   5. Der Pessimist versteht das nicht.   6. Er sitzt den ganzen Tag zu Hause.   7. Wir geben unser Wort.

I. *Change the sentences to past tense:*

EXAMPLE: Er hatte seine Wette immer gewonnen.
             Er gewann seine Wette immer.

1. Die Studenten hatten seine Schriften gelesen.   2. Man hatte über sein Buch gesprochen.   3. Die Krankheit hatte ihn ergriffen.   4. Er hatte sie wieder verlassen.   5. Sie hatten immer in der Klasse geschlafen.   6. Er hatte sie eines Tages im Theater gesehen.   7. Du hattest ihn gestern in München getroffen.

J. *Change the sentences to present tense:*

EXAMPLE: Das Drama hat uns gut gefallen.
             Das Drama gefällt uns gut.

1. Man sah ihn oft im Restaurant.   2. Sie hatten ihm immer geholfen.
3. Wir gingen nach dem Theater nach Hause.   4. Es hatte vier geschlagen.
5. Alle Kinder haben in der Klasse gesessen.   6. Er hatte zu wenig geschlafen.
7. Sie sprach nur über Psychoanalyse.

8

Personal and

Interrogative Pronouns

Nietzsche und Wagner

Friedrich Nietzsche war schon in seiner Jugend für Richard Wagner begeistert. Noch in der Schule gründete er mit zwei Freunden die „Literarische Vereinigung Germania" und kaufte mit ihnen die Noten zu Wagners Oper „Tristan". Zu Weihnachten schrieb er seiner Mutter: „Ich wünsche mir die Fotografie eines berühmten Mannes, vielleicht die von Richard Wagner." 5

Später wurden Nietzsche und Wagner Freunde. Nietzsche bewunderte Wagner grenzenlos, und dieser wieder genoß die Bewunderung eines solchen Freundes. Nietzsche war damals Professor an der Universität Basel. Er lebte in der Nähe Wagners und besuchte ihn in drei Jahren 23[1] Mal. Wagners Frau Cosima und ihre Kinder verlangten,[2] Nietzsche jedes Wochenende zu 10 sehen. „Wie geht es Ihnen, wir erwarten Sie . . . besuchen Sie uns . . . wann kommen Sie zu uns . . . der Meister spricht täglich von Ihnen", schrieb Frau Cosima immer wieder an den Freund in Basel.

Es war eine glückliche Zeit für sie alle. Nietzsche sah in Wagners Musik die Bestätigung seiner Philosophie, und Wagner fand in Nietzsches Philoso- 15 phie die Bestätigung seiner Musik. Nietzsche war nicht nur sein junger

---

1. (read) **dreiundzwanzig.**   2. **verlangten** (go from here to the infinitive, **zu sehen,** and then translate the rest of the clause).

Freund, er war fast sein Sohn, und Wagner gab ihm oft gute Ratschläge. Einmal schrieb er ihm: „Komponieren Sie eine Oper oder heiraten Sie!" Nietzsche tat beides nicht. Ja, sein Verhältnis zu Wagner wurde bald kühl
20 und kritisch. Bei[3] einem seiner Besuche brachte[4] er ihm ein Werk seines Rivalen Brahms.[5] Wagner war gekränkt und machte ihm eine Szene. Nietzsche erklärte später: „In diesem Augenblick war er nicht groß."

Warum gingen sie von nun an verschiedene Wege? Wagner war für Nietzsche nicht mehr der Seher der Zukunft wie in seiner Jugend. Er sah in ihm
25 jetzt einen Mann der Vergangenheit. Er fand die Festspiele in Bayreuth[6] furchtbar, denn man machte hier die Kunst zu einem Geschäft. Und dann erzählte ihm Wagner eines Tages von[7] seiner neuen Oper „Parsifal", einem Kunstwerk mit christlichen Ideen. „Die Leute verlangen etwas Christliches", erklärte Wagner. Das ertrug Nietzsche nicht und verließ ihn. Der Freund
30 Wagners wurde nun dessen größter[8] Feind. Er erklärte ihn und den Philosophen Schopenhauer für seine „Antipoden" und Wagners Musik für eine „Musik ohne Zukunft". 1888[9] veröffentlichte er seine Schrift „Nietzsche contra Wagner". Da stehen die Sätze: „Auf wen wirkt Wagners Musik? Auf etwas, worauf[10] ein vornehmer Künstler niemals wirkt—auf die Masse!
35 auf die Unreifen! auf die Blasierten![11] auf die Krankhaften! auf die Idioten! auf Wagnerianer!"

3. **bei** (here:) *during.* 4. **brachte** *brought.* 5. **Johannes Brahms,** German composer. 6. **Festspiele** *festivals* (In Bayreuth, Wagner had established his own opera house). 7. **von** (here:) *about.* 8. **größter** (superlative of **groß**) *greatest.* 9. (read) **achtzehnhundertachtundachtzig.** 10. **worauf** *whereupon, on which.* 11. **die Blasierten** *the blasés (ones).*

FRAGEN

1. Was gründete Nietzsche mit zwei Freunden in der Schule? 2. Was kaufte er mit ihnen? 3. Was wünschte er sich von seiner Mutter zu Weihnachten? 4. Was genoß Richard Wagner? 5. Wo lebte Nietzsche zur Zeit seiner Freundschaft mit Wagner? 6. Was verlangten Frau Cosima und ihre Kinder? 7. Wer war Frau Cosima? 8. Was schrieb sie immer wieder nach Basel? 9. Für wen war diese Zeit glücklich? 10. Was sah Wagner in Nietzsches Philosophie? 11. Und was sah Nietzsche in Wagners Musik? 12. Was war Nietzsche für Wagner? 13. Was für einen Rat gab Wagner Nietzsche? 14. Wie wurde Nietzsches Verhältnis zu Wagner? 15. Warum war Wagner gekränkt? 16. Was war Wagner für Nietzsche nicht mehr? 17. Was sah er jetzt in ihm? 18. Was verlangten die Leute in der Oper? 19. Was veröffentlichte Nietzsche? 20. Auf wen wirkt ein vornehmer Künstler niemals?

WORTSCHATZ[1]

	begeistert	enthusiastic	der **Künstler,** –	artist
	berühmt	famous	das **Kunstwerk,** –e	work of art
die	**Bestätigung,** –en	confirmation	die **Masse,** -n	mass(es)
	bewundern	to admire	in der **Nähe**	near, nearby
die	**Bewunderung,** –en	admiration	**neu**	new
	damals	at that time	**niemals**	never
	erklären	to explain; to declare	die **Noten** (*pl.*)	(musical) notes, score
	erklären für (*w. acc.*)	to declare to be	von nun an	from now on
	erwarten	to await, to expect	der **Ratschlag,** ⸗e	(bit of) advice
	fast	almost	**reif**	ripe, mature
	geht: wie geht es Ihnen?	how are you?	**unreif**	immature
das	**Geschäft,** –e	business	der **Seher,** –	seer
	glücklich	happy	der **Sohn,** ⸗e	son
die	**Grenze,** -n	limit, boundary	die **Vereinigung,** –en	society
	grenzenlos	boundlessly, immensely	die **Vergangenheit**	past
	gründen	to found	das **Verhältnis,** –se	relationship
	ja	yes	**verlangen**	to demand
	ja (*exclamation*)	indeed	**verschieden**	different
			vornehm	refined
die	**Jugend**	youth	(die) **Weihnachten** (*pl.*)	Christmas
	kränken	to hurt; to insult	zu **Weihnachten**	for Christmas
	krankhaft	sickly, morbid	**wirken**	to have an effect
	kühl	cool	die **Zukunft**	future

STRONG VERBS

betrügen	to deceive		betrog	betrogen
ertragen	to bear, tolerate	erträgt	ertrug	ertragen
finden	to find	findet	fand	gefunden
genießen	to enjoy		genoß	genossen
schneiden	to cut	schneidet	schnitt	geschnitten
sehen	to see	sieht	sah	gesehen
sitzen	to sit		saß	gesessen
stehen	to stand		stand	gestanden
tun	to do	tut	tat	getan
versprechen	to promise	verspricht	versprach	versprochen

[1] Beginning with this lesson, obvious cognates and easily recognized word combinations will no longer be listed in the lesson vocabularies. They may be found, however, in the German-English end vocabulary.

GRAMMATICAL TERMS

1. The personal pronouns in English are:

Subjective (nominative) case: *I, you, he, she, it, we, you, they.*

Objective (dative, accusative) case: *(to) me, (to) you, (to) him, (to) her*[1], *(to) it, (to) us, (to) you, (to) them.*

2. The interrogative pronouns are: *who?* and *what?* The declension of *who* is: *who, whom, (to) whom, whose.*

PERSONAL PRONOUNS

1. In conjugating a verb, the nominative forms of the personal pronoun are used: **ich, du, er, sie, es, wir, ihr, sie; Sie.** The complete declension is:

	SINGULAR					PLURAL			CONVEN-TIONAL ADDRESS
NOM.	**ich** *I*	**du** *you*	**er** *he, it*	**sie** *she, it*	**es** *it*	**wir** *we*	**ihr** *you*	**sie** *they*	**Sie** *you*
ACC.	**mich** *me*	**dich** *you*	**ihn** *him, it*	**sie** *her, it*	**es** *it*	**uns** *us*	**euch** *you*	**sie** *them*	**Sie** *you*
DAT.	**mir** *(to) me*	**dir** *(to) you*	**ihm** *(to) him, it*	**ihr** *(to) her, it*	**ihm** *(to) it*	**uns** *(to) us*	**euch** *(to) you*	**ihnen** *(to) them*	**Ihnen** *(to) you*
GEN.	**meiner** *of me*	**deiner** *of you*	**seiner** *of him, it*	**ihrer** *of her, it*	**dessen** *of it*	**unser** *of us*	**euer** *of you*	**ihrer** *of them*	**Ihrer** *of you*

The genitive forms occur only after a few verbs and adjectives requiring the genitive:

> Er schämt sich **meiner.**   *He is ashamed of me.*
> Herr, erbarme dich **unser!**   *Lord, have mercy on us.*

2. The impersonal pronoun is **man** (English *one*, as in: *One can hardly imagine*), although impersonal *they, people, you* or similar constructions are often more colloquial equivalents).

Man has no genitive; for the accusative and dative, forms of the indefinite article are used: accusative: **einen;** dative: **einem.**

> **Man sagt, er ist reich.**   *One says (they say, people say) he is rich.*
> **Man tut das nicht.**   *One doesn't do that. (It is not done).*
> **Das ärgert einen.**   *That annoys one (you, people).*
> **Er dankt einem nie.**   *He never thanks you (anyone).*

---

[1] Be sure to distinguish between the possessive adjective *her,* preceding a noun (*her* book), and the dative or accusative of the personal pronoun: I give *her* a book. I see *her.*

3. A pronoun must agree in gender and number with the noun to which it refers. Hence, **er, ihn, ihm, sie, ihr** may all be equivalent to English *it*, referring to an inanimate object:

> **er:** **Der Brief** war nicht nur groß, **er** war auch schwer.
> *The letter was not only big, it was also heavy.*

> **ihn:** Er fand **den Fehler** und verbesserte **ihn.**
> *He found the mistake and corrected it.*

> **ihm:** Er kaufte **ein altes Bild** und gab **ihm** einen neuen Rahmen.
> *He bought an old picture and gave it a new frame.*

> **sie:** **Die Stadt** ist nicht nur schön, **sie** ist auch sehr interessant.
> *The city is not only beautiful, it is also very interesting.*

> **ihr:** Er reparierte **die Maschine** und gab **ihr** etwas Öl.
> *He repaired the machine and gave it a little oil.*

4. **Sie** may mean *she, her, it, they, them*, according to its position and function in the sentence:

a. **sie** as the subject of a verb in the singular means *she* or *it: she* when referring to a female being, *it* when referring to a thing:

> **Marie** ist hier. **Sie** kommt mit uns.
> *Marie is here. She's coming with us.*
> Ich habe **eine Uhr,** aber **sie** geht nicht.
> *I have a watch but it isn't running.*

b. **sie** as the subject of a verb in the plural means *they:*

> **Meine Freunde** kommen. **Sie** haben jetzt Ferien.
> *My friends are coming. They have a vacation now.*

c. **sie** as the direct object of a verb means *her, them*, or *it: it* when referring to a thing; otherwise, the antecedent will decide whether **sie** is singular (*her, it*) or plural (*them*):

> **Marie** ist nett. Ich kenne **sie** gut.
> *Marie is nice. I know her well.*

> Wer sind **diese Männer?** Kennen Sie **sie?**
> *Who are these men? Do you know them?*

> Wo ist **meine Zeitung?** Ich kann **sie** nicht finden.
> *Where is my newspaper? I can't find it.*

5. **Ihr** may mean *you, her, it, its*, or *their*, depending on the antecedent noun to which **ihr** refers:

a. **ihr** as the subject of a verb in the plural means *you:*

> **Ihr** kommt mit. *You are coming along.*

b. **ihr** as the dative of **sie** (indirect object or object of a preposition) means (*to*) *her* or (*to*) *it:*

> Was soll ich **ihr** (Marie) geben?
> *What am I to give her?*
> Er gab **ihr** (der Maschine) etwas Öl.
> *He gave it a little oil.*

c. **ihr** as a possessive adjective, preceding a noun, means *her*, *their*, or *its*, depending on the antecedent:

> **Marie** und **ihr Freund.**   *Marie and her friend.*
> **Meine Eltern** und **ihr Freund.**   *My parents and their friend.*
> **Die Stadt** und **ihre Häuser.**   *The city and its houses.*

INTERROGATIVE PRONOUNS

The German interrogative pronouns are: **wer?** (*who?*) and **was?** (*what?*). They are declined as follows:

NOM.	**wer?**	*who?*	**was?**	*what?*
ACC.	**wen?**	*whom?*	**was?**	*what?*
DAT.	**wem?**	(*to*) *whom?*	——	
GEN.	**wessen?**	*whose?*	——	

> **Wer ist dieser Mann?**   *Who is this man?*
> **Wen meinen Sie?**   *Whom do you mean?*
> **Wem sagen Sie das?**   *To whom are you saying that?*
> **Wessen Hund ist das?**   *Whose dog is it* (*that*)?
> **Was sagen Sie?**   *What are you saying?*

RECAPITULATION OF MAIN POINTS

1. The personal pronouns in German are: **ich, du, er, sie, es, wir, ihr, sie; Sie.** For declensions, see the table in paragraph 1 above.

2. Most personal pronouns are easy to remember, but note:

euch means *you*, **ihnen** means *them;* the conventional address forms are **Sie, Ihnen,** meaning *you.*

3. **sie** may mean *she, her, they, them* (sometimes *it*): the antecedent decides.

4. ihr may mean *you, her, their:*

ihr geht	*you are going*
Was gibst du ihr?	*What are you giving her?*
ihr Buch	*her* or *their book*

5. The impersonal pronoun is **man;** for the accusative and dative, use **einen, einem.**

6. The interrogatives *who, whom, (to) whom, whose* are **wer, wen, wem, wessen.** The interrogative *what* has only one form: **was.**

ÜBUNGEN

Practice in Reading and Writing

A. *Read aloud and translate:*

1. Was habt ihr da? 2. Marie ist hier. Geben Sie ihr das Buch! 3. Wer sagt dir das? 4. Marie und ihr Freund kommen mit uns. Kommt ihr auch? 5. Sein Sohn hat ein Geschäft in Frankfurt. Es geht gut. 6. Bitten wir ihn um seine Ratschläge! Sie sind immer gut. 7. Wessen Sohn ist er? 8. Wer sagt Ihnen das? 9. Er wird euch heute nicht besuchen. 10. Ich erkläre Ihnen gerne diese Geschichte. 11. Man versteht Sie nicht, Herr Schmidt! 12. Was für eine Jugend! Verstehen Sie sie? 13. Die Jugend von heute? Was erwarten Sie von ihr? 14. Sie war grenzenlos glücklich mit ihm. 15. Er verlangte das Buch in der Bibliothek, aber man fand es nicht. 16. Nietzsche bewunderte Wagner und nannte (*called*) ihn einen Seher der Zukunft. 17. Meinen Sie seine Freundin? Ich kenne sie nicht. 18. Er hat viele Freundinnen und keiner kennt sie. 19. Wem sagen Sie das? 20. Warum erklären Sie das einem nicht? 21. Was erwartet uns in der Stadt? 22. Ich weiß nicht, wessen Sohn er ist. 23. Was erwartest du zu Weihnachten? 24. Wen hat Nietzsche bewundert?

B. *In each of the following sentences, the pronoun in heavy type means "it."* *Explain the form of the pronoun. Example:* Er findet eine Zigarette und raucht **sie.** *He finds a cigarette and smokes it:* **sie,** *meaning* it, *refers to* **die Zigarette,** *which is feminine;* **sie** *is the accusative of* **sie.**

1. Er findet ein Hemd in dem Geschäft und kauft **es.** 2. Die Maschine ist neu, und **sie** arbeitet sehr schnell. 3. Studieren Sie Nietzsches Philosophie und erklären Sie **sie** uns! 4. Ich kenne Wagners Musik, aber ich schätze **sie** nicht sehr. 5. Ich suche noch einen Platz, aber ich finde **ihn** nicht. 6. Wir haben die Bestätigung erwartet, aber wir verstehen **sie** nicht.

C. *Use the correct pronoun forms:*

EXAMPLE: (it) Das ist eine Geschichte. Kennen Sie . . . .?
Kennen Sie sie?

1. (you) Was hat er . . . . gesagt, Frau Schmidt?
2. (you) Was hat er . . . . gesagt, Kinder?
3. (her) Er gibt . . . . einen Ratschlag.
4. (him) Sie gab . . . . einen Sohn.
5. (him) Das ist mein Freund. Kennst du . . . .?
6. (them) Sie hat drei Kinder. Was geben wir . . . . zu Weihnachten?
7. (her) Er hat eine neue Freundin. Kennst du . . . .?
8. (them) Er hat immer wieder eine neue Freundin. Kennst du . . . . alle?
9. (us) Er erzählte . . . . seine Geschichte.
10. (you) Hat er . . . . seine Geschichte auch erzählt, Fritz?

D. *Translate:*

1. Does he know them? 2. He explained that to us. 3. Do they know you, Max? 4. Does she know him? 5. You say you love her. How well do you know her? 6. To whom does she say that? 7. They expect us at home. 8. He is doing that for (**für,** w. acc.) her. 9. What do you expect of (**von,** w. dat.) him? 10. What kind of advice is that? Who gave it to you? (Use present perfect, familiar). 11. Are you sure of him? 12. He is an artist, and she admires him. 13. She does not understand anybody (translate: understands nobody). 14. What do you say, and to whom do you say it? 15. This work of art is very beautiful, but I do not understand it. 16. You said she is very happy with him. 17. He always greeted me and said, "How are you?" 18. Here are all his books. Which ones have you read? 19. He lives nearby, and we see him sometimes. 20. In whose business is he working?

Oral Exercises

E. *Answer the questions using the correct pronoun:*

EXAMPLE: Geht das Geschäft sehr gut?   Ja, es geht sehr gut.
Ist die Schule sehr gut?   Ja, sie ist sehr gut.

1. Ist das Wasser kalt?
2. Ist die Luft kalt?
3. Ist das Gedicht bekannt?
4. Ist dieser Ort sehr bekannt?
5. Ist das Stück neu?
6. Ist die Musik schön?
7. Ist sein Interesse groß?
8. Ist seine Eifersucht groß?
9. Ist das Theater sehr berühmt?
10. Ist dieser Stil alt?

F. *Replace the accusative object of the following sentences with a pronoun:*

EXAMPLES: Ich verstehe das Rätsel nicht.   Ich verstehe es nicht.
          Ich verstehe die Philosophie nicht.   Ich verstehe sie nicht.

1. Du hast das Beispiel vergessen.   5. Ihr habt das Lied oft gehört.
2. Du hast den Ratschlag vergessen.   6. Ihr habt die Musik oft gehört.
3. Wir haben das Schloß erreicht.   7. Wir lieben das Privatleben.
4. Wir haben die Stadt erreicht.   8. Wir schätzen seine Freundschaft.

G. *Replace the dative object of the following sentences with a pronoun:*

EXAMPLES: Ich helfe meinem Freund.   Ich helfe ihm.
          Wir helfen unseren Freunden.   Wir helfen ihnen.

1. Du schreibst deiner Mutter.   5. Wir glauben den Philosophen nicht.
2. Er antwortet den Damen.   6. Er glaubt dieser Frau nicht.
3. Er dankt seinem Vater.   7. Es geht meiner Großmutter ganz gut.
4. Wir danken den Leuten.   8. Es geht den Mädchen ganz gut.

H. *Ask for the noun in the following sentences using an interrogative pronoun:*

EXAMPLE: Sie haben die Noten gekauft.   Was haben sie gekauft?

1. Er hat seiner Mutter geschrieben.   6. Sie genießt viel Bewunderung.
2. Der Pessimist glaubt das nicht.   7. Er schreibt seiner Freundin oft.
3. Er hat eine Oper komponiert.   8. Sie schreibt ihren Freunden oft.
4. Ihr Verhältnis war kühl und kritisch. 9. Die Dame war sehr gekränkt.
5. Er sieht den Komponisten oft.

9

Prepositions

Heinrich Heine

Heinrich Heine wurde im Jahre 1797[1] in Düsseldorf geboren und ist 1856[2] in Paris gestorben. Er war wegen seines Witzes in ganz Europa[3] berühmt, und Matthew Arnold sagte einmal in einem Essay über den Dichter: „Der Weltgeist[4] sieht die Dummheiten der Menschheit und lächelt. Dieses Lächeln
5 ist Heine."

Heine hat von sich selbst[5] gern als von dem letzten Romantiker gesprochen, und das sicher mit Recht. Er hat romantisch gelebt und romantisch geliebt— nicht nur die Frauen, sondern das Leben überhaupt. In vielen Liedern und Gedichten hat er von dem Leben und der Liebe gesungen, aber in seiner Prosa
10 lebt ein anderer Heine: da hat er mit Leidenschaft für die Freiheit, für ein liberales und demokratisches Deutschland gekämpft. Schon als junger Mann hat er daher seine Heimat verlassen und ist nach Frankreich gegangen, und hier ist er viele Jahre später nach langer Krankheit gestorben.

Heine hatte immer viele Freundinnen, auch in Paris, unter ihnen die dicke

---

1. (read) **siebzehnhundertsiebenundneunzig.**   2. (read) **achtzehnhundertsechsundfünfzig.**
3. **in ganz Europa** *in all of Europe.*   4. **Weltgeist** *World Spirit* (God).   5. **sich selbst**
himself.

Mathilde. Sie hat er schließlich geheiratet. „Morgen", schrieb er einem 15
Freund, „begehe[6] ich mit meiner Mathilde Monogamie."

Seine Mathilde war ein einfaches Mädchen aus dem Volk und sprach kein
Deutsch. Heine sprach zwar Französisch, aber schon in der Schule hatte er
die Sprachen schwer gefunden, besonders das Latein. „Die Römer haben
Glück gehabt", meinte er, „sie sprachen schon als Kinder Latein. Man hat 20
keine Zeit, erst Latein zu lernen und dann die Welt zu erobern." Im Deutschen
fand der Junge den Unterschied zwischen dem Dativ und dem Akkusativ
schwer. Später meinte er einmal: „Mein Onkel in Hamburg, der Millionär,
hat es leicht: er hat einen Diener für den Dativ und einen für den Akkusativ."

Im Exil leben ist eine schreckliche Sache, schrieb er aus Paris. „Komme[7] 25
ich einst in den Himmel, werde ich sicher auch unter den Engeln unglücklich
sein. Sie singen so schön und riechen so gut, aber sie sprechen ja[8] kein
Deutsch und rauchen keinen Kanaster.[9] Nur im Vaterland ist mir wohl."[10]

Heine kämpfte mit der Feder in der Hand gegen Intoleranz und Ungerechtigkeit. Sein Lächeln ist nicht immer das Lächeln des Weltgeistes, es 30
ist manchmal sehr bitter. Bekannt sind seine Worte über den Staat der
Zukunft. Sie klingen heute fast prophetisch: „Nur e i n Vaterland wird es
geben[11], nämlich die Erde, und nur e i n e n Glauben, nämlich das Glück auf
Erden. Es wird vielleicht nur e i n e n Hirten und e i n e Herde geben—ein
freier Hirte mit einem eisernen Hirtenstab[12] und eine gleichgeschorene, 35
gleichblökende Menschenherde! . . . Die Zukunft riecht nach Blut, nach
Gottlosigkeit und nach sehr viel Prügeln.[13] Ich rate unsern Enkeln, mit
einer dicken Rückenhaut[14] zur Welt zu kommen."

6. **begehe ich** *I commit.*   7. **komme** (translate:) *if I get.*   8. **ja** (in the middle of a clause,
assertive:) *you know.*   9. **Kanaster** ("cannister tobacco") *cheap tobacco.*   10. **ist mir wohl**
I feel well.   11. **wird es geben** *there will be.*   12. **Hirtenstab** *shepherd's staff.*   13. **Prügel**
thrashings.   14. **Rückenhaut** *skin of the back.*

FRAGEN

1. Wo wurde Heine geboren?   2. Wo ist er gestorben?   3. Was hat Matthew
Arnold einmal über ihn gesagt?   4. Wie hat Heine gelebt und geliebt?
5. Was hat er geliebt?   6. Wo findet man besonders den anderen Heine?
7. Wann hat Heine seine Heimat verlassen?   8. Wo und wann ist er gestorben?
9. Wie war Mathilde?   10. Was hat Heine einem Freund gemeldet?   11. Was
war Mathilde?   12. Wie fand der junge Heine die Sprachen?   13. Warum
haben die Römer Glück gehabt?   14. Was fand der junge Heine im Deutschen
schwer?   15. Was sagte er später über den Onkel in Hamburg?   16. Warum
wird er auch unter den Engeln unglücklich sein?   17. Was tun die Engel?

18. Wie ist sein Lächeln manchmal?　19. Was klingt heute fast prophetisch?
20. Was wird es geben?　21. Wie riecht die Zukunft?　22. Was rät Heine
seinen Enkeln?

WORTSCHATZ[1]

einst	some day (in the past *or* future)	die **Leidenschaft, –en**	passion
eisern	(of) iron	**letzt**	last
der **Engel, –**	angel	die **Liebe**	love
der **Enkel, –**	grandchild	das **Lied, –er**	song
die **Erde**	earth	die **Menschheit**	humanity
auf Erden	on earth	der **Onkel, –**	uncle
erobern	to conquer	das **Recht, –e**	right
die **Feder, –n**	pen	**mit Recht**	rightly so
(das) **Frankreich**	France	die **Sache, –n**	thing, matter
(das) **Französisch**	French	**schrecklich**	terrible
die **Freiheit, –en**	freedom	**schwer**	heavy; hard, difficult
geboren werden	to be born	**sondern** (*after negative clause*)	but, but rather
gleich	equal, even(ly)		
gleichblökend	bleating the same way	**spät**	late
		der **Staat, –en**	state
das **Glück**	good luck, happiness	die **Tafel, –n**	blackboard
Glück haben	to be lucky	**überhaupt**	in general
die **Heimat**	native land	die **Ungerechtigkeit, –en**	injustice
der **Himmel, –**	heaven		
der **Hirt, –en, –en**	shepherd	der **Unterschied, –e**	difference
kämpfen	to fight	das **Volk, ⸗er**	people
leicht	easy	die **Welt, –en**	world
es leicht haben	to have an easy time of it; to be lucky	der **Witz**	wit, humor, joke
		wohl	well
		zwar	to be sure

STRONG VERBS

fahren	to drive	**fährt**	**fuhr**	(ist) **gefahren**[2]
klingen	to ring; to sound		**klang**	**geklungen**
raten	to advise	**rät**	**riet**	**geraten**
riechen (**nach,** *w. dat.*)	to smell (of)		**roch**	**gerochen**
scheren	to shear		**schor**	**geschoren**
singen	to sing		**sang**	**gesungen**
sprechen	to speak	**spricht**	**sprach**	**gesprochen**
treten	to step	**tritt**	**trat**	(ist) **getreten**[2]

[1] From this chapter on, prepositions will no longer be listed in the Wortschatz.
[2] **fahren** and **treten** are conjugated with **sein** if not followed by a direct object.

GRAMMATICAL TERMS

Prepositions are words like: *in, under, for, with, to, against,* etc. A noun or pronoun preceded by a preposition is called a *prepositional object.*

PREPOSITIONS IN GERMAN

1. In German, prepositions govern certain cases, that is, they require the noun or pronoun dependent on them to be in a certain case form. Some prepositions govern the genitive, others the dative, and others the accusative; in addition, there are some which govern either the dative or the accusative, depending on the function of the verb in the clause.

2. Common Prepositions

a. with the genitive:[1]

anstatt (or **statt**)	*instead of*
trotz	*in spite of*
während	*during*
wegen	*on account of, because of*[2]
um . . . willen	*for the sake of*

b. with the dative:[1]

aus	*out of;* (before cities or countries:) *from*
außer	*except; besides; beside*
bei	*near; at; at* (someone's) *house; with, in the home of*
mit	*with* (together with)
nach	*after; according to; to* (before the names of cities and countries)
seit	*since; for* (duration)
von	*from; by* (authorship): *of, about*
zu	*to*

[1] Less common are the following prepositions with the genitive: **diesseits** *this side of —* **jenseits** *that side of;* **oberhalb** *above—* **unterhalb** *below;* **außerhalb** *outside of —* **innerhalb** *inside of;* **halber** *for the sake of;* **infolge** *because of;* **längs** *alongside of;* **mittels** *by means of;* **zwecks** *for the purpose of* and others; with the dative: **gegenüber** *opposite, as against;* **gemäß** *according to;* **nebst** *besides, including.*

[2] When the genitive forms combine with the preposition **wegen** (*on account of*), the final **r** of **meiner, deiner,** etc. changes to **t,** and the preposition is placed after, and attached to, the pronoun: **meinetwegen, deinetwegen, seinetwegen, ihretwegen, unsertwegen, euretwegen, ihretwegen** (*for my sake, for your sake,* etc.): **Ich tue das deinetwegen** *I do that for you* (*for your sake*). Note also the special meaning of the expression **meinetwegen** (used by itself): **Gehen wir jetzt? — Meinetwegen!** *Are we going now? — All right with me!* (*For all I care!*)

c. with the accusative:

durch	*through, by the means of*
für	*for*
gegen	*against, toward*
ohne	*without*
um	*around; at* (. . . o'clock)
wider	(literary) *against*

3. Most German prepositions (except in the genitive) have more than one meaning in English (and vice versa!), depending on the context.

Examples:

a. With the genitive:

anstatt (or **statt**) **eines Autos**   *instead of a car*
trotz seiner Angst   *in spite of his fear*
wegen dieses Herrn   *because of this gentleman*
Um (des) Himmels willen!   *For heaven's sake!*

b. With the dative:

aus: Er kommt **aus dem Hause.**   *He is coming out of the house.*
Er kommt **aus Paris.**   *He comes from Paris.*

außer: **Außer dem Großvater** war die ganze Familie da.   *Except for the grandfather the whole family was there.*
Außer ihm war niemand da.   *Besides him no one was there.*
Er ist **außer sich** vor Freude.   *He is beside himself with joy.*

bei: Godesberg **bei Bonn.**   *Godesberg near Bonn.*
Er ist **bei der Arbeit.**   *He is at work.*
bei uns (**mir, dir,** etc.)   *at our* (*my, your,* etc.) *house*
Er ist **bei seinem Freund.**   *He is with* (*at the home of*) *his friend.*

nach: **nach einer Stunde**   *after an hour*
nach Chicago   *to Chicago*
nach Einstein   *according to Einstein*
nach dem Gesetz   *according to the law*
meiner Meinung nach[1]   *in* (*according to*) *my opinion*

seit: **seit jener Zeit**   *since that time*
seit einiger Zeit[2]   *for some time* (*now*).

von: **von meinen Eltern**   *from my parents*
ein Buch **von Thomas Mann**   *a book by Thomas Mann*
Er spricht wenig **von ihr.**   *He talks little about her.*

[1] **nach,** meaning *according to,* frequently follows the noun it governs.
[2] In constructions with **seit,** the German verb is in the present tense when an action began in the past and is continuing in the present (English present perfect):

Er ist seit einiger Zeit in München.   *He has been in Munich for some time* (*now*).
Seit einer Woche arbeitet er nicht.   *He has not been working for a week.*

c. With the accusative:

durch: **durch das Fenster**   *through the window*
Er erreichte das **durch einen Trick.**   *He achieved that by means of a trick.*

gegen: Er ist **gegen einen Baum** gefahren.   *He drove against a tree.*
Er kam **gegen fünf Uhr.**   *He came toward (around) five o'clock.*

um: **um das Haus**   *around the house*
Er kommt **um fünf Uhr.**   *He is coming at five o'clock.*

4. The following prepositions govern either the dative or the accusative:

an	*on; at; in; to; up to*
auf	*on; upon; on top of; to; in; at*
hinter	*behind*
in	*in; into*
neben	*beside; next to*
über	*over; above; about*
unter	*under; below; among*
vor	*before; in front of; ago; with*[1]
zwischen	*between*

These nine prepositions refer primarily to space relationships. When direction or motion is expressed, use the accusative. When location (also definite time or duration) is expressed, use the dative:

WITH THE ACCUSATIVE (motion or direction)	WITH THE DATIVE (location; time)
Ich hänge das Bild **an die Wand.** *I am hanging the picture on the wall.*	Das Bild hängt **an der Wand.** *The picture is hanging on the wall.*
Er steigt **auf das Pferd.** *He climbs on the horse.*	Er sitzt **auf dem Pferd.** *He is sitting on the horse.*
Er kriecht **unter das Auto.** *He crawls under the car.*	Er liegt **unter dem Auto.** *He is lying under the car.*
Er geht **unter die Leute.** *He goes among (mingles with) the people.*	Er lebt **unter den Leuten.** *He lives among the people.*
Er stellt die Milch **vor die Tür.** *He puts the milk in front of the door.*	Er steht **vor der Tür.** *He is standing in front of the door.*
	Sie kommt nicht **vor dem Sommer.** (time) *She won't come before the summer.*
	Ich sah sie **vor zehn Minuten.**[2] (time) *I saw her ten minutes ago.*

[1] **Vor** is used to indicate cause: **vor Freude** *with joy;* **vor Hunger** *of hunger.*
[2] Note: **vor** preceding an expression of time always means *ago;* **vor zehn Minuten** (*ten minutes ago*) never means *for ten minutes.*

5. Many prepositions are used with certain verbs to form fixed verbal expressions. English uses prepositions similarly, but you will note that the basic meanings of the prepositions in the two languages do not necessarily coincide. Generally speaking, the prepositions governing either the dative or the accusative (except **vor**) are used with the accusative when they are dependent on verbs. Study the following common examples:

antworten auf (acc.)	*to answer* (a question)
bitten um	*to ask for* (a favor)
danken für	*to thank for*
denken an (acc.)	*to think of*
fragen nach	*to ask about*
glauben an (acc.)	*to believe in*
halten für	*to take for, consider*
halten von	*to think of* (have an opinion of)
hoffen auf (acc.)	*to hope for*
sagen zu	*to say about* (or *to*)
schreiben an (acc.)	*to write to*
sprechen von, über (acc.)	*to speak* (*talk*) *about*
warten auf (acc.)	*to wait for*

6. Some prepositions may be contracted with **dem, der,** and **das:**

WITH **dem** (DAT.):	WITH **der** (DAT.):	WITH **das** (ACC.):
an dem = am	zu der = zur	an das = ans
bei dem[1] = beim		auf das = aufs
hinter dem = hinterm		durch das = durchs
in dem = im		für das = fürs
von dem = vom		hinter das = hinters
vor dem = vorm		in das = ins
über dem = überm		über das = übers
unter dem = unterm		um das = ums
zu dem = zum		unter das = unters
		vor das = vors

7. Like **nach,** the following prepositions may be placed before or after the noun they govern, the latter being preferred in most cases:

With the genitive:	**wegen**	*because of*
With the dative:	**entgegen**	*toward, contrary to*
	gegenüber	*opposite, in the face of*
	gemäß	*according to*
With the accusative (only after a noun):	**entlang**	*along* (*side of*)
	lang	*long, for*

---

[1] Note the very common combination of **beim** with verbal nouns (infinitives used as nouns): **beim Essen** *at* (*during*) *the meal, while eating;* **beim Arbeiten** *at work, while working.*

EXAMPLES:

Entgegen seinen Wünschen ⎫ **seinen Wünschen entgegen** ⎭	*contrary to his wishes*
gegenüber dem Bahnhof ⎫ **dem Bahnhof gegenüber** ⎭	*opposite the railway station*
die Straße entlang	*along the street*
das ganze Jahr lang	*all year long, for the whole year*
viele Jahre lang	*for many years*

RECAPITULATION OF MAIN POINTS

1. German prepositions govern certain cases. The following arrangement will help you remember which cases the various prepositions govern:

GENITIVE: **anstatt (statt), trotz, während, wegen, um . . . willen**

DATIVE: **aus, außer, bei, mit, nach, seit, von, zu**

DATIVE OR ACCUSATIVE: **an, auf, hinter, in, neben, über, unter, vor, zwischen**

ACCUSATIVE: **durch, für, gegen, ohne, um, wider**

2. With prepositions governing the dative or accusative, use the accusative if the verb expresses motion or direction, the dative if the verb expresses location.

ACC.: Ich gehe **in den Park.** *I go to the park.*
DAT.: Ich bin **in dem Park.** *I am in the park.*
DAT.: Ich gehe **in dem Park** spazieren. *I go for a walk in the park.*

ÜBUNGEN

Practice in Reading and Writing

A. *Ein Gedicht von Heinrich Heine:*

Sie saßen und tranken am Teetisch,
Und sprachen von Liebe viel.
Die Herren, die waren ästhetisch,
Die Damen von zartem Gefühl.

1	**der Teetisch** **saßen**	*tea table* *past of* **sitzen**	
		tranken	*past of* **trinken** *to drink*
	4	**von zartem Gefühl**	*of delicate feeling*

5   Die Liebe muß sein platonisch,
Der dürre Hofrat sprach.
Die Hofrätin lächelt ironisch,
Und dennoch seufzet sie: Ach!

Der Domherr öffnet den Mund weit:
10   Die Liebe sei nicht zu roh,
Sie schadet sonst der Gesundheit.
Das Fräulein lispelt: Wieso?

Die Gräfin spricht wehmütig:
Die Liebe ist eine Passion!
15   Und präsentieret gütig
Die Tasse dem Herren Baron.

Am Tische war noch ein Plätzchen;
Mein Liebchen, da hast du gefehlt.
Du hättest so hübsch, mein Schätzchen,
20   Von deiner Liebe erzählt.

5	dürr	*skinny*		sonst	*otherwise*
6	der Hofrat	*Court (Privy)*	12	lispeln	*to lisp*
		Councillor		wieso?	*how come?*
7	die Hofrätin	*the Councillor's*	13	die Gräfin	*countess*
		wife		wehmütig	*in a melancholy*
8	dennoch	*nevertheless*			*way*
	seufzen	*to sigh*	15	gütig	*kindly*
9	der Domherr	*canon*	16	die Tasse	*cup*
	der Mund	*mouth*	18	da hast du gefehlt	*there you should*
10	sei	*should be*			*have been*
	roh	*coarse*	19	hättest	*would have*
11	schaden	*to damage*		Schätzchen	*sweetheart*

B. *Read aloud and translate:*

1. während des Tages   2. nach der Heimat   3. nach drei Jahren   4. ein Drama von Schiller   5. wegen des Geschäfts   6. Sie wohnen bei mir.   7. Sie wohnt bei ihren Eltern.   8. Er ist seit einer Woche in Berlin.   9. Seiner Meinung nach ist es nicht zu spät.   10. Bitte denken Sie manchmal an mich!   11. Für wen arbeitest du?   12. Er geht an die Tür und öffnet sie.   13. Er war vor zwei Tagen hier.   14. Er arbeitet unter den Amerikanern.   15. Sie leben unter Amerikanern.   16. Was halten Sie von diesem Künstler?   17. Halten Sie diesen Mann für einen Künstler?   18. Bitte warten Sie auf mich an der Ecke!   19. Wen haben Sie nach seiner Adresse gefragt?   20. Was haben Sie gegen Nietzsches Philosophie?   21. Er wohnt uns gegenüber.   22. Ich habe immer wieder gefragt, aber keiner hat auf meine Frage geantwortet.   23. Kommen Sie meinetwegen?   24. Meinetwegen kommen Sie!

C. *Schleiermacher und die Studenten*

1. Eine Dame fragte einmal den Philosophen und Theologen Schleiermacher nach den Zuhörern (*auditors, students*) in seinen Vorlesungen (*lectures*). 2. „Studenten, junge Damen und Soldaten kommen zu mir", antwortete Schleiermacher. 3. „Soldaten?" fragte die Dame erstaunt. „Was tun denn die Soldaten bei Ihnen?" 4. „Das ist sehr einfach. Die Studenten kommen wegen der Examen, die jungen Damen kommen wegen der Studenten, und die Soldaten kommen wegen der jungen Damen."

D. *In the following exercise, try to deduce the meanings of the prepositions from the context; they are not necessarily literal:*

1. Sie hat vor Eifersucht geweint. 2. Hat er schon wieder über Wagner gesprochen? 3. Er spricht immer von seiner Tante. 4. Mit anderen Worten: du kommst nicht. 5. Er ist ohne Frage sehr reich. 6. Auf eine solche Frage antworte ich nicht. 7. Aus diesem Grunde (*reason*) sage ich nein. 8. Wir nehmen Sie beim Wort, Herr Schmidt. 9. Seine Gesundheit ist aus Eisen. 10. Ich habe heute keinen Pfennig (*penny*) bei mir. 11. Auf deutsch sagt man das anders. 12. Im Englischen sagt man das nicht. 13. Im Himmel und auf der Erde. 14. Ein Vers von Wilhelm Busch: „Nichts ist schwerer (*more difficult, harder*) zu ertragen als eine Reihe (*series*) von guten Tagen." 15. Man weiß, was Heine unter Freiheit versteht.

E. *In the following sentences, prepositions are used with either the dative or the accusative. Explain each usage:*

1. Der Tod steht vor der Tür. 2. Er tritt vor die Tür. 3. Heine sagt das in einem Gedicht. 4. Er ist in seine Heimat gereist. 5. Er hat lange unter Indianern (*American Indians*) gelebt. 6. Er ist unter die Soldaten gegangen. 7. Ich schreibe Ihnen die Worte auf die Tafel (*blackboard*). 8. Die Worte stehen auf der Tafel. 9. Wir gehen dieses Jahr an den Rhein. 10. Sie leben am Rhein. 11. Er sitzt vor der Bibliothek und liest. 12. Ich lege das Telefonbuch neben das Telefon.

F. *Translate:*

1. The children believe in Santa Claus **(der Weihnachtsmann)**. 2. Wait for us; we are coming with you. 3. They are working during the day. 4. He has been (present tense!) here for a week now. 5. Say that in French! 6. Be honest, you are among friends. 7. They are standing in front of the door. 8. We are reading a play by Hauptmann. 9. The merchant is coming from Chicago and is going to New York. 10. Are you living at Mr. Schmidt's? 11. What is life without love? 12. What are you looking for behind the couch **(das Sofa)**? 13. Who is knocking on the door? 14. He wrote to his uncle and is still **(immer noch)** waiting for an answer. 15. He

asked me for a poem by Heine.   16. Heine wrote many poems about love.
17. The difference between these songs is interesting.   18. He spoke about
the difference between the Germans and the French.   19. I don't understand
much about (von) music.   20. What did Heine say about freedom?   21. He is
doing that for our sake.   22. That's alright with me!

Oral Exercises

G. *Translate:*

1. He is against his professor.   2. She is for her professor.   3. We walk
through our house.   4. He comes without his books.   5. They stand around
the house.   6. She does it for her friends.   7. We are sitting around the
teacher.   8. He is traveling through his native land.   9. She is working
without her friend.   10. He is fighting against injustice.

H. *Translate:*

1. They are against him.   2. He is for me.   3. They are working without her.
4. We are standing around him.   5. I hear it from her.   6. She is doing it
for us.   7. I am coming without them.   8. He is fighting against me.   9. We
are writing to her.   10. They are not against me.

I. *Translate:*

1. He is from this city.   2. Near my house.   3. He is coming with his mother.
4. After (the) class.   5. Since the war.   6. A poem by the poet Heine.   7. A
book from a friend.   8. The house of my father.   9. The way to the city.
10. He lives with his parents.

J. *Translate:*

1. This book is from me.   2. They are standing near him.   3. He is dancing
with her.   4. After the war.   5. A poem by her.   6. A word from us.   7. Go
to them!   8. He is coming with us.   9. Besides me she is here.

K. *Combination drill. Translate:*

1. We are not against them.   2. Is he living near them?   3. She is coming
without him.   4. The book is by him.   5. Do that for me!   6. She has it
from me.   7. They are coming with him.   8. He speaks for me.   9. They
fight against us.   10. I'll go to him.

L. *Change the sentences according to the example:*

EXAMPLE: Er geht in die Bibliothek.
            Jetzt ist er in der Bibliothek.

1. Er geht in den Hafen.
2. Er geht hinter das Haus.
3. Er geht an die Tür.
4. Er geht unter die Leute.
5. Er geht zwischen die Häuser.

6. Er geht auf den Korridor.
7. Er geht vor das Haus.
8. Er geht neben das Auto.
9. Er geht in das Theater.

10

Da- and Wo-Compounds

Albert Einstein

Die Relativitätstheorie ist etwas, wovon die meisten Leute nicht viel verstehen. Man hört zwar schon in der Schule davon—zum Beispiel, daß Albert Einstein ihr „Vater" ist. Das ist nicht viel, aber für die meisten ist es genug.

5 Wer war Albert Einstein? Ohne jede Frage einer der großen Geister unserer Zeit. Man nennt ihn gerne den Newton unseres Jahrhunderts, womit aber noch nicht alles gesagt ist, denn wir bewundern in Einstein ja nicht nur den Wissenschaftler, sondern auch und vielleicht sogar vor allem den Menschen. Als solcher stand er in der Tradition des deutschen Humanismus

10 wie Heine, denn er war, wie dieser, ein Feind aller Intoleranz und Ungerechtigkeit, worunter er selbst fast sein ganzes Leben lang zu leiden hatte.

Die Geburtsstadt Einsteins ist Ulm an der Donau[1], wo einige Jahrhunderte früher auch der berühmte Astronom Johannes Kepler[2], der Erfinder des Fernrohrs, gelebt hatte. Schon früh beschäftigte den jungen Einstein die

15 Mathematik, besonders die Algebra. „Die Algebra ist wunderbar", sagte er.

1. **Donau** *Danube*. 2. **Johannes Kepler**, 1571–1630, late-medieval astronomer (Kepler's laws).

112

„Wenn man etwas nicht weiß, nennt man es ‚X' und sucht danach." Auch die Geometrie faszinierte ihn schon in jungen Jahren. Ein Freund schenkte ihm einmal ein Buch darüber, und er las darin so begeistert wie andere seines Alters in Detektivgeschichten.

Aber nicht nur die Wissenschaft, auch Kunst, Musik und Literatur interes- 20 sierten ihn sein Leben lang. Er spielte die Geige und liebte es, mit seinen Freunden zu musizieren. Er las gerne, aber er hatte nur wenig Zeit dafür. Als Wissenschaftler wollte er nicht experimentieren, sondern denken. Eines Tages besuchte ihn ein Freund und bemerkte ein Fernrohr in seinem Zimmer. „Ah", sagte er, „das ist also[3] das Instrument, mit dem Sie das Universum 25 durchdringen!"

„Ach nein", antwortete dieser, „das Fernrohr gehört dem früheren Besitzer des Hauses", womit er Kepler meinte.

„Ja, aber womit arbeiten Sie denn?"[4] fragte der Freund.

„Damit!" antwortete Einstein und wies mit dem Finger auf die Stirn.　30

Aber auch ein großer Mathematiker rechnet nicht immer so schnell wie eine Hausfrau. Darüber gibt[5] es eine hübsche Anekdote. Während der Inflation fuhr Einstein eines Tages mit der Straßenbahn. Es war die Zeit nach dem ersten Weltkrieg, als[6] das Geld rapide im Wert sank. Von Tag zu Tag fiel die Mark im Kurs[7], und die Preise stiegen astronomisch. Schließlich hatte jeder 35 die Taschen voll von wertlosem Papiergeld. Einstein also[8] gab dem Schaffner in der Straßenbahn ein Bündel[9] Geld. Es waren mehrere Milliarden[10] Mark. Er erhielt einige Millionen zurück und begann, sie nachzurechnen.[11] Aber wer rechnet so schnell! Der Schaffner wurde ungeduldig, nahm ihm die Scheine aus der Hand[12] und zählte sie selbst noch einmal. „Richtig!" sagte 40 er dann und schüttelte den Kopf. „Ich weiß nicht, womit Sie Ihr Geld verdienen, aber ein Mathematiker sind Sie bestimmt nicht!"

Einstein hatte sogar für das Glück eine mathematische Formel. Ein Künstler malte ihn einmal und fragte dabei: „Haben Sie auch für das Glück eine Formel?"—„Jawohl", antwortete Einstein. „Sie lautet: A = X + Y + Z."[13] 45

„Und wofür stehen A, X, Y und Z?"

„A für das Glück, X für die Arbeit und Z für das Spiel."

„Und wofür steht Y?" fragte der Künstler zurück.

„Y steht für: den Mund halten!"

---

3. **das ist also** *so that is.*　4. **denn** (in a question, for emphasis: don't translate).　5. **gibt es** *there is.*　6. **als** (as conjunction at the beginning of a clause:) *when.*　7. **Kurs** *rate of exchange.*　8. **also** (begin translation with this word) *so.*　9. **Bündel** (nouns indicating quantity precede the following noun directly) *bundle of.*　10. **die Milliarde** *billion.*　11. **nachzurechnen** *to count over; to check.*　12. **ihm . . . aus der Hand** (see Aufgabe 3, 9: if a phrase refers to parts of the body or clothing, the English possessive adjective is replaced by the German article and the possessor is in the dative:) *out of his hand.*　13. For the pronunciation of these letters in German, see page 1.

FRAGEN

1. Worüber verstehen die meisten Leute nicht viel?   2. Wovon hört man schon in der Schule?   3. Wer war Albert Einstein?   4. Was nennt man ihn gerne?   5. Warum ist damit nicht alles gesagt?   6. In welcher Tradition stand er?   7. Worunter hat er fast sein ganzes Leben lang gelitten?   8. Wer hat vor Einstein schon in Ulm gelebt?   9. Was beschäftigte den jungen Einstein schon früh?   10. Warum ist die Algebra wunderbar?   11. Was schenkte ihm ein Freund einmal?   12. Was interessierte Einstein neben der Wissenschaft?   13. Was tat er gerne?   14. Warum las er nicht viel?   15. Was wollte er als Wissenschaftler nicht tun?   16. Was bemerkte der Freund in seinem Zimmer?   17. Was sagte er zu Einstein?   18. Was antwortete Einstein?   19. Worüber gibt es eine hübsche Anekdote?   20. Was geschieht in einer Inflation?   21. Was gab Einstein dem Schaffner?   22. Warum wurde der Schaffner ungeduldig?   23. Was sagte er dann zu Einstein?   24. Wofür hatte Einstein auch eine Formel?   25. Wie lautet diese Formel?   26. Wofür stehen A, X, Y und Z?

WORTSCHATZ

die **Arbeit, –en**	work	**meist**	most
bemerken	to notice	**die meisten**	most people
der **Besitzer, –**	owner	**Leute**	
bestimmt	certainly, definitely	der **Mund, ∺er**	mouth
der **Erfinder, –**	inventor	**den Mund**	(*lit.*, "to hold
das **Fernrohr, –e**	telescope	**halten**	one's mouth")
früher	earlier		to shut up
die **Geburt, –en**	birth	**nennen**	to call
die **Geburts-**	native city	**nichts**	nothing
stadt, ∺e		**rechnen**	to count; to calculate
die **Geduld**	patience	**richtig**	correct(ly)
geduldig	patient	der **Schein, –e**	bill
ungeduldig	impatient	**schenken**	to give (as a present)
gehören (*w. dat.*)	to belong to	**schütteln**	to shake
die **Geige, –n**	violin	**den Kopf**	to shake one's
das **Geld, –er**	money	**schütteln**	head (about)
das **Papier-**	paper money	(**über,** *w. acc.*)	
geld, –er		das **Spiel, –e**	play
genug	enough	die **Stirn, –en**	forehead
das **Jahrhundert, –e**	century	die **Straßenbahn,**	streetcar
jawohl	yes, indeed	**–en**	
(**er, man) kann**	(he, one) can	die **Tasche, –n**	pocket
lauten	to sound, to run	**verdienen**	to earn
malen	to paint	**versuchen**	to try
mehrere	several	der **Wert, –e**	value, worth

wertlos	worthless	zählen	to count (over)
der **Wissenschaftler,–**	scientist	**zufrieden**	satisfied
(er) **wollte**	(he) wanted to	**zusammen**	together

STRONG VERBS

durchdringen	to penetrate		durchdrang	durchdrungen
erhalten	to receive	erhält	erhielt	erhalten
fallen	to fall	fällt	fiel	ist gefallen[1]
geschehen	to happen	geschieht	geschah	ist geschehen[1]
leiden (unter, *w. dat.*)	to suffer (from)		litt	gelitten
sinken	to sink		sank	ist gesunken[1]
steigen	to climb, rise		stieg	ist gestiegen[1]
weisen	to point (to)		wies	gewiesen

DISTINGUISH BETWEEN

geben *to give* and **schenken** *to give* (as a present).

GRAMMATICAL TERMS

(See Aufgabe 8)

DA-COMPOUNDS

1. In older or more formal English, it was common to find a combination of *there* with a preposition if the pronoun object of the preposition (*it, that, them*) referred to a thing or things: *therewith, therein, thereupon*, etc., in place of *with it, in that, upon them*, or the like:

> But thou *thereon* didst only breathe . . . .

In modern German, personal pronouns referring to things or ideas and used as objects of a preposition are generally replaced by **da** (*there*), which then combines with the preposition: **damit, dafür, dagegen:**

> Ich lege einen Stein **darauf** (= auf die Zeitung).
> *I put a rock on it (= the newspaper).*

In the plural:

> Ich habe zwei Instrumente. Was kann ich **dafür** bekommen?
> *I have two instruments. What can I get for them?*

Therefore, when you come upon a form like **damit, dafür, dagegen**, etc.,

[1] Takes **sein** as auxiliary in the compound tenses.

translate: *with it* (*that* or *them*), *for it* (*that* or *them*), *against it* (*that* or *them*). Always translate the second part—the preposition—first:

2 1
Was sagst du **dazu**?   *What do you say to that?*

2 1
Was hältst du **davon**?   *What do you think of that?*

2. If the preposition to be combined with **da** begins with a vowel, an **r** is inserted between **da** and the preposition (**da r an, da r auf, da r über**):

Ich glaube nicht **daran**.   *I don't believe in it.*
Darüber hat er nichts gesagt.   *He did not say anything about that.*

3. Only prepositions governing the dative or accusative form **da**-compounds, but **ohne, außer, seit** never do:

Ich kann **ohne das** auskommen.   *I can get along without it.*

4. If a verb which requires a preposition (like **denken an**) is followed by a dependent clause, a **da**-compound is usually formed with the given preposition, but this **da**-compound often has no English equivalent:

Er dankte mir **dafür**, daß ich ihm das Buch mitgebracht hatte.
He thanked me (for the fact), that I had brought the book along for him.
Er denkt **daran**, sich ein neues Auto zu kaufen.
He thinks (of it) of buying (lit., to buy) a new car.

5. A few **da**-compounds are used idiomatically as adverbial phrases; learn them as vocabulary:

damit: *so saying; with that; with these words*
Damit ging sie.   *So saying (with these words) she left.*

darauf: *thereupon, then*
Darauf ging sie.   *Then she left.*

dabei: *and yet; at the same time; for all that*
Er kauft sich ein Auto; **dabei** hat er kaum genug zu essen.
He is buying himself a car; and yet, he has hardly enough to eat.

dagegen: *on the other hand*
Vater werden ist nicht schwer,   *To become a father is not difficult.*
Vater sein **dagegen** sehr. (W. Busch)   *To be one, on the other hand, very!*

WO-COMPOUNDS

1. Similarly, in older or more formal English, prepositions were commonly compounded with *where* (*wherewith*, *wherein*, etc. in place of *with what*, *in which*, etc.) and used in questions and relative clauses whenever *where* referred to a thing or things:

Wherewith shall it be salted?
The play's the thing *wherein* I'll catch the conscience of the king.

In modern German, especially interrogative but also relative pronouns referring to things or ideas and used with a preposition are replaced by **wo** (*where*), which then combines with the preposition:

Womit hat er dich geschlagen?
With what did he hit you?
Das ist etwas, **wovon** ich nichts verstehe.
That is something about which I understand nothing.

Therefore, when you come to a **wo**-compound, translate **wo-** as *which* (or *what*) and give the preposition its proper meaning:

Wofür halten Sie mich?   *What do you take me for?*

Notice that in colloquial English the equivalent of the German **wo**-compound is often split.

2. If the preposition to be combined with **wo** begins with a vowel, an **r** is inserted between **wo** and the preposition (**woran, worauf, worin, worüber**):

Worüber hat er gesprochen?   *About what did he speak?*
(*What did he speak about?*)

3. Only prepositions governing the dative or accusative form **wo**-compounds, but **ohne, außer, seit** do not.

4. In questions, **wo**-compounds *must* be used. There is no other way to express *for what?, in what?, with what?* etc. than by **wofür?, worin?, womit?**, etc.

In relative clauses, **wo**-compounds used to be accepted along with uncombined forms. In modern usage, however, uncombined forms are preferred, except when the relative pronoun refers to an indefinite antecedent (**das, etwas** *something*, **nichts** *nothing*, etc.):

Definite antecedent:

Das ist **eine Bank, auf der (worauf)** ich gerne sitze.
That is a bench on which I like to sit.

Indefinite antecedent:

Das ist **etwas, worüber** (über das) ich sprechen möchte.
That is something about which I would like to talk.
Wozu (or **Warum**) tust du das? **Worauf** er antwortete . . . .
Why are you doing that? Whereupon he answered . . . .

RECAPITULATION OF MAIN POINTS

1. **Da**-compounds and **wo**-compounds are used when pronoun objects of a preposition refer to things or ideas:

   > **dafür**   *for it; for that; for them*
   > **wofür**   *for what, for which*

2. **Da**-compounds replace: prepositions + personal object pronouns. **Wo**-compounds replace: prepositions + interrogative or relative pronouns.

3. Only prepositions governing the dative or accusative form **da**-compounds and **wo**-compounds. Exceptions: **ohne, außer, seit.**

4. **Wo**-compounds *must* be used in questions; they *may* occur in relative clauses.

ÜBUNGEN

Practice in Reading and Writing

A. *Read aloud and translate:*

Variation über ein Thema

1. Max und Gustav gingen einmal zusammen nach Hause (*home*) und sprachen dabei über dies und das, darunter auch die Relativitätstheorie. 2. Beide wußten (*knew*) aber nicht viel davon. 3. „Was sagst du denn dazu?" fragte Max. 4. „Wozu? Zu der Relativitätstheorie? 5. Was möchtest du denn darüber wissen (möchtest du . . . wissen *would you like to know*)?" 6. Darauf Max: „Nun, so das Prinzip!" 7. „Also, paß auf (*listen*): Du sitzt den ganzen Tag im Büro bei der Arbeit; alle anderen genießen das Leben, nur du hast nichts davon. 8. Dabei wird dir ein Tag zu einer Woche —so lang ist er. 9. Aber in den Ferien (*vacation*) ist das ganz anders; da wird dir dagegen eine Woche zu einem Tag. Das ist die Relativitätstheorie." 10. „Das ist die Relativitätstheorie? Und davon lebt Einstein?"

B. *Translate and analyze the use of* **da-** *and* **wo**-*compounds or their absence:*

1. Womit hat Einstein die Wissenschaft revolutioniert? 2. Wer versteht etwas davon? 3. Wovon verstehen nicht viele etwas? 4. Das ist eine Theorie, über die die Meinungen verschieden sind. 5. Worüber sind die

Meinungen verschieden? 6. Sind wir darüber einer Meinung? 7. Bei wem arbeitet er? 8. Wobei geschieht das? Bei der Arbeit? 9. Wovon leben diese Menschen? 10. Worüber lächelt das Mädchen die ganze Zeit? 11. Sie lächelt darüber, daß du so dumme Fragen stellst. 12. Darauf schüttelte er den Kopf. 13. Ich glaube nicht daran, daß die Zeiten wieder besser (*better*) werden. 14. Er redet immer über Politik; dabei versteht er gar nichts davon. 15. Damit sagte er „Danke schön" und ging nach Hause. 16. Was halten Sie davon? 17. Einstein? Wir lesen gerade etwas über ihn. 18. Über wen lesen Sie etwas? 19. Worüber lesen Sie etwas? 20. Wozu tust du denn das? 21. Von wem hast du das Buch erhalten?

C. *Idiomatic uses of* **da-** *and* **wo-***compounds. Find suitable English equivalents:*

1. Wofür halten Sie mich? 2. Womit kann ich Ihnen dienen (here: *help*)? 3. Dadurch wurde er der Newton unseres Jahrhunderts. 4. Worauf warten Sie jetzt? 5. Woran denken Sie gerade? 6. Woran arbeitet er zur Zeit? 7. Worüber sprechen Sie denn da? 8. Davon halte ich nicht viel. 9. Woraus besteht (bestehen aus *to consist of*) dieses Produkt? 10. Was bekommen Sie dafür? 11. Wozu arbeitest du so viel? 12. Er hat nicht viel zu essen; dabei fährt er einen Cadillac. 13. Dafür haben Sie mir zu danken. 14. Darauf kann ich nicht warten. 15. Worunter leidet sie denn? 16. Direkt daneben steht unser Haus. 17. Lesen wir noch einmal den Vers von Wilhelm Busch, von dem man so viel lernen kann: „Vater werden ist nicht schwer, Vater sein dagegen sehr."

D. *Translate; before doing so, review the information on word order in Aufgabe Eins:*

1. What do you have against these people? I have nothing against them. 2. I said (to) him that I did not believe in it. 3. Is this the telescope through which Kepler (has) looked (use: **sehen**)? 4. Wait for me; we'll go to him together. 5. What did they talk about? 6. That is a science about which I have not yet heard anything. 7. For whom are you working? 8. Many people suffer from that. 9. For what am I giving you money? 10. Nobody has time for that now. 11. I received his letter but found nothing in it. 12. About what did he shake his (the) head? 13. He did not understand anything about it. 14. He gets enough money, but what does he do with it? 15. What did you give her (as a present)? What did she say to it? 16. After that he kept his mouth shut. 17. He has a house, but he doesn't live in it. 18. I don't believe that he will have enough money for it. 19. What don't you believe in? 20. He does not think (of the fact) that these people are very poor.

Oral Exercises

E. *Answer the questions using either a preposition + a pronoun or a* **da**-*compound:*

EXAMPLES: Sprechen Sie *von Einstein?*   Ja, ich spreche *von ihm.*
           Sprechen Sie *von der Tradition?*   Ja, ich spreche *davon.*

1. Ist er mit diesen Leuten zufrieden?
2. Ist er mit dieser Detektivgeschichte zufrieden?
3. Hat sie Zeit für ihre Kinder?
4. Hat sie Zeit für Kunst und Literatur?
5. Haben Sie genug von diesen Studenten?
6. Haben Sie genug von diesem Klima?
7. Halten Sie etwas von Psychoanalyse?
8. Halten Sie etwas von diesem Psychiater?

F. *Form questions based on the following statements. Use* **wo**-*compounds where applicable:*

EXAMPLES:

Sie hat ein Buch *über Nietzsche* gelesen.   *Über wen* hat sie ein Buch gelesen?
Sie hat ein Buch *über Philosophie* gelesen.   *Worüber* hat sie ein Buch gelesen?

1. Er fährt mit seinen Freunden in die Stadt.
2. Er fährt mit der Straßenbahn in die Stadt.
3. Er hat über die Dame oft gelacht.
4. Er hat über diesen Witz oft gelacht.
5. Es gibt über Einstein eine hübsche Anekdote.
6. Er hat die Taschen voll Geld.

11

Reflexive and Impersonal Verbs

Gerhart Hauptmann[1] und Thomas Mann[2]

Es gibt in der modernen deutschen Literatur nicht viele so klare und scharfe
Gegensätze wie den Schlesier[3] Gerhart Hauptmann und den Norddeutschen
Thomas Mann. Hauptmann hatte sich schon in jungen Jahren mit seinem
sozialen Drama „Die Weber"[4] einen Namen gemacht. Zwar hatte auch
Thomas Mann schon früh seine ersten Erfolge als Schriftsteller gehabt, aber   5
er wurde doch erst viel später durch seine großen Romane in der ganzen
Welt bekannt. Für die Kunst Thomas Manns ist die Klarheit des Intellekts
das Entscheidende, für die Hauptmanns „die Seele des Volkes".

Hauptmann hatte vielleicht keinen sehr klaren, aber dafür einen sehr
auffallenden Kopf, besonders seit er sich auf Goethe frisierte. Er hielt sich   10
für den wiedergeborenen[5] Goethe. Man hat sich oft darüber lustig gemacht,
wie etwa die ziemlich respektlose Dichterin Else Lasker-Schüler, denn sie
begrüßte ihn einmal mit den Worten: „Sie sehen ja aus[6] wie die Großmutter
von Goethe!"

1. **Gerhart Hauptmann,** 1862–1946, foremost German dramatist of the Naturalist generation.   2. **Thomas Mann,** 1875–1955, one of the great novelists of modern German literature.
3. **Schlesier** *Silesian.*   4. **Die Weber** *The Weavers*, 1892, a play about the uprising of the
starving weavers in Silesia.   5. **wiedergeboren** *reborn.*   6. **Sie sehen . . . aus wie** *you look like.*

15   Man fragt sich natürlich, wie Hauptmann sich bei einer solchen Gelegenheit verhielt. Hat er sich geärgert? Gefreut hat er sich sicher nicht.

Gegensätze ziehen sich an,[7] sagt ein deutsches Sprichwort. Thomas Mann und Gerhart Hauptmann sind dafür ein gutes Beispiel. Sie kannten[8] sich gut und sind einander auch oft begegnet. Vor allem aber: sie schätzten
20 sich nicht nur als Dichter, sondern auch als Menschen. Thomas Mann hat Hauptmann in einer Rede einmal als den „König des Volkes" bezeichnet, und das bestimmt nicht nur wegen seiner großen Popularität. In den Jahren der Weimarer Republik[9] gab man den beiden gerne den Titel „Hofdichter der deutschen Republik". „Hofdichter" in einer Republik gibt es wohl nur
25 in Deutschland.

Dann aber kam der „Dritte Reich".[10] Thomas Mann begab sich, wie viele andere deutsche Schriftsteller, in die Schweiz, aber Hauptmann hatte sich gegen die Emigration entschieden. In Zürich haben sie sich dann noch einmal getroffen—man kann auch sagen: sie haben sich verfehlt. Thomas
30 Mann befand sich nämlich[11] eines Tages in einem Geschäft. Er kaufte sich irgendetwas—sagen wir: eine Krawatte. Da sagte der Verkäufer zu ihm: „Wir haben gerade noch einen anderen deutschen Dichter im Haus, Gerhart Hauptmann. Möchten Sie[12] ihn sprechen?"

„Nein", antwortete Thomas Mann, „damit warten wir besser bis nach
35 dem Ende des Dritten Reiches."

„Genau dasselbe hat Herr Hauptmann auch gesagt", meinte der Verkäufer.

7. **ziehen sich an** *attract each other*. 8. **kannten** (past of **kennen**) *knew*. 9. **Weimarer Republik** *Weimar Republic*, the period in Germany between the end of World War I and the advent of Hitler. 10. **das Dritte Reich** designation of Hitler Germany. 11. **nämlich** *namely* (translate by *for*, begin the sentence with it). 12. **möchten Sie** *would you like?*

FRAGEN

1. Was sind Gerhart Hauptmann und Thomas Mann in der modernen deutschen Literatur? 2. Wann hatte Hauptmann sich einen Namen gemacht? 3. Womit hatte er sich einen Namen gemacht? 4. Womit wurde Thomas Mann später in der ganzen Welt bekannt? 5. Was ist das Entscheidende für die Kunst Thomas Manns? 6. Was für einen Kopf hatte Hauptmann? 7. Wie frisierte er sich? 8. Wie war die Dichterin Else Lasker-Schüler? 9. Wie begrüßte sie Hauptmann einmal? 10. Was fragt man sich natürlich? 11. Was sagt ein deutsches Sprichwort? 12. Was sind Thomas Mann und Gerhart Hauptmann für dieses Sprichwort? 13. Wie verhielten sich Mann und Hauptmann zueinander? 14. Welchen Titel gab man den beiden gerne? 15. Was gibt es wohl nur in Deutschland? 16. Was tat Thomas Mann zu

Beginn des „Dritten Reichs"? 17. Was sagte der Verkäufer zu Thomas
Mann? 18. Was antwortete Thomas Mann? 19. Was hatte Hauptmann
gesagt?

WORTSCHATZ

sich ärgern	to get angry	das **Geschäft, –e**	shop
auffallend	striking	der **Hof,** ⸗**e**	court
sich begegnen	to meet	der **Hofdich-**	court poet
zu Beginn	at the beginning	**ter, –**	
begrüßen (*w. object only*)	to greet	**irgendetwas**	just something, just anything
bezeichnen	to characterize	der **Kopf,** ⸗**e**	head; (fig.) mind
bis (prep.)	until	die **Krawatte, –n**	tie
dagegen	on the other hand	**sich lustig machen (über)**	to poke fun at
doch	yet	**möchten Sie?**	would you like to?
entscheidend	decisive	die **Rede, –n**	speech
das **Entscheidende**	the decisive thing, what is decisive	der **Roman, –e**	novel
erst (*as time adverb*)	only	der **Schriftsteller, –**	writer
etwa	for instance	die **Seele, –n**	soul
sich freuen	to be glad, happy	das **Sprichwort,** ⸗**er**	proverb
sich frisieren (auf)	to do one's hair (in the manner of)	**sich verfehlen**	to miss one another
das **Gefühl, –e**	feeling	der **Verkäufer, –**	salesman
der **Gegensatz,** ⸗**e**	opposite, contrast	der **Widerspruch,** ⸗**e**	contradiction
die **Gelegenheit, –en**	opportunity, occasion	**wohl**	probably
		ziemlich	rather

STRONG VERBS

s.¹ befinden	to be		**befand s.**	**s. befunden**
s. begeben	to go	**begibt s.**	**begab s.**	**s. begeben**
s. entscheiden	to decide		**entschied s.**	**s. entschieden**
frieren	to freeze		**fror**	**gefroren**
gelingen²	to succeed		**gelang**	**ist gelungen**
s. halten für	to consider oneself	**hält s.**	**hielt s.**	**s. gehalten**
kommen	to come		**kam**	**ist gekommen**
s. treffen	to meet	**trifft s.**	**traf s.**	**s. getroffen**
trinken	to drink		**trank**	**getrunken**
s. verhalten	to behave, act	**verhält s.**	**verhielt s.**	**s. verhalten**
waschen	to wash	**wäscht**	**wusch**	**gewaschen**

Note also the expressions: **was gibt's?** *what is the matter* and **es geht** *it works, it's alright, it can be done.*

¹ **s. = sich.**
² impersonal verb.

DISTINGUISH BETWEEN

erst means *first* and *only: only* as an adverb in a time context (**erst zwanzig Jahre alt** *only twenty years old*); *first* in an enumerative sense (**erst kommt die Arbeit** *work comes first*).

etwas *something* — **etwa** *for instance; approximately.*

GRAMMATICAL TERMS

1. A reflexive verb denotes an action that is directed back upon the subject: *I excuse myself.*

2. The reflexive pronouns in English are: *myself, yourself, himself, herself, itself, ourselves, yourselves, themselves.*

3. Impersonal verbs have the indefinite pronoun *it* as a subject: *It is raining.* They are used only in the third person singular in each tense.

4. A prefix is a syllable or word placed before a root word to modify its meaning: *under*go, *with*hold.

REFLEXIVE VERBS

1. The reflexive pronouns are:

		1st person	2nd person	3rd person	Conventional Address
SINGULAR	Accusative	**mich**	**dich**	**sich**	**sich**
	Dative	**mir**	**dir**	**sich**	**sich**
PLURAL	Accusative	**uns**	**euch**	**sich**	**sich**
	Dative	**uns**	**euch**	**sich**	**sich**

The reflexive pronoun differs from personal pronouns only in the third person, both singular and plural, where it is always **sich.** Note that the accusative and dative have different forms only in the first and second persons singular.

2. To make a verb reflexive, German (like English) adds the reflexive pronoun:

ich entschuldige   *I excuse*
ich entschuldige mich   *I excuse myself, I apologize*

wir fragen	*we ask*
wir fragen uns	*we ask ourselves, we wonder (whether)*
sie setzen	*they set, place*
sie setzen sich	*they sit down*

In normal word order, the reflexive pronoun follows the verb **(wir fragen uns),** but when the verb comes first in a clause (as in questions or commands), the reflexive pronoun follows the subject:

Entschuldigst du dich nicht?	*Don't you excuse yourself (apologize)?*
Setzen Sie sich, bitte!	*Sit down, please.*

3. Since most German verbs require an accusative object, the reflexive pronoun is mostly in the accusative. A few verbs are constructed with the dative, and the reflexive pronouns then are also in the dative **(ich helfe ihm** *I help him;* **Ich helfe mir** *I help myself.).* Examples:

REFLEXIVE PRONOUNS

in the accusative	in the dative
ich entschuldige mich *I excuse myself*	**ich helfe mir** *I help myself*
du entschuldigst dich	**du hilfst**[1] **dir**
er entschuldigt sich	**er hilft sich**
wir entschuldigen uns	**wir helfen uns**
ihr entschuldigt euch	**ihr helft euch**
sie entschuldigen sich	**sie helfen sich**
Sie entschuldigen sich	**Sie helfen sich**

In conventional address, the reflexive pronoun **sich** is not capitalized.

4. The reflexive pronoun is in the dative when a direct object follows:

Ich baue **mir** ein Haus.	*I am building myself a house.*
Kaufst du **dir** ein Kleid?	*Are you buying yourself a dress?*

The reflexive pronoun is also in the dative when the direct object is a part of the body or an article of clothing; if the possessor is the subject of the sentence, German uses the definite article with the direct object where English normally requires a possessive adjective:

	Ich wasche mir die Hände.	*I wash my hands.*
	Ich kämme mir die Haare.	*I comb my hair.*
	Du putzt dir die Zähne.	*You brush your teeth.*
	Ich ziehe mir die Schuhe an.	*I put on my shoes.*
But:	**Ich ziehe mir seine Schuhe an.**	*I put on his shoes.*

[1] **helfen** is a strong verb and changes its stem vowel in the second and third persons singular; see Aufgabe 7.

5. Reflexive verbs are more common in German than in English. It is important to note that the addition of a reflexive pronoun may change the meaning of a verb:

erinnern	*to remind*	**sich erinnern**	*to remember*
fürchten	*to fear*	**sich fürchten**	*to be afraid*
denken	*to think*	**sich** (dat.) **denken**	*to imagine*

The addition of a preposition may also affect the meaning of a reflexive verb. Note especially:

sich freuen auf	*to look forward to; to anticipate*
sich freuen über	*to be happy about*
Ich freue mich auf das Buch.	*I am looking forward to the book.*
Ich freue mich über das Buch.	*I am happy about the book.*

6. **Selber** or **selbst** are sometimes added to the reflexive pronouns (but also to personal pronouns: **ich selbst** *I myself*) to intensify the reflexive; both words are invariable and may be used interchangeably:

> Er lobt **sich selbst** (or **selber**). *He praises himself.*
> Ich verstehe **mich selber** nicht. *I don't understand myself.*

7. **Selbst** (but *not* **selber**) means *even* when it precedes a word: **selbst ich** (*even I*), **selbst dann** (*even then*):

> **Selbst ein Blinder** kann das finden! *Even a blind man can find that!*

8. The reflexive pronoun **sich** is often the equivalent of English *each other* or *one another*. To avoid ambiguity, **sich** may be replaced by **einander:**

> Sie geben **sich** (or **einander**) die Hand.
> *They shake hands.* (lit., give each other the hand).
> Sie sehen **einander** im Spiegel.
> *They see one another in the mirror.*

9. Reflexive verbs take **haben** to form their compound tenses (exception: **sich begegnen** *to meet*):

> Ich habe mich gewaschen.
> *I washed myself.*
> Du hast dir damit nicht geholfen.
> *You didn't help yourself with that (by doing that).*

10. The imperative of reflexive verbs is regular. The reflexive pronoun **sich** follows **Sie** in conventional address:

> **Setze dich! Setzt euch! Setzen Sie sich!** *Sit down.*

IMPERSONAL VERBS

1. Impersonal verbs are used in the third person singular with the pronoun subject **es.** Many of these verbs express or describe phenomena of nature:

blitzen:	**es blitzt**	*it is lightening*	**hageln:**	**es hagelt**	*it is hailing*
dämmern:	**es dämmert**	*it is dawning*	**regnen:**	**es regnet**	*it is raining*
donnern:	**es donnert**	*it is thundering*	**schneien:**	**es schneit**	*it is snowing*
frieren:	**es friert**	*it is freezing*	**tauen:**	**es taut**	*it is thawing*

Similarly in all other tenses: **es regnet, es hat geregnet, es hatte geregnet, es wird regnen, es wird geregnet haben,** etc.

2. Certain verbs are frequently used in impersonal constructions to express mental or physical states:[1]

es freut mich	*I am glad*	**es geht mir gut**	*I am well*
es friert mich	*I am cold*	(**schlecht,** etc.)	(*not well,* etc.)
es gefällt mir	(lit., *it pleases me*)	**es geschieht**	*it happens*
	I like it	**es tut mir leid**	*I am sorry*
es gelingt mir	*I succeed*	**es ist mir übel**	*I feel sick*

3. Since impersonal constructions cannot be conjugated, the pronoun object changes to indicate the appropriate person:

es freut **mich**[2]	*I am glad*	es gelingt **mir**	*I succeed*
es freut **dich**	*you are glad*	es gelingt **dir**	*you succeed*
es freut **ihn (sie)**	*he (she) is glad*	es gelingt **ihm (ihr)**	*he (she) succeeds*
es freut **uns**	*we are glad*	es gelingt **uns**	*we succeed*
es freut **euch**	*you are glad*	es gelingt **euch**	*you succeed*
es freut **sie**	*they are glad*	es gelingt **ihnen**	*they succeed*
es freut **Sie**	*you are glad*	es gelingt **Ihnen**	*you succeed*

4. Note the following impersonal constructions:

> **es klingelt** (from **klingeln** *to ring a bell*) *there is a ring*
> **es klopft** (from **klopfen** *to knock*) *there is a knock (on the door)*

5. Es gibt (*there is, there are*) is a common impersonal expression. It is always followed by an accusative object, which may be either singular or

---

[1] The subject **es** is often omitted in these expressions; the pronoun object is then placed before the verb: **mich freut, mir gelingt, mir ist übel.** Some of these verbal expressions are more commonly used in personal constructions: **Ich freue mich, ich friere;** gefallen and gelingen, however, must be used in personal constructions if the object is expressed: **Dieser Roman gefällt mir** *I like this novel;* **Das Experiment ist ihm gelungen** *He succeeded with the experiment.*

[2] **Es freut mich** and some other impersonal expressions may introduce a clause: **Es freut mich, Sie zu sehen.** *I am glad to see you.*

plural. If the object is singular, **es gibt** means *there is;* if it is plural, it means *there are:*

Es gibt heute keine Milch.	*There is no milk today.*
Es gibt dieses Jahr keine Äpfel.	*There are no apples this year.*
Eine solche Straße gibt es nicht.	*There is no such street.*
Solche Straßen gibt es nicht.	*There are no such streets.*

Memorize all tense forms of **es gibt:**

es gibt (present)	*there is, there are*
es gab (past)	*there was, there were*
es wird geben (future)	*there will be*
es hat gegeben (pres. perf.)	*there has (have) been, there was*
es hatte gegeben (past. perf.)	*there had been*
Rare: **es wird gegeben haben** (fut. perf.)	*there will have been*

6. **Es gibt** is used to express general existence; **sein** is used, with or without anticipatory **es,** to refer to specific facts or situations:

es gibt:	**Es gibt Leute, die das nicht glauben.**
	There are people who don't believe that.
	Es gibt keine Löwen am Nordpol.
	There are no lions at the North Pole.
sein (without **es**):	**Dreihundert Leute sind im Theater.**
	Three hundred people are in the theater.
sein (with **es**):	**Es sind dreihundert Leute im Theater.**[1]
	There are three hundred people in the theater.

The **es gibt** construction is also used when referring to food:

Es gibt heute Pfannkuchen.
We'll have pancakes today.

---

[1] In this construction, the impersonal pronoun **es** is used as an anticipatory subject of the sentence for the sake of emphasis or formality, as we say in English: *There is a man at the door.* It may be followed by the verb in the singular or in the plural, depending on the "real" subject of the sentence. Examples:

Es irrt der Mensch, solang er strebt. (Goethe: *Faust*)
Man errs as long as he strives.
Es ist ein Ros' entsprungen . . . (German Christmas carol)
A rose sprang up . . .
Es sind viele Fehler gemacht worden. (for: Viele Fehler sind gemacht worden).
Many mistakes have been made.

Note that **es** is not omitted in the **es gibt** construction when it is inverted:

Am Nordpol **gibt es** keine Löwen.
There are no lions at the North Pole.

RECAPITULATION OF MAIN POINTS

1. Reflexives often change the meaning of the verb:

Nonreflexive: **Ich erinnere ihn.**   *I remind him.*
Reflexive: **Ich erinnere mich.** *I remember.*

2. Most reflexive verbs take the accusative. The pattern is:

ich—(verb)—**mich**	wir—(verb)—**uns**
du—(verb)—**dich**	ihr—(verb)—**euch**
er or sie—(verb)—**sich**	sie—(verb)—**sich**

If the verb takes the dative, only two forms differ: **ich**—(verb)—**mir** and **du**—(verb)—**dir.**

3. **selbst** or **selber** may be added to a reflexive pronoun for emphasis:

Er lobt sich selber.   *He praises himself.*

4. **selbst** preceding a specific word means *even:*

Selbst ich weiß das.   *Even I know that.*

5. Impersonal verbs have **es** for their subject: **Es regnet.** *It is raining.* This **es** is not translated in impersonal constructions like:

Es gelingt ihm.   *He succeeds*
Es freut mich.   *I am glad.*

6. Es gibt means *there is* or *there are* depending on the object (singular or plural):

Es gibt einen Gott.   *There is a God.*
Es gibt keine Götter.   *There are no gods.*

ÜBUNGEN

Practice in Reading and Writing

A. *Read aloud and translate:*

Die Uniform des Generals Wrangel

1. Der Diener des Generals Wrangel in der Armee Friedrichs des Großen (*Frederick the Great*) befand sich eines Tages im Garten des Hauses.   2. Er hatte die Uniform des Generals zu säubern (*clean*): er klopfte (*beat*) sie,

bürstete (*brushed*) sie und gab sich alle Mühe (sich Mühe geben *to take pains*) damit.   3. Da zeigte sich ein Mann an der Gartentür, kam mit einem Brief (*letter*) in der Hand zu ihm und sagte: „Hier, beeilen Sie sich (*hurry up*)! Geben Sie dem General sofort diesen Brief."   4. Der Diener hängte die Uniform an einen Nagel (*nail*) und begab sich mit dem Brief ins Haus.   5. Wrangel nahm den Brief, setzte sich damit ans Fenster und las: 6. „Wenn es gelingt, dann ist es gut. Wenn es nicht gelingt, dann ist es auch gut."   7. „Der Kerl (*fellow*) ist wohl verrückt (*crazy*)!" meinte Wrangel. „Geh und erkundige dich (sich erkundigen *to inquire*), was er will!"   8. Der Diener ging, war aber nach einem Augenblick schon wieder zurück: „Es ist gelungen", erklärte er. „Der Kerl hat die Uniform gestohlen (stehlen *to steal*)."

B. *Translate:*

1. Entschuldigen Sie mich, bitte!   2. Wir werden uns bei ihm noch entschuldigen.   3. Amüsieren Sie sich gut!   4. Habt ihr euch gestern (*yesterday*) abend gut amüsiert?   5. Die Gestalt hatte sich langsam am Fenster entlang bewegt (sich bewegen *to move*).   6. Viele Gäste befanden sich im Hofgarten.   7. Sie hatte sich gestern nicht sehr gut befunden.   8. Wo befindet sich sein Geschäft?   9. Er macht sich immer über uns lustig.   10. Erinnerst du dich noch an die Geschichte mit dem General Wrangel?   11. Mensch ärgere dich nicht!   12. Es gibt wirklich Leute, die sagen: ich begebe mich nach Hause!   13. Wenn ich mich nicht irre, ist das ein Widerspruch.   14. Ich schäme mich ein wenig für ihn.   15. Er interessiert sich gar nicht für Musik.   16. Er hat sich schon wieder verlobt (sich verloben *to get engaged*).   17. Das wundert mich gar nicht.   18. Alle Kinder freuen sich auf Weihnachten.   19. Die Kinder freuen sich über ihre Geschenke (*presents*).   20. Ich habe mir seinen letzten Roman gekauft.   21. Mir ist davon sehr übel geworden.   22. Das tut mir wirklich leid!   23. Wenn es klingelt, öffnen Sie bitte die Tür!   24. Es klopfte, und der Alte stand an der Tür.   25. Was gibt es heute zu essen?   26. Sokrates sagt: „Kenne dich selbst!"   27. Er selbst war da.   28. Selbst er war da.   29. Wenn Deutsche sich treffen, schütteln sie sich die Hand.   30. Sie hatten einander so gern!   31. Wir sehen uns sicher morgen.   32. Was hat es heute bei euch gegeben?   33. Es donnert und blitzt, aber es regnet nicht.   34. Mich friert; ich fürchte, ich erkälte mich.   35. Es gibt Situationen, über die man sich leicht ärgert.   36. Ich kann mir nicht denken, daß das geht.   37. Es geht nicht.   38. Ich denke mir das ganz einfach.   39. Sie hatte sich erkältet, aber jetzt geht es ihr wieder gut.   40. Es ist ihm immer wieder gelungen, genug Geld zu bekommen.   41. Ihm gelingt auch alles!   42. Seine Rede hat mir nicht gefallen.   43. Gefällt Ihnen meine Krawatte?   44. Es freut mich, Sie kennenzulernen.   45. Es kommen heute abend viele Leute.   46. Das versteht sich von selbst (lit., *by itself, easily*).   47. Das lernt sich leicht.   48. Es ist nicht alles Gold, was (*that*) glänzt (*glitters*).

übel werden: to get sick (#21)
leid tun: to be sorry about (22)

C. *Distinguish between* **nach Hause** *and* **zu Hause:**

1. Wann kommst du heute abend nach Hause?   2. Ich bin am Wochenende immer zu Hause.   3. Ich freue mich, nach Hause zu kommen.   4. Wir fanden sie nicht zu Hause.   5. Fritz kommt nach der Schule nach Hause.

D. *Translate:*

1. He is washing his hands.   2. He is buying himself a necktie.   3. Why do you get angry?   4. We are looking forward to his visit.   5. She is happy about his visit.   6. How are you (first use **sich befinden,** then **gehen**) today, Mr. Schmidt?   7. Do you remember how he always poked fun at us?   8. Why don't you sit down?   9. Even he doesn't understand this novel.   10. When they meet, they shake hands.   11. Such a shop does not exist.   12. There are two physicians in our town.   13. I did not succeed in finding (translate *to find*) his address.   14. Was there a knock on the door?   15. There are many Americans who (**die**—verb at the end!) speak German.   16. Not many people are here today.   17. There are many children in these houses.   18. There had been much unrest at that time.   19. There will be no milk tomorrow.   20. That does not happen everywhere.

Oral Exercises

E. *Complete the sentences:*

EXAMPLE: Ich ärgere mich, und du ärgerst dich.

1. Du wunderst dich, und er . . . .
2. Er hat sich verliebt, und sie . . . .
3. Sie macht sich darüber lustig, und wir . . . .
4. Wir begegnen uns im Restaurant, und ihr . . . .
5. Ihr befindet euch im Geschäft, und sie . . . .
6. Sie beeilen sich endlich, und ich . . . .
7. Ich amüsiere mich leider nicht, und du . . . .

F. *Complete the sentences:*

EXAMPLE: Ich putze mir die Schuhe, und du putzt dir die Schuhe.

1. Du kämmst dir das Haar, und er . . . .
2. Er hat sich dafür entschieden, und sie . . . .
3. Sie hat sich ein Buch geholt, und wir . . . .
4. Wir wünschen uns ein Auto, und ihr . . . .
5. Ihr begegnet euch, und sie . . . .
6. Sie helfen sich, und ich . . . .
7. Ich habe mir eine Geige gekauft, und du . . . .

gern haben (mögen): to be fond, to like (30)
s. erkälten: to catch a cold (34)
einfach: simple (38)

G. *Insert the proper form—***nach Hause** *or* **zu Hause***—in the following sentences:*

1. Ich bleibe heute . . . .   2. Warum gehst du nicht . . . .?   3. Er arbeitet immer . . . .   4. . . . . reden wir deutsch.   5. Warum besuchen Sie mich nicht einmal . . . .?   6. Manchmal komme ich früh . . . .

Lessons 6 through 11

1 Weak Verbs and Reflexive Verbs

A. All you need to know about a weak verb to use it in all its tenses is the infinitive. The present tense, the past, and the past participle are all formed from the verb stem, which is the infinitive minus the infinitive ending:

STEM	ENDING
sag	**en**

B. The endings for the present and the past of weak verbs are very similar:

PRESENT	PAST
ich sage	ich sag**te**
du sagst[1]	du sag**test**
er sagt[1]	er sag**te**
wir sagen	wir sag**ten**
ihr sagt[1]	ihr sag**tet**
sie sagen	sie sag**ten**

If we disregard the addition of **t** to the stem of weak verbs in the past (which corresponds to English *-ed*), the endings differ only in the third person singular.

[1] An **e** is inserted before the endings in certain verbs. Review these deviations on page 72.

133

C. Reflexive verbs are formed by placing the appropriate reflexive pronoun: **mich (mir), dich (dir), sich, uns, euch, sich** after the verb form: **ich entschuldige mich.** In questions and imperatives, the reflexive pronoun follows the personal pronoun: Hat **er sich** entschuldigt? Entschuldigen **Sie sich!,** but it is placed after the verb if the subject is a noun: Hat **sich** der Mann entschuldigt?

D. In some reflexive constructions, the pronoun is translated:

> **Ich entschuldige mich.**   *I excuse myself.*

In others, it is not:

> **Ich erinnere mich.**   *I remember.*

E. The suffix **-ieren** is added to non-Germanic verbal stems: **studieren, telefonieren.** The regular endings are added to **-ier;** such verbs do not use the past participle prefix **ge-:** Ich habe **telefoniert.**

F. In translating German tense forms into English, note that the German present tense may be equivalent to the future tense in English and the German present perfect to an English simple past.

G. Translate and identify the tenses:

1. Was hast du ihm gesagt?   2. Ich fahre morgen nach New York.   3. Das habe ich nicht gesagt.   4. Hast du schon telegrafiert?   5. Wir haben seine Worte diskutiert.   6. Was diskutiert er?   7. Ich frage dich und du antwortest mir.   8. Wann haben Sie sich erkältet?   9. Hat Fritz sich schon wieder erkältet?   10. Ich habe mich darüber gefreut.   11. Hat es geklopft?   12. Amüsieren Sie sich gut!   13. Du wirst das kennen.   14. Er schüttelte den Kopf.   15. Er sagte etwas und sie lächelte nur.   16. Hat sie eigentlich gelächelt?

2 Impersonal Verbs

A. Impersonal verbs are used only in the third person singular: **es regnet** *it rains.* The object pronoun is changed to express the person:

> **es freut mich**   *I am glad*
> **es freut uns**   *we are glad,* etc.

B. Note the common constructions with **es gibt** (*there is, there are*), followed by a direct object, which becomes the subject in English:

> **Es gibt in Massachusetts keine Elefanten.**
> *There are no elephants in Massachusetts.*
> Or: *Elephants do not exist in Massachusetts.*

C. Impersonal verbs refer either to conditions in nature or to emotional situations: **Es regnet** *it rains;* **es tut mir leid** *I am sorry.* The latter are usually rendered by personal constructions in English.

D. Translate:

1. Es gibt hier nicht viel Musik.   2. Diesen Sommer hat es nicht viel Regen (*rain*) gegeben.   3. Gibt es ein solches Drama?   4. Das gibt es nicht!   5. Es hat diesen Sommer viel geregnet.   6. Dieser Dichter gefällt mir.   7. Wie gefällt er Ihnen?   8. Ihm gelingt das Experiment.   9. Das gelingt ihm nicht. 10. Hat es geklopft?   11. Es klingelt schon wieder!   12. Es freut mich, daß Sie kommen.   13. Seine Worte haben mich gefreut.   14. Wie geht es Ihnen? 15. Danke, mir geht es auch gut.

3 Strong Verbs

A. To conjugate a strong verb, one has to know its principal parts: the infinitive, the first person singular of the past, the past participle: **stehen** (*to stand*), **stand, gestanden.**

B. Some strong verbs change their stems also in the second and third persons singular of the present tense. In such cases, the strong verb has four principal parts: **essen** (*to eat*), **ißt, aß, gegessen.**

C. The endings for strong verbs in the present are the same as for weak verbs; in the past tense they differ in that the first and third persons singular have no endings:

ich **gab**	wir **gaben**
du **gabst**	ihr **gabt**
er **gab**	sie **gaben**

D. Translate:

1. Was liest du da?   2. Er hält eine Rede.   3. Sie haben das Geld genommen. 4. Alle haben im Krieg sehr gelitten.   5. Sie wird täglich besser.   6. Er begab sich nach Berlin.   7. Nimm das Buch und lies das Gedicht von Heine! 8. Bei wem schläft er heute?   9. Waren Sie einmal in Rom?   10. Er hat viele Sprachen gesprochen.   11. Der Gebildete (*the educated*) spricht mehr als eine Sprache.   12. Er verlor seine Großmutter vor einem Jahr.   13. Man tut das nicht!   14. Er hat sich immer sehr intelligent verhalten.   15. Er fährt immer zu schnell.   16. Hast du das Buch bekommen?   17. Er vergißt alles; er wird sicher Professor.   18. Man hat ihn für einen Deutschen gehalten.   19. Trifft er uns in der Stadt?   20. Die Temperatur ist den ganzen Tag gestiegen.

4 Prepositions

A. Review the basic meanings of the prepositions and their most common idiomatic uses (Aufgabe 9).

B. Translate:

1. durch das Fenster   2. während dieser Zeit   3. mit seiner Arbeit   4. wegen seines Vaters   5. um das Haus   6. ohne meine Frau   7. aus dem Haus 8. Seit einer Woche ist er in Berlin.   9. Vor zwei Jahren war er bei seinem Freund in Köln.   10. Dieses Gedicht ist von Heine.   11. Ihrer Meinung nach ist das nicht wahr.   12. Nach der Deutschstunde gehe ich nach Hause. 13. Er sitzt bei seiner Freundin.   14. Wir wohnen außerhalb der Stadt. 15. Bei uns sagt man das nicht.   16. Sie ist im Haus.   17. Sie geht in das Haus.   18. Er sitzt auf dem Pferd.   19. Er setzt sich auf das Pferd.   20. Fritz kommt am Sonntag.

5 Personal Pronouns; Da- and Wo-Compounds

A. Review the personal pronouns (Aufgabe 8).

B. Recall the different meanings for **sie:**

she:	Lächelt **sie?**	*Is she smiling?*
her:	Kennst du **sie?**	*Do you know her?*
they:	Lächeln **sie?**	*Are they smiling?*
them:	Kennst du **sie?**	*Do you know them?*
it:	**Sie** (die Uhr) geht nicht.	*It isn't running.*

Note that the context will often determine the meaning.

C. Remember the different meanings for **ihr:**

As a possessive adjective:

her:	Ist das **ihr Buch?**	*Is that her book?*
their:	Ist das **ihr Buch?**	*Is that their book?*
its:	Die Zeit und **ihre Probleme.**	*The time (age) and its problems.*

As a personal pronoun:

you:	Geht **ihr** schon?	*Are you going already?*
her:	Was gibst du **ihr?**	*What are you giving her?*
it:	Ich gebe **ihr** (der Maschine) Öl.	*I give it oil.*

D. When **da** is compounded with a preposition, translate **da** by *it* or *that*.

Similarly, when **wo** is compounded with a preposition, translate **wo** by *which* or *what*.

E. Translate:

1. Wer sind sie? 2. Wer sind Sie? 3. Wer ist sie? 4. Kennt ihr ihn? 5. Ich kenne euch! 6. Ich gebe dir alles. 7. Was kann ich Ihnen geben? 8. Was kann ich ihnen geben? 9. Sie tut es nicht seinetwegen. 10. Meinetwegen kannst du (*you can*) gehen. 11. Was gibt er ihr? 12. Was gibt sie ihm? 13. Das Auto ist gut. Ich kaufe es. 14. Die Maschine ist kaputt (*broken*); reparieren wir sie! 15. Meine Freunde? Kennst du sie? 16. Das Mädchen ist da; er kommt mit ihr. 17. Ich habe einen Bleistift und schreibe damit. 18. Womit schreibst du? 19. Darauf habe ich keine Antwort. 20. Eine Antwort? Es geht auch ohne sie.

12

Intransitive Verbs with »sein«

Der Wissenschaftler als Schriftsteller: Georg Christoph Lichtenberg[1]

Lichtenberg war für seine Zeitgenossen vor allem der kleine, verwachsene[2] Professor der Physik und Astronomie in Göttingen, Lehrer einer ganzen Generation von Naturwissenschaftlern. Seine eigene wissenschaftliche Leistung aber war gering und ist heute überhaupt vergessen. Nur die Leistung
5 des Schriftstellers Lichtenberg hat die Zeiten überlebt.[3] Durch die genaue Beobachtung und Beschreibung des Menschen und seiner Verhältnisse ist er ein Vorläufer Nietzsches und der modernen Psychologie geworden.

In einem Jahrhundert der philosophischen Spekulation war er einer der ersten, die als Wissenschaftler wirklich experimentierten. Er besaß eine
10 berühmte Sammlung physikalischer Apparate und liebte es, seinen Studenten während der Vorlesung die physikalischen Phänomene zu demonstrieren. Das ist gut, meinte er, damit die Studenten nicht einschlafen. Und sie sind, wie wir hören, bei ihm nicht eingeschlafen. Es waren vor allem elektrochemische Experimente, oft auch Experimente mit Gasen. Besonders lebendig
15 waren seine Vorlesungen offenbar, wenn er Ballons mit Gas füllte und

1. 1742–1799. 2. **verwachsen** *hunchbacked.* 3. **überlebt** *outlived.*

explodieren ließ. Die Bürger Göttingens waren daran gewöhnt, daß es im Hause des Professors donnerte und krachte. Und noch an etwas anderes hatten sie sich zu gewöhnen: an den Blitzableiter[4] auf seinem Haus, den ersten Blitzableiter in Deutschland. Sie waren darüber zuerst sehr erschrocken. War das nicht gegen den Willen Gottes? Hören wir Lichtenberg 20 selbst: „Daß in den Kirchen gepredigt wird,[5] macht deswegen die Blitzableiter auf ihnen nicht unnötig." Das sind die Worte eines freien Geistes in einer dogmatischen Zeit.

Als Astronom hat Lichtenberg sich besonders mit dem Mond beschäftigt und eine erste Mondkarte hergestellt. Dafür hat man später einen Mondkrater 25 nach ihm genannt.[6]

Lichtenberg ist im Jahre 1742[7] als siebzehntes[8] Kind eines Pastors in der Nähe von Darmstadt geboren. Der Vater liebte es, seine Predigten durch Betrachtungen über Physik und Astronomie zu beleben. Auch bei ihm ist man bei der Predigt offenbar nicht eingeschlafen. Er unterrichtete seine Kinder 30 selbst in Mathematik und Physik. Das große Erlebnis für den jungen Lichtenberg waren seine beiden Reisen nach England. In London haben sich ihm die Augen für die große Welt geöffnet, im Gegensatz zu den kleinen Verhältnissen zu Hause in Deutschland. In England aber ist er vor allem zum deutschen Schriftsteller geworden. „Ich bin eigentlich nach England ge- 35 gangen", schreibt er, „um[9] deutsch schreiben zu lernen." Seine Beschreibungen Englands und englischer Verhältnisse sind immer noch Meisterwerke der deutschen Literatur. Er ist nicht nur tief in den Geist Englands, sondern auch in den der englischen Literatur eingedrungen. Der Satiriker Sterne ist immer sein Vorbild geblieben. Die Resultate seiner Beobachtungen und 40 Erfahrungen liegen heute in den Tausenden von Aphorismen vor uns, als sein eigentliches Lebenswerk.

4. **der Blitzableiter** *lightning rod.*   5. **gepredigt wird** (passive, translate: *that they preach*). 6. **genannt** *named.*   7. (read:) **siebzehnhundertzweiundvierzig.**   8. **siebzehntes** *seventeenth.* 9. **um . . . zu** *in order to.*

FRAGEN

1. Wer war Lichtenberg für seine Zeitgenossen?   2. Was ist heute vergessen? 3. Was hat dagegen die Zeiten überlebt?   4. Wodurch ist er ein Vorläufer Nietzsches geworden?   5. Was liebte er?   6. Warum ist das gut?   7. Was für Experimente machte er vor allem?   8. Wann waren seine Vorlesungen offenbar besonders lebendig?   9. Woran waren die Bürger Göttingens gewöhnt?   10. Worüber waren sie zuerst erschrocken?   11. Können Sie uns

den Aphorismus Lichtenbergs über den Blitzableiter und die Kirche geben?
12. Was hat Lichtenberg mit dem Mond gemacht?   13. Wie belebte der
Vater Lichtenbergs seine Predigten?   14. Worin unterrichtete er seine Kinder?
15. Was war das große Erlebnis des jungen Lichtenberg gewesen?   16. Warum
ist Lichtenberg eigentlich nach England gegangen?   17. Was sind immer noch
Meisterwerke der deutschen Literatur?   18. Welcher englische Schriftsteller
ist immer Lichtenbergs Vorbild geblieben?   19. Kennen Sie Lawrence Sterne?
Haben Sie etwas von ihm gelesen?   20. Wo finden Sie heute die Resultate
von Lichtenbergs Beobachtungen und Erfahrungen?

WORTSCHATZ

etwas anderes	something else	**krachen**	to bang
beleben	to enliven	**lebendig**	lively, alive
die **Beobachtung,**	observation	die **Leistung, –en**	achievement
–en		das **Meisterwerk, –e**	masterpiece
die **Beschreibung,**	description	**möglich**	possible
–en		der **Mond, –e**	moon
brauchen	to need	die **Mond-**	moon chart
der **Bürger, –**	citizen	**karte, –n**	
damit (*conjunc-*		**nötig**	necessary
tion, verb at		**unnötig**	unnecessary
the end!)	so that	**offenbar**	apparently
deswegen	for that reason	**predigen**	to preach
die **Erfahrung, –en**	experience (*from*	die **Predigt, –en**	sermon
	which one learns)	die **Reise, –n**	trip, journey
die **Erlaubnis, –se**	permission, permit	die **Sammlung, –en**	collection
das **Erlebnis, –se**	experience (*as chance*	die **Straße, –n**	street
	happening)	**tief**	deep(ly)
erwachen	to wake up	**unterrichten**	to instruct, teach
füllen	to fill	das **Verhältnis, –se**	condition
gering	slight, small	das **Vorbild, –er**	model, ideal
sich gewöhnen	to get accustomed	der **Vorläufer, –**	precursor
(an) (*w. acc.*)	(used) to	die **Vorlesung, –en**	(university) lecture
herstellen	to produce, manu-	der **Wagen, –**	car
	facture	der **Zeitgenosse, –n,**	contemporary
die **Kirche, –n**	church	**–n**	
der **Krach, ⸗e**	(thundering) noise	**zuerst**	at first

STRONG VERBS

beschreiben	to describe		**beschrieb**	**beschrieben**
besitzen	to own, possess	**besitzt**	**besaß**	**besessen**
bitten (um,	to ask (a favor)		**bat**	**gebeten**
w. acc.)				
eindringen[1]	to penetrate, (enter) into	**dringt ein**	**drang ein**	**ist eingedrungen**
einschlafen[1]	to go to sleep	**schläft ein**	**schlief ein**	**ist eingeschlafen**

[1] These verbs are combined with separable prefixes which go to the end of the clause in
which the verb occurs in a present or past (simple tenses).

entstehen	to originate, be caused		entstand	ist entstanden
erschrecken	to be frightened, startled	erschrickt	erschrak	ist erschrocken
fliegen	to fly		flog	ist geflogen
lassen	to let	läßt	ließ	gelassen
liegen	to lie (*position*)		lag	gelegen
scheinen	to seem, appear; to shine		schien	geschienen
schlafen	to sleep	schläft	schlief	geschlafen
wachsen	to grow	wächst	wuchs	ist gewachsen
werden	to become	wird	wurde	ist geworden

GRAMMATICAL TERMS

1. *Transitive* verbs take a direct object: He *said nothing*, I *saw him*.

2. *Intransitive* verbs do not take a direct (but may take an indirect) object: He *comes, goes, travels, dies*, etc.

INTRANSITIVE VERBS WITH "SEIN"

1. The perfect tenses of transitive verbs are formed with **haben,** and so are the perfect tenses of many intransitive verbs:

> TRANSITIVE: Er **hat** das Fenster **geöffnet.**
> INTRANSITIVE: Er **hat** im Hotel **geschlafen.**

2. The perfect tenses of many intransitive verbs, however, both weak and strong, are formed with **sein.** Dictionaries and vocabularies generally indicate verbs conjugated with **sein** by adding "**(s.)**" or "**ist**" after the infinitive or before the past participle:

> **reisen (s.)** *to travel*
> **sterben, i, a, ist gestorben** *to die*

3. Intransitive verbs conjugated with **sein** include:

a. verbs which express a change of position or motion (like **reisen** *to travel;* **wandern** *to hike*, etc.);

b. verbs which express a change of condition (like **einschlafen** *to go to sleep;* **erwachen** *to wake up;* **sterben** *to die*, etc.);

c. the verbs **sein** *to be* **(ich bin, ich war, ich bin gewesen), bleiben** *to remain* **(ich bleibe, ich blieb, ich bin geblieben),** and **werden** *to become* **(ich werde, ich wurde, ich bin geworden).**

Many intransitive verbs of motion and change of position or condition are strong verbs.

4. The perfect tenses of an intransitive verb with **sein** (example: **reisen** *to travel*):

PRESENT PERFECT:	ich bin gereist	wir sind gereist
	du bist gereist	ihr seid gereist
	er ist gereist	sie sind gereist
PAST PERFECT:	ich war gereist	wir waren gereist
	du warst gereist	ihr wart gereist
	er war gereist	sie waren gereist
FUTURE PERFECT:	ich werde gereist sein	wir werden gereist sein
	du wirst gereist sein	ihr werdet gereist sein
	er wird gereist sein	sie werden gereist sein

5. Some verbs may be conjugated with either **haben** or **sein,** depending upon whether they are used transitively or intransitively; examples:

treten: (transitive:) *to kick* (somebody); (intransitive:) *to step*

Er hat mich getreten. *He kicked me.*
Er ist ins Zimmer getreten. *He stepped into the room.*

fahren: *to drive* (transitive or intransitive)

Ich habe ihn gefahren. *I drove him.*
Ich bin nach New York gefahren. *I drove to New York.*

6. When translating a perfect tense with a form of **sein,** look for the past participle before translating the auxiliary. If the past participle is derived from an intransitive verb of motion or of change of condition or position, render the auxiliary by the appropriate form of English *to have* (unless, of course, English requires the simple past tense):

Er **war** aus tiefem Schlaf **erwacht.**
He had awakened from a deep sleep.
Er **ist** mir immer nach Hause **gefolgt.**
He (has) always followed me home.
Er **ist** sofort **aufgewacht.**
He woke up at once.

RECAPITULATION OF MAIN POINTS

1. All transitive and most intransitive verbs are conjugated with **haben** in the perfect tenses. Intransitive verbs conjugated with **sein** are: **sein, bleiben, werden,** and verbs expressing:

a. a change of position or motion,
b. a change of condition.

2. Remember: German **ist** is generally equivalent to *is* and **war** to *was*, but with intransitive verbs German **ist** becomes *has* and **war** *had*:

>Er **ist** alt. *He is old.*
>Er **ist** schon **angekommen.** *He has already arrived.*
>
>Es **war** kalt. *It was cold.*
>Es **war** kalt **geworden.** *It had gotten cold.*

ÜBUNGEN

Practice in Reading and Writing

A. *Read aloud and translate:*

Der Amerikaner in Moskau

1. Ein Amerikaner ist einmal im Auto nach Moskau gefahren. 2. Die Russen sind immer sehr freundlich zu ihm gewesen und haben ihn oft zu sich gebeten. 3. Er hat sein Auto dann auf der Straße gelassen und ist ins Haus gegangen. 4. Bei seiner Rückkehr (*upon his return*) haben immer einige Russen interessiert um sein Auto gestanden. 5. Da hat ihn einmal einer der Russen gefragt: „Sagen Sie, bitte, wie haben Sie diesen Wagen gekauft?" 6. „Oh", meinte der Amerikaner, „ich bin einfach in ein Geschäft gegangen und habe ihn gekauft." 7. „Und wer hat Ihnen dafür die Erlaubnis gegeben?" 8. „Eine Erlaubnis habe ich dafür nicht gebraucht." 9. „Und wo sind Sie um eine Erlaubnis für Benzin eingekommen (einkommen um *to apply for*)?" 10. „Auch für Benzin braucht man keine Erlaubnis." 11. Da ist der Russe sehr erstaunt gewesen und hat gefragt: „Und in einem solchen Chaos können Sie leben?"

B. *Translate and identify the tense of each verb form:*

1. Er hatte keine Zeit. 2. Er hatte keine Zeit gehabt. 3. Er ist Soldat. 4. Sie sind im Krieg Soldaten gewesen. 5. Er hat die Frage des Arztes nicht gehört. 6. Wer ist mit ihr in die Stadt gegangen? 7. Wann sind sie in die Stadt eingedrungen? 8. Wir waren den ganzen Tag zu Hause. 9. Wir haben nicht viel zu essen. 10. Wir haben nicht viel gegessen. 11. Wohin seid ihr dieses Jahr gefahren? 12. Wir werden dieses Jahr nach Europa fahren. 13. Wir sind eine Woche in München geblieben und dann nach Wien geflogen. 14. Sie sind sich in der Kirche begegnet. 15. Sie haben nicht sehr laut gesprochen; wir sind darüber eingeschlafen. 16. Die Studenten haben wieder viel Krach gemacht. 17. Er war drei Jahre bei seinem Onkel in einem kleinen Dorf in Norddeutschland. 18. Er war drei Jahre lang bei seinem Onkel in einem kleinen Dorf in Norddeutschland gewesen.

19. Sie ist nicht lange bei ihrer Familie.   20. Sie ist nicht lange bei ihrer Familie geblieben.   21. Er wird wohl nicht gern in Berlin geblieben sein. 22. Ich bin sehr erschrocken, als ich die Geschichte gehört habe.   23. Das kleine Mädchen ist gut gewachsen.   24. Manche Märchen (*fairy tales*) enden: und wenn sie nicht gestorben sind, dann leben sie noch heute.   25. Seine Beschreibungen sind in England entstanden.   26. Ich bin erst spät eingeschlafen und schon früh aufgewacht (aufwachen *to wake up*).

C. *Explain why the verbs in the following sentences are conjugated with* **sein** *or* **haben:**

1. Wir haben uns in der Stadt getroffen.   2. Wir sind uns in der Stadt begegnet.   3. Sie haben sich die Hand gegeben.   4. Lichtenberg hat das englische Theater genau beschrieben.   5. Lichtenberg ist in Göttingen gestorben.   6. Ich habe noch nie einen Volkswagen gefahren!   7. Der kleine Max ist im letzten Jahr sehr gewachsen.   8. Wie lange sind Sie in München geblieben und was haben Sie da gemacht?   9. Er wird wohl schon eingeschlafen sein.   10. Wir sind in seine Gedanken nicht eingedrungen.

D. *Translate* (*use compound tenses where possible*):

1. They stayed a day in New York and then flew to Europe.   2. We heard the music when (**als**) we came into the room.   3. What has become of (**aus**) him? Did he die?   4. Why did the students always go to sleep in his lectures? 5. Where have you been? We don't see you anymore.   6. He told us about his experiences in Germany.   7. His descriptions have become very famous. 8. Lichtenberg was already very interested in the moon; his moon chart remained in use (**im Gebrauch**) for a long time.   9. Did you get frightened when you heard the noise in (**auf**) the street?   10. Did you wash your hands, Fritz?   11. I heard something else.   12. He preached every Sunday in the same church.   13. How was your trip? How long did you stay in Paris? 14. He did not get used to life in America.   15. He said that Lichtenberg's observations were very exact.   16. They valued Lichtenberg as a scientist and as a writer.   17. These models originated in Germany.   18. The collection has not grown very (much).   19. Goethe had many precursors, and many followed him.   20. Why were the citizens of Göttingen afraid of the lightning rod on Lichtenberg's house?

Oral Exercises

E. *Change the sentences to present perfect:*

EXAMPLE: Er fährt im Auto nach Moskau.
            Er ist im Auto nach Moskau gefahren.

1. Wir gehen in ein Geschäft.
2. Sie ist sehr freundlich zu ihm.
3. Ich bleibe eine Woche hier.
4. Er wird Wissenschaftler.
5. Die Leute sind sehr erstaunt.
6. Er tritt in das Zimmer.
7. Alle gehen in die Stadt.
8. Er erwacht jeden Morgen um sechs Uhr.
9. Es wird sehr kalt.

F. *Combination drill. Change the sentences to present perfect using either* **haben** *or* **sein:**

1. Ich fahre ihn nach München.
2. Ich fahre heute nach München.
3. Er kommt heute mit seinen Freunden.
4. Er wartet hier auf seine Freunde.
5. Wir sind heute abend zu Hause.
6. Wir bleiben heute abend zu Hause.
7. Das Kind wächst in diesem Jahr sehr.
8. Das Kind lächelt manchmal.
9. Er tanzt oft mit ihr.
10. Er geht oft mit ihr ins Theater.

13

Prefixes

Else Lasker-Schüler[1]

Else Lasker-Schüler war nicht nur eine der wirklich bedeutenden Dichterinnen zu Beginn unseres Jahrhunderts, sie war überhaupt ein menschliches und soziales Phänomen. Mitten in der Großstadt[2] Berlin führte sie ein Leben der Phantasie wie im Märchen. „Ich bin in Theben[3] geboren", erklärte
5 sie, „auch wenn ich in Elberfeld zur Welt kam, im Rheinland." Sie gab sich exotische Namen: „Jussuf von Theben" oder „Tino von Bagdad", und ihre Freunde redeten sie gerne als „Prinz von Theben" an. Das klingt vielleicht amüsant, aber es ist auch tragisch. Einer ihrer Freunde, selbst ein Schriftsteller, erinnerte sich später: keiner nahm ihr ihr metaphysisches Flirten mit
10 einer breiten, fluktuierenden Menge übel, besonders da[4] es Frucht abwarf: Liebesgedichte oft hohen[5] Ranges. Zwei andere Freunde haben sich einmal im Café geohrfeigt, denn der eine hatte erklärt: ihren Gedichten fehlte das „Mentale". Diese Szene spielte sich in dem berühmten „Café des Westens" ab, wo die jungen Genies jeden Tag zusammenkamen, diskutierten,

---

1. Born 1869 in Elberfeld, today Wuppertal, died 1945 in Jerusalem. 2. **Großstadt** *metropolis* (a German **Stadt** becomes a **Großstadt** when it exceeds 100,000 inhabitants).
3. **Theben** *Thebes* (in Egypt). 4. **da** (here conj.) *since*. 5. **hohen** (from **hoch**) *high, great*.

Zeitschriften gründeten und sich aus ihren Werken vorlasen. Im Volksmund[6] 15
hieß es „Café Größenwahn".[7]

Gottfried Benn[8], der führende Lyriker dieser expressionistischen Genera-
tion, hat die Erscheinung der Lasker-Schüler einmal so beschrieben: Rote
Samtjacke[9], mit Goldknöpfen[10] und schwarzer Jockeymütze[11], dazu seidene
Hosen, Sandalen mit kleinen Glöckchen, die[12] bei jedem Schritt klingelten, 20
und eine Menge unechten Schmucks[13] an Armen und Hals. Zu Beginn des
Ersten Weltkrieges lief sie mit einer schwarz-weiß-roten Fahne um den Hals
in den Straßen von München herum. „Lieber Prinz von Theben", redete eine
Freundin sie an, „sind Sie denn[14] so patriotisch?"—„Nein", war die Antwort,
„aber ohne meine Schärpe[15] halten mich die Leute für eine Spionin." Das 25
alles kommt uns heute sehr bekannt vor. Wir übertreiben sicher nicht, wenn
wir Else Lasker-Schüler als eins der ersten „Blumenkinder" bezeichnen.

Hinter ihrer Exotik aber verbarg sich bei ihr ein warmes Herz. Einmal
begegnete ihr eine andere junge Dichterin auf der Straße. Das Mädchen war
gerade sehr unglücklich. „Mein liebes Kind", tröstete Else Lasker-Schüler 30
sie, „schreiben Sie ein schönes Gedicht. Aus jedem Leid muß ein Gedicht
erblühen[16], das dazu[17] da ist, eines anderen Leid zu mildern." Besonders
hübsch ist die Episode mit dem Dramatiker Carl Zuckmayer[18]. Zuckmayers
erstes Stück hatte seine Uraufführung, aber es fiel durch. Er saß selbst im
Theater, Else Lasker-Schüler neben ihm. Sie wollte[19] auch ihn trösten und 35
begann, ihm Schokolade in den Mund zu schieben, ein Stück nach dem
andern. Zuckmayer aber haßte Süßigkeiten. Ihm wurde ganz übel davon,
aber er war, wie er sich ausdrückte, ihrer „Caritas"[20] hoffnungslos ausgeliefert. „Ein einziger Schnaps wäre[21] mir lieber gewesen", erklärte er in
seiner Autobiographie. 40

6. **Im Volksmund** (lit., mouth of the people) *colloquially.* 7. **Größenwahn** *megalomania.*
8. 1886–1956. 9. **Samtjacke** *velvet jacket.* 10. **Goldknöpfe** *gold buttons.* 11. **Jockeymütze** *jockey's cap.* 12. **die** (relative pronoun) . . . **klingelten** *which tinkled.* 13. **unechten
Schmucks** *of costume jewelry.* 14. **denn** (in a question which implies a negative answer)
really. 15. **Schärpe** *scarf.* 16. **erblühen** *blossom (up).* 17. **das dazu da ist . . . zu mildern**
which has the purpose of lessening. 18. Born 1896, a leading contemporary German
dramatist. 19. **sie wollte** *she wanted to.* 20. **Caritas** (Latin) *compassion.* 21. **wäre mir
lieber gewesen** *I would have preferred.*

FRAGEN

1. Was war Else Lasker-Schüler? 2. Was für ein Leben führte sie? 3. Wo
war sie zur Welt gekommen? 4. Wo ist sie geboren, ihren eigenen Worten
nach? 5. Wo liegt Elberfeld? 6. Wie heißt Elberfeld heute? 7. Welche
Namen gab sie sich gerne? 8. Wie redeten ihre Freunde sie manchmal an?

9. Finden Sie das amüsant? 10. Was ist das aber auch? 11. Was tat ihr metaphysisches Flirten? 12. Was für Früchte warf es ab? 13. Warum haben sich die beiden Freunde im Café des Westens geohrfeigt? 14. Was taten die jungen Genies im Cafés des Westens? 15. Wie heißt das Café des Westens im Volksmund? 16. Beschreiben Sie die Erscheinung der Lasker-Schüler! 17. Wie lief Else Lasker-Schüler zu Beginn des Ersten Weltkriegs in München herum? 18. Warum tat sie das? 19. Wie kann man Else Lasker-Schüler heute bezeichnen? 20. Was sagte sie zu dem unglücklichen Mädchen? 21. Was tat Else Lasker-Schüler während der Uraufführung? 22. Was erklärte Zuckmayer in seiner Autobiographie?

WORTSCHATZ

sich ab/spielen[1]	to take place
ab/werfen (wirft ab, warf ab, abgeworfen)	to throw off; to yield
an/reden	to address
auch wenn	even though, although
sich aus/drücken	to express oneself
aus/liefern	to deliver
bedeutend	significant, important, distinguished
die Blume, –n	flower
breit	broad, wide, large
durch/fallen (fällt durch, fiel durch, ist durchgefallen)	to fail, "flunk"
sich erinnern	to remember
die Erscheinung, –en	appearance
die Fahne, –n	flag
fehlen (w. dat., impers.)	to be lacking
ihren Gedichten fehlt	her poems are lacking (in)
der Fortschritt, –e	progress
die Frucht, ≠e	fruit
die Glocke, –n	bell
der Hals, ≠e	neck
hassen	to hate
herum- (prefix)	around
herum/laufen (läuft herum, lief herum, ist herumgelaufen)	to run around
die Hoffnung, –en	hope
hoffnungslos	hopeless(ly)
die Hose, –n (often in plural)	pants
das Leid	sorrow
lieb	dear
das Märchen, –	fairy tale
die Menge, –n	mass, great number of (people or things)
mitten in	in the middle of
die Ohrfeige, –n	box on the ear
sich ohrfeigen	to box one another's ears
rot	red
der Schnaps, ≠e	(cheap) liquor
der Schritt, –e	step
schwarz	black
die Seide	silk
seiden	silken
der Spion, –e (fem.: die Spionin, –nen)	spy
süß	sweet
die Süßigkeiten (usually in the plural)	sweets
trösten	to comfort
übel/nehmen (nimmt übel, nahm übel, übelgenommen)	to hold against; to take amiss

[1] A slash indicates a separable prefix.

übel werden (*impers.*)	to get sick	die **Uraufführung,** **–en** die **Zeitschrift, –en**	premiere, first per- formance periodical

STRONG VERBS

an /fangen	to begin	**fängt an**	**fing an**	**angefangen**
graben	to dig	**gräbt**	**grub**	**gegraben**
heißen	to be called		**hieß**	**geheißen**
laufen	to run	**läuft**	**lief**	ist **gelaufen**
schieben	to shove, push		**schob**	**geschoben**
schweigen	to be silent		**schwieg**	**geschwiegen**
übertreiben	to exaggerate		**übertrieb**	**übertrieben**
s. verbergen	to hide	**verbirgt s.**	**verbarg s.**	s. **verborgen**
vergessen	to forget	**vergißt**	**vergaß**	**vergessen**
vor /kommen	to seem, occur; to strike		**kam vor**	ist **vorgekommen**
vor /lesen	to read aloud, recite	**liest vor**	**las vor**	**vorgelesen**
werfen	to throw	**wirft**	**warf**	**geworfen**

DISTINGUISH BETWEEN

das Lied, –er *song*   **das Leid, die Leiden** *suffering*

GRAMMATICAL TERMS

In English, prefixes are added to verbs to modify or change their basic meanings: to come: to *be*come, to *over*come. An adverb or preposition may also be attached to a verb without, however, affecting its basic meaning: to come *back;* to come *in.*

PREFIXES IN GERMAN

1. The basic meaning of a verb may or may not be modified by the use of a prefix. Prefixes consist of: *to begin to*

   a. syllables like **be-, ge-, er-: be**kommen *to get*
   b. adjectives like **hoch: hoch**heben *to lift up*
   c. prepositions like **an, auf, in: an**kommen *to arrive*
   d. adverbs like **zurück, wieder: zurück**kommen *to return, come back*
   e. verbs, as in **kennen**lernen *to become acquainted with;* **spazieren**gehen *to go for a walk.*

2. German is rich in verbs modified by prefixes. German prefixes are either

inseparable or separable, according to whether they do or do not separate from the verb in certain tenses:

| INSEPARABLE: | bekommen | Er **bekommt** nichts. |
| SEPARABLE: | ankommen | Er **kommt** morgen **an.** |

The separable prefix always takes the word accent (**ạnkommen**), while verbs with inseparable prefixes are accented on the stem (**bekọmmen**).

INSEPARABLE PREFIXES

1. The prefixes **be-, emp-,**[1] **ent-, er-, ge-, hinter-, miß-, ver-,** and **zer-** are inseparable from the verb stem.

2. All forms of verbs with inseparable prefixes are accented on the *stem*, never on the prefix.

3. In the past participle, verbs with inseparable prefixes omit the prefix **ge-:**[2]

INFINITIVE		PAST PARTICIPLE
bekommen	*to get*	**bekommen**
erkennen	*to recognize*	**erkannt**
verstehen	*to understand*	**verstanden**

4. Unlike separable prefixes, inseparable prefixes have no independent meanings of their own. Note, however, that the prefix **be-** makes intransitive verbs transitive without affecting their meaning, and that **zer-** (occasionally also **ver-**) usually imparts a negative or destructive element to the verb:

be-: **antworten** (intrans.); **beantworten** (trans.) *to answer*

Intransitive: Ich **antworte** ihm. *I answer him.*
Transitive: Ich **beantworte** seine Frage. *I answer his question.*

zer-: **stören** *to disturb;* **zerstören** *to destroy*
brechen *to break;* **zerbrechen** *to break to pieces*

---

[1] The prefix **emp-** is a variation of **ent-:** **emp-** occurs only when the stem of the verb begins with **f: empfangen** *to receive.*

[2] Verbs with the inseparable prefix **ge-** have the same past participle as their basic verbs. The context decides from which infinitive such a past participle is derived:

fallen	**fiel**	ist **gefallen**	*to fall*
gefallen	**gefiel**	**gefallen**	*to please*
hören	**hörte**	**gehört**	*to hear*
gehören	**gehörte**	**gehört**	*to belong*

ver-:   **brennen** *to burn;* **verbrennen** *to burn down, burn up*

But   **stehen** *to stand;* **verstehen** *to understand*
       leben *to live;* **verleben** *to spend one's life*

SEPARABLE PREFIXES

1. The separable prefix is a word in its own right (preposition, adverb, or verb). Often it retains its original meaning and does not alter the basic meaning of the verb with which it is combined. In certain instances, however, it does affect the meaning of the compound verb, without regard to the meaning of the root verb:

hören	*to hear*	**aufhören**	*to stop*
bringen	*to bring*	**umbringen**	*to kill*

2. The separable prefix separates from the verb in main clauses in the *present*, *past*, and *imperative*. A separated prefix usually stands at the end of the clause:

INFINITIVE: **aufstehen**   *to get up*
PRESENT: ich **stehe** früh **auf**   *I get up early*
PAST: er **stand** spät **auf**   *he got up late*
IMPERATIVE: **steh(e)** bitte **auf!**, **steht** bitte **auf!**, stehen Sie bitte auf!   *please get up!*

In dependent clauses, no separation takes place. Both prefix and verb are at the end and are written together:

Er weiß, daß ich immer spät **aufstehe.**
He knows that I always get up late.

3. Dictionaries and glossaries list verbs with separable prefixes under the prefix. Thus, in the sentence,

Hier **stellte** man die erste Taschenuhr **her.**
Here they manufactured the first pocket watch.

the meaning of *manufacture* will be found under **herstellen,** not under **stellen.** This applies also to a verb compounded with another verb:

Er **lernte** sie vor einigen Jahren in Berlin **kennen.**
He made her acquaintance in Berlin a few years ago.

The meaning of *to make the acquaintance of* will be found under **kennenlernen.**

RULE: Read a sentence to the end. If there is a separable prefix, you are dealing with a compound verb, to be looked up under the prefix.

4. The past participle of verbs with separable prefixes is formed by attaching the prefix **ge-** to the stem of the verb:

INFINITIVE	PAST PARTICIPLE
kommen	gekommen
ankommen	angekommen

5. If the infinitive of a verb with a separable prefix is preceded by **zu** (*to*), **zu** is inserted between the prefix and the stem of the verb:

> Er plant, morgen **zurückzukommen.**
> *He plans to come back tomorrow.*

6. **Hin** and **her** are frequently used as separable prefixes: **hin** indicates movement away from the speaker, **her** movement toward the speaker.[1] They often combine with other prefixes:

Geh hin! *Go (there)*		**Komm her!** *Come here.*	
Geh hinaus! *Go out.*		**Komm herein!**[2] *Come in.*	
Hinaus! (colloquial: **Raus!**)[3] *Get out.*		**Herein!** *Come in!*	

Used adverbially, **hin und her** means *back and forth.*

7. The use of inseparable and separable prefixes in the various tenses is illustrated in the following synopsis:

	INSEPARABLE	SEPARABLE
PRESENT	Ich **verstehe** alles.	Ich **stehe** früh **auf.**
PAST	Ich **verstand** alles.	Ich **stand** früh **auf.**
FUTURE	Ich **werde** alles **verstehen.**	Ich **werde** früh **aufstehen.**
PRES. PERF.	Ich **habe** alles **verstanden.**	Ich **bin** früh **aufgestanden.**
PAST PERF.	Ich **hatte** alles **verstanden.**	Ich **war** früh **aufgestanden.**
FUT. PERF.	Ich **werde** alles **verstanden haben.**	Ich **werde** früh **aufgestanden sein.**

VARIABLE PREFIXES

1. The prefixes **durch-, über-, um-, unter-, voll-,** and **wieder-** are variable; that is, they may be either inseparable or separable.

---

[1] **Hin** and **her** must be added to adverbs of space when motion is involved: **dort** *there;* but: **dorthin** *there (thither);* **hierher** *here (hither),* etc.
[2] The preposition **in,** when used with the accusative (motion), becomes **ein** as a prefix: **einsteigen** *to get in.*
[3] Short for **heraus,** substituting for **hinaus** as more suitable for energetic pronunciation.

2. If the variable prefix is inseparable, the compound verb has a figurative meaning:[1]

wiederhọlen	*to repeat*
Wiederholen Sie das bitte!	*Please repeat that.*

3. If the variable prefix is separable, the compound verb usually retains its literal meaning:

wịederholen	*to get back*
Morgen hole ich mir mein Buch wieder.	*Tomorrow I'll get my book back.*

RECAPITULATION OF MAIN POINTS

1. The inseparable prefixes are: **be-, emp-, ent-, er-, ge-, hinter-, miß-, ver-, zer-.** Verbs with an inseparable prefix have past participles without the prefix **ge-.** Inseparable prefixes never carry a voice stress.

2. Separable prefixes are words in their own right (adverbs, prepositions, verbs). In compounds, both verb and prefix usually retain their basic meanings. However, the addition of a prefix may change the basic meaning of a verb. The prefix separates from the verb in the present and past tenses in main clauses and in the imperative. When separated, the prefix stands at the end of the clause. In the past participle, the prefix **ge-** is placed between the separable prefix and the stem of the verb; in the infinitive, **zu,** when needed, is treated in the same manner.

3. **Durch-, über-, um-, unter-, voll-** and **wieder-** are variable prefixes. Usually, they are inseparable when the verb is used in a figurative sense, separable when its meaning is literal.

4. Look up a verb with a prefix under the prefix.

ÜBUNGEN

Practice in Reading and Writing

A. *Read aloud and translate:*

---

[1] Note, however, that some verbs with variable prefixes used inseparably retain a literal meaning:

      Er **durchlief** den Wald.   *He ran through (crossed) the forest.*

Die Rolle der Frau in der Weltgeschichte

1. Wir haben uns bis jetzt fast nur mit den großen Männern der deutschen Literatur beschäftigt. 2. Wir waren in Gefahr gewesen, die Frauen ganz zu vergessen. 3. Sie werden ja so leicht vergessen! 4. Wir haben von Heine und Nietzsche gelesen, Hauptmann, Mann und Brecht sind uns begegnet, und von anderen berühmten Leuten werden wir noch hören. 5. Da ist nun wohl die Frage erlaubt: hat es in Deutschland denn nur Männer und keine Frauen gegeben? 6. Oder gehört die Frau, wie man sagt, wirklich nur in die Küche, und nicht auch in die Literaturgeschichte? 7. Jeder aber wird sicher gerne zugeben: ohne die Frauen wäre auch den Männern ihr Leben lang nicht viel eingefallen. 8. Stellen wir uns nur einen Heine ohne die hübschen Mädchen vor! 9. Aus jedem seiner Gedichte lächelt uns ein süßes Köpfchen entgegen. 10. Da redet er sie an, sie selber aber schweigen. 11. Schon diese Situation kommt uns etwas unnatürlich vor, denn in Wirklichkeit haben sie natürlich nicht so viel geschwiegen. 12. Sie haben vielleicht sogar immer das letzte Wort gehabt—aber nicht sie, sondern die Männer haben das dann aufgeschrieben. 13. Das Resultat ist als Literatur bekannt. 14. Und doch haben sich die Frauen über diese schlechte Behandlung nicht viel, oder doch nicht sehr laut beklagt. 15. Es scheint, diese Rolle hat ihnen sogar ganz gut gefallen. 16. Nun haben aber die Frauen in unserer Zeit angefangen, selbst an der Literatur aktiv teilzunehmen. 17. Nicht nur die Mädchen, auch die Männer werden nun angedichtet. 18. Wir können das als „Fortschritt" bezeichnen. 19. Es fragt sich dann nur, was wir vom Fortschritt halten. 20. So oder so, die Welt wird deswegen nicht gleich untergehen.

2	**die Gefahr, –en**	*danger*
5	**erlauben**	*to permit*
6	**die Küche, –n**	*kitchen*
7	**zugeben (i, a, e)**	*to admit*
	ein /fallen (ä, ie, a, ist) (impers.)	*to occur to, have an idea*
	wäre . . . eingefallen	*would have occurred to*
8	**sich vor/stellen**	*to imagine*
9	**entgegen/lächeln**	*to smile at*
11	**vor/kommen (a, o, ist)**	*to seem*
12	**auf/schreiben (ie, ie)**	*to write down*

14	**schlecht**	*bad*
	die Behandlung	*treatment*
	sich beklagen	*to complain*
16	**teil/nehmen an**	*to participate (in)*
17	**werden angedichtet**	*are being addressed in poetry*
18	**der Fortschritt**	*progress*
19	**fragt sich (idiom)**	*the question is*
20	**so oder so**	*(this way or that) whatever we may think of it*
	gleich	*immediately*
	unter /gehen	*to go down; to perish*

B. *Translate (using the end vocabulary for unfamiliar verbs with prefixes):*

1. Er drückt sich immer sehr genau aus. 2. Er ist im Examen durchgefallen. 3. Wir sind den ganzen Tag in der Stadt herumgelaufen. 4. Man erinnert sich später nicht mehr genau an seine Kinderjahre. 5. Im 19. (neunzehnten) Jahrhundert sind viele Deutsche nach Amerika ausgewandert. 6. Ich nehme

ihm diese Bemerkung (*remark*) sehr übel. 7. Haben Sie mir diese Worte wirklich übelgenommen? 8. Er hat die Sache schrecklich übertrieben. 9. Warum muß er immer alles übertreiben? 10. Er hat uns seine Gedichte vorgelesen. 11. Lesen Sie mir das bitte laut vor! 12. Ihm ist von all dem Bier schrecklich übel geworden. 13. Fritz hat von seinem Lehrer eine Ohrfeige bekommen. 14. Sie haben sich auf der Straße geohrfeigt. 15. Die Uraufführung findet morgen statt (stattfinden, a, u, *to take place*). 16. Wann hat die Uraufführung stattgefunden? 17. Das Stück wird morgen uraufgeführt (uraufführen *to put on for the first time*). 18. Diese Affaire hat seine Autorität ganz untergraben. 19. Er hat sich nicht sehr klar ausgedrückt. 20. Drücken Sie diesen Gedanken etwas klarer (*more clearly*) aus! 21. Wo hat sich diese Geschichte abgespielt? 22. Was wird all diese Arbeit abwerfen? 23. Sie hat nicht viel abgeworfen. 24. Sie kamen jeden Tag in demselben Café zusammen. 25. Werden wir morgen wieder zusammenkommen? 27. Beschreiben Sie mir die Erscheinung der jungen Dame! 28. Er hat uns das oft beschrieben. 29. Können Sie mir das beschreiben? 30. Diese Geschichte kommt mir sehr bekannt vor. 31. Wer hat an der Sache teilgenommen? 32. Er verlebte seine Kindheit in Berlin. 33. Wo hat er sie verlebt? 34. Er war seinen Feinden hoffnungslos ausgeliefert. 35. Wann wird die Post (*mail*) ausgeliefert?

teilnehmen: to participate

C. *Translate:*

1. Did this first performance please you? 2. She had fallen on the street but got up again. 3. The bell was ringing, but I did not hear it (use present perfect). 4. This book had belonged to my grandmother. 5. Don't forget to stop (with) your work. 6. Did you get to know the poet personally? 7. After one day he came back. 8. When did he come back? 9. He described her appearance closely. 10. He repeated the description once again. 11. Please get the periodical back for me. 12. He told us his story but I did not understand it. 13. Where do they produce this cheap liquor? 14. He spent a few years in Germany. 15. They became acquainted with him on the street one day. 16. He always arrived on time. 17. Formerly he liked to recite poems. 18. They did not answer my questions correctly. 19. I did express myself clearly, but he did not take it amiss. 20. It is healthy to get up early.

Oral Exercises

D. *Change the sentences to present tense:*

EXAMPLES: Es wird mir vielleicht einfallen. Es fällt mir vielleicht ein.
Ich werde mir alles überlegen. Ich überlege mir alles.

verleben: to spend one's life (or time)

1. Wir werden das sofort aufschreiben. 2. Wir werden alles ganz genau beschreiben. 3. Er wird seine Kinder selbst unterrichten. 4. Die Welt wird nicht untergehen. 5. Sie wird ihre Gedichte vorlesen. 6. Sie werden sich daran erinnern. 7. Er wird im Examen durchfallen. 8. Alle werden das übelnehmen. 9. Sie wird alle meine Fragen beantworten. 10. Sie werden ihn bald kennenlernen.

E. *Change the sentences to present perfect:*

EXAMPLES: Er kommt heute in München an.
Er ist heute in München angekommen.

Er bekommt von dem Mädchen eine Ohrfeige.
Er hat von dem Mädchen eine Ohrfeige bekommen.

1. Wir gehen jeden Tag spazieren. 2. Die Arbeit fängt an. 3. Er lernt sie in Nürnberg kennen. 4. Er verspricht ihr einfach alles. 5. Der Schnaps untergräbt seine Gesundheit. 6. Er vergißt die Zeitschrift. 7. Sie läuft in der Stadt herum. 8. Wir nehmen ihm das nicht übel. 9. Sie kommen diese Woche zurück. 10. Sie bekommen die Bücher in der Bibliothek.

14

Irregular Weak Verbs

Till Eulenspiegel

Wenn in Deutschland einer anderen Leuten gerne Streiche spielt, nennt man
ihn einen „Eulenspiegel", und jedes Kind weiß, daß Till Eulenspiegel ein
großer Spaßmacher[1] war. Vielen ist er durch Richard Strauß' Tondichtung
„Till Eulenspiegels lustige Streiche" bekannt.

Till Eulenspiegel war der Sohn eines Bauern aus Braunschweig[2] in Nord- 5
deutschland. Er war zu seiner Zeit so berühmt wie die Braunschweiger Wurst.
Ein Volksbuch[3] aus dem 16.[4] Jahrhundert erzählt von seinen vielen lustigen
Streichen. Es war ein gutes Buch für lange Winterabende, wenn—wie es im
Vorwort heißt—die Mäuse unter die Bänke rennen, das Feuer im Ofen lustig
brennt und die gebratenen Birnen gut schmecken. Das Buch war sehr beliebt 10
und findet sich in vielen Übersetzungen, denn man kannte Till nicht nur in
Deutschland, sondern auch in Holland, Frankreich, Italien, Dänemark und
Polen. In Polen war Till sogar der Freund und Hofnarr[5] König Kasimirs.
Auch in England war er berühmt. Man nannte ihn da „Owl Glass", denn man
meinte, daß Eule „owl" bedeutet und Spiegel „looking glass". Aber „Eulen- 15
spiegel" kommt wahrscheinlich von dem französischen Wort für „Schelm".

1. **Spaßmacher** *joker, prankster.* 2. **Braunschweig** *Brunswick.* 3. **Volksbuch** *book of
popular stories, "chapbook."* 4. 16. (read:) **sechzehnten** *sixteenth.* 5. **Hofnarr** *court
jester.*

Aber wenden wir uns Till selbst zu! Auf dem Markt einer Stadt traf er einmal einen Bauern mit einem schönen grünen Tuch. Er fragte ihn, wo er wohnte. Der Bauer nannte ihm den Namen eines Dorfes, und Till behauptete
20 darauf, aus derselben Gegend zu sein. „Warte hier auf mich", sagte er zu ihm, „wir haben denselben Weg und können zusammen nach Hause gehen." Dann rannte er zu zwei Freunden; der eine von ihnen war Advokat.[6] Till dachte sich mit ihnen einen Plan aus, dem Bauern das Tuch abzuschwindeln.[7] Dann ging er zum Markt zurück und machte sich mit dem Bauern auf den
25 Weg.[8] Sie waren noch nicht weit gekommen, da wollte Till wissen, wieviel der Bauer für das schöne blaue Tuch bezahlt hatte. Der antwortete: „Zwei Taler,[9] aber das Tuch ist nicht blau, sondern grün, wie jeder Dummkopf sehen kann."

„Nun, ich bin aber kein Dummkopf", wandte Till ein, „und ich behaupte
30 immer noch, daß das Tuch blau ist."

„Hast du denn keine Augen im Kopf?" rief der Bauer. „Das Tuch ist grün!"

„Wenn das Tuch grün ist", erwiderte Till, „dann gebe ich dir fünf Taler. Aber wenn es blau ist, dann gibst du mir das Tuch."

35 „Gut", meinte der Bauer nach einigem Bedenken, „wenn das Tuch nicht grün ist wie Gras, gebe ich es dir."

Nun trafen sie den ersten der Freunde Tills und fragten ihn nach der Farbe des Tuches. Tills Freund sagte natürlich blau, aber der Bauer wollte die Entscheidung nicht anerkennen und das Tuch nicht hergeben. „Ihr steckt beide
40 unter einer Decke",[10] erklärte er.

„Nun", meinte Till, „da kommt ein Advokat. Wenden wir uns an den!"

„Geehrter[11] Herr[12] Advokat", begann der Bauer, „ich habe eine große Bitte. Ich weiß natürlich, daß dieses Tuch grün ist, grün wie Gras, aber die beiden hier behaupten, es ist blau. Sagen Sie uns bitte, ob es blau oder grün
45 ist."

Der Advokat bedachte sich nicht lange. „Ich habe zwar Besseres[13] zu tun, als meine Zeit mit Dummheiten zu verbringen. Aber ich will euch helfen, und so erkläre ich denn, daß das Tuch selbstverständlich blau ist, wie jeder Dummkopf sehen kann."

50 Der Bauer dankte dem Advokaten und wandte sich dann wieder an Till: „Das ist nun ein Advokat", sagte er, „und ich sehe daher ein, daß ihr doch nicht unter einer Decke steckt." Und so bekam Till das Tuch.

6. **Advokat** (old word for **Rechtsanwalt**) *lawyer*. 7. **das Tuch abzuschwindeln** *to swindle (the peasant) out of the cloth.* 8. **machte sich . . . auf den Weg** *started out on the road.* 9. **Taler** (old monetary unit; the word "dollar" is derived from it). 10. **steckt . . . unter einer Decke** (lit., are under one blanket) *are in cahoots.* 11. **Geehrter** (lit., honorable) *my dear.* 12. **Herr** (note that in German **Herr** precedes a title in an address). 13. **Besseres** *something better.*

FRAGEN

1. Was weiß jedes Kind? 2. Wodurch ist Till Eulenspiegel vielen bekannt? 3. Wer war Till Eulenspiegel? 4. Wie berühmt war er zu seiner Zeit? 5. Wofür war das Volksbuch gut? 6. Was tun die Mäuse an langen Winterabenden? 7. Was tut das Feuer? 8. Wo kannte man Till überall? 9. Was war Till in Polen? 10. Warum nannte man ihn in England „Owl Glass"? 11. Wen traf Till eines Tages auf dem Markt einer Stadt? 12. Was behauptete er? 13. Was sagte Till zu dem Bauern? 14. Was tat Till dann? 15. Was wollte Till wissen? 16. Was antwortete der Bauer? 17. Was wandte Till ein? 18. Was rief der Bauer nun? 19. Was erwiderte Till darauf? 20. Was meinte der Bauer schließlich? 21. Was fragten sie den ersten Freund Tills? 22. Was sagte dieser Freund? 23. Was wollte der Bauer nicht tun? 24. Wie redete der Bauer den zweiten Freund an? 25. Was antwortete der Advokat? 26. Was sagte der Bauer schließlich?

WORTSCHATz

an/erkennen	to accept; to recognize	die Gegend, –en	region
		grün	green
aus/denken	to think up	es heißt (in)	it says (in)
die Bank, ⹋e	bench	her/geben (gibt her, gab her, hergegeben)	to hand over
der Bauer, –n (or –s), –n	peasant, farmer		
bedenken	to reflect	lange (time adverb)	for a long time
sich bedenken	to ponder, hesitate		
das Bedenken	reflection	lustig	merry, gay
bedeuten	to mean	der Markt, ⹋e	market (place)
beliebt	popular	ob (conj.)	whether
bezahlen	to pay	der Ofen, ⹋	stove, oven
die Birne, –n	pear	der Schelm, –e	rascal
die Bitte, –n	request	schmecken	to taste
blau	blue	selbstverständlich	of course, naturally
doch	after all	der Spiegel, –	mirror
die Dummheit, –en	stupidity	der Streich, –e	prank
der Dummkopf, ⹋e	dumbbell, blockhead	das Tier, –e	animal
einiges (neuter sing.; plural: einige)	some	die Tondichtung, –en	tone poem
		das Tuch, ⹋er	cloth
		die Übersetzung, –en	translation
ein/sehen (sieht ein, sah ein, eingesehen)	to come to realize, to understand	verbringen	to spend
		das Vorwort, –e	foreword, introduction
ein/wenden	to object		
die Entscheidung, –en	decision	wahrscheinlich	probably
		weit	far
erwidern	to answer	die Wurst, ⹋e	sausage
die Farbe, –n	color	sich zu/wenden	to turn to
das Feuer, –	fire	der Zweck, –e	purpose

STRONG VERBS

braten	to roast	**brät**	**briet**	**gebraten**
helfen	to help	**hilft**	**half**	**geholfen**
rufen	to call		**rief**	**gerufen**
schreien	to scream		**schrie**	**geschrie(e)n**

DISTINGUISH BETWEEN

kennen and **wissen: kennen** is *to know* in the sense of "to be acquainted with"
        wissen is *to know* in the sense of "to have knowledge of"

die Bank, plural **die Bänke,** *bench*
die Bank, plural **die Banken,** *bank*

IRREGULAR WEAK VERBS

1. A few verbs, known as "irregular weak verbs," change their stem vowel in the past tense and in the past participle, but they are otherwise conjugated like regular weak verbs:

EXAMPLE: **kennen** *to know*

PRESENT	PAST	PAST PARTICIPLE
ich kenne *I know*	ich kannte *I knew*	**gekannt** *known*
du kennst	du kanntest	
er kennt	er kannte	
wir kennen	wir kannten	
ihr kennt	ihr kanntet	
sie kennen	sie kannten	

2. The irregular weak verbs are:

brennen	*to burn*	**brannte**	**gebrannt**
kennen	*to know*	**kannte**	**gekannt**
nennen	*to name*	**nannte**	**genannt**
rennen	*to run*	**rannte**	**gerannt**
senden (nach)	*to send (for)*	**sandte (sendete)**	**gesandt (gesendet)**
wenden	*to turn*	**wandte (wendete)**	**gewandt (gewendet)**
bringen	*to bring*	**brachte**	**gebracht**
denken	*to think*	**dachte**	**gedacht**

Senden and **wenden** also form regular weak past tenses and past participles, as the above table shows; the two sets of forms are interchangeable.

3. The verb **wissen** (*to know*) has all the characteristics of an irregular weak verb, but different forms in the singular of the present tense, and the stem vowel is **u** in the past and past participle:

PRESENT	PAST	PAST PARTICIPLE
ich weiß	ich wußte	**gewußt**
du weißt	du wußtest	
er weiß	er wußte	
wir wissen	wir wußten	
ihr wißt	ihr wußtet	
sie wissen	sie wußten	

4. Two German verbs express the idea of "to know": **wissen** and **kennen.** **Wissen** is used in the sense of "to know a fact," **kennen** in the sense of "to be acquainted with." **Kennen** may be followed only by a direct object, **wissen** also by a dependent clause:

Kennst du ihn?	*Do you know him?*
Ich **weiß** nicht, wo er wohnt.	*I don't know where he lives.*
Nur wer die Sehnsucht **kennt,**	*Only he who knows longing*
Weiß, was ich leide. (Goethe)	*knows what I suffer.* (In English: "None but the lonely heart . . .")

5. Irregular weak verbs, despite their limited number, assume additional meanings through prefixes that are attached to them. Note the following common combinations:

brennen:	**ab /brennen**	*to burn down*
	an /brennen	*to burn* (food when cooking)
	durch /brennen (colloq.)	*to run away*
	verbrennen	*to burn* (off)
	sich verbrennen	*to burn oneself*
kennen:	**an /erkennen**	*to recognize, appreciate*
	bekennen	*to confess*
	erkennen (an, *w. dat.*)	*to recognize* (*by*), *realize* (*from*)
	verkennen	*to misjudge, misunderstand*
nennen:	**ernennen**	*to nominate, appoint*
rennen:	**fort /rennen** ⎫ **(von, aus)**	*to run away* (*from*)
	weg /rennen ⎭	
senden:	**fort /senden** ⎫ **(von, aus)**	*to send away*
	weg /senden ⎭	
	nach /senden	*to forward*
wenden:	**sich ab /wenden (von)**	*to turn away* (*from*)
	an /wenden (auf, *w. acc.*)	*to apply* (*to*)
	ein /wenden (gegen)	*to object* (*to*)
	sich um /wenden	*to turn around*
	verwenden	*to use*
bringen:	**an /bringen**	*to put in* (*on*), *fix*
	bei /bringen (colloq.)	*to teach*
	heraus /bringen	*to publish*
	hervor /bringen	*to produce*
	mit /bringen	*to bring along, bring as a present*

	um /bringen	*to kill*
	unter /bringen	*to put up, shelter*
	verbringen	*to spend* (time)
	vor /bringen	*to utter, bring up*
	zu /bringen	*to spend* (time)
denken:	aus /denken	*to think up*
	bedenken	*to consider*
	durch /denken, durchdenken	*to think through*
	gedenken (w. gen.)	*to remember; to plan*
	nach /denken (über, *w. acc.*)	*to ponder, reflect* (*on*)

RECAPITULATION OF MAIN POINTS

1. Irregular weak verbs change their stem vowel in the past tense and in the past participle to **a.** Otherwise they are conjugated like regular verbs.

2. **Wissen** is conjugated in the present tense as follows:

ich **weiß**	wir **wissen**
du **weißt**	ihr **wißt**
er **weiß**	sie **wissen**

In the past and past participle, its stem vowel is **u;** otherwise it is conjugated like a regular weak verb.

3. **Wissen** (*to know*) is "to know a fact," "have knowledge of," **kennen** "to be acquainted with"; only **wissen** can be followed by a dependent clause.

ÜBUNGEN

Practice in Reading and Writing

A. *Read aloud and translate* (*with the help of the list of prefixed verbs on pages 161–162*):

„Sprechen Sie Schimpanse?"

1. Ein deutscher Anthropologe hat vor einigen Jahren ein Buch herausgebracht unter dem Titel „Sprechen Sie Schimpanse?". 2. Dieser Anthropologe hatte die Sprache der Schimpansen studiert und dabei erkannt, daß jeder Laut des Schimpansen etwas bedeutet. 3. Man meint, man versteht einen Hund oder eine Katze, aber was wissen wir wirklich von der Sprache der Tiere? 4. Wir denken dabei nicht daran, daß man einem Papagei

deutsche oder englische Wörter beibringen kann. 5. Wir haben bei dieser Bemerkung vielmehr an die Sprache der Tiere selbst gedacht. 6. Woran erkennen wir eine jede Sprache? An ihren Lauten. 7. Ich habe einmal einen Mann gekannt, der seine Zeit damit verbrachte, die Sprache der Raben zu lernen. 8. Wenden Sie nicht ein, daß nicht jede Tiersprache eine Lautsprache ist! 9. Das hat man immer schon gewußt. 10. Die Bienen zum Beispiel verwenden dafür einen Tanz. 11. Eine Biene findet ein Feld mit Blumen, und die anderen Bienen erkennen an ihrem Tanz, wo das Feld ist. 12. Ist Ihnen der Ausdruck bekannt: „Stumm wie ein Fisch"? 13. Dieser Ausdruck verkennt die Natur der Fische genauso wie der bekannte: „Er trinkt wie ein Fisch". 14. Natürlich bringt ein Fisch keine Laute hervor, aber er hat dafür eine Zeichensprache. 15. Auch die Menschen verwenden solche Zeichensprachen. 16. Die Siedler des amerikanischen Westens haben eine Zeichensprache angewandt, wenn sie mit den Indianern handelten. 17. Jedem Jungen, der die „Lederstrumpfgeschichten" kennt, ist diese Zeichensprache bekannt. 18. In manchen Ländern verwenden die jungen Damen ihre Fächer zu demselben Zweck, und heute kennt man auch die sogenannte Körpersprache. 19. Leider erkennen die Universitäten solche Sprachen nicht als Fremdsprachen an. 20. Bedenken Sie, man könnte die Sprache der Schimpansen für diesen Zweck verwenden!

2	der Laut, –e	*sound*		14	das Zeichen, –	*sign*
3	der Hund, –e	*dog*		16	der Siedler, –	*settler*
	die Katze, –n	*cat*			der Indianer, –	*American Indian*
	das Tier, –e	*animal*			handeln	*to trade*
4	der Papagei, –en	*parrot*		17	der Junge, –n, –n	*boy*
5	die Bemerkung, –en	*remark*			die Lederstrumpf-geschichten	*Leatherstocking Tales*
	vielmehr	*rather*		18	der Fächer, –	*fan*
7	der Rabe, –n	*raven*			der Zweck, –e	*purpose*
10	die Biene, –n	*bee*			sogenannt	*so-called*
	der Tanz, ⸗e	*dance*		19	die Fremdsprache, –n	*foreign language*
12	der Ausdruck, ⸗e	*expression*				
	stumm	*silent*				

B. *Translate and give the infinitives of the verb forms in italics (watch for separated prefixes):*

1. Entschuldigen Sie, ich habe Sie nicht *erkannt*. 2. Erst habe ich *gedacht*, Sie sind Ihr Bruder. 3. Dann *dachte* ich: Nein, Sie sind es selbst. 4. Und jetzt *erkenne* ich Sie endlich: Ja, Sie sind Ihr Bruder! 5. Man hat diesen Dichter lange *verkannt*. 6. Er hat sich zum Katholizismus *bekannt*. 7. Sie *ernannten* ihn zum Präsidenten. 8. Ich habe meine Kinderjahre auf dem Land (*in the country*) *verbracht*. 9. Man *erkannte* seine Leistung überall an. 10. Einen solchen Mann kann man immer *verwenden*. 11. Worüber *denken* Sie jetzt nach? 12. Sie haben den Diktator schließlich *umgebracht*. 13. Er *wandte* sich um und *erkannte* sie sofort. 14. Die beiden sind eines Tages zusammen *durchgebrannt*. 15. Was *senden* Sie da jetzt ab? 16. Man kann

sich diese Verben selbst *beibringen.* 17. Er *brachte* ihr etwas aus Paris mit. 18. Wo haben Sie die letzte Woche *verbracht?* 19. Ich habe sie im Bett *zugebracht.* 20. Wir *bringen* euch in einem guten Hotel unter. 21. Er *nannte* mir seinen Namen. 22. Ich *wende* mich mit meiner Bitte an Sie! 23. Sie *verbringt* wirklich den ganzen Tag in der Sonne und ist schon sehr *eingebrannt (sunburned).* 24. Eine gute Hausfrau läßt das Essen nicht *anbrennen.*

C. *Distinguish between* **kennen** *and* **wissen.** *Complete with the appropriate form of either:*

1. _____ Sie, wo er wohnt? 2. _____ du ihn? 3. Ich _____ ihn nicht aber ich _____, daß er kein Dummkopf ist. 4. _____ Sie die Geschichte von Till Eulenspiegel? 5. _____ Sie, wer die Musik dazu geschrieben hat? 6. Ich habe von seinem Tode nichts _____. 7. _____ Sie diesen Mann? 8. _____ Sie, wer er ist?

D. *Translate:*

1. She burned herself. 2. One day they ran away. 3. Do you know this color? I don't recognize it. 4. I know that it is blue. 5. We have no objection to it (translate: We have nothing to object against it). 6. He brought along a book. 7. He gave (use **nennen**) me his name. 8. They notified **(benachrichtigen)** his parents that he had run away. 9. The farmer turned around, but nobody was there. 10. I have thought about your request. 11. Excuse (me), but I don't know you. 12. I really don't know who **(wer)** you are. 13. Were you spending this year in Germany? 14. The peasant did not recognize his cloth. 15. They sent for **(nach)** a doctor, and he came immediately. 16. We like to put him up in our house. 17. Who knows whether he is at home? 18. When he comes home, he works for a while in his garden.

Oral Exercises

E. *Change the sentences to past tense:*

EXAMPLE: Er nennt ihm den Namen der Stadt.
　　　　　Er nannte ihm den Namen der Stadt.

1. Der Bauer bringt das Tuch mit. 2. Der Schelm denkt sich einen Streich aus. 3. Er bedenkt sich nicht lange. 4. Wir wissen das wirklich nicht. 5. Die Häuser brennen alle ab. 6. Die Mäuse rennen unter die Bänke. 7. Du erkennst die Entscheidung nicht an. 8. Wir wenden nichts dagegen ein. 9. Der Schelm bringt ihm viele Streiche bei.

F. *Change the sentences to present perfect:*

EXAMPLE: Wir bringen alle Leute im Hause unter.
Wir haben alle Leute im Hause untergebracht.

1. Sie denkt über dieses Problem nach.   2. Er wendet die Theorie an.   3. Der Schelm brennt wieder einmal durch.   4. Er bringt den Mann auf der Straße um.   5. Wir wissen wenig über ihn.   6. Er nennt sich Advokat.   7. Man erkennt ihn an seinem grünen Tuch.   8. Sie senden ihn bald fort.   9. Wir bringen ihm die Birnen mit.

15

Adjectives

Günter Grass[1]

Durch Günter Grass hat die deutsche Literatur nach dem Zweiten Weltkrieg ihren alten guten Namen wiedergewonnen. Sein erster, ziemlich langer, sehr origineller Roman, „Die Blechtrommel",[2] hat die Leser in aller Welt fasziniert.

Grass ist jedoch nicht nur ein ausgezeichneter Schriftsteller. Man kann
5 sich sogar mit gutem Grund fragen: in welcher Kunst hat er eigentlich nicht gearbeitet? Mit zwanzig Jahren erlernte er zunächst das Handwerk eines Steinmetzen.[3] Dann besuchte er die Düsseldorfer Kunstakademie und lernte da zeichnen und modellieren. Gleichzeitig war er Mitglied einer Jazzkapelle[4] und spielte in Düsseldorfer Lokalen. Damals schrieb er auch seine
10 ersten Gedichte und kurze Theaterszenen sowie Ballette.

Heute sind seine epischen, lyrischen, dramatischen und graphischen Arbeiten den Lesern moderner deutscher Literatur gut bekannt. Grass hat nämlich noch jedes seiner Bücher mit einer eigenen Zeichnung für den Schutzumschlag[5] versehen. Der kleine Oskar[6] mit seiner großen Blechtrom-

1. Born in Danzig, 1927.   2. **Die Blechtrommel** *The Tin Drum.*   3. **Steinmetz** *stonecutter.*
4. **Jazzkapelle** *jazz band.*   5. **Schutzumschlag** *dust jacket.*   6. **der kleine Oskar** the hero of *The Tin Drum.*

mel, dem spitzen Papierhelm[7] und dem runden, offenen Mündchen trommelt 15
durch die ganze Welt. Auch die Bände seiner Gedichte enthalten Illustrationen
von Grass.

Heute spielt Günter Grass nicht mehr auf dem Waschbrett.[8] Er macht auch
keine Skulpturen mehr. „Das ist so anstrengend wie Romanschreiben", sagt
er. „Man arbeitet acht Studen am Tag und hat dann erst eine Kniescheibe[9] 20
fertig."

Dafür hat Grass sich in den letzten Jahren politisch sehr engagiert. Er
arbeitet für die Sozialdemokratische Partei, schreibt für ihre Kandidaten
Wahlreden und nimmt auch selbst an den Wahlkämpfen teil. Er hat sogar
katholische Nonnen aufgefordert, sozialdemokratisch zu wählen! Das war 25
für deutsche Nonnen etwas ganz Neues.

Auch in den Zeiten zwischen den Wahlen in der Bundesrepublik[10] ist
Grass politisch aktiv. Er schickt nicht nur seine Bücher in die Welt, sondern
reist auch selbst gern in alle Himmelsrichtungen. Einige Zeit hat er in Paris
gelebt, und dort ist auch seine „Blechtrommel" entstanden. 30

Eine seiner ersten Reisen führte den noch unbekannten Autor nach Polen.
Dafür brauchte er aber ein offizielles Dokument, und so bat er einen be-
kannten polnischen Kritiker um eine Einladung. Zum Beweis für sein
Dichtertum[11] schickte er ihm in seinem Brief zwei seiner Gedichte mit.[12]
Er bekam seine Einladung und sandte seinem Gastgeber darauf folgendes 35
Telegramm: „Komme Sonntag mittag stop Trage blaues Hemd stop Günter
Grass."

Aber am Sonntag mittag kommen in Warschau zwei Züge an verschiedenen
Bahnhöfen und zwei Flugzeuge verschiedener Gesellschaften aus Berlin an.
Der polnische Kritiker war in einiger Verlegenheit. Er konnte nicht gut an 40
vier Stellen zur selben Zeit sein. Schließlich entschied er sich für den Hauptbahnhof. Aber seine Verlegenheit wuchs, als[13] mehr als zweihundert blaue
Hemden aus dem Berliner Zug sprangen. Eine ostdeutsche Studentenorganisation machte an diesem Tag einen Ausflug nach Polen, und alle ihre
Mitglieder trugen blaue Hemden als Uniform. Den zahllosen Hemden aber 45
folgte ganz zuletzt noch ein einzelnes blaues Hemd. Der Wartende fühlte sich
erleichtert: „Herr Grass! Sie sind wirklich ein Dichter! Das hat mir Ihr
Telegramm bewiesen."

7. **Papierhelm** *paper helmet.* 8. **Waschbrett** *washboard.* 9. **Kniescheibe** *knee cap.* 10. **Bundesrepublik** *Federal Republic.* 11. **sein Dichtertum** *his being a poet.* 12. **mit** (as prefix) *along.* 13. **als** (as conjunction) *when.*

FRAGEN

1. Was hat die deutsche Literatur durch Günter Grass wiedergewonnen?
2. Wie war der erste Roman von Günter Grass? 3. Wen hat „Die Blechtrommel" fasziniert? 4. Was kann man sich mit gutem Grund fragen?
5. Was tat Günter Grass in Düsseldorf? 6. Wann schrieb er seine ersten
Gedichte? 7. Was ist den Lesern der modernen deutschen Literatur heute
gut bekannt? 8. Womit hat Grass jedes seiner Bücher versehen? 9. Wer
trommelt durch die ganze Welt? 10. Warum macht Grass heute keine
Skulpturen mehr? 11. Was hat er statt dessen getan? 12. Beschreiben Sie,
wie Günter Grass sich politisch engagiert hat! 13. Was hat er mit den
katholischen Nonnen getan? 14. Was tut Grass gern? 15. Wo ist „Die
Blechtrommel" entstanden? 16. Worum bat er einen bekannten polnischen
Kritiker? 17. Warum schickte er ihm zwei Gedichte mit? 18. Was für ein
Telegramm sandte er darauf? 19. Wie viele Züge und Flugzeuge aus Berlin
kommen am Sonntag in Warschau an? 20. Warum war der polnische
Kritiker in Verlegenheit? 21. Warum wuchs seine Verlegenheit? 22. Warum
waren alle diese blauen Hemden in Warschau? 23. Was sagte der Wartende
zu dem letzten blauen Hemd?

WORTSCHATZ

anstrengend	strenuous		main railroad
auf /fordern	to exhort		station)
der **Ausflug, ⸗e**	excursion	der **Himmel, –**	sky, heaven
ausgezeichnet	excellent	**jedoch**	however
der **Bahnhof, ⸗e**	railroad station	**kurz**	short
der **Band, ⸗e**	volume (of books)	das **Lokal, –e**	public place (of en-
der **Beweis, –e**	proof		tertainment)
zum Beweis	as proof	das **Mitglied, –er**	member
der **Brief, –e**	letter	**mittag**	(at) noon
die **Einladung, –en**	invitation	die **Nonne, –n**	nun
einzeln	single	**offen**	open
erleichtern	to relieve	der **Osten**	the East
fertig	ready, finished	**spitz**	pointed
das **Flugzeug, –e**	airplane	die **Stelle, –n**	place
folgen	to follow	die **Stunde, –n**	hour
fühlen	to feel	**trommeln**	to drum
der **Gastgeber, –**	host	die **Verlegenheit, –en**	embarrassment
die **Gesellschaft, –en**	company	die **Wahl, –en**	election
gleichzeitig	at the same time	der **Wahl-**	election campaign
der **Grund, ⸗e**	ground, reason	**kampf, ⸗e**	
das **Handwerk, –e**	craft	**wählen**	to vote; to elect
das **Haupt, ⸗er**	head; *as prefix:* main	der **Wirt, –e**	host
	(der **Hauptbahnhof**	die **Zahl, –en**	number
		zahllos	innumerable

zeichnen	to draw	zuletzt	at the end
die **Zeichnung, –en**	drawing	zunächst	first (of all)
der **Zug, ≠e**	train	zwanzig	twenty

STRONG VERBS

an/kommen	to arrive		**kam an**	ist **angekommen**
beweisen	to prove		**bewies**	**bewiesen**
ein/laden	to invite	**lädt ein**	**lud ein**	**eingeladen**
enthalten	to contain	**enthält**	**enthielt**	**enthalten**
fangen	to catch, capture	**fängt**	**fing**	**gefangen**
gewinnen	to win		**gewann**	**gewonnen**
springen	to jump		**sprang**	ist **gesprungen**
stehlen	to steal	**stiehlt**	**stahl**	**gestohlen**
teil/nehmen	to participate	**nimmt teil**	**nahm teil**	**teilgenommen**
tragen	to wear, carry	**trägt**	**trug**	**getragen**
versehen (mit)	to provide (with)	**versieht**	**versah**	**versehen**

DISTINGUISH BETWEEN

die **Uhr** *clock* (also used to indicate time: **zwei Uhr** *two o'clock*)
die **Stunde** *hour*

der **Band** (plural: **die Bände**) *volume* and **das Band** (plural: **die Bänder**) *ribbon*

GRAMMATICAL TERMS

1. A descriptive adjective is a word which indicates the quality or condition of a thing or being: a *good* book, an *attractive* woman, the *American* flag.

2. An adjective is in attributive position when it precedes the noun it modifies. The above-mentioned adjectives are all in attributive position; they are called *attributive adjectives*.

3. An adjective is in predicate position when a verb separates it from the noun it modifies: The woman was *attractive* but not very *pleasant*. *Attractive* and *pleasant* are called *predicate adjectives*.

ADJECTIVES IN GERMAN

1. A predicate adjective never has an ending:

Er ist **stark** aber **dumm.**
He is strong but stupid.

2. Adjectives after **Der**-Words

If preceded by a **der**-word, an attributive adjective has the following (so-called "weak") endings:

	SINGULAR			PLURAL
	Masculine	Feminine	Neuter	(all genders)
NOM.	e	e	e	
ACC.	en	e	e	en
DAT.	en	en	en	
GEN.	en	en	en	

The weak adjective endings are **-e** in five cases (all singular), **-en** in all others.

Examples:

	SINGULAR		
	Masculine	Feminine	Neuter
NOM.	der gute Mann	die gute Frau	das gute Kind
ACC.	den guten Mann	die gute Frau	das gute Kind
DAT.	dem guten Mann(e)	der guten Frau	dem guten Kind(e)
GEN.	des guten Mannes	der guten Frau	des guten Kindes

	PLURAL
NOM.	die guten Männer (Frauen, Kinder)
ACC.	die guten Männer (Frauen, Kinder)
DAT.	den guten Männern (Frauen, Kindern)
GEN.	der guten Männer (Frauen, Kinder)

A good way to master these adjective endings is to memorize the three forms: **der gute Mann, die gute Frau, das gute Kind,** because they cover all five cases in which the adjective ending is **-e;** in all other combinations, it is **-en.**

3. Adjectives after **Ein**-Words

If an **ein**-word precedes an adjective, the above set of weak adjective endings changes in only three case forms: *nominative masculine, nominative* and *accusative neuter* (in the singular), where the endings are:

	MASCULINE	NEUTER
NOM.	kein guter Mann	kein gutes Kind
ACC.		kein gutes Kind

The complete set of (so-called "mixed") adjective endings after **ein**-words:

	SINGULAR			PLURAL
	Masculine	Feminine	Neuter	
NOM.	er	e	es	
ACC.	en	e	es	*en*
DAT.	en	en	en	
GEN.	en	en	en	

The endings in the plural remain **-en** for all cases.

Examples:

	SINGULAR		
	Masculine	Feminine	Neuter
NOM.	kein guter Mann	keine gute Frau	kein gutes Kind
ACC.	keinen guten Mann	keine gute Frau	kein gutes Kind
DAT.	keinem guten Mann	keiner guten Frau	keinem guten Kind
GEN.	keines guten Mannes	keiner guten Frau	keines guten Kindes
	PLURAL		
NOM.	keine guten Männer (Frauen, Kinder)		
ACC.	keine guten Männer (Frauen, Kinder)		
DAT.	keinen guten Männern (Frauen, Kindern)		
GEN.	keiner guten Männer (Frauen, Kinder)		

4. To master these adjective endings, memorize: **kein guter Mann, keine gute Frau, kein gutes Kind;** in all other combinations with **ein**-words, the adjective endings are **-en.**

5. Unpreceded Adjectives

Adjectives not preceded by either a **der**-word or an **ein**-word take the so-called "strong" adjective endings, which are identical with the endings used for the declension of **dieser** (see page 28), except in the genitive singular, masculine, and neuter, where it is **-en:**

	SINGULAR			PLURAL
	Masculine	Feminine	Neuter	(all others)
NOM.	er	e	es	e
ACC.	en	e	es	e
DAT.	em	er	em	en
GEN.	en	er	en	er

Examples:

	SINGULAR			PLURAL
	Masculine	Feminine	Neuter	(all genders)
NOM.	süßer Wein	frische Butter	reines Wasser	arme Leute
ACC.	süßen Wein	frische Butter	reines Wasser	arme Leute
DAT.	süßem Wein	frischer Butter	reinem Wasser	armen Leuten
GEN.	süßen Weines	frischer Butter	reinen Wassers	armer Leute

6. Some adjectives change their basic stem forms slightly when inflected:

a. **Hoch** (*high*) drops **c** when an ending is added: ein **hoher** Baum *a tall tree.*

b. Adjectives ending in **-er**, **-el**, or **-en** often drop **e** before inflectional endings:

dunkel	*dark:*	ein **dunkles** Haus	*a dark house*
edel	*noble:*	ein **edler** Mann	*a noble man*
offen	*open:*	ein **offnes** (or **offenes**) Fenster	*an open window*
tapfer	*brave:*	ein **tapfrer** (or **tapferer**) Soldat	*a brave soldier*
teuer	*expensive:*	**teure** Bücher	*expensive books*

Be sure to restore this dropped **e** before looking up the adjective in a dictionary or vocabulary: der **tapfre** Mann, look up: **tapfer.**

c. Adjectives in **-e** (**weise** *wise*) drop this **e** before inflectional endings: **weise, weisen, weisem, weises,** etc.

d. Some adjectives ending in **-s** drop this **s** when inflected:

anders	*other(wise):*	das **andere** Haus	*the other house*
links	*left:*	die **linke** Hand	*the left hand*
rechts	*right:*	die **rechte** Hand	*the right hand*

7. Two or more adjectives modifying the same noun have the same ending:

ein schönes, reiches Land   a beautiful, rich country

8. The plural adjectives **andere** (*other*), **einige** (*a few*), **mehrere** (*several*), **wenige** (*few*), and **viele** (*many*) are treated like attributive adjectives not preceded by a **der-** or **ein-**word, that is, they take strong endings, as do the adjectives following them.

Alle, however, is a plural **der-**word (singular: **jeder**); hence, descriptive adjectives following **alle** require weak endings.[1]

9. After **etwas** (*something*), **viel** (*much*), and **nichts** (*nothing*), capitalized adjectives are used as neuter nouns and take the strong endings for neuter adjectives; **etwas, viel,** and **nichts** remain unchanged:

etwas Schönes	*something beautiful*
viel Gutes	*much* (*that is*) *good*
nichts Interessantes	*nothing interesting*

Wir haben **von nichts Besonderem** gesprochen.
We talked about nothing special (*in particular*).

10. The adjectives **mehr** (*more*), **viel** (*much*), **wenig** (*little*, in quantity) are not declined in the singular:

Ich habe wenig Geld.   I have little money.

11. Adjectival nouns (that is, adjectives used as nouns) are declined like adjectives; their endings are weak, strong, or mixed according to the rules discussed. Examples:

	SINGULAR		PLURAL
(with **der**:)	der Deutsche	*the German*	die Deutschen
	den Deutschen		die Deutschen
	dem Deutschen		den Deutschen
	des Deutschen		der Deutschen
(with **ein-**word:)	kein Deutscher	*no German*	keine Deutschen
	keinen Deutschen		keine Deutschen
	keinem Deutschen		keinen Deutschen
	keines Deutschen		keiner Deutschen
(without **der-** or **ein-** word:)	Deutsche	*Germans*	
	Deutsche		
	Deutschen		
	Deutscher		

[1] If a **der-** or **ein-**word follows **alle,** it takes the strong endings: alle **diese** Leute; alle **unsere** Kinder.

Similarly: **der Kleine** (*the little man*), **die Dicke** (*the fat woman*), **ein Weiser** (*a wise man*), **unsere Verwandten** (*our relatives*—from: **verwandt** *related*), and others.

12. Adjectival nouns in the masculine refer to men, in the feminine to women, in the neuter to things or abstractions:

der Gute	*the good man*	**der Deutsche**	*the German* (*man*)
die Gute	*the good woman*	**die Deutsche**	*the German* (*woman*)
das Gute	*that which is good*	**das Deutsche**	*that which is German, the German language*[1]

13. Adjectives derived from names of places add **-er** to the name; they are always capitalized, and the ending remains uninflected in all cases:

das **Heidelberger** Schloß	*the castle at Heidelberg*
die **Wiener** Wurst	*Vienna sausage*
der **Berliner** Schnellzug	*the Berlin express*
Ich besuche meine **New Yorker** Freunde.	*I visit my New York friends.*

RECAPITULATION OF MAIN POINTS

1. After **der**-words, the adjective endings are **-en** in all cases except the following five:

		MASC.	FEM.	NEUTER
SING.:	NOM.	e	e	e
	ACC.		e	e

2. After **ein**-words, the adjective endings are **-en** in all cases except the following five:

		MASC.	FEM.	NEUTER
SING.:	NOM.	er	e	es
	ACC.		e	es

3. If the adjective is not preceded either by a **der**-word or an **ein**-word, its endings are identical with those of **dieser,** except in the genitive singular, masculine and neuter:

[1] In this meaning, the form **das Deutsch** is also used.

	MASC.	NEUTER
GEN. SING.:	**en**	**en**

4. Rule of thumb for adjective endings after **der-** and **ein-**words:

der gute Mann	**die** gute Frau	**das** gute Kind
ein guter Mann	**eine** gute Frau	**ein** gutes Kind

In all article-adjective-noun combinations which begin with any other article form, the ending is **-en.**

ÜBUNGEN

Practice in Reading and Writing

A. *Read aloud and translate:*

Eine kleine Geschichte

1. Ein Geisteskranker geht eines schönen Tages in dem großen Garten eines Krankenhauses spazieren. 2. Schließlich setzt er sich gemütlich an ein schönes rundes Blumenbeet. 3. In der einen Hand hat er eine lange Angel. 4. Während er in der warmen Sonne sitzt, hält er die Angel über das runde Blumenbeet. 5. Am offenen Fenster eines Zimmers sitzt der Direktor des Krankenhauses, ein freundlicher Mann, und wundert sich über das sonderbare Benehmen des armen Kranken. 6. Nach einer Weile kommt er heraus und tritt neben den Kranken. 7. Der Kranke aber „fischt" ruhig weiter. 8. „Ein schöner Tag heute, wie?", sagt er zu dem fischenden Mann. 9. Dieser aber antwortet gar nicht auf die freundlichen Worte. 10. Endlich fragt der Direktor: „Nun, guter Mann, wie viele haben Sie heute schon gefangen?" 11. „Sie sind der dritte", erklärt der Kranke.

1	**der Geisteskranke,** **–n**	*mental patient*	5	**sich wundern** **(über,** *w. acc.***)**	*to be surprised (at)*
	das Krankenhaus, **⸚er**	*hospital*		**sonderbar**	*strange*
2	**gemütlich**	*comfortable*		**das Benehmen**	*behavior*
	rund	*round*	7	**weiter** (as prefix)	*to go on (fishing,*
	das Beet, –e	*(flower) bed*			*etc.)*
3	**die Angel, –n**	*fishing rod*	8	**wie?**	*isn't it?*
4	**während** (conj.)	*while*	11	**dritte**	*third*

B. *Translate:*

1. ein dicker Mann 2. eine dicke Dame 3. ein offenes Hemd 4. Was für ein interessanter Mann! 5. die Söhne reicher Familien 6. die Gesund-

heit amerikanischer Kinder   7. das Leben eines berühmten Künstlers   8. Er
war das Kind armer Leute.   9. Das Neue ist selten (*seldom*) wahr, und das
Wahre ist selten neu.   10. Die alten Griechen (*Greeks*) idealisierten das
Gute, das Wahre und das Schöne.   11. Man ist zu jungen Damen immer
höflich (*polite*).   12. Er stellte eine wirklich dumme Frage.   13. Wir lesen
jeden Tag eine Berliner Zeitung (*newspaper*).   14. Kennen Sie das Heidel-
berger Schloß?   15. Schon wieder Wiener Würstchen?   16. August der
Starke war König von Sachsen (*Saxony*).   17. Es gibt viele Anekdoten über
August den Starken.   18. Das Leben Augusts des Starken war sicher sehr
amüsant.   19. „Morgen, morgen, nur nicht heute", sagen alle faulen (*lazy*)
Leute.   20. Faule (*rotten*) Äpfel sind ungesund.   21. Ein Bekannter meines
Onkels schreibt für eine New Yorker Zeitung.   22. Eine Bekannte von mir
raucht Zigarren!   23. die Vereinigten (*United*) Staaten von Amerika   24. das
Alte und das Neue Testament   25. Was wissen Sie von der deutschen
Grammatik?   26. die Grammatik des Deutschen   27. Die deutsche Gram-
matik ist nicht schwer.   28. Ich lese gerade Nietzsches *Jenseits von Gut und
Böse* (*evil*).   29. Nietzsche war einer der großen deutschen Philosophen.
30. Er war ein großer deutscher Philosoph.

C. *Identify the case endings of the attributive adjectives:*

1. eine kleine Nachtmusik   2. seine beiden Söhne   3. unser neues Haus
4. jede kleine Stadt   5. mit jedem hübschen Mädchen   6. mein junger
Freund   7. Sie hat immer das letzte Wort.   8. Er sucht ein modernes Haus.
9. der Autor eines bekannten Romans   10. Wir wohnen in einer kleinen
Stadt.   11. Till gab ihm sein grünes Tuch.   12. Ich mache gerne lange
Reisen.   13. die blauen Augen seiner kleinen Tochter   14. Was halten Sie
von diesem dicken Roman?   15. Er kommt ohne seine kleine Freundin.

D. *Translate:*

1. an old man   2. two old men   3. my little brother   4. a young lady   5. fat
people   6. The rooms in our new house are not very large.   7. Don't catch
cold by (**an**) the open window.   8. One sees many poor (people) in large
cities.   9. How do you like modern music?   10. What a strange question!
11. Old streets are usually narrow (**eng**), and the houses in old streets are
high.   12. Not everybody has a rich uncle in America!   13. There is something beautiful everywhere.   14. I find nothing interesting in his new book.
15. He received a high offer (**das Angebot**) for his old car.   16. He wrote a
long letter to his parents.   17. I like to have a good breakfast in my own
room.   18. German is not a difficult language.

Oral Exercises

E. *For the following exercises, review the rule-of-thumb for adjective endings:*

der gute Mann   die gute Frau   das gute Kind
ein guter Mann   eine gute Frau   ein gutes Kind

Change the following sentences:

EXAMPLES: Der Brief ist lang.   Das ist der lange Brief.
           Mein Brief ist lang.   Das ist mein langer Brief.

1. Die Illustration ist modern.
2. Seine Illustration ist modern.
3. Das Telegramm ist kurz.
4. Dein Telegramm ist kurz.
5. Der Roman ist originell.
6. Sein Roman ist originell.
7. Das Hemd ist blau.
8. Mein Hemd ist blau.
9. Die Reise ist weit.
10. Deine Reise ist weit.
11. Das Handwerk ist alt.
12. Ein Handwerk ist alt.
13. Der Ausflug ist schön.
14. Unser Ausflug ist schön.
15. Die Akademie ist berühmt.
16. Ihre Akademie ist berühmt.
17. Der Beweis ist gut.
18. Euer Beweis ist gut.

F. *Combine the sentences:*

EXAMPLES: Hier kommt der Freund der Studentin. Sie ist hübsch.
           Hier kommt der Freund der hübschen Studentin.

           Wir glauben dem Arzt. Er ist berühmt.
           Wir glauben dem berühmten Arzt.

1. Das ist das Buch des Schriftstellers. Er ist berühmt.
2. Sie kommt mit ihrem Onkel. Er ist lustig.
3. Das ist das Ende des Konzerts. Es ist modern.
4. Sie heiratet einen Kaufmann. Er ist reich.
5. Das ist das Telegramm unseres Gastgebers. Er ist ungeduldig.
6. Wir sprechen von seiner Rede. Sie ist interessant.
7. Das ist das Werk eines Schriftstellers. Er ist respektlos.
8. Du imitierst meinen Lehrer. Er ist originell.
9. Er ist der Autor dieses Buches. Es ist bekannt.
10. Sie spricht von ihrem Professor. Er ist alt.

G. *Combination drill. Continue in the same manner:*

1. Hier ist der Brief. Er ist lang.
2. Hier ist ein Brief. Er ist kurz.
3. Ich schreibe einen Brief. Er ist begeistert.
4. Ich gehe in ein Konzert. Es ist modern.
5. Du kennst das Konzert. Es ist berühmt.
6. Das ist ein Ausflug. Er ist schön.
7. Das ist unsere Akademie. Sie ist alt.
8. Ihr kennt diese Akademie. Sie ist berühmt.

 9. Er ist Mitglied einer Akademie. Sie ist bedeutend.
10. Sie kennen diesen Schriftsteller. Er ist jung.
11. Das ist ein Schriftsteller. Er ist beliebt.
12. Sie spricht von einem Schriftsteller. Er ist komisch.
13. Er ist der Autor dieses Buches. Es ist bekannt.
14. Hier ist sein Roman. Er ist originell.
15. Das ist ihre Arbeit. Sie ist gut.
16. Sie heiratet einen Professor. Er ist dick.
17. Sie wohnen in ihrem Haus. Es ist elegant.
18. Das ist ihr Haus. Es ist schön.

H. *Change the singular nouns to plural:*

EXAMPLES: Sie sehen hier die moderne Illustration.
           Sie sehen hier die modernen Illustrationen.

           Sie sehen hier eine moderne Illustration.
           Sie sehen hier moderne Illustrationen.

           Wir kennen die Bücher des bekannten Schriftstellers.
           Wir kennen die Bücher der bekannten Schriftsteller.

           Wir kennen die Bücher eines bekannten Schriftstellers.
           Wir kennen die Bücher bekannter Schriftsteller.

1. Du sprichst mit dem beliebten Professor. 2. Du sprichst mit einem
beliebten Professor. 3. Sie hat diese gute Übersetzung gemacht. 4. Sie hat
eine gute Übersetzung gemacht. 5. Ich habe die Romane dieses ausgezeichneten Autors gelesen. 6. Ich habe die Romane eines ausgezeichneten
Autors gelesen. 7. Sie haben das offizielle Dokument bekommen. 8. Alle
Mitglieder tragen ein blaues Hemd. 9. Sie nehmen an dem lauten Wahlkampf teil. 10. Wir machen eine weite Reise.

16

Comparison of Adjectives;

Adverbs

Franz Kafka[1]

Franz Kafka verbrachte fast die ganzen einundvierzig[2] Jahre seines Lebens in seiner Heimatstadt Prag. Damals war er noch ein ziemlich unbekannter Autor. Er las manchmal einigen Freunden aus seinen Manuskripten vor, aber er veröffentlichte wenig und nur kleinere Werke. Er verlangte sogar, daß man nach seinem Tod alle seine Manuskripte verbrannte.   5

Heute sehen wir in Kafka einen der größten Dichter unseres Jahrhunderts. Seine Romane, die längeren und die kürzeren Erzählungen, seine Tagebücher und sogar viele seiner zahllosen Briefe sind Kunstwerke höchsten Ranges.

Kafka war ein äußerst liebenswürdiger Mensch. Einmal traf er in einem 10 Park ein weinendes kleines Mädchen und fragte es freundlich: „Warum weinst du denn?"[3]

„Ich habe meine liebste Puppe verloren", antwortete das Mädchen unter fließenden Tränen. Kafka aber fand sofort den richtigen Trost: „Du hast deine Puppe gar nicht verloren", sagte er. „Sie macht nur gerade eine größere 15 Reise. Ich weiß das, denn ich habe eben einen Brief von ihr bekommen."

---

1. German novelist (1883–1924). 2. *forty-one*. 3. **denn**—in a question, for emphasis; here best rendered by beginning the question with: *but* . . .

„Hast du den Brief bei dir?" fragte das Kind.

„Nein", sagte Kafka, „ich habe ihn zu Hause gelassen, aber ich werde ihn dir morgen mitbringen." Kafka ging nach Hause und schrieb den Brief.
20 Und er schrieb in den folgenden Tagen noch mehrere Briefe im Namen der Puppe. Er arbeitete sie so genau und mit derselben Konzentration aus wie seine Erzählungen und Romane. Dann brachte er sie mit in den Park und las sie dem kleinen Mädchen vor, denn es ging noch nicht in die Schule. In den Briefen erzählte die Puppe, daß sie jetzt lieber eine Zeitlang woanders
25 lebte. Sie wurde nämlich rasch größer, sie hatte Wichtigeres zu tun, und zuletzt heiratete sie sogar. Das kleine Mädchen war über diese Briefe äußerst glücklich und vergaß seinen Schmerz.

Kafka hatte überhaupt viel Sinn für Humor. Natürlich waren ihm die Stunden des Schreibens die liebsten, aber er war auch ein sehr genauer
30 Beamter. Er arbeitete in einer Versicherungsgesellschaft. Nach einigen Jahren beförderte man ihn und zwei andere Kollegen in eine höhere Stellung mit besserer Bezahlung. Das verlangte aber einen Besuch der drei Angestellten beim Präsidenten der Gesellschaft. Einer der beiden Kollegen Kafkas hielt die Dankrede.[4] Der Präsident saß würdig an seinem Schreibtisch, mit seinem
35 weißen Bart und einem etwas dicken Bauch, fast würdiger noch als der Kaiser selbst. Kafka mußte[5] lachen, und er lachte immer mehr und immer heftiger, so daß der Besuch fast in einer Katastrophe endete. Die drei flohen zuletzt aus dem Zimmer.

Am lustigsten war Kafka in der Gesellschaft seiner Freunde. Er reiste gern
40 mit ihnen, aber sie hatten nie genug Urlaub und noch weniger Geld. Dadurch bekam Kafka die Idee für eine neue Art von Reiseführern[6] mit dem Titel „Billig durch die Schweiz" oder „Billig in Paris". Er machte aus dem Adjektiv einen Mann und für diesen Mann die verschiedensten Pläne. Mit „Billig" brauchte der Reisende weniger Zeit und Geld, er hatte mit ihm überhaupt
45 nicht die geringsten Probleme, denn „Billig" wußte alles: er kannte das beste Hotel zum niedrigsten Preis, das einfachste Transportmittel,[7] er wußte, wo man das kleinste Trinkgeld gab und am leichtesten Freikarten[8] für das Theater bekam. „Billig" gab sogar Sprachunterricht, und er gab ihn nach folgendem Prinzip: es ist unmöglich, eine fremde Sprache richtig zu lernen,
50 daher lehren wir sie lieber gleich falsch.

Leider fand sich[9] für diesen „Billig" kein Verleger.

---

4. **hielt die Dankrede** *made the speech of appreciation* (lit. *thanks*). 5. **mußte** *had to*.
6. **Reiseführer** *travel guide*. 7. **Transportmittel** *means of transportation*. 8. **Freikarten** *free tickets*. 9. **fand sich** *could be found*.

FRAGEN

1. Wo verbrachte Franz Kafka fast sein ganzes Leben? 2. Was tat er manchmal? 3. Was veröffentlichte er während seines Lebens? 4. Was verlangte er kurz vor seinem Tode? 5. Was sind seine Romane? 6. Sind nur seine Romane Kunstwerke höchsten Ranges? 7. Wen traf er einmal in einem Park? 8. Was fragte er das kleine Mädchen? 9. Was antwortete die Kleine? 10. Welchen Trost fand Kafka für sie? 11. Warum wußte er das? 12. Hatte er den Brief bei sich? 13. Was sagte er zu dem kleinen Mädchen? 14. Was tat er an den folgenden Tagen? 15. Wie arbeitete er diese Briefe aus? 16. Was tat er mit diesen Briefen? 17. Warum las das Mädchen die Briefe nicht selbst? 18. Was erzählte die Puppe in den Briefen? 19. Wie reagierte das Mädchen auf die Briefe? 20. War Kafka nur ein genauer Schriftsteller? 21. Was tat man nach einigen Jahren? 22. Was mußten die drei Kollegen tun? 23. Beschreiben Sie den Präsidenten. 24. Was tat Kafka? 25. Was tat er gern mit seinen Freunden? 26. Warum bekam Kafka die Idee für eine neue Art von Reiseführern? 27. Wie war die Idee dieser Reiseführer? 28. Was wußte Billig alles? 29. Nach welchem Prinzip gab Billig Sprachunterricht? 30. Warum können wir diese Reiseführer heute nicht kaufen?

WORTSCHATZ

der **Angestellte, –n,** **–n** ein **Angestellter**	employee	**hoch** der **Kaiser, –** **klug**	high emperor clever
die **Art, –en** **äußerst**	kind, manner extremely	**lehren** (cf. der **Lehrer**)	to teach
der **Bart, ⸗e**	beard	**liebenswürdig**	charming
der **Bauch, ⸗e**	stomach, belly	**lieber**	rather
der **Beamte, –n, –n** ein **Beamter**	official, civil servant	**lieber sein** (w. dat.)	to prefer
befördern	to promote	**mit /bringen** (irr. wk.)	to bring along
die **Bezahlung, –en**	pay(ment)	**niedrig**	low
billig	cheap	**noch nicht**	not yet
die **Erzählung, –en**	story, tale	**rasch**	quick(ly)
falsch	("false"), wrong, in- correct	der **Schmerz, –ens, –en**	pain, sorrow
fremd	foreign, strange	der **Schreibtisch, –e**	desk
geringst-	least	der **Sinn, –e (für)**	sense (of)
gleich	right away; even(ly); same; presently	der **Sprachunterricht** die **Stellung, –en**	language instruction position
heftig	violent	das **Tagebuch, ⸗er**	diary

die **Träne, –n**	tear	die **Versicherung,**	insurance
das **Trinkgeld, –er**	tip	**–en**	
der **Trost**	comfort	**wichtig**	important
überhaupt nicht	not at all	**woanders**	somewhere else
der **Urlaub**	leave, furlough	**würdig**	worthy, dignified
der **Verleger, –**	publisher	**eine Zeitlang**	for a while

STRONG VERBS

erscheinen	to appear	**erschien**	**ist erschienen**
fliehen	to flee	**floh**	**ist geflohen**
fließen	to flow	**floß**	**ist geflossen**

DISTINGUISH BETWEEN

die Art *kind, manner* and **die Kunst** *art*
in die Schule *to school* and **in der Schule** *in school*
in die Kirche *to church* and **in der Kirche** *in church*

GRAMMATICAL TERMS

1. An adjective may be in the *positive, comparative,* or *superlative* degree:

POSITIVE: *good* food
COMPARATIVE: *better* food
SUPERLATIVE: *best* food

2. Adverbs are words which modify and qualify a verb, an adjective, or another adverb: He drives *fast*. It is *very* good. He writes *extremely* well.

COMPARISON OF ADJECTIVES

1. Comparative
  a. To form the comparative of an adjective, add **-er** to the positive degree:

POSITIVE: **reich**   COMPARATIVE: **reicher**

Never form a German comparative by using a construction with **mehr** (*more*).

  b. If the adjective is attributive, the proper case ending is added to the comparative form:

POSITIVE	COMPARATIVE
der reiche Mann	der reichere Mann
ein reicher Mann	ein reicherer Mann

c. **So . . . wie** (*as . . . as*) is used with adjectives in the positive degree, **als** (*than*) after comparatives:

POSITIVE: Er ist **so alt wie** ich. *He is as old as I* (*am*).
COMPARATIVE: Er ist **älter als** ich. *He is older than I.*

d. English "the . . . the," connecting two comparatives, is **je . . . desto** or **je . . . umso; je** precedes the first comparative, **desto** (or **umso**) the second:

Je mehr desto besser. *The more the better.*

If **je . . . desto** (or **umso**) connects two clauses, the **je** clause has the finite verb at the end (dependent word order), the **desto** (or **umso**) clause requires inversion:

Je mehr ich diesen Dichter **lese, umso besser verstehe ich** ihn.
The more I read this poet, the better I understand him.

e. **Immer** (lit., *always, ever*) directly preceding a comparative is best rendered by repeating the comparative in English:

immer besser   *better and better*

f. Comparatives are also used to express the idea of "rather" when no real comparison is made; they are then mostly used with the indefinite article:

ein **älterer** Herr   *a rather old* (*elderly*) *gentleman*
eine **längere** Zeit   (*for*) *a rather long* (*for quite some*) *time.*

2. Superlative

a. To form the superlative of an attributive adjective, add **-st** to the positive and then the proper adjective ending:[1]

reich: der reich**ste** Mann
schön: sein schön**stes** Buch

If the adjective in the positive ends in **d,**[2] **t, s, sch, ß, z,** or **tz,** add **-est** to the positive and then the adjective ending:

laut: die laut**este** Stimme   *the loudest voice*
heiß: der heiß**este** Sommer   *the hottest summer*

---

[1] After the indefinite article **ein,** the superlative is frequently formed with **höchst** (lit., *most highly*), since no specific comparison is made:

eine **höchst amüsante** Geschichte   *a highly* (*or most*) *amusing story.*

[2] This does not apply to present participles used as adjectives:

der spannend**ste** Roman   *the most exciting novel*

Make sure that the superlative has the required adjective ending, whether it is in attributive or predicate position; in the predicate, the superlative adjective is treated as a pronoun—the ending must agree with the noun, which is not expressed but understood:

ATTRIBUTE: Dies ist sein **schönstes** Buch.
PREDICATE: Dies Buch ist sein **schönstes** (Buch).

b. If a superlative in the predicate is used in a general sense (as in: It is *best* not to spend any money.), an invariable form consisting of the positive plus the ending **-sten** is used, preceded by **am**; in such a construction, English usually employs a superlative without article:

In diesem Laden sind die Lebensmittel **am billigsten.**
In this shop the groceries are cheapest.
Im Sommer ist es in den Bergen **am schönsten.**
In summer it is most beautiful in the mountains.

This **am . . . sten** form can never be used attributively.

3. Irregularities in the Comparison of Adjectives

   a. Adjectives ending in **-e** drop this **-e** before adding comparative endings:

leise	*soft*	leiser
böse	*bad; angry*	böser

   b. Some monosyllabic adjectives of common occurrence take the Umlaut in the comparative and superlative:

arm	*poor*	**ärmer**	der (die, das) **ärmste**
alt	*old*	**älter**	der (die, das) **älteste**

   To this group belong:

dumm[1]	*stupid*		**lang**	*long*
hart	*hard*		**rot**[1]	*red*
jung	*young*		**scharf**	*sharp*
kalt	*cold*		**schwach**	*weak*
klug	*clever*		**schwarz**	*black*
krank[1]	*sick, ill*		**stark**	*strong*
kurz	*short*		**warm**	*warm*

   c. The following adjectives are irregular in comparison:

groß	*big, tall*	**größer**	der (die, das) **größte**
gut	*good*	**besser**	der (die, das) **beste**

[1] Some monosyllabic adjectives (like **dumm, krank, rot**) may be used with or without Umlaut in the comparative and superlative: **roter** or **röter.**

hoch	*high*	**höher**	der (die, das) **höchste**
nah(e)	*near*	**näher**	der (die, das) **nächste**
viel[1]	*much*	**mehr**[1]	der (die, das) **meiste**[2]

ADVERBS

1. In German, adverbs ordinarily have no endings and are therefore indistinguishable in form from uninflected adjectives:

ADJECTIVE: Sie ist **schön.** *She is beautiful.*
ADVERB: Sie singt **schön.** *She sings beautifully.*

2. The suffix **-weise** (lit., *in a manner*), preceded by **-er-,** is added to many adjectives to form common adverbs:[3]

glücklicherweise *fortunately*
dummerweise *stupidly enough*

3. To form the comparative of an adverb, add **-er** to the positive degree; for the superlative, use the **am . . . sten** form:

POSITIVE: Ich fahre **schnell.** *I drive fast.*
COMPARATIVE: Du fährst **schneller.** *You drive faster.*
SUPERLATIVE: Er fährt **am schnellsten.** *He drives fastest.*[4]

4. The comparison of the common adverb **gern(e)** (lit., *gladly*) is irregular; **gern** (or **gerne**) is used in conjunction with verbs to express the idea of "to like to":

gern(e)   **lieber**   **am liebsten**

The following examples show how these forms compare with English:

Ich trinke gern(e) Wasser.   *I like to drink water.*
Ich trinke lieber Milch.   *I prefer to drink milk.*
Am liebsten trinke ich Kaffee.   *Best of all I like to drink coffee.*

---

[1] **Viel** (singular) and **mehr** (singular and plural) do not use declensional endings: Ich habe nicht **viel** Geld; Hast du **mehr** Geld? Wer hat heute **viel** Zeit?
[2] Note also the construction: **die meisten** (*most of*): **die meisten Kinder** *most (of the) children.*
[3] Note also the adverbial phrase **auf . . . Art und Weise** or **auf . . . Weise** (*in a . . . manner*): Er hat **auf anständige (Art und) Weise** gehandelt. *He acted in a decent manner.*
[4] The English adverbial phrase *in a most . . . manner* is equivalent to the construction **aufs . . . -ste:** Er weigerte sich **aufs heftigste.** *He refused in a most violent manner.*

RECAPITULATION OF MAIN POINTS

1. The comparative is formed by adding **-er** to the adjective in the positive degree. The inflectional endings for the comparative are the same as for the positive: der reich**e** Mann; ein reicher**er** Mann.

2. The superlative is formed by adding **-st** (or **-est**) to the adjective in the positive degree; the regular inflectional endings of the adjectives are then added: die dümm**ste** Antwort. If the superlative is used in a general sense and stands in the predicate, the **am . . . -sten** form is used: Die Lebensmittel sind hier **am billigsten.** *The groceries are cheapest here.*

3. In the positive and comparative, adverbs have the same forms as uninflected adjectives; in the superlative, the form is always **am . . . -sten.**

ÜBUNGEN

Practice in Reading and Writing

A. *Read aloud and translate:*

Der Nachtbesuch

1. In einer kleinen Stadt lebte einmal ein sehr tüchtiger Arzt. 2. Eines Nachts—das Städtchen lag schon in tiefstem Schlaf—klingelte es bei ihm. 3. Es klingelte einmal, es klingelte zweimal, es klingelte dreimal, und jedesmal klingelte es etwas lauter und etwas länger. 4. Schließlich erschien der Kopf des Arztes im obersten Fenster des Hauses. 5. „Was gibt's?" fragte er mit sehr verschlafener Stimme. 6. „Wieviel nehmen Sie für einen Besuch nicht weiter als zehn Kilometer von hier?" fragte die Stimme von unten zurück. 7. „Zu so später Stunde—zehn Mark", war die Antwort des Arztes. 8. „Nicht mehr und nicht weniger." 9. „Gut", meinte der Mann auf der Straße— höchst erfreut, wie es schien. 10. „Am besten, wir fahren sofort. Es ist höchste Zeit." 11. Der Arzt erschien nach einer Weile in der Haustür, sie stiegen zusammen in seinen Wagen, und bald fuhren sie mit höchster Geschwindigkeit durchs Land. 12. Nach weniger als zehn Minuten sagte der Mann zu dem Arzt: „So, da sind wir." 13. Dann gab er ihm zehn Mark und erklärte: „Den Kilometer für eine Mark; billiger geht es kaum." 14. „Nur der Tod selbst ist noch billiger", antwortete der Arzt lachend. 15. „Billiger kaum", meinte der Mann, „aber nur der Tod fährt noch schneller als Sie." Und auch er lachte laut. 16. Wer zuletzt lacht, lacht am besten, dachte er dabei. 17. „Und wo ist nun unser armer Patient?" fragte endlich der Arzt. „Wir lachen hier und der Ärmste muß warten." 18. „Entschuldigen Sie,

Herr Doktor", sagte der Mann darauf, „einen Patienten gibt es hier glücklicherweise nicht. 19. Wir haben hier sogar mehr Ärzte als Kranke. 20. Aber das Taxi in der Stadt verlangte zwanzig Mark für die Fahrt, und so fuhr ich lieber mit Ihnen." (Adapted from *Das Buch des Lachens*, by Wilhelm Scholz.)

1	**tüchtig**	*capable*	6	**unten**	*below*
2	**der Schlaf**	*sleep*	11	**die Geschwindig-**	*speed*
4	**oberst** (from **oben**	*uppermost*		**keit, –en**	
	upstairs)		13	**es geht kaum**	*it can hardly be done*
5	**verschlafen**	*sleepy*	20	**die Fahrt, –en**	*trip*
	die Stimme, –n	*voice*			

B. *Translate and give the positive adjective forms from which the following comparatives and superlatives are derived:*

1. Es wird immer kälter. 2. Lieber heute als morgen. 3. Am besten spielt er Hamlet. 4. Am liebsten glauben wir den Leuten, die uns sagen, was wir gerne hören. 5. Die neuesten Nachrichten (*news*). 6. Von allen Komponisten war er der produktivste. 7. Am glücklichsten war er auf der Universität (note the expression: auf der Universität). 8. Wenn die Not (*need*) am größten, ist Gottes Hilfe (*help*) am nächsten. 9. Der Nächste, bitte! 10. Die meisten Leute wissen das. 11. Dummerweise erinnere ich mich nicht daran. 12. Sagen Sie das noch einmal, aber einfacher. 13. Dieser Winter ist der kälteste. 14. Dieser Winter ist am kältesten. 15. Dies ist der kälteste Winter, an den sich die ältesten Leute im Dorf erinnern können. 16. Der Held des Romans ist ein kleiner Mann aus dem Volk. 17. Ein kleinerer Schreibtisch ist mir lieber. 18. Ich werde möglicherweise morgen zu Ihnen kommen. 19. Er versteht das so gut wie jeder andere und manches sogar noch besser. 20. Er ist besser als die meisten Schriftsteller.

C. *Is the adjective in the following sentences positive or comparative?*

1. Was für ein kleiner Mann! 2. ein moderner Mensch 3. ein reicher Kaufmann 4. mit lauterer Stimme 5. die Kinder armer Eltern 6. das Urteil (*judgment*) weiserer Männer 7. ein warmer Tag 8. Wer von ihnen ist intelligenter? 9. Das ist wirklich ein intelligenter Mann! 10. Der alte König war immer noch sehr tapfer (*brave*). 11. Wer war tapferer als er? 12. Das Leben wird immer teurer. 13. Ein teurer Wagen! 14. Dies Messer (*knife*) ist schärfer. 15. ein scharfer Hund.

D. *Adverb or adjective?*

1. Sie wird immer *dicker*. 2. Am *liebsten* ist mir jetzt ein Glas Wasser. 3. Dieser Weg ist am *kürzesten*. 4. Das haben Sie sehr *dumm* gemacht. 5. Sie singt wirklich sehr *schön*. 6. Bleibe, wie du heute bist, der Himmel dir dann *sicher* ist. 7. Sie sagte das sehr *laut*. 8. Ihre Stimme war sehr *laut*. 9. Er sprach sehr *klug* (*clever*). 10. Er handelte (*acted*) auf eine sehr *kluge* Weise.

E. *Translate:*

1. Berlin is the largest city in Germany.   2. He was extremely popular with **(bei)** the farmers.   3. It is getting warmer and warmer.   4. He always falls in love with younger girls.   5. He is as old as I but much stronger.   6. Life in Germany is cheapest.   7. The more they demand, the more expensive it gets.   8. Women live longer than men; they work less.   9. Life is simpler in **(auf)** the country, but it is more interesting in the city. 10. Most people marry only once.   11. He did that in the most polite manner.   12. The more intelligent, the better.   13. Do you like to read such stories or do you prefer others? 14. Most people like best to have large rooms.   15. I think **(glauben)** he expects a larger tip.   16. She is the prettiest, nicest, and also the most intelligent girl here.   17. You did that very well, better than the best candidate for the position.   18. Most people have only one car, but after the next election they will have two in every garage.   19. That is the highest mountain in our region; you find higher ones only in the Alps **(die Alpen).** 20. The best is good enough for me.

Oral Exercises

F. *Change the adjective (a) to comparative, (b) to superlative:*

EXAMPLES: Er findet ein billiges Hotel. (a) Aber ich . . . .
                                                  Aber ich finde ein billigeres Hotel
                                                        als er.
                                              (b) Und Oskar . . . .
                                                  Oskar findet das billigste Hotel.

1. Er hat heftige Schmerzen. Aber ich . . . .
                        Und der Pessimist . . . .
2. Wir fahren ein schnelles Auto. Aber ihr . . . .
                        Und der Student . . . .
3. Sie steigt auf einen hohen Berg. Aber ich . . . .
                        Und der Junge . . . .
4. Ich lese ein wichtiges Dokument. Aber du . . . .
                        Und der Spion . . . .
5. Er ist ein liebenswürdiger Mensch. Aber du . . . .
                        Und der Kritiker . . . .
6. Ihr wohnt in einem alten Haus. Aber wir . . . .
                        Und der Schriftsteller . . . .
7. Sie bekommt viel Geld. Aber er . . . .
                        Und die Blumenkinder . . . .
8. Du hast einen großen Schreibtisch. Aber ich . . . .
                        Und der Präsident . . . .

9. Wir bekommen eine gute Bezahlung. Aber ihr . . . .

               Und der Wissenschaftler . . . .

10. Er besitzt einen teuren Ring. Aber ich . . . .

             Und die vornehme Dame . . . .

G. *Change the following adverbs and predicate adjectives* (*a*) *to comparative,* (*b*) *to superlative:*

EXAMPLE: Er reist viel. Aber ich . . . .

        Ich reise mehr als er.

        Und die Sekretärin . . . .

        Die Sekretärin reist am meisten.

1. Das Mädchen lacht laut. Aber er . . . .

         Und die Großmutter . . . .

2. Die Studenten sprechen gut deutsch. Aber ihr . . . .

           Und der Professor . . . .

3. Sie wohnt nah. Aber wir . . . .

       Und der Angestellte . . . .

4. Er liest gern. Aber Oskar . . . .

       Und der Kritiker . . . .

5. Er ist schlau. Aber der Spion . . . .

       Und der Mörder . . . .

6. Dieser Herr ist vornehm. Aber diese Dame . . . .

         Und der polnische Kritiker . . . .

7. Er verlangt viel. Aber der Arzt . . . .

        Und der Psychoanalytiker . . . .

8. Der Roman ist interessant. Aber das Drama . . . .

        Und die Oper . . . .

9. Er ist klug. Aber die Studentin . . . .

       Und der Angestellte . . . .

10. Diese Leute sind arm. Aber wir . . . .

        Und Oskar . . . .

Review 3

Lessons 12 through 16

1. <u>Sein</u> as Auxiliary Verb for Perfect Tenses

A. Most verbs use **haben** as the auxiliary for the perfect tenses. Those verbs using **sein** are generally intransitive verbs denoting a change of position or condition and the verbs **sein, werden,** and **bleiben.**

B. Forms of **sein** used in perfect tenses are translated by forms of *to have.*

C. Translate. Watch the use of **haben** and **sein** in the perfect-tense forms:

1. Ich habe die Erfahrung gemacht. 2. Er ist in Rom gestorben. 3. Hast du das Geräusch gehört? 4. Sie sind in seiner Vorlesung eingeschlafen. 5. Was hatte Lichtenberg bewiesen? 6. Wann sind Sie gekommen? 7. Wie lange ist er hier geblieben? 8. Ich habe keine Zeit gehabt.

2. Inseparable and Separable Prefixes

A. Most inseparable prefixes are mere syllables. They never separate from the verb, but it is not always possible to anticipate how they will change the meaning of the root verb.

B. Separable prefixes are words in their own right. Sometimes it is possible to tell how they change the meaning of a root verb, sometimes not. In case of doubt, consult a dictionary or vocabulary and remember to look up the verb under the prefix.

C. Translate and give the infinitives:

1. Wie hat Else Lasker-Schüler ihre letzten Jahre verlebt?   2. Sie besaß nicht viel Geld.   3. Zuckmayers Stück war durchgefallen.   4. Eine Freundin redete sie an.   5. Wo hat sich das abgespielt?   6. Daran erinnere ich mich nicht.   7. Was bedeutet dieses Wort?   8. Wem hat das Buch einmal gehört?   9. Haben Sie ihn gehört?   10. Lesen Sie mir das bitte laut vor!

3. Irregular Weak Verbs

A. Irregular weak verbs change their stem vowel from **e** to **a** in the past and past participle; otherwise they are conjugated like weak verbs, except **bringen, denken,** and **wissen.**

B. The present tense of **wissen** is irregular: **ich weiß, du weißt, er weiß.**

C. Kennen means *to know* in the sense of "to be acquainted with": **Sie kennt ihn. Wissen** is *to know a fact*. **Wissen** is always used when a dependent clause follows: **Ich weiß, daß er kommt.**

D. Translate and give the infinitives:

1. Was hat er ihr mitgebracht?   2. Kannten Sie dies Gedicht?   3. Wußten Sie, daß es von Heine ist?   4. Wußten Sie, wer es geschrieben hat?   5. Kennen Sie den Herrn?   6. Er hat mir seinen Namen genannt, aber ich habe ihn nicht gekannt.   7. Sie haben viele Leute umgebracht.   8. Hast du das Buch zurückgebracht?   9. Ich habe nicht gewußt, daß Sie den Mann gekannt haben.   10. Daran habe ich nicht gedacht.   11. Er hat sich den Finger verbrannt.   12. Er wandte sich um.

4. Adjectives

A. Remember the line: **der gute Mann, die gute Frau, das gute Kind.** These are the cases in which the adjective has the ending **-e** when it is preceded by a **der**-word; in all others, the ending is **-en.**

B. Remember the line: **ein guter Mann, eine gute Frau, ein gutes Kind:** these are the cases in which the adjective ending is NOT **-en** when the adjective follows an **ein**-word.

C. Do not confuse the ending **-er** of an adjective which follows an **ein**-word with the comparative ending **-er:** ein **junger** Mann; er ist **jünger** als sie.

D. Immer with a comparative is best rendered in English by repeating the comparative: **immer besser** *better and better;* **immer schöner** *more and more beautiful.*

E. Am . . . sten is the superlative for predicate adjectives and adverbs:

Das ist **am interessantesten.**
That is most interesting.

Sie singt **am schönsten.**
She sings most beautifully.

F. Translate and explain the adjective endings:

1. Sein alter Bruder. 2. Sein älterer Bruder. 3. Mein lieber Sohn. 4. Ich esse lieber Wurst. 5. Eine anstrengende Gesellschaft. 6. Eine anstrengendere Gesellschaft. 7. Das Bild einer jungen Frau. 8. Das Bild einer jüngeren Frau. 9. Die Bilder jüngerer Frauen. 10. Ein gut geschriebener Brief. 11. Lesen Sie bitte diesen gut geschriebenen Brief. 12. Haben Sie viele so gut geschriebene Briefe? 13. Es wird immer besser.

17

Modal Auxiliaries

Georg Friedrich Händel[1]

Die deutsche Musik ist weltberühmt. In beinahe jedem Konzert kann man Werke von Bach, Beethoven, Brahms, Mozart, Haydn, Schubert, Strauß, Wagner oder anderen großen Komponisten hören. Wagner war lange einer der beliebtesten unter ihnen, besonders bei der Jugend. Viele aber mögen Wagner nicht, und man kann sicher sagen, daß Wagners Musik noch heute 5 eine Sache des persönlichen Geschmacks ist. Dagegen dürfte[2] es nur wenige Menschen geben, die wirklich kein Ohr für Mozart oder Haydn haben. Auch Händel, den[3] man allerdings zur englischen Musikgeschichte rechnen kann, war Deutscher. Er war in Halle[4] geboren, ist aber schon als junger Mann nach London gegangen, wo er in hohem Alter gestorben ist und in der 10 Westminster Abbey begraben liegt. Trotzdem hat er nie gut Englisch gekonnt, und wenn er wütend wurde, soll er in vier oder fünf Sprachen geschimpft haben.

Wir dürfen uns mit Recht über die Energie wundern, mit der[5] einige der großen Meister der Musik gearbeitet haben. Händel vermochte, sein großes 15 Oratorium „Messias" in ungefähr drei Wochen zu beenden. Er hat es zum

1. 1685–1759. 2. **es dürfte . . . geben** *there probably are.* 3. **den** *whom.* 4. **Halle** city near Leipzig, in East Germany. 5. **mit der** *with which.*

ersten Mal in Dublin aufführen lassen, und zwar als Wohltätigkeitskonzert[6]
für Krankenhäuser und Gefängnisse. Wie groß das Interesse an diesem
Konzert war, läßt sich daran erkennen, daß die Damen an diesem Abend
20 keine Reifröcke[7] tragen durften, denn so viele Leute wie möglich sollten
Platz finden können.

Später führte man den „Messias" auch in London auf, wo König Georg II.
(der Zweite) beim Halleluja-Chor aufgestanden sein soll. Seitdem pflegt man
während dieses Chores zu stehen.

25 Händel war eine sehr imposante Figur. Er konnte sehr liebenswürdig sein,
ließ sich aber auch leicht aufbringen. Er soll einmal so wütend geworden
sein, daß er eine Pauke[8] ergriff und sie nach dem Dirigenten warf. Ein
anderes Mal mochte eine italienische Sängerin eine Arie nicht, die[9] Händel
für sie geschrieben hatte. Da rief er ihr zu: „Madame, ich weiß, daß Sie
30 ein Teufel sind, aber ich bin Beelzebub, der Herr der Teufel", und wollte
sie aus dem Fenster werfen. Andere Zeiten, andere Sitten! Ein englischer
Sänger wollte sich Händels Behandlung nicht gefallen lassen und drohte, auf
das Klavier zu springen. „Tun Sie das", erklärte Händel, „ich kann es
dann in allen Zeitungen bekanntmachen lassen. Sicher kommen mehr Leute,
35 Sie springen zu sehen als singen zu hören."

Trotzdem war Händel sehr beliebt und ein großer Künstler. Beethoven
soll ihn sogar für den größten Musiker aller Zeiten gehalten haben. Wir
fragen uns freilich: was will ein so extravagantes Urteil wirklich besagen?
Wahrscheinlich nicht mehr als: ich mag Händel.

6. **Wohltätigkeitskonzert** *benefit concert.*   7. **Reifröcke** *crinolines.*   8. **Pauke** *drum.*   9. **die**
which.

FRAGEN

1. Wo kann man Werke deutscher Komponisten hören?   2. Können Sie
einige der großen deutschen Komponisten nennen?   3. Was hat Händel
komponiert?   4. Bei wem war Wagner lange besonders beliebt?   5. Was ist
Wagners Musik noch heute?   6. Wo ist Händel geboren und wo ist er
gestorben?   7. Wo liegt er begraben?   8. Was soll Händel getan haben, wenn
er wütend war?   9. Worüber dürfen wir uns wundern?   10. Wann hat
Händel den „Messias" beendet?   11. Als was hat er den „Messias" zum
ersten Mal aufführen lassen?   12. Woran läßt sich erkennen, wie groß das
Interesse an diesem Konzert war?   13. Warum durften die Damen an diesem
Abend keine Reifröcke tragen?   14. Was soll König Georg bei der Aufführung des „Messias" in London getan haben?   15. Was hat Händel einmal

getan, als er sehr wütend wurde?   16. Was rief er der italienischen Sängerin zu?   17. Was drohte der Sänger zu tun?   18. Was antwortete Händel? 19. Wofür soll Beethoven Händel gehalten haben?   20. Was wollte Beethoven damit vielleicht nur sagen?

WORTSCHATZ

auf/bringen (brachte auf, aufgebracht) (irr. wk.)	to excite, upset	**(es) läßt sich, ließ sich, etc., (impers.)**	(it) can be, could be
auf/führen	to perform	das **Mal, –e**	time (enumerative)
beenden (used only w. object)	to finish (something)	**zum ersten Mal**	for the first time
die **Behandlung, –en**	treatment	das **Ohr, –en**	ear
beinahe	almost	**pflegen (zu)**	to be accustomed (used) to
bekannt/machen	to announce	**schimpfen**	to scold; to rail
besagen	to mean, signify	die **Sitte, –n**	custom
der **Dirigent, –en, –en**	conductor	der **Teufel, –**	devil
drohen	to threaten	**trotzdem**	nevertheless
erkennen (irr. wk.) (**an**, w. dat.)	to recognize (from)	**ungefähr**	approximately
		das **Urteil, –e**	judgment
freilich	to be sure, however	**vermögen (vermag, vermochte, vermocht)**	to be able to
sich gefallen lassen (ä, ie, a)	to put up with		
das **Gefängnis, –se**	prison	**sich wundern (über)**	to marvel (at)
imposant	impressive	**wütend**	furious, angry
das **Klavier, –e**	piano	die **Zeitung, –en**	newspaper
das **Krankenhaus, ⸗er**	hospital	**zwar**	to be specific; to be sure

STRONG VERBS

auf/stehen	to get up, rise		**stand auf**	ist **aufgestanden**
begraben	to bury	**begräbt**	**begrub**	**begraben**
heben	to lift, pick up		**hob**	**gehoben**
leihen	to lend		**lieh**	**geliehen**

MODAL AUXILIARIES

dürfen	to be permitted to	**darf**	**durfte**	**gedurft**
können	to be able to	**kann**	**konnte**	**gekonnt**
mögen	to like to	**mag**	**mochte**	**gemocht**
müssen	to have to	**muß**	**mußte**	**gemußt**
sollen	to be obliged to	**soll**	**sollte**	**gesollt**
wollen	to want to	**will**	**wollte**	**gewollt**

DISTINGUISH BETWEEN

das Mal and **die Zeit** *time:* **das Mal** is *time* only in the enumerative sense (**einmal** *once,* **zwei Mal** *twice,* etc.); **Zeit** is *time* measured by the clock.

GRAMMATICAL TERMS

1. *Mood* is the attribute of a verb which shows the speaker's attitude or feeling towards what he is saying.

2. *Modal auxiliaries* are verbs which express certain of these attitudes or feelings: obligation, ability, desire, permission: I *may* go, but I *cannot;* yet I *must.*

3. Modal auxiliaries in English are called "defective" because they exist in certain tense forms only (*may, might; can, could; must;* etc.). Infinitives and other tense forms are obtained by means of verbal phrases: I was permitted to, I will be able to, I was obliged to, etc.

MODAL AUXILIARIES IN GERMAN

1. There are six modal auxiliaries in German. Unlike the few "defective" English modals, German modals can be fully conjugated in all tenses. Except for the singular of the present tense, they are conjugated like weak verbs. The auxiliary for the perfect tenses is **haben.**

The six modal auxiliaries and their basic meanings are:

dürfen	*to be permitted (allowed) to*	**durfte**	**gedurft**
können	*to be able to*	**konnte**	**gekonnt**
mögen	*to like to*	**mochte**[1]	**gemocht**[1]
müssen	*to have to*	**mußte**	**gemußt**
sollen	*to be (supposed, obliged) to*	**sollte**	**gesollt**
wollen	*to want to*	**wollte**	**gewollt**

In the infinitive all modal auxiliaries have Umlaut except **sollen** and **wollen;** this Umlaut is dropped in the past and past participle.

2. The present tense of modal auxiliaries is irregular in the singular:

ich **darf**	ich **kann**	ich **mag**	ich **muß**[2]	ich **soll**	ich **will**
(*I may*)	(*I can*)	(*I like*)	(*I must*)	(*I am to*)	(*I want to*)

[1] Note the stem change in these forms.
[2] Be careful to distinguish between **ich muß** (*I must*) and **ich mußte** (*I had to*).

| du **darfst** | du **kannst** | du **magst** | du **mußt** | du **sollst** | du **willst** |
| er **darf** | er **kann** | er **mag** | er **muß** | er **soll** | er **will** |

but regular in the plural:

wir **dürfen**	wir **können**	wir **mögen**	wir **müssen**	wir **sollen**	wir **wollen**
ihr **dürft**	ihr **könnt**	ihr **mögt**	ihr **müßt**	ihr **sollt**	ihr **wollt**
sie **dürfen**	sie **können**	sie **mögen**	sie **müssen**	sie **sollen**	sie **wollen**

3. Modal Auxiliaries Without Dependent Infinitives

In contrast to English, German modal auxiliaries can be used without a dependent infinitive in expressions in which the dependent infinitive is understood.

Compare the following most frequent tense forms of the German modal auxiliaries (used without a dependent infinitive) with the English:

ich **darf** das.	*I am permitted (allowed) to do that; I may do that.*
ich **durfte das.**	*I was permitted (allowed) to do that.*
ich **habe das gedurft.**	*I was (have been) permitted (allowed) to do that.*
ich **werde das dürfen.**	*I will be permitted (allowed) to do that.*
ich **kann das nicht.**	*I am not able to (cannot) do that.*
ich **konnte das nicht.**	*I was not able to (could not) do that.*
ich **habe das nicht gekonnt.**	*I was not (have not been) able to do that.*
ich **werde das nicht können.**	*I shall not be able to do that.*
ich **mag sie sehr.**	*I like her very much.*
ich **mochte sie sehr.**	*I liked her very much.*
ich **habe sie sehr gemocht.**	*I (have) liked her very much.*
ich **muß nach Hause.**	*I have to (must) go home.*
ich **mußte nach Hause.**	*I had to go home.*
ich **habe nach Hause gemußt.**	*I (have) had to go home.*
ich **werde nach Hause müssen.**	*I shall have to go home.*
ich **soll in die Schule.**	*I am (supposed, obliged) to go to school.*
ich **sollte in die Schule.**	*I should, ought to, was (supposed, obliged) to go to school.*
ich **will in die Stadt.**	*I want to go to town.*
ich **wollte in die Stadt.**	*I wanted to (never: would!) go to town.*
ich **habe in die Stadt gewollt.**	*I (have) wanted to go to town.*

4. Modal Auxiliaries with Infinitives

Dependent infinitives used after a modal auxiliary are not preceded by

zu.[1] Compare the English verbs in verbal phrases which perform the function of the German modal auxiliaries and require "to" before the dependent infinitive:

> Er **kann (muß, soll, will,** etc.) das **machen.**
> *He is able (has, is supposed, wants,* etc.) *to do that.*

5. If a modal auxiliary in a perfect tense is used with a dependent infinitive, the regular past participle of the modal changes to a form identical with the infinitive: **gekonnt** becomes **können, gedurft** becomes **dürfen,** etc. The resulting combination looks like (and is often called) a "double infinitive":

PRESENT TENSE:	Ich kann **arbeiten.**	*I can work.*
PRESENT PERFECT:	Ich habe **arbeiten können.**	*I have been able to work.*

Of these two "infinitives" the dependent infinitive precedes. Examples:

WITHOUT DEPENDENT INFINITIVE	WITH DEPENDENT INFINITIVE
Ich **habe** das nie **gekonnt.**	Ich **habe** das nie **tun können.**
I have never been able to do that.	*I have never been able to do that.*
I have never been able to.	
Sie **hatte** es nicht **gewollt.**	Sie **hatte** es nicht **sagen wollen.**
She hadn't wanted it.	*She hadn't wanted to say it.*
Das **haben** wir nie **gedurft.**	Das **haben** wir nie **tun dürfen.**
We were never permitted (to do) that.	*We were never permitted to do that.*

6. A "double infinitive" usually stands last in any clause, main or dependent. In dependent clauses, the auxiliary immediately precedes both infinitives. Note the following dependent clauses and compare them with the main clauses in 5 above:

> Er weiß, **daß ich das nie habe tun können.**
> Er weiß, **daß sie es nicht hat sagen wollen.**
> Er weiß, **daß du das nie wirst tun dürfen.**

7. When the German modal auxiliary is used without a dependent infinitive, **es** is frequently added to refer to the infinitive omitted:

> **Er kann Klavier spielen.**   *He can play the piano.*
> **Aber ich kann es nicht.**   *But I cannot.*

8. Four other verbs share some of the characteristics of modal auxiliaries:

a. dependent infinitives follow them without **zu;**

[1] This does not apply to modals modified by prefixes, the most common of which is **vermögen** (*to be able to*): **Er vermochte das nicht einzusehen.** *He could not understand that.*

b. in perfect tenses, the past participle usually changes to a form identical with the infinitive, forming a "double infinitive":

helfen *to help*

Ich habe den Brief **schreiben helfen.** (not: **geholfen**)
I helped write the letter.

hören *to hear*

Hast du ihn nicht **kommen hören?** (not: **gehört**)
Didn't you hear him come (or coming)?

lassen *to let, have (something done)*[1]

Ich habe mir die Haare **schneiden lassen.** (not: **gelassen**)
I had my hair cut.
Er hat sie nicht **mitkommen lassen.**
He did not let her come along.
Er hat sein Auto **reparieren lassen.**
He had his auto repaired.

sehen *to see*

Hast du ihn je **arbeiten sehen?** (not: **gesehen**)
Did you ever see him work (or working)?

9. Factual and Hypothetical Meanings of Modal Auxiliaries

We have learned that the basic meanings of the six German modal auxiliaries are:

PERMISSION:	**dürfen**	*to be permitted (allowed) to*
ABILITY:	**können**	*to be able to*
DESIRE:	**mögen**	*to like to*
NECESSITY:	**müssen**	*to have to*
OBLIGATION:	**sollen**	*to be (supposed) to*
INTENTION:	**wollen**	*to want to*

These basic meanings, however, apply only to factual statements, that is, when the speaker or writer refers to facts: **Ich kann kommen.** *I can come.* **Ich will essen.** *I want to eat.*

10. As in English, modal auxiliaries may also be used to express mere opinions, suppositions, or doubts, with different meanings. Contrast the following sentences:

ABILITY: **Er kann deutsch sprechen.**
He can speak German. (It is a fact that he speaks German.)

---

[1] Remember that **lassen** can also mean *to leave:* **Er hat sie immer allein gelassen.** *He always left her alone.*

ASSUMPTION: **Das kann richtig sein.**
That may be correct. (It is the speaker's assumption that it is correct.)

11. The six German modal auxiliaries and their meanings in hypothetical statements:[1]

dürfen (so used in the subjunctive only)

| probability: | **Das dürfte wahr sein.** | *That might be true.* |
| | **Das dürfte wahr gewesen sein.** | *That might have been true.* |

können[2]

| assumption: | **Das kann (mag) richtig sein.** | *That may be correct.* |
| | **Das kann (mag) richtig gewesen sein.** | *That may have been correct.* |

mögen[2]

| assumption: | **Es mag (kann) falsch sein.** | *It may be wrong.* |
| | **Es mag (kann) falsch gewesen sein.** | *It may have been wrong.* |

müssen

| opinion: | **Er muß viel Geld haben.** | *He must have much money.* |
| | **Er muß viel Geld gehabt haben.** | *He must have had much money.* |

sollen

| hearsay or supposition: | **Er soll heute hier sein.** | *He is said to be here today.* |
| | **Er soll gestern hier gewesen sein.** | *He is said to have been here yesterday.* |

wollen

| doubtful claims: | **Er will reich sein.** | *He claims to be rich.* |
| | **Er will reich gewesen sein.** | *He claims to have been rich.* |

Sometimes only the context determines in which sense a modal auxiliary is used.

12. Idiomatic Uses of Modal Auxiliaries

dürfen

requests: **Darf ich Sie um das Salz bitten?**
May I ask you for the salt? (*Please pass the salt.*)

---

[1] Note that, in hypothetical statements referring to the past, the German (as the English) modals retain present-tense forms, while the dependent infinitive changes to past infinitive:
   Das kann richtig **gewesen sein.**   *That may have been correct.*

[2] **Können** and **mögen** in this use are interchangeable.

negative commands: **Das darfst du nicht tun.**
You must not do that.

können

politeness: **Können (könnten) Sie mir bitte helfen?**
(indicative or subjunctive) *Can (could) you help me, please?*

mögen

wish: **Ich möchte jetzt gehen.**
(subjunctive) *I would like to go now.*

sollen

command: **Du sollst den Mund halten!**
(*You are to*) *keep your mouth shut!*
Du sollst nicht stehlen!
Thou shalt not steal!

obligation: **Er soll (sollte) das eigentlich wissen.**
(indicative or subjunctive) *He really should (ought to) know that.*

RECAPITULATION OF MAIN POINTS

1. There are six modal auxiliaries in German: **dürfen, können, mögen, müssen, sollen, wollen.**

2. The conjugation of modal auxiliaries is irregular only in the singular of the present tense: **ich darf, ich kann, ich mag, ich muß, ich soll, ich will.** In addition, **mögen** changes the **g** of its stem to **ch** in the past and in the past participle: **mochte, gemocht.**

3. Characteristics of modal auxiliaries:

    a. Modal auxiliaries take the past participle in the present perfect when they are used without a dependent infinitive, that is, when the dependent infinitive is understood;

    b. the so-called "double infinitive" occurs when the modal is used in a perfect tense and another infinitive depends on it; in such a construction the regular past participle of the modal normally changes to a form identical with the infinitive: Er hat **kommen können.** *He was (has been) able to come.*

    c. dependent infinitives are not preceded by **zu.**

4. The "double infinitive" is also used with the verbs **helfen, hören, lassen sehen** (the so-called semimodal auxiliaries).

5. A "double infinitive" usually stands last in a clause; in a dependent clause it is preceded by the auxiliary:

> Ich glaube, daß er nicht **hat kommen können.**
> *I believe that he has not been able to come.*

ÜBUNGEN

Practice in Reading and Writing

A. *Read aloud and translate:*

Das Wunderkind Mozart

1. Wolfgang Amadeus Mozart war schon als Kind ein erstaunlicher Musiker und konnte verschiedene Instrumente spielen. 2. Bereits mit vier Jahren wollte er ein ganzes Klavierkonzert komponieren. 3. Es wurde dann aber so schwer, daß niemand es zu spielen vermochte. 4. Der kleine Mozart aber sagte: „Drum ist's ein Konzert; man muß so lange exerzieren, bis man es treffen kann; sehen Sie, so muß es gehen!" 5. Dann setzte er sich hin und spielte mit seinen viel zu kurzen Fingern, aber man konnte doch erkennen, was er wollte. 6. Mozarts Gehör soll unglaublich fein gewesen sein. 7. Er soll gehört haben, wenn eine Violine einen halben Viertelton zu tief gestimmt war. 8. Als er bei einem Hauskonzert die zweite Violine spielen wollte aber nicht durfte, sagte er: „Um die zweite Violine zu spielen, muß man es doch nicht gelernt haben." 9. Das Wunderkind machte viele Reisen durch Europa, und an jedem Hof sah und hörte man ihn und seine Schwester Nannerl musizieren. 10. Man hat ihn auch in vielen Städten spielen hören. 11. In Wien ließ die Kaiserin Maria Theresia den Sechsjährigen vor der kaiserlichen Familie spielen. 12. Er mochte die Kaiserin so gern, daß er auf ihren Schoß sprang und sie abküßte. 13. Der Fußboden im kaiserlichen Schloß war aber so glatt, daß man sehr vorsichtig gehen mußte. 14. Der

	das Wunderkind,	*child prodigy*	8	**um . . . zu spielen**	*in order to play*
	−er			**die Kaiserin, – nen**	*empress*
1	**erstaunlich**	*amazing*	11	**der Sechsjährige,**	*six-year-old boy*
4	**drum**	*that's why*		**−n**	
	treffen	(here:) *to hit*		**kaiserlich**	*imperial*
5	**sich hin/setzen**	*to sit down*	12	**der Schoß, ⸗e**	*lap*
6	**das Gehör**	*hearing*		**ab/küssen**	*to cover with kisses*
	unglaublich	*unbelievably*	13	**der Fußboden, ⸗**	*floor*
7	**halb**	*half*		**glatt**	*slippery*
	der Viertelton, ⸗e	*quarter tone*		**vorsichtig**	*carefully*
	stimmen	(here:) *to tune*			

kleine Sechsjährige konnte das noch nicht und fiel hin.   15. Die Prinzessin Marie Antoinette, die später die unglückliche Königin von Frankreich werden sollte, hob ihn auf.   16. „Sie sind brav", sagte der kleine Mozart zu ihr, „ich will Sie heiraten."   17. Als Musiker war er sehr stolz und hat am liebsten nur vor Musikkennern spielen mögen.   18. Als der Kaiser einmal neben ihm am Klavier stand und ihm da zuhören wollte, fragte Mozart nach dem Komponisten Wagenseil.   19. „Der versteht es", soll er gesagt haben.   20. Wagenseil mußte kommen, und erst jetzt begann Mozart zu spielen.

14	**hin/fallen (ä, ie, a, ist)**	*to fall down*	
15	**auf/heben (o, o)**	*to pick up*	
16	**brav**	(here:) *kind*	
17	**stolz**	*proud*	
18	**zu/hören**	*to listen to*	
	fragen nach	*to ask for*	

B. *Translate:*

1. Sie darf alles, was sie will.   2. Wir müssen jetzt nach Hause.   3. Er will das nicht wissen.   4. Er will das nicht gewußt haben.   5. Sie mußte sofort ins Krankenhaus.   6. Ich mag keine Milch.   7. Er wollte es ihr sagen, aber er konnte es nicht.   8. Was ich sagen wollte: Können Sie morgen kommen?   9. Er soll ein Dummkopf sein.   10. Können Sie mir sagen, wo ich eine Krawatte kaufen kann?   11. Die Liebe soll eine Dummheit sein; aber wer will sein ganzes Leben lang vernünftig (*reasonable*) bleiben?   12. Du sollst nicht töten!   13. Ich habe mir einen neuen Anzug (*suit*) machen lassen.   14. Er wollte mit, aber er durfte nicht.   15. Man darf in der Bibliothek nicht rauchen.   16. Darf man das bei euch?   17. Man sollte das wirklich nicht tun.   18. Können Sie mir vielleicht zehn Dollar leihen?   19. Ich kann, aber ich will nicht!   20. Ich soll ihn heute abend besuchen.   21. Ich muß ihn heute abend besuchen.   22. Der Arzt hat ihn noch nicht wieder aufstehen lassen.   23. Haben Sie ihn einmal schimpfen hören?   24. In welcher Zeitung hat er das bekanntmachen lassen?   25. Ich glaube, daß ich sie einmal habe tanzen sehen.   26. Ich muß jetzt in die Stadt.   27. Was mußt du jetzt tun?   28. Mußtest du wirklich in die Stadt?   29. Was soll ich ihm sagen?   30. Ich habe ihm das sagen sollen.

C. *Give the proper form of the modal auxiliary for the expressions in parentheses:*

1. (*wants to*) Er ...... seine Arbeit tun.   2. (*know*) Ich ...... Deutsch.   3. (*Do you know*) ...... Englisch?   4. (*likes*) Sie ...... Klaviermusik nicht.   5. (*must*) Du ...... diesen Dirigenten einmal hören.   6. (*may*) Fritz ...... nicht auf der Straße spielen.   7. (*has been able to*, pres. perf.) ...... er das aufführen?   8. (*is said to be*) Er ...... sehr berühmt sein.   9. (*had to*) Er ...... für eine Woche in die Stadt.   10. (*had to*, pres. perf.) Ich ...... mir das gefallen lassen.   11. (*could, wanted*) Er ...... alles, was er ....   12. (*were permitted*) Wir ...... ihn nur einmal im Krankenhaus besuchen.

D. *Which form of the past participle do you have to use?*

1. (lassen) Wir haben das bekanntmachen .... 2. (dürfen) Wir haben das nicht .... 3. (wollen) Er hat auf das Klavier springen ...... 4. (können) Er hat es nicht sagen .... 5. (sehen) Hast du mich nicht springen ......? 6. (mögen) Er hat Wagner nie .... 7. (wollen) Seine Frau hat ihm die Haare schneiden .... 8. (können) Sie hat die ganze Woche nicht singen .... 9. (können) Hast du es ......? 10. (sehen) Hast du sie kommen ......?

E. *Translate:*

1. I have to go home now. 2. He had to stay at home. 3. I would like to see his new piano. 4. His wife wanted (pres. perf.) to visit him in the hospital. 5. We heard her coming but did not see her leaving (pres. perf.). 6. They say that is impossible. 7. Can you tell me where she is? 8. We had to leave. 9. Did they have to do that (pres. perf.)? 10. May I visit you in your office? 11. I wanted (past) to read that book but I was never able to (pres. perf.) get it. 12. He claimed to have been in (the) town. 13. Did you like the concert? This woman can play! 14. He is said to have composed the aria for her, but she could not sing it. 15. He had to (pres. perf.) announce his concert in the paper. 16. Which paper would you like to read? 17. Why did he want to see you? 18. We have to put up with everything.

Oral Exercises

F. *Begin the following sentences with the subjects indicated:*

EXAMPLE: Wir können das sicher sagen. Man . . . .
            Man kann das sicher sagen.

1. Ihr sollt ihn für einen guten Künstler halten. Er . . . .
2. Sie können verschiedene Instrumente spielen. Ich . . . .
3. Wir müssen Klavier spielen lernen. Er . . . .
4. Ihr sollt den Mund halten. Du . . . .
5. Du darfst das Stück nicht vorspielen. Ihr . . . .
6. Wir können das nicht wissen. Du . . . .
7. Ich will nach England reisen. Wir . . . .
8. Sie müssen das alles gelernt haben. Er . . . .
9. Er mag diesen Leuten nicht vorspielen. Wir . . . .

G. *Change the sentences to present perfect:*

EXAMPLES: Sie will es nicht.   Sie hat es nicht gewollt.
         Sie will es nicht sagen.   Sie hat es nicht sagen wollen.

1. Er kann nicht gut Englisch. 2. Er kann nicht gut Englisch sprechen.
3. Sie mag ihn nicht. 4. Sie mag ihn nicht küssen. 5. Ihr sollt das nicht.
6. Ihr sollt das nicht tun. 7. Er muß das bestimmt. 8. Er muß das bestimmt
lernen. 9. Du darfst das nicht. 10. Du darfst das nicht essen.

H. *Change the sentences to present perfect:*

EXAMPLES: Man hört ihn oft.   Man hat ihn oft gehört.
          Man hört ihn oft musizieren.   Man hat ihn oft musizieren hören.

1. Wir helfen ihm. 2. Wir helfen ihm arbeiten. 3. Sie läßt ihn nicht allein.
4. Sie läßt ihn nicht gehen. 5. Er sieht sie jeden Tag. 6. Er sieht sie jeden
Tag in die Universität gehen. 7. Wir hören ihn manchmal. 8. Wir hören
ihn manchmal Klavier spielen.

I. *Hypothetical use of modal auxiliaries. Change the present infinitive to past
infinitive. Then translate the sentence into English:*

EXAMPLE: Er muß eine Violine haben.   Er muß eine Violine gehabt haben.
                                      He must have had a violin.

1. Er soll oft wütend werden. 2. Sie will das nicht wissen. 3. Das mag
richtig sein. 4. Er soll ihn für einen großen Musiker halten. 5. Das kann
sein. 6. Sein Deutsch soll sehr gut sein. 7. Das dürfte wahr sein. 8. Er
soll in vier oder fünf Sprachen schimpfen.

18

The Passive

Der Freiherr[1] von Münchhausen

Hieronymus Karl Friedrich Freiherr von Münchhausen wird heute gerne als einer der größten Lügner aller Zeiten bezeichnet. Und doch war dieser lustige Jäger und tapfere Soldat kein gewöhnlicher Schwindler. Denn wenn wirklich gut gelogen wird, wird das Lügen zur Kunst. Münchhausen war im
5 Russisch-Türkischen[2] Krieg gewesen, und nach seiner Rückkehr pflegte er die unglaublichsten Geschichten über seine Abenteuer in Rußland und in der Türkei zu erzählen. Natürlich wußten seine Freunde recht gut, daß diese Geschichten mehr oder weniger frei erfunden waren. Das machte aber nichts, denn es kam ja nur darauf an, daß man sich bei einer Flasche Wein gut unter-
10 hielt. Münchhausens Geschichten wurden dann mit anderen zusammen in einem Buch unter dem Titel „Vademecum[3] für lustige Leute" veröffentlicht.
Aber wirklich berühmt wurde der Freiherr erst in England. Dort erschien nämlich ein Buch unter dem Titel „The Original Adventures of Baron Münchhausen". Es war von einem deutschen Professor Raspe aus Kassel[4] herausge-
15 geben worden, denn der Herr Professor brauchte Geld. Daß ein Professor Geld brauchte, war natürlich nichts Neues. Dieser Professor aber hatte eine

---

1. **Freiherr** *baron* (Münchhausen lived from 1720 to 1797).   2. **im Russisch-Türkischen Krieg** *in the Russo-Turkish War* (1768–1774).   3. **Vademecum** (Latin) *handbook*.   4. **Kassel** city in the West German state of Hesse.

etwas originelle Art, sich Geld zu verdienen. So originell war seine Methode, daß die Polizei ein Auge auf ihn warf und er Deutschland verlassen mußte. Übrigens hat er auch England später wieder verlassen und ist nach Irland gegangen, wo er dann gestorben ist und begraben wurde.   20

Raspes Buch kam dann nach Deutschland und wurde von dem Dichter Gottfried August Bürger[5] frei übersetzt. Es erfreute sich bei den deutschen Lesern einer großen Beliebtheit, trotz seines langen Titels: „Wunderbare Reisen zu Wasser und zu Lande, Feldzüge und lustige Abenteuer des Freiherrn von Münchhausen, wie er dieselben bei einer Flasche Wein im Zirkel 25 seiner Freunde zu erzählen pflegt".

Ein solches Abenteuer sah ungefähr folgendermaßen aus: Der Freiherr wurde einmal von den Türken gefangen und als Sklave an den Sultan verkauft. Er mußte nun jeden Tag die Bienen des Sultans auf die Weide[6] treiben. Einmal aber wurde eine Biene plötzlich von zwei Bären angefallen. Münch- 30 hausen warf seine Axt nach den Bären, aber sie flog an den Bären vorbei bis auf den Mond. Er pflanzte daher schnell eine türkische Bohne, und diese wuchs sofort bis zum Mond hinauf. Er kletterte daran auf den Mond und holte sich seine Axt wieder. Aber als er wieder herunterklettern wollte, war die Bohne verdorrt. Er nahm daher Stroh und machte sich daraus einen 35 Strick, und den band er an einem Horn des Mondes fest. Aber der Strick war nicht lang genug, und jedes Mal, wenn Münchhausen ans Ende kam, mußte er ihn oben abschneiden und unten wieder anbinden. So kam er beinahe bis zur Erde, aber nur beinahe—denn als er noch in den Wolken war, riß der Strick. Da war nun nichts mehr zu machen: Münchhausen fiel 40 und fiel, tief in die Erde hinein. Das Loch, das[7] er im Fallen machte, war so tief, daß er nicht herausklettern konnte. Glücklicherweise aber waren ihm in der langen Zeit die Fingernägel so lang gewachsen, daß er damit eine Treppe graben konnte. Und so kam er schließlich wieder auf die Erde zurück.

5. 1747–1794.   6. **auf die Weide treiben** *to drive to pasture.*   7. **das** (rel. pron.) *which.*

FRAGEN

1. Als was wird der Freiherr von Münchhausen heute gerne bezeichnet? 2. Was hat Münchhausen in Rußland gemacht? 3. Was pflegte er nach seiner Rückkehr aus Rußland zu erzählen? 4. Wodurch wurde Münchhausen in England berühmt? 5. Von wem war das Buch herausgegeben worden? 6. Warum mußte der Herr Professor Raspe Deutschland verlassen? 7. Wie originell war Raspes Methode, sich sein Geld zu verdienen? 8. Von wem wurde Raspes Buch frei ins Deutsche übersetzt? 9. Von wem

wurde Münchhausen einmal gefangen? 10. Was mußte Münchhausen für den Sultan tun? 11. Werden Bienen gewöhnlich auf die Weide getrieben? 12. Von wem wurden die Bienen angefallen? 13. Was warf Münchhausen nach den Bären? 14. Wohin flog die Axt? 15. Wie kam Münchhausen auf den Mond? 16. Wachsen türkische Bohnen wirklich schneller als Bostoner Bohnen? 17. Was tat Münchhausen, als die Bohne verdorrt war? 18. Wo war er, als der Strick riß? 19. Was tat Münchhausen nun mit dem Strick? 20. Wie kam er wieder aus dem tiefen Loch heraus?

WORTSCHATZ

ab- (*pref.*)	off	das macht nichts	that makes no difference
das **Abenteuer, –**	adventure		
an /kommen	to matter	der **Nagel, ⸗**	nail
(a, o)(ist) auf		**oben**	above; upstairs
(*w. dat.*)		**pflanzen**	to plant
der **Bär, –en, –en**	bear	die **Polizei**	police
die **Biene, –n**	bee	**recht**	quite
die **Bohne, –n**	bean	die **Rückkehr**	return
sich erfreuen	to enjoy	der **Strick, –e**	rope
(*w. gen.*)		das **Stroh**	straw
der **Feldzug, ⸗e**	campaign	**tapfer**	brave
fest- (*pref.*)	on, fast	die **Treppe, –n**	stairs, staircase
fest /binden (a, u)	to attach to; to fasten	**übersetzen**	to translate
		übrigens	by the way
die **Flasche, –n**	bottle	**unglaublich**	unbelievable
folgendermaßen	as follows	**unten**	below, downstairs
gewöhnlich	ordinary	**sich (gut) unter-**	to have a good time
herunter- (*pref.*)	down	**halten (ä, ie, a)**	
der **Jäger, –**	hunter	**verdorren**	to dry up, wither
klettern	to climb	**verkaufen**	to sell
das **Loch, ⸗er**	hole	**vorbei-** (*pref.*)	past
der **Lügner, –**	liar	**wieder-** (*pref.*)	back
		die **Wolke, –n**	cloud

STRONG VERBS

an /fallen	to attack	**fällt an**	**fiel an**	**angefallen**
aus /sehen	to look (like)	**sieht aus**	**sah aus**	**ausgesehen**
binden	to bind		**band**	**gebunden**
erfinden	to invent		**erfand**	**erfunden**
heraus /geben	to edit; to publish	**gibt heraus**	**gab heraus**	**herausgegeben**
lügen	to (tell a) lie		**log**	**gelogen**
reißen	to tear		**riß**	**gerissen**
treiben	to drive, engage in		**trieb**	**getrieben**
s. unterhalten (mit)	to have a good time; to converse, to talk to	**unterhält s.**	**unterhielt s.**	**s. unterhalten**

DISTINGUISH BETWEEN

unter (preposition) *under* and **unten** (adverb) *below, downstairs*

GRAMMATICAL TERMS

1. In the active voice, the subject performs the action: *The people elect* a president.

2. In the passive voice, the subject is acted upon: *a president is elected* by the people.

Note how in changing from the active to the passive the direct object of the active sentence (*a president*) becomes the subject of the passive sentence.

3. In English, the auxiliary verb for the passive is *to be: is* elected; the agent or instrument of the passive action is introduced by the preposition *by: by the people.*

THE PASSIVE IN GERMAN

1. In German, **werden** is the auxiliary verb of the passive voice. Accordingly, **werden** is the verb that is conjugated and used with the past participle of the main verb:[1]

> Die Geschichte **wird** von vielen Leuten **geglaubt.**
> *The story is (being) believed by many people.*

2. The verb **loben** (*to praise*) may serve as an illustration for the conjugation of a verb in the present tense of the passive:

ich **werde gelobt** *I am (being) praised*	wir **werden gelobt**
du **wirst gelobt**	ihr **werdet gelobt**
er **wird gelobt**	sie **werden gelobt**

3. A synopsis of **gelobt werden** (*to be praised*):

PRESENT TENSE:	ich **werde gelobt**
PAST TENSE:	ich **wurde gelobt**
FUTURE TENSE:	ich **werde gelobt werden**
PRESENT PERFECT TENSE:	ich **bin gelobt worden**
PAST PERFECT TENSE:	ich **war gelobt worden**
FUTURE PERFECT TENSE:	ich **werde gelobt worden sein.**

---

[1] Do not confuse forms of **werden** (*to be*) used in the passive with those used in the future (Er **wird** es **glauben.** *He will believe it.*) or with the independent verb **werden** (Er **wird** alt. *He is getting old;* Er **wurde** Ingenieur. *He became an engineer*).

Since **werden** is an intransitive verb conjugated with **sein,** the auxiliary for the compound tenses of any verb in the passive is **sein.**

In the passive voice, the past participle of **werden** is **worden** (not **geworden**).

4. The agent (*by whom* something is done) is expressed by **von** (with the dative) and the instrument (*by means of which* something is done) by **durch** (with the accusative):

> Das Lied wurde **von vielen Soldaten** gesungen.
> *The song was (being) sung by many soldiers.*
> Der Patient wurde **durch die Medizin** geheilt.
> *The patient was cured by means of (through) the medicine.*

When the agent or instrument cannot be clearly differentiated, either **von** or **durch** may be used:

> Die Firma ist **von einer** (or **durch eine**) **Bank** finanziert worden.
> *The firm was financed by (through) a bank.*

5. The impersonal pronoun **man** is not expressed when an active sentence is changed into a passive sentence:

> ACTIVE: **Man befragt ihn** selten.   *They consult him rarely.*
> PASSIVE: **Er wird** selten **befragt.**   *He is rarely consulted.*

6. As in English, the direct (accusative) object of the active sentence becomes the (nominative) subject of the passive sentence and determines the form of the auxiliary **werden:**

> ACTIVE: **Man singt diese Lieder** hier oft.
> PASSIVE: **Diese Lieder werden** hier oft **gesungen.**
>   *These songs are (being) sung here often.*

The dative object of an active sentence, however, is retained in the passive and does not determine the form of the auxiliary **werden;** a sole dative object requires that the auxiliary **werden** be in the third person singular:

ACTIVE	PASSIVE
Man hilft ihm nicht.	**Ihm wird** nicht **geholfen.**[1]
One does not help him.	*He is not being helped.*
Man glaubt diesen Leuten nicht.	**Diesen Leuten wird** nicht **geglaubt.**[1]
One does not believe these people.	*These people are not (being) believed.*

---

[1] If the dative object in a passive sentence *follows* the auxiliary **werden,** the pronoun **es** functions as a substitute for the missing subject:

> **Es wird ihm** nicht **geholfen.**
> **Es wird diesen Leuten** nicht **geglaubt.**

7. The passive is often used in German for impersonal statements like "There was loud talking and laughing." The substitute for the missing subject is **es:**

> **Es wurde laut gesprochen und gelacht.**

The German past participles **(gesprochen, gelacht)** are equivalent to English verbal nouns (*talking, laughing*); when the sentence has (or allows for) an inversion, **es** is omitted:

> **Es wird in Deutschland mehr gesungen als hier.**
> or: **In Deutschland wird mehr gesungen als hier.**
> *There is more singing in Germany than here.*

8. When the agent is not specified, German prefers certain impersonal *active* constructions where English normally uses the passive:

a. a construction with **man:**

> **Man denkt (glaubt, sagt), daß . . . .**
> *It is thought (believed, said) that . . . .*
> **Man hat es nicht lesen können.**
> *It could not be read.*

b. an active infinitive with **zu** after a form of **sein** (where English uses a passive infinitive):

> **Was war zu machen?** *What was to be done?*
> **Wie ist das zu verstehen?** *How is that to be understood?*

c. a reflexive construction (with an indefinite or abstract subject):

> **Das versteht sich** (von selbst).
> (Lit., *That is understood by itself.*) *That goes without saying.*
>
> **Deutsch lernt sich** sehr leicht.
> *German is easily learned.*

d. **sich lassen**[1] with the infinitive:

> **Das läßt sich nicht beweisen.**
> *That cannot be proved.*

9. Only a construction consisting of a form of **werden** with a past participle constitutes a genuine passive. Forms of **sein** are also used with the past participle, but these are not true passives: rather, they describe conditions that may be the result of a passive action. Compare:

---

[1] Constructions with **läßt sich (ließ sich,** etc.) are very common, and it is good practice to translate them automatically by *can* (*could*, etc.) and then changing the following German active infinitive to the passive infinitive in English (*be done*, etc.).

Das Haus wird aus Stein **gebaut.**   **Das Haus ist** aus Stein **gebaut.**
The house is being built of stone.   *The house is built of stone.*

You are dealing with a genuine passive when you can add "being" in the English translation:

<table>
<tr><td>GENUINE PASSIVE</td><td>APPARENT PASSIVE</td></tr>
<tr><td>Die Fenster werden geschlossen.</td><td>Die Fenster sind geschlossen.</td></tr>
<tr><td>The windows are being closed.</td><td>The windows are closed.</td></tr>
</table>

RECAPITULATION OF MAIN POINTS

1. The German passive requires the use of the auxiliary **werden** with the past participle of a main verb:

> **Der Präsident wird gewählt.**   *The president is being elected.*

Remember: **werden** alone is: *to become,* or *to be getting;*
werden plus infinitive: *will* (future tense);
werden plus past participle: some form of *to be* must be used.

2. In the perfect tenses, the auxiliary is **sein,** and the past participle of **werden** is shortened to **worden:** Der Präsident **ist gewählt worden.**

3. Fix in mind the pattern: **ist . . . worden:** *has been*
war . . . worden: *had been*

4. The agent in a passive sentence is expressed by **von** (with the dative), the instrument by **durch** (with the accusative):

> Der Präsident ist **vom Volk** gewählt worden.
> *The president was elected by the people.*
> Das Haus ist **durch einen Agenten** verkauft worden.
> *The house was sold through an agent.*

5. A form of **sein** combined with a past participle of the main verb does not constitute a genuine passive but rather describes a condition resulting from a passive action; such a construction is sometimes called an "apparent passive":

> GENUINE PASSIVE: Die Fenster **werden geschlossen.**
> *The windows are being closed.*
> APPARENT PASSIVE: Die Fenster **sind geschlossen.**
> *The windows are closed.*

6. Fix in mind the common patterns:

Es läßt sich zeigen.	*It can be shown.*
Es ist zu beweisen.	*It is to be proved.*

ÜBUNGEN

Practice in Reading and Writing

A. *Read aloud and translate:*

Hoffmanns Erzählungen

1. Ernst Theodor Amadeus Hoffmann—er nannte sich „Amadeus" aus Verehrung für Mozart—muß als ein später Romantiker bezeichnet werden. 2. Er hat sich nicht nur als Dichter und Schriftsteller einen Namen gemacht, sondern wird auch als Kritiker, Komponist, Karikaturist und selbst als kluger Jurist geschätzt. 3. Er hat viel komponiert, sogar Opern, aber seine Musik wird heute nicht mehr gespielt. 4. Durch den Dichter Hoffmann aber sind viele Dichter in der ganzen Welt immer wieder inspiriert worden, unter ihnen Victor Hugo in Frankreich und Edgar Allan Poe und Hawthorne in Amerika. 5. Hoffmann selbst wurde dann von Jacques Offenbach, der der französischen Musikgeschichte zuzurechnen ist, aber in Deutschland geboren war, in seiner bekannten Oper „Hoffmanns Erzählungen" auf die Bühne gebracht. 6. Offenbach war vom französischen Theaterpublikum wegen seiner Operetten immer schon verwöhnt worden, aber in den letzten Jahren seines Lebens wurde er dann noch von dem Ehrgeiz gepackt, auch als ernsthafter Opernkomponist anerkannt zu werden. 7. Aus den Erzählungen des Dichters Hoffmann ließ sich, wie er glaubte, der Stoff für eine Oper über das tragische Schicksal des Künstlers gewinnen. 8. Als die Oper begonnen wurde, war Offenbach schon ein kranker Mann, aber er hoffte bis zuletzt, die Aufführung in Paris noch zu erleben. 9. Er ist dann doch schon vor der ersten Aufführung gestorben. 10. Die Oper wurde kurz nach seinem Tode in Paris begeistert aufgenommen. 11. Dann aber wurde sie vom Unglück verfolgt. 12. Bei der zweiten Aufführung in Wien brannte das Theater ab, und man glaubte, das Werk war verhext. 13. Lange Zeit wurde die Oper

1	**die Verehrung**	*devotion*	7	**der Stoff, –e**	*material, subject*
2	**der Jurist, –en, –en**	*lawyer*		**das Schicksal, –e**	*fate*
5	**die Bühne, –n**	*stage*	8	**erleben**	*to experience*
6	**die Operette, –n**	*light opera, operetta*	10	**auf/nehmen (i, a, o)**	*to receive*
	verwöhnen	*to spoil*	11	**das Unglück**	*misfortune*
	der Ehrgeiz	*ambition*		**verfolgen**	*to pursue*
	ernsthaft	*serious*	12	**verhexen** (from **die Hexe** *witch*)	*to bewitch*

dann nicht mehr aufgeführt.   14. Nur die bekannte Barkarole wurde noch gespielt, die von Offenbach ursprünglich für eine seiner Operetten komponiert worden war.   15. Doch auch die Barkarole wurde vom Unglück verfolgt.   16. Die Kaiserin von China hatte sich nämlich in die Melodie verliebt, und so sollte sie eines Tages von Musikanten am Hof in Peking gespielt werden.   17. So europäische Musik ließ sich aber von chinesischen Musikanten damals noch nicht spielen.   18. Man erzählte sich, die Kaiserin sei furchtbar wütend geworden.   19. Man sagt, sie hat die Musikanten bis auf den letzten Mann köpfen lassen.

14	**ursprünglich**	*originally*	19	**bis auf**	*down to*
18	**sei geworden**	*had become*		**köpfen**	*to behead*

B. *Translate:*

1. Von wem ist das Buch übersetzt worden?   2. Oben wird der Strick abgeschnitten und unten wieder angebunden.   3. Es wurde ein tiefes Loch gegraben.   4. Deutsch lernt sich nicht in einer Woche!   5. Das läßt sich nicht machen.   6. Es versteht sich von selbst, daß wir die Aufführung sehen.   7. Da ist nichts zu machen.   8. Die Pflanze ist sehr gewachsen.   9. Einem solchen Menschen ist nicht zu helfen.   10. Wie läßt sich die Axt vom Mond herunterholen?   11. Das Buch ließ sich nicht besser übersetzen.   12. Das Buch läßt sich nicht besser übersetzen.   13. Es wird heutzutage (*nowadays*) weniger gearbeitet.   14. Früher ist mehr gearbeitet worden.   15. Ich werde kommen, wenn ich gerufen werde.

C. Von *or* **durch?** *Insert the correct preposition in the following sentences:*

1. _____ wem ist diese Geschichte?   2. Das Buch wurde _____ einem Dichter übersetzt.   3. Man ließ ihn _____ die Polizei suchen.   4. Ihm wurde _____ seine Verwandten geholfen.   5. Das wurde _____ die Zeitung bekannt gemacht.   6. Die Bohne wurde _____ Münchhausen gepflanzt.   7. Wo _____ ist er bekannt geworden?   8. Die Regierung wird _____ dem Volk gewählt.

D. *Translate:*

1. They will not be caught this time.   2. Shakespeare was translated by Tieck.   3. The beans had been planted and they grew very fast.   4. Can that be done easily (use construction with **sich lassen**)?   5. He is having a desk made.   6. The most unbelievable stories were being told by him.   7. By whom was the book read in Germany?   8. They climbed into the old house and were caught there by the police.   9. There was much drinking upstairs.   10. A new method was invented and the work done much faster.   11. The bear was attacked by a bee.   12. This book must be translated into good German.   13. During the Middle Ages witches were being burned in public.   14. The Barkarole is still being played on the radio.   15. The lightning rod was

invented by Benjamin Franklin, but it was brought to Germany by Lichtenberg. 16. That cannot be described (use construction with **sich lassen**) in (**mit**) a few words. 17. We shall discuss this problem; I am sure it can be solved. 18. This boy has always been spoiled by his mother.

Oral Exercises

E. *Change the sentences from active to passive. Do not express the agent:*

EXAMPLES: Man schließt das Fenster.   Das Fenster wird geschlossen.
        Man schließt die Fenster.   Die Fenster werden geschlossen.

1. Man gibt das Buch heraus. 2. Man gibt die Bücher heraus. 3. Man braucht das Geld jetzt. 4. Man braucht die neuen Methoden jetzt. 5. Man veröffentlicht die Geschichten auch in England. 6. Man veröffentlicht das Buch auch in England. 7. Man erkennt den Dichter an. 8. Man erzählt hier die unglaublichsten Geschichten.

F. *Change the sentences to passive:*

EXAMPLES: Man droht dem Kritiker.   Dem Kritiker wird gedroht.
        Man droht den Kritikern.   Den Kritikern wird gedroht.

1. Man glaubt dem Schwindler nicht.   2. Man glaubt den Schwindlern nicht.
3. Man antwortet diesen Leuten überhaupt nicht. 4. Man hilft dem alten Mann wirklich. 5. Man dankt den Mitgliedern endlich. 6. Man antwortet mir überhaupt nicht.

G. *Change the sentences to passive:*

EXAMPLE: Bei uns tanzt man gern.   Bei uns wird gern getanzt.

1. Bei euch lacht man oft.   4. Am Abend arbeitet man nicht.
2. Bei ihnen redet man zuviel.   5. Hier raucht man gar nicht.
3. Hier lügt man wirklich gut.

H. *Combination drill. Continue in the same manner:*

1. Man fragt diese Leute überhaupt nicht. 2. Man antwortet diesen Leuten überhaupt nicht. 3. Hier spricht man überhaupt nicht. 4. Man glaubt dem Schwindler nichts. 5. Hier lügt man wirklich gut. 6. Man erzählt hier die unglaublichsten Geschichten. 7. Man dankt allen Mitgliedern. 8. Man fragt alle Mitglieder. 9. Hier arbeitet man nicht viel.

I. *Change the sentences to passive. Pay special attention to the tenses:*

EXAMPLES: Man glaubte ihm einfach nicht.
        Ihm wurde einfach nicht geglaubt.

Man hat alle seine Bücher gelesen.
Alle seine Bücher sind gelesen worden.

Man hatte die unglaublichsten Geschichten erzählt.
Die unglaublichsten Geschichten waren erzählt worden.

1. Man machte den Strick aus Stroh.
2. Man hat die Axt wiedergeholt.
3. Man hatte diese Geschichten erfunden.
4. Man hat das Buch frei übersetzt.
5. Man kaufte die Bücher sogar in London.
6. Man hatte ihn oft danach gefragt.

J. Change the sentences to passive. State the agent:

EXAMPLE: Professor Raspe veröffentlichte die Geschichten.
    Die Geschichten wurden von Professor Raspe veröffentlicht.

1. Zwei Bären haben Münchhausen angefallen.   2. Münchhausen hat die Axt wiedergeholt.   3. Kein Mensch glaubt diese Geschichten.   4. Die Leute kaufen diese Bücher gern.   5. Hoffmann hat diese Oper komponiert.   6. Das Publikum hatte sie begeistert aufgenommen.   7. Das Unglück hat ihn verfolgt.

19

Relative Pronouns

Immanuel Kant[1]

Kant, mit dem ein Zeitalter in der Geschichte der Philosophie zu Ende ging und ein neues begann, ist in Königsberg in Ostpreußen[2] geboren, einer Stadt, die er sein ganzes Leben lang nicht verlassen hat. Die Familie des Vaters stammte aus Schottland, wo sie sich „Cant" geschrieben hatte. Kant selbst war das vierte[3] von elf Kindern, von denen aber sechs schon in jungen 5 Jahren gestorben sind.

Im 18.[4] Jahrhundert, das wir das Zeitalter der „Aufklärung"[5] nennen, hatte man bis zu Kant geglaubt, mit dem Verstand alles erklären zu können. Für diese Zeit war alles vernünftig, was der Mensch mit seinem Kopf fassen konnte, aber niemand hatte bisher gefragt, wie es denn in diesem Kopf selbst 10 aussah. Kant war der erste, der das Denken selbst kritisch untersuchte und damit nicht nur dessen Gesetze, sondern auch die Grenzen, denen es unterlag, fand, was ihn mehr als einmal mit den herrschenden Ideen, besonders auf dem Gebiete der Religion, in Konflikt brachte. Sein Hauptwerk, in dem er sein kritisches System entwickelte, ist die „Kritik der reinen Vernunft" aus 15 dem Jahre 1781.[6]

1. German philosopher, 1724–1804. 2. **Ostpreußen** *East Prussia.* 3. **vierte** *fourth.* 4. **18.,** (read:) **achtzehnten.** 5. **Aufklärung** *Enlightenment.* 6. **1781,** (read:) **siebzehnhunderteinundachtzig.**

Die Genauigkeit bestimmte aber nicht nur sein Denken, sondern auch sein ganzes Leben, was uns von vielen seiner Zeitgenossen bezeugt wird. Er ging abends pünktlich um zehn Uhr zu Bett und stand ebenso pünktlich morgens
20 um fünf Uhr auf. Auch der Einrichtung[7] des Bettes stand er kritisch gegenüber. „Das Bett ist das Nest einer Menge von Krankheiten", erklärte er einmal. Nach dem Aufstehen nahm er ein leichtes Frühstück zu sich, welches aus einer Tasse Kaffee und einer Pfeife Tabak bestand, was wir kaum als besonders gesund empfinden werden. Den Vormittag verbrachte er arbeitend
25 hinter seinem Schreibtisch. Um ein Uhr ging er zum Essen, in jüngeren Jahren in einem Restaurant, später bei sich zu Hause, und dazu lud er sich dann gerne einige Freunde ein, mit denen er sich lange, bis vier oder gar fünf Uhr, unterhielt. Über alles durfte dabei gesprochen werden, sogar über die Küche und das Kochen—nur nicht über die Philosophie. Kant, der
30 nicht nur das Gespräch liebte, sondern auch gerne gut aß, interessierte sich sehr für die Geheimnisse der Kochkunst, besonders in der Gegenwart von Frauen. Einer seiner Freunde schlug ihm einmal vor, auch eine „Kritik der Kochkunst" zu schreiben.

Nach dem Essen machte er dann seinen täglichen Spaziergang, bei dem er
35 immer denselben Weg nahm. Er soll aus diesem Grunde seine Schwester, die in einem Teil der Stadt wohnte, der nicht an seinem Weg lag, vierundzwanzig Jahre nicht gesehen haben. So pünktlich erschien er in den Straßen der Stadt, daß die Königsberger ihre Uhren nach ihm stellen konnten.

Kant hat nie geheiratet. Er war kein Weiberfeind,[8] aber er stand doch
40 auch den Frauen recht kritisch gegenüber. „Die Damen kommen nicht in den Himmel", erklärte er einmal kategorisch, „denn schon in der Offenbarung[9] Johannis heißt es an einer Stelle: es war eine Stille von einer halben Stunde. So etwas läßt sich aber, wo Frauenzimmer[10] sind, gar nicht als möglich denken." Zweimal soll er trotzdem ans Heiraten gedacht haben,
45 aber dafür brauchte er so viel Zeit, daß die Frauen schon verheiratet oder weggezogen waren, als er seinen Entschluß endlich gefaßt hatte. So lebte er denn allein, nur mit seinem Diener, dessen Name Lampe war. Wie Diogenes[11] seine Laterne, so hatte Kant seinen Lampe. Lampe war ziemlich dumm, aber offenbar sehr arrogant. Kant mußte ihn schließlich gehen lassen,
50 aber er konnte ihn doch nicht vergessen. Er war nun auch schon etwas alt und zerstreut geworden und schrieb sich daher ein Memorandum, das er auf seinen Schreibtisch stellte, und das lautete: „Lampe muß vergessen werden!"

---

7. **Einrichtung** *set-up, provision, institution.*   8. **Weiberfeind** *antifeminist.*   9. **Offenbarung Johannis** *Revelation according to St. John.*   10. **Frauenzimmer** *women, females* (in modern German a derogatory term!).   11. **Diogenes** *Greek philosopher who walked through the streets of Athens with a lantern in his hand in search of truth.*

FRAGEN

1. Was ging mit Kant zu Ende? 2. Ist Kant viel gereist? 3. Welches Kind der Familie war Kant? 4. Wie viele Geschwister hatte er? 5. Was hatte man im 18. (achtzehnten) Jahrhundert bis zu Kant geglaubt? 6. Was war für diese Zeit vernünftig? 7. Was hatte bisher niemand gefragt? 8. Worin war Kant der erste? (construct your answer around: darin daß . . .). 9. Was fand Kant damit? 10. Was ist die „Kritik der reinen Vernunft"? 11. Was wird uns von seinen Zeitgenossen bezeugt? 12. Wann ging Kant zu Bett und wann stand er auf? 13. Warum stand er der Einrichtung des Bettes kritisch gegenüber? 14. Woraus bestand Kants Frühstück? 15. Wo hat Kant zu Mittag gegessen? 16. Worüber unterhielt man sich beim Essen? 17. Was schlug einer seiner Freunde Kant einmal vor? 18. Warum soll er seine Schwester vierundzwanzig Jahre lang nicht gesehen haben? 19. War Kant ein Weiberfeind? 20. Was sagte er von den Damen? 21. Warum hat er die beiden Male nicht geheiratet? 22. Mit wem lebte er zusammen? 23. Warum mußte Kant Lampe schließlich gehen lassen? 24. Was stand auf dem Memorandum, das er sich schrieb? 25. Was tat er mit diesem Memorandum?

WORTSCHATZ

abends	in the evening	**kochen**	to cook, boil
bestimmen	to determine	**kritisch gegen-**	to be critical toward
bezeugen (from:	to attest	**über /stehen**	
der Zeuge		die **Küche, –n**	kitchen
witness)		**morgens**	in the morning
bisher	until now	die **Pfeife, –n**	pipe
zu Ende gehen	to come to an end	**rein**	pure, clean
der **Entschluß,**	decision	der **Spaziergang, ⸗e**	walk
Entschlüsse		**stammen (aus)**	to come from, hail
einen Ent-			from
schluß fassen	to make a decision	**stellen**	to place; *of clocks:*
entwickeln	to develop		to set
so etwas	something like that	**still**	quiet
fassen	to grasp	die **Stille**	quiet, quietness
das **Frühstück, –e**	breakfast	die **Tasse, –n**	cup
gar	even	der **Teil, –e**	part
das **Gebiet, –e**	realm, region	die **Uhr, –en**	clock
die **Gegenwart**	presence; present	**um . . . Uhr**	at . . . o'clock
	(tense)	**sich unterhalten**	to converse; to en-
die **Geschwister** (*pl.*)	brothers and sisters	**(unterhält sich,**	gage in conversa-
das **Gesetz, –e**	law	**unterhielt sich,**	tion
das **Gespräch, –e**	conversation	**sich unter-**	
herrschen	to prevail	**halten)**	

unterliegen	to underlie, be sub-	der **Vormittag, –e**	forenoon, morning
(unterlag,	jected to	**weg-** (*prefix*)	away
unterlegen)		**weg/ziehen (zog**	to move away
untersuchen	to investigate	**weg, ist wegge-**	
die **Vernunft**	(critical) reason	**zogen)**	
vernünftig	reasonable	**zerstreut**	absent-minded
der **Verstand**	reason, intelligence	**zu sich nehmen**	to partake (of)

STRONG VERBS

bestehen (aus)	to consist of		**bestand**	**bestanden**
empfinden	to feel (to be)		**empfand**	**empfunden**
erfahren	to find out, experience	**erfährt**	**erfuhr**	**erfahren**
essen	to eat	**ißt**	**aß**	**gegessen**
verbieten	to forbid		**verbot**	**verboten**
vor/schlagen	to suggest	**schlägt vor**	**schlug vor**	**vorgeschlagen**
ziehen	to move; to pull		**zog**	**(ist) gezogen**

DISTINGUISH BETWEEN

das Café *café, coffee house* and **der Kaffee** *coffee*

der Entschluß and **die Entscheidung** *decision*. **Die Entscheidung** is a decison between things on hand, hence a choice; **der Entschluß** is a decision for something yet to come.

die Vernunft and **der Verstand** *reason*. In colloquial German the two words are used more or less interchangeably, with preference given to **der Verstand**; a clear distinction is made in philosophy, where **die Vernunft** is *reasoning ability*. German for *common sense* is: **der gesunde Menschenverstand** (not **Vernunft**).

GRAMMATICAL TERMS

1. *Relative pronouns* refer (relate) to a noun in the preceding clause; such pronouns are: *who, whom, whose, which, that:*

> Kant was a man *who* greatly influenced his age.

2. The word to which the relative pronoun refers is the *antecedent:*

> *The walk* which Kant took everyday . . . .

3. The case of the relative pronoun depends on its function in the relative clause it introduces:

> He complained to *the mayor, who investigated the case.*
> He had dinner with *the friends whom he had invited.*

In the first example, the relative pronoun (*who*) is the subject, in the second it (*whom*) is the object of the verb in the relative clause.

RELATIVE PRONOUNS IN GERMAN

1. The relative pronouns are **der, die, das,** and their declension is the same as that of the demonstrative pronouns (see Aufgabe 4):

	SINGULAR			PLURAL
	Masc.	Fem.	Neuter	(all genders)
NOM.	der	die	das	die
ACC.	den	die	das	die
DAT.	dem	der	dem	denen
GEN.	dessen	deren	dessen	deren

These relative pronouns refer to specific or definite antecedents:

der Mann, der . . .   *the man who . . .*

Forms of the relative pronouns are easily distinguished from those of the demonstrative pronouns because they begin a (relative) clause and are, therefore, preceded by a comma:

Er hat es nur **denen** (demonstrative) gesagt, **denen** (relative) er traute.
He told only those whom he trusted.

2. Welcher, welche, welches may also be used as relative pronouns, except that they form no genitives; in the genitive, forms of **der, die, das** must be used. The relative pronouns **welcher, welche, welches** are less common than **der, die, das:**

	SINGULAR			PLURAL
	Masc.	Fem.	Neuter	(all genders)
NOM.	welcher	welche	welches	welche
ACC.	welchen	welche	welches	welche
DAT.	welchem	welcher	welchem	welchen
GEN.	dessen	deren	dessen	deren

3. Relative pronouns agree in number and gender with their *antecedents,* but their cases are determined by their *function* (subject, object) in the (relative) clause:

(sing.)

⟵──── (dat.)

Kant, mit dem ──⟶ **ein Zeitalter zu Ende ging . . .**

⟵

(masc.)

The following examples are limited to masculine singular cases:

NOMINATIVE: **Kant, der (welcher)** nicht nur das Gespräch liebte . . .
Kant, who not only loved conversation . . .

ACCUSATIVE: **Kant, den (welchen)** jeder in Königsberg kannte . . .
Kant, whom everyone in Königsberg knew . . .

DATIVE: **Kant, dem (welchem)** einmal einer seiner Freunde vorschlug . . .
Kant, to whom one of his friends once suggested . . .

GENITIVE: **Kants Diener, dessen Name** Lampe war . . .
Kant's servant, whose name was Lampe . . .

4. Relative clauses are dependent clauses which are set off by commas and in which the finite verb stands at the end. A relative pronoun may *never* be omitted in German (as it may in English):

> **Das Buch, das ich mir gekauft habe, war nicht teuer.**
> *The book (that) I bought was not expensive.*

5. The indefinite relative pronouns are **wer** and **was.** They refer to antecedents that are general or indeterminate. They cannot be used in place of **der, die, das.**

a. **Wer** is used much like English *he who* or *whoever* in an indefinite relative clause; the main clause follows it and begins with a demonstrative pronoun (usually omitted in the nominative but not in other cases):

> **Wer nicht arbeitet,** (der) soll auch nicht essen.
> *He who doesn't work is not to eat either.*

> **Wer einmal lügt,** dem glaubt man nicht.
> (lit., *He who lies once is not believed.*)
> *Nobody believes anybody who has once lied.*

b. **Was** (*what, that which, that*) is used as a relative pronoun when:

1. no antecedent exists; it then has the meaning of "whatever":

> Wir tun, **was wir können.**
> *We will do what (whatever) we can.*

2. an indefinite neuter antecedent like **alles, nichts, etwas** precedes:

> **Alles, was er sagt,** ist Unsinn.
> *All (that) he says is nonsense.*

3. a neuter adjective in the superlative used as noun precedes it:

> Das ist **das Beste, was man darüber sagen kann.**
> *That is the best that can be said about it.*

4. it sums up, or derives a conclusion from a preceding clause; **was** then usually means "a fact that" or "a thing that":

Kant hat ein Zeitalter beendet, **was wir erst heute richtig verstehen.**
Kant terminated an age, a fact we understand correctly only today.

Just as the definite relative pronoun, the indefinite relative pronoun can never be omitted in German.

RECAPITULATION OF MAIN POINTS

1. The definite relative pronouns are **der, die, das.** They are declined like demonstrative pronouns.

2. The relative pronouns **welcher, welche, welches** are less common than **der, die, das.** In the genitive, forms of **der, die, das** must be used.

3. The relative pronoun agrees with its antecedent in gender and number, but its case is determined by its function in the relative clause.

4. Relative pronouns are never omitted in German.

5. The indefinite relative pronoun **wer** is equivalent to *he who, whoever.*

6. The indefinite relative pronoun **was** is used when no antecedent precedes; after indefinite neuter antecedents like **alles, etwas, nichts;** after neuter adjectives in the superlative used as nouns **(das Beste);** and when summing up a preceding clause (where **was** is equivalent to *a fact that* or *something that*).

7. Wer and **was** may never be used in place of the definite relative pronouns **der, die, das** or **welcher, welche, welches.**

ÜBUNGEN

Practice in Reading and Writing

A. *Read aloud and translate:*

Der uneingeladene Gast

1. Johann Georg Hamann, der wie Kant in Königsberg lebte, hatte manchmal

sonderbare Ideen. 2. Eines Tages hatte er einen Freund eingeladen, mit dem er einen schönen Rehbraten essen wollte, den ihm einer seiner Verehrer geschenkt hatte. 3. Da öffnete sich die Tür und ein junger Mann erschien, dessen Gesellschaft Hamann nicht ausstehen konnte. 4. Der junge Mann sah den Braten, den der Diener schon auf den Tisch gestellt hatte, und zeigte sich bereit, mit den beiden Freunden Platz zu nehmen, was Hamann aber unbedingt verhindern wollte. 5. Schließlich nahm er den jungen Mann beiseite und flüsterte ihm ins Ohr: „Sie kennen doch die Tungusen, von denen man sagt, daß sie Hundebraten essen? 6. Wir Europäer haben gegen Hundebraten eine Art Abneigung—was mein Freund hier vernünftig findet, ich aber nicht. 7. Heute will ich ihm nun beweisen, daß die Abneigung gegen Hundebraten, die so viele Leute haben, ohne Grund ist. 8. Was da auf dem Tisch steht, hält er für einen Rehbraten. 9. Was es wirklich ist, darf er erst nach dem Essen erfahren. 10. Sie, von dessen Urteil wir beide viel halten, müssen daher unbedingt mit uns essen; bitte, nehmen Sie Platz!" 11. „Ein interessantes Experiment", meinte der junge Mann etwas unsicher, „dem ich gerne beiwohnen würde, wozu ich heute aber leider gar keine Zeit habe." 12. Damit verabschiedete er sich schnell, und Hamann und dessen Freund, dem er die Geschichte während der Mahlzeit erzählte, haben noch oft darüber gelacht.

1	sonderbar	*strange*		**die Tungusen**	*Tungus* (Mongols
2	der Rehbraten, –	*roast venison*			of Eastern
3	ausstehen können	*to be able to stand*			Siberia)
4	bereit	*ready*	6	**die Abneigung, –en**	*aversion*
	unbedingt	*absolutely*	11	**bei/wohnen** (*w. dat.*)	*to attend*
	verhindern	*to prevent*		**würde**	*would*
5	flüstern	*to whisper*	12	**sich verabschieden**	*to take leave*
				die Mahlzeit, –en	*meal*

B. *Translate:*

1. In England ist alles erlaubt, was nicht verboten ist. 2. In Deutschland ist alles verboten, was nicht erlaubt ist. 3. In Frankreich ist alles erlaubt, was verboten ist. 4. Wer nicht kann, was er will, muß wollen, was er kann. 5. Das ist das Beste, was darüber bisher geschrieben worden ist. 6. Ich glaube dir alles, was du sagst. 7. Das ist etwas, was ich noch nicht gehört habe. 8. Es gibt da nichts, was Sie nicht wissen dürfen. 9. Was er gesagt hat, weiß ich nicht. 10. Wer das ist, weiß ich nicht. 11. Wer sich selbst hilft, dem wird geholfen. 12. Ich verstehe nichts von dem, was Sie da sagen. 13. Er ist gestern in Boston gewesen, was er gar nicht geplant hatte. 14. Er hatte die Angewohnheit (*habit*), in jeder Gesellschaft, in der er sich befand, über Politik zu reden. 15. Viele Bücher, die für die Ewigkeit (*eternity*) geschrieben wurden, haben nicht einmal eine zweite Auflage (*edition*) erlebt. 16. Von der Architektur, von der er so gerne redete, verstand er fast gar nichts. 17. Kennen Sie die Dichter, deren Werke wir lesen wollen?

18. Wer kennt die Frau, deren Mann in unserem Geschäft arbeitet?   19. Theodor Storm, der Autor von „Immensee", ist der Dichter derer, die gerne sentimentale Geschichten lesen.   20. Was wissen wir von all denen, mit denen wir jeden Tag zusammenkommen?   21. Das sind Gedanken, welche Sie schon bei Lichtenberg finden.   22. Welche Gedanken finden sich bei Lichtenberg nicht!   23. Niemand von denen, die das Stück gesehen haben, hat es wirklich verstanden.

C. *Supply the correct form of the relative pronoun:*

1. (*who*) Der Student, _____ heute hier war, war lange krank.   2. (*whose*) Der Mann, _____ Name ich vergessen habe, ist etwas zerstreut.   3. (*whom*) Ihr Freund, _____ sie lange nicht gesehen hatte, kam.   4. (*to whom*) Das Mädchen, _____ ich das Buch gegeben habe, heißt Marie.   5. (*whom*) Die Studentin, mit _____ er gesprochen hat, ist sehr intelligent.   6. (*which*) Die Stadt, in _____ er arbeitet, ist nicht weit von Berlin.   7. (*whose*) Der Philosoph, _____ Werk wir studieren, war Deutscher.   8. (*whom*) Die Leute, von _____ ich lange nicht gehört habe, waren in Europa.   9. (*which*) Der Spaziergang, _____ er jeden Tag machte, war ziemlich lang.   10. (*whom*) Die Freunde, mit _____ er zu essen pflegte, waren seine Kollegen.   11. (*whom, whom*) Der Diener, ohne _____ er nicht leben und _____ er nicht vergessen konnte, war früher Soldat gewesen.   12. (*which*) Das Relativpronomen ist etwas, _____ er nicht verstehen kann!

D. *Translate:*

1. He does not want to read a book he cannot understand.   2. He had made a plan that was really very reasonable.   3. Whoever can understand this philosopher must be a philosopher himself.   4. History is something that one should learn in school.   5. His lectures are on (**über**) Germany, of which I know very little.   6. His lectures lasted two hours, which was too long for most (of the people).   7. Lichtenberg married a woman whom he had taken into his house as a little girl and with whom he fell in love later. 8. Goethe later acted similarly, which shocked (**schockieren**) the society of Weimar.   9. He took trips during which he collected many rocks.   10. These are the rocks which he later fit (**ein/fügen**) into his collections.   11. Only those who know Germany well can follow his descriptions.   12. Fritz is inviting everybody who can come.   13. There are women who forget nothing they have heard.   14. Those were impressions I shall never forget.   15. Is that all you have to say?   16. Is that the breakfast he always talks about? 17. That is the last I have heard of him.   18. These then (**also**) are the relative pronouns over which we have stumbled (**stolpern über**) so often.

Oral Exercises

E. *Change the following sentences to relative clauses. Begin each sentence with* **Kant ist der Philosoph, . . .:**

EXAMPLE: Er lebte im achtzehnten Jahrhundert.
Kant ist der Philosoph, der im achtzehnten Jahrhundert lebte.

1. Über ihn gibt es viele Anekdoten.   2. Mit ihm beginnt ein neues Zeitalter.
3. Seine Heimat ist Ostpreußen.   4. Er hatte viele Interessen.   5. Für ihn war Genauigkeit alles.   6. Nach ihm haben die Königsberger ihre Uhren gestellt.   7. Sein Diener hieß Lampe.   8. Er hatte keine Zeit für Frauen.
9. Mit ihm endete die Aufklärung.

F. *Change the following sentences to relative clauses. Begin each sentence with* **Ich habe eine Freundin, . . .:**

EXAMPLE: Sie spricht gut Deutsch.
Ich habe eine Freundin, die gut Deutsch spricht.

1. Mit ihr studiere ich.
2. An sie denke ich oft.
3. Ihr helfe ich gern.
4. Sie hilft mir auch gern.
5. Von ihr habe ich dieses Buch bekommen.
6. Sie ist noch sehr jung.
7. Ihre Schwester heißt Maria.
8. Sie finde ich interessant.
9. Ihre Eltern habe ich kennengelernt.

G. *Change the following sentences to relative clauses. Begin each sentence with* **Hier kommen die Leute, . . .:**

EXAMPLE: Sie haben eine lange Reise gemacht.
Hier kommen die Leute, die eine lange Reise gemacht haben.

1. Für sie haben wir Zeit.
2. Von ihnen hören wir viel.
3. Ihr Interesse ist groß.
4. Mit ihnen diskutieren wir gern.
5. Ihnen glauben wir alles.
6. Sie verstehen wir gut.
7. Ihre Reise ist wunderbar gewesen.

20

Word Order; Conjunctions

Der Dreißigjährige[1] Krieg

Der Dreißigjährige Krieg (1618 bis 1648)[2] hat als Religionskrieg begonnen, als das letzte Kapitel in der Geschichte der Reformation. Die beiden[3] Parteien, die protestantische und die katholische, mußten erst, wie es scheint, miteinander um die Macht ringen, ehe sie in Frieden zusammenleben konnten. Aber schon früh hatten die politischen Fragen die religiösen immer mehr 5 verdrängt. Obwohl nämlich Gustav Adolf[4] mit seinen Schweden im Namen der Reformation in Deutschland erschienen war, war er in Wirklichkeit gekommen, weil er sein kleines Schweden zu einer europäischen Großmacht zu machen beabsichtigte. Aber nicht nur Deutschland, Österreich und Schweden waren miteinander im Krieg, sondern auch Frankreich, 10 Spanien, England, Dänemark und Holland. Wir haben wirklich jeden Grund, den Dreißigjährigen Krieg als den ersten Weltkrieg zu bezeichnen.

Deutschland war durch seine Lage, in der Mitte Europas, zum Schlachtfeld besonders geeignet. Immer wieder drangen die Armeen von allen Seiten durch das Land, von Norden nach Süden, von Westen nach Osten. 15

---

1. **Dreißigjährige** *Thirty Years'*. 2. (read:) **sechzehnhundertachtzehn bis sechzehnhundertachtundvierzig.** 3. **die beiden** (note that German prefers **beide** as an adjective where English uses the numeral *two*). 4. **Gustav Adolf** *Gustavus Adolphus* (1594–1632, king of Sweden).

Wie Heuschrecken[5] stürzten sie sich auf alles und fraßen es auf. Wenn auch einige Teile Deutschlands, wie etwa die Stadt Hamburg, in diesen langen Krieg, der eigentlich aus vier oder fünf verschiedenen Kriegen bestand, nicht hineingezogen wurden, so sind andere fast vollkommen zerstört
20 worden. Zu Beginn des Krieges hatte Deutschland achtzehn Millionen Einwohner, nach dessen Ende jedoch nur noch vier. Aber nicht nur Menschen waren gemordet, Städte zerstört, Felder verwüstet, sondern auch das Leben selbst war verwildert,[6] die kulturelle Entwicklung des Landes unterbrochen. Der Landsknecht[7] war der Herr im Land, und Soldatsein war sein Beruf.
25 Außerdem hat man geschätzt, daß einer Armee von 40 000[8] Mann[9] ein Troß[10] von 140 000[11] Männern, Frauen und Kindern folgte, die von dem Sold und der Beute der Soldaten lebten. Hans Jakob Christoffel von Grimmelshausen[12] hat uns in seinem großen Roman vom „Abenteuerlichen Simplizissimus", einer Geschichte seiner eigenen Kindheit und Jugend
30 während des Krieges, ein lebendiges Bild von den Zuständen der Zeit gegeben.

Das Schicksal der Stadt Magdeburg ist besonders interessant, indem es uns zeigt, wie wenig das menschliche Leben damals wert war. Tilly, der Feldherr Kaiser Ferdinands,[13] hatte die Stadt belagert, während die Magdeburger auf die Hilfe der Schweden warteten. Als Tilly die Stadt schließlich
35 nahm, hatten seine Soldaten freie Hand, denn eine eroberte Stadt war nach damaligem Kriegsrecht[14] die Beute des Siegers. Nachdem aber die Soldaten in die Stadt eingedrungen waren, fingen einige Häuser bei der Plünderung[15] Feuer, und niemand war da, es zu löschen. Vor ihren Augen sahen die Soldaten ihre Beute verbrennen, und damit begann ein Morden
40 und Brennen ohne Beispiel. Am Ende blieb von der Stadt nichts als die Kathedrale und ein großer, glimmender Aschenhaufen.[16]

5. **Heuschrecken** *locusts.* 6. **verwildert** *laid bare* (made "wild"). 7. **Landsknecht** *mercenary.* 8. (read:) **vierzigtausend.** 9. **Mann** (does not form a grammatical plural when used as a unit of measurement). 10. **Troß** *camp following.* 11. (read:) **hundertvierzigtausend.** 12. **Grimmelshausen** 1610 or 1625–1676, German novelist; his *Abenteuerlicher Simplizissimus* is the first German novel of more than national interest. 13. Ferdinand II, 1578–1637, became Holy Roman Emperor in 1619. 14. **Kriegsrecht** *law of war.* 15. **Plünderung** *sack.* 16. **Aschenhaufen** *heap of ashes.*

FRAGEN

1. Wie hat der Dreißigjährige Krieg begonnen? 2. Was mußten die beiden Parteien tun, ehe sie in Frieden zusammenleben konnten? 3. Was hatte die religiösen Fragen schon früh immer mehr verdrängt? 4. Warum war Gustav Adolf in Wirklichkeit nach Deutschland gekommen? 5. Welche Länder

waren miteinander im Krieg? 6. Als was können wir den Dreißigjährigen Krieg bezeichnen? 7. Wodurch war Deutschland zum Schlachtfeld besonders geeignet? 8. Wie drangen die Armeen durch das Land? 9. Warum waren sie wie Heuschrecken? 10. Was tun Heuschrecken? 11. Gab es Teile Deutschlands, die in den Krieg nicht hineingezogen wurden? 12. Wie viele Einwohner hatte Deutschland zu Beginn und am Ende des Krieges? 13. Was war zerstört, verwüstet und verwildert? 14. Was hat uns Grimmelshausen in seinem ,,Abenteuerlichen Simplizissimus" gegeben? 15. Warum ist das Schicksal der Stadt Magdeburg besonders interessant? 16. Was tat Tilly? 17. Was taten die Magdeburger? 18. Warum hatten Tillys Soldaten schließlich freie Hand? 19. Warum hat man die brennenden Häuser nicht gelöscht? 20. Was blieb am Ende von der Stadt?

WORTSCHATZ

belagern	to besiege, lay siege to	die **Mitte**	middle, center
der **Beruf, –e**	profession	(das) **Österreich**	Austria
die **Beute**	booty	**schätzen**	to estimate
das **Bild, –er**	picture	das **Schicksal, –e**	fate
damalig (*adj.*)	at (of) that time	die **Schlacht, –en**	battle
sich eignen (für, zu)	to be suited (for)	das **Schlachtfeld, –er**	battlefield
geeignet	suited	der **Sieger, –**	victor
der **Einwohner, –**	inhabitant	der **Sold**	(army) pay
die **Entwicklung, –en**	development	**sich stürzen (auf, w. acc.)**	to descend (violently)(upon)
(er)morden	to murder	**verdrängen**	to supplant, to displace
erobern	to conquer		
der **Feldherr, –n, –(e)n**	general	**verwüsten** (*from: die Wüste desert*)	to devastate
die **Hilfe**	help		
das **Kapitel, –**	chapter	**vollkommen**	complete(ly)
die **Lage**	situation, location	**wert**	worth
löschen	to extinguish	die **Wirklichkeit, –en**	reality
die **Macht, ⸗e**	power	der **Zustand, ⸗e**	condition

STRONG VERBS

dringen	to push; to penetrate		**drang**	ist **gedrungen**
fressen	to eat[1]	**frißt**	**fraß**	**gefressen**
glimmen	to glow		**glomm**	**geglommen**
ringen (um)	to fight (for); to wrestle		**rang**	**gerungen**
unterbrechen	to interrupt	**unterbricht**	**unterbrach**	**unterbrochen**

Remember the names of the four directions: **der Norden, der Süden, der Osten, der Westen.**

[1] Used of animals and animal-like eating.

GRAMMATICAL TERMS

1. A *main* (principal or independent) *clause* is a sentence unit consisting of one or more subjects and a predicate (a verb or a verbal expression) that can stand by itself:

> He was standing at the corner.
> A table and five chairs are in the room.

2. A *dependent* (or subordinate) *clause* also consists of one or more subjects and a verb, introduced usually by a subordinate conjunction or a relative pronoun which characterize the clause as an incomplete sentence unable to stand by itself:

> DEPENDENT CLAUSE   MAIN CLAUSE
> Although he was standing at the corner,   we didn't see him.

3. *Conjunctions* connect words, phrases, or clauses:

> He *and* I were standing at the corner, *but* she didn't see us.
> We didn't see him *while* he was standing at the corner.

4. Conjunctions are *coordinating* when they connect words, phrases, or clauses of equal value (for example: two nouns, two pronouns, two dependent clauses, two main clauses):

> He *and* I were standing at the corner, *but* she didn't see us.

5. Conjunctions are *subordinating* when they introduce a dependent clause:

> We didn't see him *because* he was standing behind a car.

WORD ORDER: MAIN CLAUSES

1. Word Order Review

We have already learned that the finite verb takes the second position in German main clauses, but that the subject usually follows the verb if the clause begins with an element other than the subject (an object, adverb, prepositional phrase, or a dependent clause):

FIRST POSITION	SECOND POSITION	
Der Dichter	**hörte**	diese Geschichte von seiner Mutter.
Diese Geschichte	**hörte**	der Dichter von seiner Mutter.
Von seiner Mutter	**hörte**	der Dichter diese Geschichte.
Weil ich es nicht wußte,	**hat**	er es mir gesagt.

2. The Split Predicate

    a. We have further seen that separable prefixes, infinitives, and past participles stand at the end of a main clause:

SEPARABLE PREFIX:	Er **geht** nie ohne seine Frau **aus.**
	He never goes out without his wife.
INFINITIVE:	Er **möchte** ohne seine Frau **ausgehen.**
	He would like to go out without his wife.
PAST PARTICIPLE:	Er **ist** gestern ohne seine Frau **ausgegangen.**
	He went out without his wife yesterday.

We call these forms **(geht . . . aus, möchte . . . ausgehen, ist . . . ausgegangen)** split predicates.

Occasionally the second part of a split predicate is followed by an afterthought or the second part of a comparison:

> Er ist gestern ausgegangen, **aber nicht mit seiner Frau.**
> *He went out yesterday, but without his wife.*
> Er ist schneller gelaufen **als sein Bruder.**
> *He ran faster than his brother.*

    b. The following verbs with their verbal complements are treated like split predicates:

      1. **sein** or **werden** with predicate adjectives:

beliebt sein:	Er **ist** überall **beliebt.**
	He is popular everywhere.
reich werden:	Er **wurde** schnell **reich.**
	He got rich fast.

      2. **sein** or **werden** with a predicate noun:

Student sein:	Er **ist** jetzt **Student.**
	He is a student now.
Professor werden:	Er **wird** nächstes Jahr **Professor.**
	He will be a professor next year.

      3. a verb in combination with a directive (a prepositional phrase which answers the question **wohin?**):

nach Hause gehen:	Wir **gehen** bald **nach Hause.**
	We are going home soon.

      4. expressions like the following:

Klavier spielen:	Sie **spielt** sehr gut **Klavier.**
	She plays the piano very well.

Deutsch sprechen: Er **spricht** jetzt gut **Deutsch.**
He speaks German well now.
Kaffee trinken: Alle **trinken** um 4 Uhr **Kaffee.**
Everybody drinks coffee at 4 o'clock.

3. Position of Direct and Indirect Objects

    a. If both objects are nouns, the indirect object usually precedes the direct object:

        Er gab **dem Mann das Geld.**   *He gave the man the money.*
                           or *He gave the money to the man.*

    But the sequence may be reversed, if the direct object is preceded by a definite article and the indirect object by an **ein-**word and if the indirect object is emphasized:

        Er gibt **das Buch einem Studenten.**
        He gives the book to a student.
        Er gibt **das Geld seinem Sohn.**
        He gives the money to his son.

    b. If both objects are personal pronouns, the direct object precedes:

        Er gab **es ihm.**
        He gave it to him.

    c. If one object is a noun and one a pronoun, the pronoun object precedes:

        Er gab **es seinem Sohn.**
        He gave it to his son.
        Er gab **ihm das Geld.**
        He gave him the money.

4. Contrary to English, adverbs and adverbial phrases of time precede those of place:

        Werden Sie **morgen in der Stadt** sein?
        Will you be in town tomorrow?
        Ist er **jetzt zu Hause?**
        Is he at home now?

By and large, the sequence of adverbs and adverbial phrases is: time—manner—place:

	TIME	MANNER	PLACE
Er kam	**heute**	**schnell**	**nach Hause.**

He came home quickly today.

5. Position of **nicht**

Nicht negates either a predicate (and thereby an entire sentence) or various parts of the sentence.

a. Position of **nicht** negating the entire sentence:

After objects:

> Er gibt dem Studenten das Buch **nicht.**
> *He doesn't give the student the book.*
> Er gibt es ihm **nicht.**
> *He doesn't give it to him.*

After expressions stating specific time, like **heute, jetzt, diese Woche:**

> Wir kommen heute **nicht.**
> *We are not coming today.*
> Er arbeitet diese Woche **nicht.**
> *He doesn't work this week.*

In sentences with split predicates, before the second part:

> Er hat dem Studenten das Buch **nicht** gegeben.
> *He didn't give the student the book.*
> Er hat diese Woche **nicht** gearbeitet.
> *He didn't work this week.*
> Er spricht **nicht** Deutsch.
> *He doesn't speak German.*

Before prepositional phrases:

> Sie sind heute **nicht zu Hause.**
> *They are not at home today.*
> Ich antworte ihm **nicht auf seinen Brief.**
> *I do not answer his letter.*

Before adverbs:

> Wir haben **nicht viel** gearbeitet.
> *We didn't work much.*
> Wir arbeiten **nicht viel.**
> *We don't work much.*
> Er fährt **nicht schnell.**
> *He doesn't drive fast.*

b. Position of **nicht** emphatically negating various parts of the sentence.

Nicht precedes the emphasized part, usually followed by a clause with **sondern:**

Er liest das Buch **nicht.** Er liest die Zeitung.
Er liest **nicht das Buch, sondern die Zeitung.**
He reads not the book, but the newspaper.

Er geht **nicht** in die Stadt. Sie geht in die Stadt.
Nicht er geht in die Stadt, **sondern sie.**
It is not he, but she who is going to town.

Er arbeitet diese Woche **nicht.** Er arbeitet nächste Woche.
Er arbeitet **nicht diese, sondern nächste Woche.**
He doesn't work this week, but next week.

Note that **nicht** usually precedes **jeder** and **alle:**

Ich kenne **nicht jeden (nicht alle)** Menschen.
I don't know everybody.

WORD ORDER: DEPENDENT CLAUSES

1. Dependent clauses are usually introduced by subordinating conjunctions, including interrogatives and relative pronouns. In dependent clauses the finite verb stands last:

Ich sagte es ihm, **weil er es noch nicht gehört hatte.**
I told him because he had not heard it.

2. Exceptions are:

a. The finite verb stands before a double infinitive:

Er glaubt, daß ich es nicht **habe tun können.**

b. When the conjunction **daß** is omitted, the word order of main clauses is used:

With **daß:**   Ich weiß, **daß** er das Buch **nicht gelesen hat.**
Without **daß:**   Ich weiß, **er hat** das Buch **nicht gelesen.**

c. When **wenn** (*if*) is omitted, the verb comes first (inverted word order):

With **wenn:**   **Wenn er** nach Hause **kommt,** ist alles gut.
Without **wenn:**   **Kommt er** nach Hause, (dann) ist alles gut.

3. Separable prefixes are joined to the finite verb at the end of a dependent clause:

Ich glaube, daß er morgen **ankommt.**

The rules for the sequence of objects, adverbs, and the position of **nicht** in main clauses also apply to dependent clauses.

CONJUNCTIONS

1. Coordinating Conjunctions

a. Coordinating conjunctions do not affect word order:

Er konnte den Ring nicht kaufen, **denn er hatte kein Geld bei sich.**
He couldn't buy the ring, because he had no money with him.
Heute ist er nicht gekommen, **aber morgen kommt er bestimmt.** (Inversion
because of adverb)
He didn't come today but he'll certainly come tomorrow.

b. The principal coordinating conjunctions are:

aber	*but, however*	**oder**	*or*
allein	*yet, however*	**sondern**	*but, but rather*
denn	*for, because*	**und**	*and*

entweder . . . oder[1]	*either . . .* or
weder . . . noch[1]	*neither . . . nor*

c. Observe especially these coordinating conjunctions:

1. **Aber** and **sondern** both mean *but;* **sondern** may follow a negation
   and suggests the idea of "on the contrary":

   Ich wartete auf ihn, **aber er kam nicht.**
   I waited for him but he didn't come.
   Ich wartete nicht auf ihn, **sondern ging sofort nach Hause.**[2]
   I didn't wait for him but (on the contrary) went home right away.

2. Distinguish between the conjunction **allein** (*yet, however*) and the
   adverb **allein** (*alone*); the word order used in the clause decides:
   after the conjunction, the word order is dependent, after the adverb
   (if it begins the clause) it is inverted:

   CONJUNCTION: **Allein er konnte** es nicht tun.   *Yet he couldn't do it.*
   ADVERB: **Allein konnte er** es nicht tun.   *He could not do it alone.*

[1] **Weder . . . noch,** when introducing clauses, are followed by inverted word order; **entweder,**
when introducing a clause, may have normal or inverted word order:

> **Weder er noch sie** weiß es. (Not introducing a clause)
> *Neither he nor she knows it.*

But: **Weder weiß er** es, **noch kann er** es sich denken.
> *He neither knows nor can imagine it.*

> **Entweder kommst du** mit (or: **du kommst** mit), **oder ich gehe allein.**
> *Either you come along, or I'll go alone.*

[2] Note also the common combination **nicht nur . . ., sondern auch** (*not only . . . but also*):

> **Napoleon besiegte nicht nur Österreich, sondern auch viele andere Länder.**
> *Napoleon defeated not only Austria but also many other countries.*

2. Subordinating Conjunctions

a. Subordinating conjunctions introduce dependent clauses in which the verb is at the end (dependent word order). The principal subordinating conjunctions are:

als	*when*[1]	**obgleich, obschon, obwohl**	*although*
bevor	*before*[1]	**seit, seitdem**	*since* (temporal)
bis	*until*	**sobald**	*as soon as*
da	*since, because*	**so daß**	*so that*
damit	*so that*	**während**	*while*[1]
daß	*that*	**(wann**[3]	*when*)
ehe	*before*[1]	**weil**	*because*
falls	*if, in case*	**wenn**	*if, when(ever)*
indem	*while, in that*[2]	**wenn auch (wenn . . . auch)**	*although, even though*
nachdem	*after*[1]	**wenn . . . nicht**	*unless*
ob	*whether*	**wie**	*as*

b. Note the differences in the use of **als, wann, wenn:**

als (*when*) refers to a single event in the past:

> **Als er das hörte,** wurde er sehr wütend.

wann (*when, at what time*) is used for questions, direct or indirect:

> **Wann kommt er?**
> Wissen Sie, **wann er kommt?**

wenn (*when, whenever, at the time when*) is used if the verb is (1) in the present or future; (2) for repeated action in the present, past, or future (*whenever*), sometimes combined with **immer;** (3) in conditional clauses (*if*):

(1) **Wenn er kommt,** müssen wir ihn freundlich begrüßen.
   When he comes, we have to greet him in a friendly manner.
(2) **(Immer) wenn er zu uns kommt (kam),** begrüßen (begrüßten) wir ihn freundlich.
   Whenever he comes (came) to us, we greet(ed) him in a friendly manner.
(3) **Wenn er käme,** müßten wir ihn freundlich begrüßen.
   If he were coming, we would have to greet him in a friendly manner.

c. Distinguish the subordinating conjunction **da** (*since, because*) from the adverb **da** (*there, then*); the conjunction **damit** (*so that*) from the **da**-compound **damit** (*with that*); and the conjunction **während** (*while*) from the preposition **während** (*during*):

---

[1] Often followed by + -*ing* form of the verb.
[2] Often equivalent to *by* + *ing*-form of verb:

> Sie können das lernen, **indem Sie gut aufpassen.**
> *You can learn it by paying close attention.*

[3] **Wann** is not a conjunction but an interrogative; it is included here to set it off from **als** and **wenn.**

da: **Da er es selbst sah,** glaubte er es.
            Since he saw it himself, he believed it.
            Da sah er es.   *Then he saw it.*

damit: Geben Sie mir die Werkzeuge, **damit ich arbeiten kann.**
            Give me the tools so that I can work.
            Damit kann ich arbeiten. *I can work with that.*

während: **Während ich schlief,** regnete es.
            While I was sleeping, it rained.
            Während der Nacht regnete es. *It rained during the night.*

3. **Ob** (*whether*) may be used without an antecedent main clause; it is then equivalent to *I* (*we*, etc.) *wonder whether:*

        Ob er heute wohl kommt? *I wonder whether he'll come today.*

Auch in the conjunction **wenn auch** is frequently separated from **wenn**:

        Wir gehen aus, **wenn** das Wetter **auch** schlecht ist.
        We'll go out even if the weather is bad.

4. Contrary to English, German uses the present tense in subordinate clauses introduced by **seit (seitdem)** when the action began in the past and is continuing in the present:[1]

        Seit (seitdem) er hier ist, ist er krank.
        Since he has been here, he has been sick.

RECAPITULATION OF MAIN POINTS

1. A characteristic feature of the German sentence is the split predicate. Split predicates may consist of:

    a. a verb and a separable prefix: Er **geht** heute **aus.**
    b. an auxiliary verb or a modal and a past participle or an infinitive: Er **ist** heute **ausgegangen.** Er **will** heute **ausgehen.**
    c. A specific group of verbs with verbal complements: Er **ist** überall sehr **beliebt.** Er **spielt** sehr gut **Klavier.**

2. Of two noun objects, the indirect usually precedes; of two pronoun objects, the direct precedes; if one object is a noun and the other a pronoun, the pronoun comes first.

3. The sequence of adverbs usually is: time—manner—place.

[1] See also Lesson 6, page 68.

4. Dependent Word Order

The word order for dependent clauses is the same as the normal word order for main clauses, except that the finite verb is at the end:

Wenn ihr das Buch morgen **mitbringt,** wird sie sich sehr freuen.

5. Coordinating conjunctions do not affect word order; subordinating conjunctions introduce dependent clauses in which the verb is at the end.

6. If the entire sentence is negated, **nicht** is usually placed before the second part of the predicate, before adverbs, predicate adjectives, predicate nouns, and prepositional phrases (except expressions stating specific time). **Nicht** is usually placed after objects and expressions stating specific time.

ÜBUNGEN

Practice in Reading and Writing

    A. *Read aloud and translate:*

Vor der Himmelstür

1. Als wir noch jung waren, haben wir alle die Märchen der Brüder Grimm gelesen. 2. Entweder haben wir sie selbst gelesen, oder unsere Mütter haben sie uns vorgelesen oder erzählt. 3. Ob Sie sich wohl jemals die Frage gestellt haben, wer diese Brüder Grimm eigentlich waren? 4. Auch sie gehören unter die Romantiker, obgleich sie moderne Philologen und strenge Wissenschaftler waren. 5. Sie haben nicht nur die „Deutschen Hausmärchen" gesammelt, sondern sich noch mit anderen Arbeiten einen Namen gemacht. 6. Noch im Alter hat einer der Brüder, Jakob, das deutsche Wörterbuch begonnen, das so groß geplant war, daß es erst Generationen später, nach dem Zweiten Weltkrieg, fertig geworden ist. 7. Als die letzten Bände erschienen, waren die ersten schon veraltet. 8. Das ganze Werk ist so groß, daß Sie es sich nicht auf den Schreibtisch stellen können, auch wenn Sie das Geld dazu hätten. 9. Jakob Grimm hat sein Wörterbuch für Bibliotheken geschrieben, nachdem er mit seinem Bruder Wilhelm die Märchen für das Volk gesammelt hatte. 10. Sie kennen sicher Märchen wie „Hänsel und Gretel", „Rotkäppchen" und „Aschenbrötel", aber viele der kleineren

3	**jemals**	*ever*	6	**das Wörterbuch, ⸗er**	*dictionary*
4	**streng**	*strict*	7	**veraltet**	*outdated*
5	**sammeln**	*to collect*	8	**hätten**	*had*

Märchen kennen Sie wohl nicht. 11. Wie ist es zum Beispiel mit dem Märchen vom armen Bäuerlein und dem reichen Mann? 12. Nachdem sie beide am selben Tag gestorben waren, sind sie zusammen vor der Himmelstür erschienen. 13. Sankt Peter hat die Tür geöffnet, jedoch nur den reichen Mann gesehen, nicht aber auch das arme Bäuerlein. 14. So durfte der reiche Mann hereinkommen, während das arme Bäuerlein warten mußte, bis die Tür wieder geöffnet wurde. 15. Indem es da stand und hörte, wie die Engel sangen und musizierten und der ganze Himmel den reichen Mann begrüßte, ist es sehr traurig geworden, bis es dann überall wieder still wurde und Sankt Peter wieder an der Tür erschien. 16. Er wollte nur nachsehen, ob wieder jemand an der Himmelstür wartete. 17. Da hat er denn das arme Bäuerlein gesehen und hereingelassen. 18. Wieder ist große Freude im Himmel gewesen, allein niemand hat gesungen oder Musik gemacht. 19. Da ist das arme Bäuerlein noch trauriger geworden und hat gefragt, ob denn im Himmel die Reichen auch besser behandelt werden, genauso wie unten auf der Erde. 20. „Oh nein", hat Sankt Peter geantwortet, „aber arme Bäuerlein wie du kommen alle Tage in den Himmel, während so ein reicher Herr nur einmal alle hundert Jahre hereinkommt."

10	**Rotkäppchen**	*Little Red Riding Hood*	16	**nach /sehen (ie, a, e)**	*to have a look; to check*
	Aschenbrötel	*Cinderella*		**jemand**	*someone*
11	**das Bäuerlein, –**	*diminutive of* **der Bauer**	18	**die Freude**	*joy*
15	**traurig**	*sad*	19	**behandeln**	*to treat*

B. *Translate:*

1. Obgleich der Dreißigjährige Krieg als Religionskrieg begonnen hatte, war er doch mehr gewesen als das. 2. Es war nicht nur eine Frage der Religion gewesen, sondern vor allem der Macht. 3. Ob Sie das auch so in der Schule gelernt haben? 4. Viele Leute, sagt man, lesen nur, damit sie nicht denken müssen. 5. Damit ist aber nicht gesagt, daß die, die nicht lesen, mehr denken. 6. Indem sie lesen, denken sie. 7. Münchhausen erzählte seine Geschichten, obwohl er genau wußte, daß niemand sie glaubte. 8. Seine Freunde freuten sich über diese Geschichten, wenn sie auch kein Wort davon glaubten. 9. Während der Kongreß in Wien tanzte, machte Napoleon seine Pläne. 10. Nachdem er in Frankreich gelandet war, marschierte er sofort auf Paris zu. 11. Manche Menschen können weder sprechen noch zuhören. 12. Nimmt man ein Glas Wasser und legt ein Blatt (*sheet*) Papier darauf, so kann man das Glas Wasser umkippen (*to turn upside down*), ohne daß das Wasser herausläuft. 13. Es fragt sich aber, ob Sie dieses schöne Experiment auf Mutters bester Tischdecke (*tablecloth*) machen sollen. 14. Es ist eine gute Idee, damit zu warten, bis sie den Tisch abgedeckt (*cleared*) hat. 15. Als sie das hörte, lachte sie. 16. Wenn sie das hörte, lachte sie. 17. Ich weiß nicht, wann Sie das gehört haben.

C. *Connect the following sentences with the conjunctions in parentheses. Change the word order where necessary:*

1. Tillys Soldaten verwüsteten die Stadt. (nachdem) Sie hatten sie erobert. 2. Er redete die ganze Zeit. (denn) Niemand unterbrach ihn. 3. Sie belagerten die Stadt. (aber) Sie konnten sie nicht erobern. 4. Der Dreißigjährige Krieg bestand nicht aus einem Krieg. (sondern) Er bestand aus vier oder fünf Kriegen. 5. Tilly wurde General. (nachdem) Der Kaiser hatte mit Wallenstein gebrochen. 6. Er verschonte (*spared*) die Stadt. (damit) Die Soldaten konnten sie plündern. 7. Die Stadt brannte. (während) Die Soldaten plünderten sie. 8. Die Soldaten plünderten die Stadt. (wenn auch) Sie brannte. 9. Sie versuchten, das Feuer zu löschen. (bis) Sie hatten kein Wasser mehr. 10. (entweder . . . oder) Die Stadt wird verschont. Sie wird zerstört.

D. *Translate:*

1. He eats everything when he is well. 2. The soldiers devastated the city when they saw that they could not plunder it. 3. It has been estimated (use *man*) that 14 million inhabitants died during the war. 4. Have you forgotten to ask him whether he has set his watch? 5. A war interrupts the development of a country because the cultural life is destroyed. 6. Not Schiller but Goethe was the greatest German poet, which everyone knows. 7. You have to translate these sentences so that you learn to use the conjunctions properly. 8. I am going to Austria because I have never been to Vienna and Salzburg. 9. Berlin does not lie in the center of Germany but it is the greatest German city. 10. What was the situation in Germany after the war had ended? 11. I wonder whether he will interrupt me again. 12. They will not invite you until you have learned to be punctual. 13. One wonders whether this is really a fairy tale or not. 14. They hoped that they could displace enough water. 15. They went to Frankfurt after the war, although they knew that the city was more or less destroyed. 16. Most people went home when they saw how late it was. 17. They will either go to Boston or stay home. 19. I shall wait until you come home.

Oral Exercises

E. *Negate the following sentences with* **nicht:**

1. Kennen Sie Wallensteins Schicksal? 2. Diese Parteien ringen um die Macht. 3. Sie können in Frieden zusammenleben. 4. Die Stadt Hamburg ist zerstört worden. 5. Das menschliche Leben war damals viel wert. 6. Die Landsknechte belagerten diese Stadt. 7. Er kam gestern nach Wien. 8. Er wurde General. 9. Kennen Sie diesen General? 10. Sie kamen in dieser Woche nach Magdeburg.

F. *Begin the following sentences with dependent clauses:*

1. Die Soldaten ermordeten die Einwohner, als sie in die Stadt eindrangen.
2. Ich weiß nicht, ob er für einen solchen Beruf selbständig genug ist.
3. Sie kennen das Schicksal Wallensteins, wenn Sie Schillers Drama lesen.
4. Schiller hat seinen „Wilhelm Tell" geschrieben, obgleich er nie in der Schweiz (*Switzerland*) gewesen ist.   5. Sie müssen Schnitzler lesen, bevor Sie nach Österreich fahren.

G. Als, wann, wenn; *insert the correct conjunction:*

1. _____ das Feuer ausbrach, versuchte man, es zu löschen.   2. _____ eine Stadt erobert wurde, war sie die Beute der Soldaten.   3. Man fragte sich, _____ eigentlich das Feuer ausgebrochen war.   4. _____ die Magdeburger Hilfe brauchten, wandten sie sich an Gustav Adolf.   5. _____ Sie nach Österreich kommen, werden Sie sehen, wie verschieden die Deutschen und die Österreicher sind.   6. Wissen Sie schon, _____ Sie nach Österreich fahren werden?

21

Numerals

Shakespeare und die Deutschen

Eine Theatersaison[1] in den deutschsprechenden Ländern, also in Deutschland, Österreich und der Schweiz, bringt etwa 2000 Schauspielpremieren[2] an ungefähr 200 Theatern. An den hundert wichtigsten Bühnen werden in einem Jahr allein 50 Dramen Shakespeares neu einstudiert.

5   Das ist die Folge einer langen kulturhistorischen Entwicklung, die um das Jahr 1600 begann. Schon vor seinem Tode wurde Shakespeare durch die sogenannten „englischen Komödianten" (d.h.[3] Schauspieler) in Deutschland eingeführt. Sie waren aus England gekommen und zogen nun mit ihren Stücken, vor allem mit Shakespeare-Dramen, von Hof zu Hof und von
10 Stadt zu Stadt. Zuerst spielten sie Shakespeare noch auf englisch, später in schlechten deutschen Übersetzungen, bis die englischen Schauspieler nach dem Dreißigjährigen Krieg mehr und mehr durch deutsche ersetzt wurden und schließlich ganz aus den Truppen verschwanden.

    Bis in die Mitte des 18. Jahrhunderts und zum Teil noch länger war es
15 Sitte, Shakespeare in solchen Bearbeitungen auf die Bühne zu bringen. Der gute Geschmack der Zeit duldete das Grausame und Schreckliche bei Shake-

---

1. **Theatersaison** *theater season.* 2. **Schauspielpremiere** *first performances (of a play).*
3. **d.h.** = **das heißt** *that is (to say).*

speare nicht. So wurde noch in den neunziger Jahren in Weimar[4] ein „Macbeth" gespielt, in dem die Rolle des Königs Duncan ganz gestrichen war.

Die erste vollständige und erstaunlich genaue Übersetzung Shakespeares erschien in 13 Bänden während der zweiten Hälfte des 18. Jahrhunderts, und 20 zwar in den Jahren 1775 bis 1782. Sie wurde dann noch einmal bearbeitet und 16 Jahre später, von 1798 bis 1806, in 12 Bänden neu herausgebracht. Ihr Verfasser war Johann Joachim Eschenburg (1743–1820), ein höchst belesener und angesehener Professor der Literatur in Braunschweig. Wie ernst Eschenburg seine Arbeit nahm, geht daraus hervor,[5] daß man nach seinem 25 Tode 400 Bände zum Thema Shakespeare in seiner Bibliothek fand. Eschenburg konnte sich allerdings auf wichtige Vorarbeiten[6] stützen. Zwischen 1762 und 1766 hatte nämlich der große Dichter und Schriftsteller der Aufklärung Christoph Martin Wieland (1733–1813) seine berühmte Überstezung von 22 Stücken Shakespeares in 8 Bänden veröffentlicht. 30

Wielands Übersetzungen waren, wie Eschenburgs, in Prosa, und hatten sich bemüht, den Geist Shakespeares dem des eleganten 18. Jahrhunderts anzupassen. Sie haben einen großen Einfluß auf die Generation von jungen Dichtern gehabt, mit der zu Ende des Jahrhunderts eine neue Zeit begann, die wir als europäische Frühromantik[7] bezeichnen können, und die in 35 Deutschland den Namen „Sturm und Drang"[8] trägt. Zu diesen Dichtern gehörten auch der junge Goethe und der junge Schiller. Ihnen genügte der Aufklärungs-Shakespeare Wielands und Eschenburgs nicht mehr: sie wollten den richtigen, historischen Shakespeare wiederentdecken. Der Student Goethe hielt 1771 eine enthusiastische Rede „Zum Shakespeare-Tag" und folgte in 40 seinem eigenen ersten Schauspiel, „Götz von Berlichingen" (1771), ganz dem Vorbild Shakespeares.

D i e[9] Form aber, in der Shakespeare den heutigen Deutschen bekannt ist, ist die der sog.[10] Schlegelschen Übersetzung. Sie ist von den Romantikern August Wilhelm Schlegel (1767–1845), Ludwig Tieck (1773–1853) und einigen 45 anderen gegen Ende des 18. und zu Beginn des 19. Jahrhunderts in Blankversen[11] geschaffen worden. Der vollständige Text der Übersetzung erschien zum esten Mal in neun Bänden in den zwanziger und dreißiger Jahren des vorigen Jahrhunderts und ist seitdem immer wieder nachgedruckt worden. Wenn die Helden und Heldinnen Shakespearescher[12] Dramen den Deutschen 50 augenscheinlich ebenso bekannt sind wie den Engländern, verdanken sie

---

4. **Weimar** city in central Germany, major literary center in the eighteenth century; seat of the constituant assembly of the Weimar Republic (1919–1933).   5. **geht daraus hervor, daß** *becomes clear from the fact that.*   6. **Vorarbeiten** *preparatory work.*   7. **Frühromantik** *Early Romanticism.*   8. **Sturm und Drang** *Storm and Stress* (so named after a play of the time).   9. Note how in German printed words are frequently spaced for emphasis. 10. **sog.** = **sogenannt** *so-called.*   11. **Blankversen** *blank verses.*   12. Note how adjectives are derived from names by adding the suffix **-(i)sch,** plus ending.

das zum großen Teil dieser Übersetzung, die man eine der größten Leistungen in der Übersetzungsliteratur aller Völker genannt hat.

Vergleichen Sie die folgenden Zitate aus der Schlegelschen Shakespeare-
55 Übersetzung mit den englischen Texten:

Sein oder nicht sein, das ist hier die Frage. („Hamlet")

Dies war der beste Römer unter allen. („Julius Cäsar")

Nicht durch die Schuld der Sterne, lieber Brutus,
Durch eigne Schuld nur sind wir Schwächlinge.[13]
60 *It is not in our stars but in*
ourselves that we are underlings. („Julius Cäsar")

Nimm vor des Märzen Idus dich in acht!
Beware the Ides of March. („Julius Cäsar")

Was ist ein Name? Was uns Rose heißt,
65 wie es auch hieße[14] würde lieblich duften.
What's in a name? A rose by any other
name would smell as sweet. („Romeo und Julia")

13. **Schwächlinge** lit., *weaklings.*   14. lit., *however it were called.*

FRAGEN

1. Was sind die deutschsprechenden Länder?   2. Wie viele Dramen Shakespeares werden in einem Jahr an den hundert wichtigsten Bühnen neu einstudiert?   3. Was ist eine Premiere?   4. Wann begann diese kulturhistorische Entwicklung?   5. Von wem wurde Shakespeare in Deutschland eingeführt?   6. Was taten diese englischen Schauspieler?   7. Wie spielten sie ihren Shakespeare?   8. Wie lange war es Sitte, Shakespeare in solchen schlechten Bearbeitungen aufzuführen?   9. Was duldete der Geschmack des 18. Jahrhunderts nicht?   10. Was hat man noch in den neunziger Jahren in Weimar getan?   11. Wodurch ist Weimar bekannt?   12. Von wem ist die erste vollständige Übersetzung Shakespeares ins Deutsche?   13. Wann wurde sie bearbeitet?   14. Wer war Eschenburg?   15. Woher weiß man, wie ernst Eschenburg seine Arbeit nahm?   16. Auf wen konnte Eschenburg sich mit seiner Arbeit stützen?   17. Was hat Wieland getan?   18. Was ist der „Sturm und Drang"?   19. Was wollten die Dichter der neuen Generation?   20. Was tat Goethe?   21. In welcher Form ist den heutigen Deutschen Shakespeare bekannt?   22. Wann ist die Schlegelsche Übersetzung vollständig erschienen?   23. Wie hat man diese Übersetzung genannt?

WORTSCHATZ

sich in acht nehmen (i, a, o) (vor)	to beware (of)	die Folge, –n	consequence
		genügen (*w. dat.*)	to satisfy
angesehen	respected	grausam	cruel
an/passen	to adapt	die Hälfte, –n	half
die Aufklärung	Enlightenment	heutig (*adj. derived from heute*)	today's
die Auflage, –n	edition		
augenscheinlich	apparently	nach/drucken	to reprint
bearbeiten	to rework, to revise	null	zero
die Bearbeitung, –en	adaptation, revision	eine Rede halten (ä, ie, a)	to make a speech
belesen	well-read		
sich bemühen	to make an effort, to attempt	das Schauspiel, –e	play
die Bühne, –n	stage	schlecht	bad, poor
dulden	to tolerate	die Schuld, (–en)	guilt; debt
der Einfluß, ⸗sse	influence	soviel	as far as
ein/führen	to introduce	sich stützen (auf)	to lean on, to rely on, to be based on
ein/studieren	to rehearse		
entdecken	to discover	zum Teil (*abbr.* z.T.)	in part, partly
wieder/entdecken	to rediscover	zum großen Teil	to a large extent
ernst	serious(ly)		
ersetzen	to replace	verdanken	to owe
erstaunlich	astonishing(ly), amazing(ly)	der Verfasser, –	author
		vollständig	complete
die Ferien (*pl.*)	vacation	vorig (*adj. derived from vor*)	last, previous

Note the expression: **auf deutsch (englisch,** etc.) *in German* (*English,* etc.); the prefix **wieder** is usually equivalent to the English prefix *re-*.

STRONG VERBS

schaffen	to create	schuf	geschaffen
streichen	to cut; to stroke; to paint	strich	gestrichen
vergleichen	to compare	verglich	verglichen
verschwinden	to disappear	verschwand	ist verschwunden

NUMERALS IN GERMAN

Most German numerals are cognates of the corresponding English numerals. Memorize the cardinal numbers and note how ordinal numbers, adverbs, and fractions are derived from them; pay special attention to the few irregularities that are in heavy type. Numbers of more than four digits are split from the right into groups of three; groups are separated by spaces, not by commas—50 354:

CARDINAL NUMBERS		ORDINAL NUMBERS	ORDINAL ADVERBS		FRACTIONS	
0	Null					
1	eins		**erste**	**erstens** *firstly*		
2	zwei		zweite	zweitens *secondly*	1/2	halb (die Hälfte)
3	drei		**dritte**	**drittens** *thirdly*	1/3	ein **Drittel**
4	vier		vierte	viertens *fourthly*	1/4	ein Viertel
5	fünf	der	fünfte	etc.	1/5	ein Fünftel
6	sechs	die	sechste		1/6	ein Sechstel
7	sieben	das	**sieb(en)te**		1/7	ein **Sieb(en)tel**
8	acht		**achte**		1/8	ein **Achtel**
9	neun		neunte			
10	zehn		zehnte			
11	elf		elfte			
12	zwölf		zwölfte			
13	dreizehn		dreizehnte			
14	vierzehn		vierzehnte			-tel
15	fünfzehn		fünfzehnte			
16	**sechzehn**		**sechzehnte**			
17	**siebzehn**		siebzehnte			
18	achtzehn		achtzehnte			
19	neunzehn		neunzehnte			
20	zwanzig		zwanzigste		1/20	ein Zwanzigstel
21	einundzwanzig					
22	zweiundzwanzig					
30	**dreißig**					
31	einunddreißig					
40	vierzig	der				
50	fünfzig	die				
60	**sechzig**	das				
70	**siebzig**					
80	achtzig					
90	neunzig		-ste			-stel
100	hundert					
101	hunderteins					
102	hundertzwei					
188	hundertacht- undachtzig					
200	zweihundert					
300	dreihundert					
1000	tausend					
2000	zweitausend					

2222   zweitausendzweihundertzweiundzwanzig

1 000 000   eine Million[1], -en

1 000 000 000   eine Milliarde, -n (English *billion*)

1 000 000 000 000   eine Billion, -en (English *trillion*)

[1] Combinations above one million are separated as follows: 2 005 347 = **zwei Millionen fünftausenddreihundertsiebenundvierzig.**

CARDINAL NUMBERS

1. **Eins** is used only in counting (**eins, zwei, drei,** etc.) and in giving the time when **Uhr** is omitted:

Es ist **viertel vor eins.**   *It is a quarter to one.*

But: **Um ein Uhr.**   *At one o'clock.*

In all other instances, the indefinite article **ein, eine, ein** is used with the correct case endings. To avoid ambiguity, **ein** is generally spaced or italicized when the numeral rather than the indefinite article is meant; modern usage tends to favor italics:

Nur e i n (*ein*) Brief ist angekommen.
Only one letter has arrived.

2. If numbers, both cardinal and ordinal, are to be spelled out, they are written in one word, no matter how long such a word would be. The practice of spelling out numbers is rare, but it may be found in documents:

tausendsechshundertvierundachtzig

1684   or

sechzehnhundertvierundachtzig

3. In giving a date, **hundert** may not be omitted (contrary to English):

1963 = **neunzehnhundertdreiundsechzig**

Also, when giving a date in German, it is not possible simply to use the preposition "in" before the number (as in English); either use the number of the year alone or place the phrase **im Jahre** before it:

Sie ist **1952** geboren.

Sie ist **im Jahre 1952** geboren.   *She was born in 1952.*

Note also the expression: **die 20er (zwanziger) Jahre,** *the Twenties.*

4. Starting with 21, German differs from English: the units digit precedes the tens digit:

einundzwanzig, zweiundzwanzig, dreiundzwanzig, etc.

hunderteinundzwanzig, etc.

tausendeinhunderteinundzwanzig, etc.

ORDINAL NUMBERS

1. Ordinals are formed from cardinals by adding **-te** to the numbers 2 to 19, and **-ste** from 20 on.

2. Ordinals are treated like regular adjectives, that is, they take the adjective endings in the various cases, numbers, and genders:

> Sie ist seine **zweite** Frau.
> *She is his second wife.*
> Wir wohnen im **fünften** Haus links.
> *We live in the fifth house to the left.*

3. Ordinals are followed by a period when expressed in figures. In reading or speaking, substitute the correct ending:

> **der 3. Mai**   (read:) **der dritte Mai**
> **der 15. August** (read:) **der fünfzehnte August**
> die Fehler **in der 2. (zweiten) Auflage**
> *the mistakes in the second edition*
> die Geburt **seines 4. (vierten) Kindes**
> *the birth of his fourth child*

A similar practice applies to titles of rulers:

> **Friedrich II. (der Zweite)**
> **Paul VI. (der Sechste)**

4. Note the following expressions referring to dates:

> **Den wievielten haben wir heute?**
> *What is today's date?*
> **Heute ist der 15. (fünfzehnte) April.**
> **Wir haben heute den 15. (fünfzehnten) April.**
> *Today is the 15th of April.*

In letterheads:

> **München, den 6. (sechsten) Juni 1971**
> *Munich, June 6, 1971*

5. Ordinal adverbs are formed by adding **-ens** to the ordinal numbers. Only the adverbs derived from the first few ordinals are in common use: **erstens** *firstly, in the first place;* **zweitens; drittens,** etc.

FRACTIONS

1. In German, decimals are indicated by commas (not periods):

> 1,5   (read:) **ein(s) Komma fünf**   *(1.5)*
> 1,05   (read:) **ein(s) Komma Null fünf** *(1.05)*

2. Fractions from 1/3 on are formed by adding **-tel** (up to 1/19) and **-stel** (from 1/20 on) to the cardinal numbers:

> 2/5   (read:) **zwei Fünftel**
> 3/10   (read:) **drei Zehntel**
> 1/25   (read:) **ein Fünfundzwanzigstel**

Notice the expressions for $1\frac{1}{2}$: **anderthalb** or **eineinhalb.**

3. Use fractions like regular nouns, **das Drittel, des Drittels, die Drittel.** Note the spelling: **drei Viertel** or **dreiviertel.**

4. Note the following usage of **halb** and **die Hälfte:**

a. **der halbe Apfel** ⎫
b. **die Hälfte des Apfels** ⎬ *half (of) the apple*
c. **die Hälfte der Äpfel**   *half (of) the apples*

In general, for half of one item (a, b), either the adjective **halb** or the noun **die Hälfte** may be used; for half of a quantity (c), only the noun **die Hälfte.**

OTHER NUMERIC FORMS AND EXPRESSIONS

1. English *time(s)* in the enumerative sense is **-mal** or **das Mal** (*not* **Zeit!**):

zum ersten Mal	*for the first time*
einmal, zweimal, dreimal, etc.	*once, twice, three times, etc.*
noch einmal	*once more, once again*
diesmal	*this time*
jedesmal	*each time, every time*
das letzte Mal	*the last time*

2. Signs used in arithmetic:

> $2 + 2 = 4$ (read:) **Zwei plus** (or **und**) **zwei ist** (or **gleich**) **vier.**
> $5 - 3 = 2$ (read:) **Fünf minus** (or **weniger**) **drei ist** (or **gleich**) **zwei.**
> $6 \cdot$ (or $\times$) $6 = 36$ (read:) **Sechs mal sechs ist** (or **gleich**) **sechsunddreißig.**
> $4 :$ (or $\div$) $2 = 2$ (read:) **Vier (geteilt) durch zwei ist** (or **gleich**) **zwei.**

RECAPITULATION OF MAIN POINTS

1. Ordinal numbers are formed from cardinal numbers by adding **-te** to the numbers 2 through 19, **-ste** from 20 on. Irregular are: **der erste, der dritte,**

der achte, der sechzehnte, der siebzehnte, and there are some other irregurities in spelling.

2. Ordinals take regular adjective endings:

> der **10. (zehnte)** April
> Er kauft sich sein **zweites** Haus.

3. Fractions add **-tel** from 3 to 19, **-stel** from 20 on. 1/2 is either **halb** or **die Hälfte.** Fractions are ordinary nouns: **das Drittel, des Drittels, die Drittel.**

4. Decimals are indicated by a comma and not by a period: **1,5 = ein(s) Komma fünf.**

ÜBUNGEN

Practice in Reading and Writing

A. *Read aloud and translate:*

Japanisches Deutsch

1. Lange vor dem 1. Weltkrieg besuchte einmal ein deutsches Kriegsschiff einen japanischen Hafen. 2. Es muß so um 1900 gewesen sein. 3. Erst seit 1853 war Japan nämlich für europäische Schiffe offen. 4. Zu Ende des 19. und zu Beginn des 20. Jahrhunderts war die deutsche Politik dann sehr japanfreundlich. 5. Das deutsche Kriegsschiff kam also nach Japan und gleich am 1. Tag machte ihm der japanische Admiral einen offiziellen Besuch. 6. Er kam an Bord, gefolgt von einem guten Dutzend hoher Offiziere. 7. Der deutsche Kapitän sprach natürlich nicht e i n Wort Japanisch. 8. Er mußte aber etwas sagen, und so murmelte er: ,,Achtzehn, neunzehn, zwanzig''. 9. Der höfliche Japaner machte eine tiefe Verbeugung und antwortete laut und klar: ,,Einundzwanzig, zweiundzwanzig, dreiundzwanzig''.

1	**das Schiff, –e**	*ship*	9	**die Verbeugung, –en**	*bow*
8	**murmeln**	*to murmur*			

B. *Read aloud and translate:*

Noch etwas über Shakespeare und die Deutschen

1. Die erste deutsche Übersetzung eines Shakespeareschen Werkes war, soviel wir wissen, Caspar Wilhelm von Borcks Übersetzung des ,,Julius Cäsar'' aus dem Jahre 1741. 2. Wieland übersetzte zwischen 1762 und 1766

22 Werke Shakespeares in Prosa. 3. Die 2. Auflage der Eschenburgschen Shakespeare-Übersetzung erschien schon 1780 in 24 Bänden. 4. Die ersten Schlegelschen Übersetzungen erschienen 1797, und bis 1810 hatten er und seine romantischen Freunde 17 Stücke übersetzt. 5. Im Jahre 1936 ist „Hamlet" 287mal in Deutschland aufgeführt worden. 6. Die bedeutendste moderne Shakespeare-Übersetzung ins Deutsche ist die von Friedrich Gundolf. 7. Sie ist zwischen 1908 und 1914 in 10 Bänden unter dem Titel „Shakespeare in deutscher Sprache" erschienen.

C. *Translate:*

1. Sogar ein Mohammedaner hat gewöhnlich nur e i n e Frau. 2. Schon mit einer zweiten vermehren (*increase*) sich seine Probleme unnötig. 3. Erstens glaube ich das nicht, und zweitens beweist es nichts. 4. Man kann sagen: die Hälfte der Studenten ist hier, aber nicht: die halben Studenten sind hier. 5. Man müßte sich dann nämlich fragen: mit welcher Hälfte sind sie hier? 6. Man nennt seine Frau manchmal: meine bessere Hälfte, aber das ist natürlich nur eine Redensart. 7. Er hat seine Arbeit nur halb getan. 8. Das Sprichwort sagt: Einmal ist keinmal; das heißt: wenn man etwas nur einmal tut, ist es so gut wie gar nicht getan. 9. Weihnachten fällt auf den 25. Dezember. 10. Goethe wurde am 28. August 1749 geboren und ist am 22. März 1832 gestorben. 11. Er wurde also etwas mehr als 82 Jahre alt. 12. Ostern fällt 1972 auf den 2. April, 1973 auf den 22. April. 13. Die Ferien beginnen am 1. Juni. 14. Bismarck war deutscher Kanzler unter Wilhelm I. und Wilhelm II. 15. Ich habe heute ein dreiviertel Stunden gearbeitet. 16. Meine Frau hat anderthalb Liter Milch gekauft. 17. Anderthalb ist dasselbe wie 1,5. 18. Am wievielten haben Sie Geburtstag? 19. Sie starb am Morgen des 16. September. 20. Ein Ganzes hat sechs Sechstel. 21. Ein Tausendstel ist nur ein sehr kleiner Teil eines Ganzen. 22. Immanuel Kant war das 4. von elf Kindern.

D. *Complete the following sentences:*

1. Mein Geburtstag ist am _____. 2. Der Geburtstag meiner Mutter ist am _____. 3. Der Geburtstag meines Vaters ist am _____. 4. Heute ist der _____. 5. Das Jahr beginnt am _____. 6. Der Sommer beginnt am _____. 7. Ich habe _____ Dollar und _____ Cents in der Tasche; wieviel ist das, wenn eine Mark 27 Cents wert ist? 8. Wenn ich allein ins Kino (*to the movies*) gehe, kostet mich das _____.

E. *Translate:*

1. Spring begins on March 21. 2. Fritz is the second of five children. 3. What date was it yesterday? 4. Our book has three parts, and we are now in the third. 5. In the first place I have no money, and in the second, I don't like to go to the movies on a 13th, especially when the 13th is a

Friday.   6. This is my second breakfast today; I do not often have two breakfasts.   7. We are living on **(in)** 10th Street.   8. Don't you know this street? It is (the) 12th Street.   9. I have told you (this) three times already. 10. Must I tell (it to) you ten times?   11. It was in **(an)** the evening of September 2.   12. September has 30 days, but August has 31.   13. A German pound has 500 grams **(das Gramm)**[1] and an American pound has 453.59. 14. On which page of our book are we? We are on page 252.   15. She arrived on the 15th and left on the 20th.   16. Many millions died during the Thirty Years' War.   17. This page is now two-thirds full.   18. Life was very gay during the 90's.

Oral Exercises

F. *Read and answer:*

$10 + 6 =$	$40 + 9 =$	$410 - 30 =$
$7 + 4 =$	$100 - 1 =$	$1000 + 100 =$
$20 - 3 =$	$99 + 7 =$	$1000 + 1500 =$
$30 + 36 =$	$200 + 200 =$	$1000 + 1566 =$
$70 + 7 =$	$350 + 100 =$	$20\,000 + 15\,000 =$
$53 - 4 =$	$600 - 50 =$	$37\,000 + 3\,000 =$
$90 - 2 =$	$700 + 77 =$	

G. *Change the pattern sentence using the cues:*

EXAMPLE: Mai, 8   Wir kommen am achten Mai an.

1. Mai, 3	5. Mai, 11	8. Mai, 23
2. Mai, 7	6. Mai, 16	9. Mai, 21
3. Mai, 1	7. Mai, 12	10. Mai, 30
4. Mai, 17		

---

[1] Nouns expressing units of measurement do not form plurals when used in numbers: **50 Gramm; 25 Mark.**

22

Time and Year

Wieviel Uhr ist es?

In der deutschen Übersetzung von „Julius Cäsar" sagt Brutus: „Still! Zählt
die Glocke!",[1] und Cassius antwortet: „Sie hat drei geschlagen." Das ist
natürlich ein Anachronismus, denn die Römer hatten zwar Sonnenuhren,[2]
Sanduhren,[3] ja sogar Wasseruhren, aber es hat in Rom niemals drei „geschlagen". Wir können uns heute die Welt ohne Uhren und Uhrenschlagen 5
kaum noch vorstellen. Unzählige Male am Tage hören, sagen oder denken
wir: wieviel Uhr ist es? Und dann wollen wir nicht wissen, wo die Sonne am
Himmel steht, denn wir sind ja keine Pfadfinder,[4] sondern ob es schon zehn
Minuten vor halb drei oder erst zehn nach zwei ist. Deshalb sehen wir auf die
Uhr. Das können wir fast überall, denn Uhren befinden sich auf Kirchtürmen, 10
an Rathäusern und Straßenecken, in Büros, in Kinos, in Küchen, in Wohn-
zimmern und am Arm.

Schon am frühen Morgen werden wir von Uhren tyrannisiert, wenn neben
unserem Bett der Wecker rasselt, und wir möchten noch gerne ein Viertelstündchen länger schlafen. Von diesem Augenblick an geht es Minute um 15
Minute und Stunde um Stunde mit der Uhr durch den Tag. Um wieviel

---

1. **Glocke,** (here, old fashioned): *clock.* 2. **Sonnenuhren** *sun dials.* 3. **Sanduhren** *hour
glasses.* 4. **Pfadfinder** (lit., *path finders*) *scouts.*

Uhr muß ich auf dem Bahnhof sein? Der Autobus geht alle zehn Minuten. Ich komme drei Minuten zu spät zum Bahnhof, und der Zug, der sonst immer Verspätung hat, ist gerade heute einmal pünktlich abgefahren. Der

20 nächste geht[5] erst in dreiviertel Stunden. Mittags wollen wir uns—wieder pünktlich!—um zwölf oder halb eins zum Essen treffen, das Abendbrot steht um Viertel nach sechs oder Viertel vor sieben auf dem Tisch, und den „Fünf-Uhr-Tee" gibt es—wie den Nachmittagskaffee—manchmal schon um vier. Für das, was ich gerne tun möchte, habe ich „keine Zeit".

25 Was schenken wir einem Mädchen, das wir gern haben? Einen Ring oder eine Armbanduhr. Was erben wir vom Großvater? Eine dicke goldene Taschenuhr. Die Taschenuhr ist übrigens eine deutsche Erfindung, die aus Nürnberg stammt. Weil sie ursprünglich die Form eines Eis hatte, hieß sie früher das „Nürnberger Ei".

30 Seit der Erfindung des elektrischen Lichts hat die Nacht an Bedeutung ge-wonnen: wir arbeiten tagsüber, damit wir des Abends und des Nachts das Leben genießen können. In früheren Zeiten war das Stadtleben von der Dauer des Tageslichts bestimmt. Man stand früh auf. Friedrich der Große[6] zum Beispiel stand im Sommer morgens um vier und im Winter um fünf

35 Uhr auf, und Lichtenberg verhielt sich ähnlich, wie wir gesehen haben. Abends um neun war fast alles dunkel. Nachts gab es keine Straßenbe-leuchtung,[7] nur in ein paar Wirtshäusern brannten vor Mitternacht noch trüb die Kerzen. Der Nachtwächter[8] wanderte dann durch die Straßen und rief die Stunden aus. Das war „die gute alte Zeit"—eine Zeit, in der Schiller[9]

40 noch schreiben konnte: „Die Uhr schlägt keinem Glücklichen."

5. **gehen** (of trains, etc.) *to leave.* 6. **Friedrich der Große** *Frederick the Great* (King of Prussia, 1740–1786). 7. **Straßenbeleuchtung** *street lighting.* 8. **Nachtwächter** *night watch-man.* 9. **Friedrich Schiller,** 1759–1805, foremost German dramatist of the classical period.

FRAGEN

1. Was sagt Brutus in der deutschen Übersetzung von „Julius Cäsar"? 2. Was antwortet Cassius? 3. Warum ist das ein Anachronismus? 4. Was können wir uns heute kaum noch vorstellen? 5. Was sagen oder denken wir unzählige Male am Tage? 6. Was wollen wir dann nicht wissen? 7. Warum wollen wir das nicht wissen? 8. Was wollen wir dann wirklich wissen? 9. Wo befinden sich Uhren? 10. Haben Sie selbst eine Uhr? 11. Was für eine Uhr haben Sie? 12. Warum tyrannisiert uns der Wecker am frühen Morgen? 13. Um wieviel Uhr müssen Sie in dieser Deutsch-stunde sein? 14. Wann essen Sie zu Mittag? 15. Mit wem essen Sie zu Mittag? 16. Wann steht bei Ihnen das Abendbrot auf dem Tisch? 17. Um

wieviel Uhr gibt es den „Fünf-Uhr-Tee"?   18. Wofür hat man „keine Zeit"?
19. Wo wurde die Taschenuhr erfunden?   20. Wie hieß sie deswegen früher?
21. Seit wann hat die Nacht an Bedeutung verloren?   22. Wovon war das
Stadtleben früher bestimmt?   23. Wann ist Friedrich der Große aufgestanden und wann ist er zu Bett gegangen?   24. Wann ist Lichtenberg aufgestanden?   25. Was war die „gute alte Zeit"?

WORTSCHATZ

das **Abendbrot**	supper	die **Mitternacht, ⸗e**	midnight
ähnlich	similar(ly)	**nachmittags**	in the afternoon
der **Anfang, ⸗e**	beginning	die **Nacht, ⸗e**	night
die **Armbanduhr, –en**	wrist watch	**des Nachts**	at night
auf/wachen	to wake up	**ein paar**	a few
die **Bedeutung, –en**	meaning, signifi-	**rasseln**	rattle
	cance	das **Rathaus, ⸗er**	city hall
die **Dauer**	duration	**sonst**	otherwise, at other
dreiviertel	three quarters		times
dunkel	dark	**tagsüber**	during the day
das **Ei, –er**	egg	der **Tisch, –e**	table
erben	to inherit	**trüb**	dim(ly)
die **Erfindung, -en**	invention	**unzählig**	innumerable
der **Feiertag, –e**	holiday	**ursprünglich**	original(ly)
der **Frühling, –e**	spring	**Verspätung haben**	to be late
gerade heute	of all days today	die **Viertelstunde,**	quarter of an hour
(**gerade er,**	(of all people he,	**–n**	
etc.)	etc.)	der **Vogel, ⸗**	bird
heilig	holy	**von ... an** (*prep.*)	from ... on
je	each	**sich vor/stellen**	to imagine
die **Kerze, –n**	candle	**wecken**	to (a)waken
das **Kino, –s**	movie house	der **Wecker**	alarm (clock)
der **Kirchturm, ⸗e**	church tower, steeple	das **Wirtshaus, ⸗er**	inn
das **Licht, –er**	light	das **Wohnzimmer, –**	living room

STRONG VERBS

ab/fahren	to depart	**fährt ab**	**fuhr ab**	**ist abgefahren**
biegen	to bend		**bog**	**gebogen**
gleiten	to slide		**glitt**	**geglitten**
reiben	to rub		**rieb**	**gerieben**
schlagen	to strike, hit, beat	**schlägt**	**schlug**	**geschlagen**
wiegen	to weigh		**wog**	**gewogen**

TIME IN GERMAN

1. Time Indications

IN ENGLISH	IN GERMAN		OFFICIAL TIME
		Es ist . . .	
3:00	3.00 or 3⁰⁰	drei Uhr	drei Uhr
3:10	3.10 or 3¹⁰	zehn (Minuten) nach drei	drei Uhr zehn
3:15	3.15 or 3¹⁵	Viertel nach drei, or	
		(ein) Viertel (auf) vier	drei Uhr fünfzehn
3:20	3.20 or 3²⁰	zwanzig nach drei, or	
		zehn vor halb vier	drei Uhr zwanzig
3:25	3.25 or 3²⁵	fünf vor halb vier	drei Uhr fünfundzwanzig
3:30	3.30 or 3³⁰	halb vier	drei Uhr dreißig
3:35	3.35 or 3³⁵	fünf nach halb vier	drei Uhr fünfunddreißig

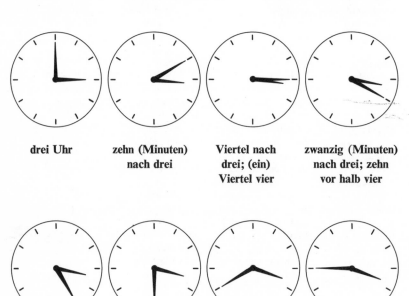

drei Uhr	zehn (Minuten) nach drei	Viertel nach drei; (ein) Viertel vier	zwanzig (Minuten) nach drei; zehn vor halb vier

fünf vor halb vier; drei Uhr fünfundzwanzig	halb vier	zwanzig vor vier; zehn nach halb vier	Viertel vor vier; dreiviertel vier

3:40	3.40 or 3⁴⁰	zwanzig vor vier, or	
		zehn nach halb vier	drei Uhr vierzig
3:45	3.45 or 3⁴⁵	Viertel vor vier, or	
		dreiviertel vier	drei Uhr fünfundvierzig
3:50	3.50 or 3⁵⁰	zehn vor vier	drei Uhr fünfzig
3:55	3.55 or 3⁵⁵	fünf vor vier	drei Uhr fünfundfünfzig

a. The word **Uhr** is normally used with the full hour, but not with any other time indication: **drei Uhr,** but: **fünf nach drei.**

b. The word **Minuten** is usually omitted: **fünf** (Minuten) **vor vier.**

c. The half hour is counted in relation to the following hour: **halb vier** (3:30), **halb fünf** (4:30).

d. Official time in Germany is on the twenty-four-hour basis: 3:20 p.m. is **15.20** or **15^{20}**. It is used in time tables, on the radio, etc.

2. Note the following phrases and expressions used in referring to time:

alle zehn Minuten	*every ten minutes*
Wie spät ist es?	
Wieviel Uhr ist es?	*What time is it? What's the time?*
Es ist genau sechs Minuten vor sieben.	*It is exactly six minutes to seven.*
Um wieviel Uhr kommst du?	*At what time are you coming?*

and the verbs and verbal expressions:

nach /gehen *to be slow*	**Unsere Küchenuhr geht nach (vor).**
vor /gehen *to be fast*	*Our kitchen clock is slow (fast).*
richtig (or **falsch**) **gehen**	**Meine Uhr geht richtig (falsch).**
to be correct or *wrong*	*My watch is correct (wrong).*
stellen *to set*	**Ich muß meine Uhr stellen.**
	I have to set my watch.
zu spät kommen	*to be late*

3. Adverbial Expressions of Time

a. in the genitive, to express indefinite time:

eines Tages	*one day*
eines Morgens	*one morning*
eines Nachts (although	*one night*
Nacht is feminine!)	

b. in the accusative, to express definite time and duration of time:

München, **den 21. September.**
Munich, September 21.
Er hat **den ganzen Tag** (lang) gearbeitet.
He worked all day (long).

DAYS, WEEKS, MONTHS, SEASONS

1. Days of the Week

der **Sonntag**	*Sunday*		der **Montag**	*Monday*

der **Dienstag**	*Tuesday*	der **Freitag**	*Friday*
der **Mittwoch**	*Wednesday*	der **Samstag** }	
der **Donnerstag**	*Thursday*	der **Sonnabend** }	*Saturday*

2. Division of the Day

der **Morgen**[1]	*morning*	der **Abend**	*evening*
der **Vormittag**	*forenoon*	die **Nacht**	*night*
der **Mittag**	*noon*	die **Mitternacht**	*midnight*
der **Nachmittag**	*afternoon*		

Only the following greetings exist: **guten Morgen! Guten Tag! Guten Abend! Gute Nacht!**

3. Adverbs Referring to Days

gestern	*yesterday*	**vorgestern**	*day before yesterday*
heute	*today*	**übermorgen**	*day after tomorrow*
morgen	*tomorrow*		

4. Note also the following expressions:

acht Tage	*a week*
heute in acht Tagen	*a week from today*
heute vor acht Tagen	*a week ago today*
vierzehn Tage	*two weeks*
morgen in vierzehn Tagen	*two weeks from tomorrow*
gestern vor vierzehn Tagen	*two weeks ago yesterday*

5. Adverbs Referring to Divisions of the Day[2]

morgens	*in the morning*	**nachmittags**	*in the afternoon*
vormittags	*in the forenoon*	**abends**	*in the evening*
mittags	*at noon*	**nachts**	*at night*

6. Time adverbs are combined as follows:

früh morgens	*early in the morning*	**heute nacht**	*tonight; last night*[3]
morgen früh	*tomorrow morning*	**letzte Nacht**	*last night*
heute früh }	*this morning*	**gestern abend**	*yesterday evening, last night*
heute morgen }			
heute abend	*this evening, tonight*	**morgen abend**	*tomorrow evening*

[1] Distinguish between **der Morgen** (*morning*), **morgen** (*tomorrow*), and **morgens** (*in the morning*).

[2] Instead of the following adverbs, nouns may be used adverbially in the genitive: **des Morgens, des Vormittags, des Mittags,** etc.; also **des Nachts**.

[3] **Heute nacht** (usually *tonight*) means *last night* when the verb is in the past:

Ich habe **heute nacht** schlecht geschlafen.
I slept badly last night.
But: Das Flugzeug geht **heute nacht**.
The plane leaves tonight.

7. Months and Seasons

a. **der Monat** (plural: **die Monate**) *month:*

(der) **Januar**	**April**	**Juli**	**Oktober**
Februar	**Mai**	**August**	**November**
März	**Juni**	**September**	**Dezember**

b. **die Jahreszeit** (plural: **die Jahreszeiten**) *season:*

der **Frühling** (–e)⎱
das **Frühjahr** (–e)⎰ *spring*   der **Herbst** (–e) *fall*

der **Sommer** (–) *summer*   der **Winter** (–) *winter*

8. The article must always be used with nouns indicating days, division of days, months, and seasons:

am Sonntag	**am Morgen**	**im August**	**im Winter**
on Sunday	*in the morning*	*in August*	*in winter*

Note the preposition **um** (*at*) in time indications (**um 12 Uhr), am** when speaking of days (**am Samstag),** and **in** when referring to months (**im Januar).**

9. Feiertage (*festivals and holidays*):

(die) **Weihnachten** (fem. sing. or plural)	*Christmas*
Fröhliche Weihnachten!	*Merry Christmas!*
das **Neujahr**	*New Year*
Fröhliches Neujahr!	*Happy New Year!*
(das, die) **Ostern** (sing. or plural)	*Easter*
der **Ostersonntag**	*Easter Sunday*
Fröhliche Ostern!	*Happy Easter!*
(das, die) **Pfingsten** (sing. or plural)	*Whitsunday, Pentecost*

ÜBUNGEN

Practice in Reading and Writing

A. *Read aloud and translate:*

1. In Deutschland beginnt Weihnachten am 24. Dezember.   2. Man nennt diesen ersten Feiertag den „Heiligen Abend".   3. Weihnachten, Ostern und Pfingsten haben je zwei Feiertage, den ersten und den zweiten Feiertag. 4. Pfingsten kommt sieben Wochen nach Ostern.   5. Der Abend vor Neujahr

heißt Silvester. 6. Der Karneval beginnt offiziell am 11. im 11. Monat um elf Uhr nachts und endet mit Aschermittwoch (*Ash Wednesday*). 7. Ich gehe übermorgen in die Stadt. 8. Er hatte vorgestern Geburtstag. 9. Morgen abend wollen wir ins Kino. 10. Abends sitzen wir immer zu Hause. 11. Er kommt morgen früh an. 12. Wir haben uns gestern nachmittag getroffen. 13. Wir treffen uns jeden Nachmittag zum Tee. 14. Gestern abend haben sie „Hamlet" gegeben. 15. Heute nacht wird es frieren. 16. Heute nacht hat es gefroren. 17. Heute abend gehen wir ins Theater. 18. Vormittags gehe ich zur Universität und nachmittags wird gearbeitet! 19. Vor acht Tagen hatten wir Weihnachten. 20. In vierzehn Tagen gibt es Ferien, Gottseidank. 21. Der Morgen war schön, aber am Nachmittag regnete es. 22. Am Montag werden wir etwas über die Anfänge der Psychoanalyse lesen. 23. Ich habe das heute morgen schon gelesen. 24. Im August kommt meine Großmutter, und sie bleibt dann bis zum Oktober. 25. Im Frühling singen die Vögel. 26. Ich habe mich heute um fünf vor halb sechs wecken lassen (sich wecken lassen *to have oneself awakened*). 27. Um Viertel vor fünf klingelte es. 28. Können Sie in einer Viertelstunde bei mir sein? 29. Der Zug fährt um 20^{12}. 30. Wir kommen bestimmt noch vor Mitternacht nach Hause. 31. Acht mal acht ist vierundsechzig. 32. Die größte Hitze haben wir im Juli. 33. Meine Uhr geht fünf Minuten vor. 34. Die Rathausuhr geht immer nach und niemand stellt sie. 35. Um wieviel Uhr eßt ihr zu Mittag?

B. *Read and give the times in colloquial German:*

1. Es ist jetzt genau 1.10. 2. Wir essen pünktlich um 6.45. 3. Wir haben von 10.00 bis 10.45 Deutsch. 4. Heute morgen bin ich um 6.30 aufgewacht. 5. Das Kino fängt um 19.15 an. 6. Um 8.35 ist das Licht ausgegangen. 7. Wecken Sie mich bitte um 7.10. 8. Das Theater ist um 23.25 aus. 9. Die Eier müssen bis 6.06 kochen. 10. Die Aufführung beginnt um 7.45.

C. *Translate:*

1. When did you set your watch? 2. The train will arrive two hours late (translate *late* by: **mit . . . Verspätung**). 3. He suffered terribly, but the danger was over **(vorüber)** in the evening. 4. All day long the heat was terrible. 5. Can I see you tomorrow morning at 9:30? 6. The shops in Paris are open at night. 7. Please remind me of it in two weeks. 8. A week ago we celebrated my mother's 50th birthday. 9. I like to go to the movies at night. 10. In our little town one gets nothing to eat after 10:00 at night. 11. Our kitchen clock is always ten minutes fast. 12. Your wrist watch is slow, you must set it. 13. It gets dark now around six o'clock. 14. He gave me the correct time before he went away. 15. Don't poke fun at my old watch, it is always correct. 16. We have exactly twelve minutes; the train leaves **(gehen)** at 18:09. 17. How do you celebrate Christmas in your family?

Oral Exercises

D. *Answer the questions*:

EXAMPLE:
Der zwölfte Monat ist der Dezember. Welches ist der erste Monat?
Der erste Monat ist der Januar.

1. Der dritte Monat ist der März. Welches ist der zweite Monat?
2. Der siebte Monat ist der Juli. Welches ist der sechste Monat?
3. Der elfte Monat ist der November. Welches ist der zehnte Monat?
4. Der siebte Monat ist der Juli. Welches ist der achte Monat?
5. Der zweite Monat ist der Februar. Welches ist der dritte Monat?

E. *Answer the questions:*

EXAMPLE: Jetzt ist es zwei Uhr. Wieviel Uhr ist es in einer Stunde?
In einer Stunde ist es drei Uhr.

1. Jetzt ist es halb vier. Wieviel Uhr ist es in einer halben Stunde?
2. Jetzt ist es Viertel vor sieben. Wieviel Uhr ist es in einer Viertelstunde?
3. Jetzt ist es halb elf. Wieviel Uhr ist es in einer Stunde?
4. Jetzt ist es acht Uhr. Wieviel Uhr war es vor einer halben Stunde?
5. Jetzt ist es Viertel nach sechs. Wieviel Uhr war es vor einer Viertelstunde?
6. Jetzt ist es Viertel vor eins. Wieviel Uhr war es vor drei Viertelstunden?
7. Jetzt ist es halb sechs. Wieviel Uhr ist es in drei Viertelstunden?

F. *Continue in the same manner, but use the official way of indicating time:*

EXAMPLE: Jetzt ist es 19 Uhr 45. Wieviel Uhr ist es in 15 Minuten?
In 15 Minuten ist es 20 Uhr.

1. Jetzt ist es 20 Uhr 18. Wieviel Uhr war es vor 10 Minuten?
2. Jetzt ist es 23 Uhr 30. Wieviel Uhr ist es in 30 Minuten?
3. Jetzt ist es 16 Uhr 20. Wieviel Uhr war es vor 15 Minuten?
4. Jetzt ist es 13 Uhr 15. Wieviel Uhr ist es in 30 Minuten?
5. Jetzt ist es 15 Uhr 20. Wieviel Uhr ist es in 10 Minuten?
6. Jetzt ist es 0 Uhr 10. Wieviel Uhr war es vor 10 Minuten?
7. Jetzt ist es 13 Uhr 10. Wieviel Uhr war es vor 15 Minuten?
8. Jetzt ist es 17 Uhr 55. Wieviel Uhr ist es in 5 Minuten?
9. Jetzt ist es 14 Uhr 15. Wieviel Uhr ist es in 30 Minuten?

Review 4

Lessons 17 through 22

1 Modal Auxiliaries

A. Modal auxiliaries are conjugated like weak verbs except in the singular of the present tense. Review these present tense forms (pages 196–197).

B. In the perfect tenses, modal auxiliaries with a dependent infinitive form past participles which are identical in form with the infinitive; ich **habe** nicht **schlafen können.**

C. The verbs **gehen** and **tun** are often omitted with modal auxiliaries when the intention is clear: **Ich kann das** (for: **ich kann das tun**). *I can do that.* **Ich will nach Berlin** (reisen). *I want to go to Berlin.* Modal auxiliaries then form the present perfect regularly: Ich **habe** das **gekonnt.**

D. Since the modal auxiliaries in English are defective, always go back to the basic meaning of the modal to arrive at the proper form. Distinguish between the meanings of modal verbs in factual and in hypothetical statements.

E. Translate:

1. Er mußte gehen.   2. Er sollte gestern kommen, aber er hat es vergessen.

3. Ich mag das nicht.   4. Mußt du mit?   5. Mußtest du mit?   6. Ich will das auch.   7. Ich habe das nie gekonnt.   8. Sie kann Englisch.   9. Sie hat das nicht tun wollen.   10. Sie will das nicht getan haben.   11. Er hat sein Auto reparieren lassen.   12. Ich möchte nur wissen, wovon diese Leute eigentlich leben.   13. Dürfte ich Sie um eine Antwort bitten?   14. Ich lasse mir das Buch kommen.   15. Es soll in Berlin geregnet haben.   16. Hast du ihn einmal schimpfen hören?   17. Du solltest etwas früher kommen.   18. Du solltest das Buch gelesen haben.   19. Ich möchte jetzt nach Hause.

2 The Passive

A. Be sure you know the various uses of **werden:**

1. **werden** alone is *to become; to grow; to get:* **Arzt werden** *to become a doctor;* **älter werden** *to grow older;* **reich werden** *to get rich.*

2. **werden** combined with an infinitive indicates future or probability.

3. **werden** with the past participle of a verb expresses the passive. Translate **werden** with the appropriate form of *to be* in the passive: **es wird gesagt** *it is said.*

B. Von and **durch** in passive constructions express agent and instrument, respectively; both mean *by.*

C. In the perfect tenses of the passive, the past participle of **werden** is **worden: Ich bin gefragt worden.** *I have been asked.*

D. The **ist zu** construction is equivalent to an English passive: **Was ist da zu machen?** *What is there to be done?*

E. Läßt sich usually means *can be:* **Das läßt sich leicht machen.** *That can easily be done.*

F. Translate. Identify the verbs and state whether they are active or passive:

1. Man wird nie jünger.   2. Man ist einmal jünger gewesen.   3. Wann wurde er geboren?   4. Du wirst nicht gefragt.   5. Du wirst vielleicht krank werden.   6. Er ist alt geworden.   7. Er ist nicht gefragt worden.   8. Er ist früh berühmt geworden.   9. Wird das Buch ins Englische übersetzt werden?   10. Wird das Buch ins Englische übersetzt?   11. Es ist nicht zu glauben.   12. Das läßt sich leicht beweisen.   13. Ich habe mir den Weg zeigen lassen.   14. Der Kranke ist sofort ins Krankenhaus zu bringen.   15. Der Kranke ist sofort ins Krankenhaus gebracht worden.   16. Diese Frage läßt sich nicht so leicht beantworten.   17. Dieses Buch liest sich leicht.   18. Das wird richtig sein.

3 Relative Pronouns

A. Der, die, das, dessen, deren, etc. are used as demonstrative or relative pronouns. In relative clauses the verb is at the end of the clause.

B. Welcher, welche, welches are rarely used as relative pronouns, and they have no genitive forms; in the genitive, **dessen, deren, dessen** (plural: **deren**) are used.

C. Wer as indefinite relative pronoun means *he who, whoever.* **Was,** its neuter form, means *what, that which, a fact that, something that.*

D. Translate and make sure that you recognize the difference between relative, indefinite relative, and demonstrative pronouns:

1. Das ist eine Frage, die ich nicht beantworten kann. 2. Otto ist jemand, dem man nicht glauben kann. 3. Es gibt Familien, in denen die Kinder immer das letzte Wort haben. 4. Es war einmal ein König, der hatte eine schöne Tochter. 5. Das sind Leute, mit denen wir nichts zu tun haben. 6. Mit denen haben wir nichts zu tun. 7. Wer das sagen kann, hat das Buch nicht verstanden. 8. Das ist etwas, was ich nicht verstehe. 9. Er hat nicht telefoniert, was sie nicht verstehen kann. 10. Das ist das Beste, was er geschrieben hat.

4 Word Order and Conjunctions

A. Be sure you know the difference between coordinating and subordinating conjunctions (see pages 235 and 236).

B. Remember: indirect noun objects ordinarily precede direct noun objects. If both objects are pronouns, the order is reversed; if one is a noun and the other a pronoun, the pronoun precedes the noun.

C. Nicht usually follows objects and expressions stating specific time and precedes prepositional expressions, adverbs, and the second part of a predicate.

D. Review the use of **als, wann,** and **wenn,** all of which mean *when* in different contexts (see page 236).

E. Distinguish between the conjunction **damit** (*so that*) and the **da-**compound **damit** (*with it, with that*); be sure you know the difference between **da** meaning *then, there,* or *since.*

F. Translate:

1. Er sagt es nicht, weil er es nicht weiß.   2. Er sagt es nicht, denn er weiß es nicht.   3. Wenn ich kann, komme ich.   4. Wann kommst du?   5. Ich war schon da, als er kam.   6. Da sie hier ist, kommt er wohl auch.   7. Er tut das, damit er etwas zu tun hat.   8. Damit hat er nichts zu tun.   9. Indem er das sagte, hörten wir das Geräusch.   10. Er gab dem Soldaten seinen Sold.   11. Er gab ihn ihm.   12. Er gab ihm seinen Sold.

5   Expressions of Time

Translate:

1. Dreimal drei ist neun.   2. Den wievielten haben wir heute?   3. Heute ist der 14. Juni.   4. Am 4. Juli haben wir keine Schule.   5. Morgen früh muß ich zur Arbeit, aber am Nachmittag gehe ich ins Kino.   6. Heute in acht Tagen ist ihr Geburtstag.   7. Vor vierzehn Tagen hatten wir Weihnachten.   8. Wir essen immer um halb sieben zu Abend.   9. Im 19. Jahrhundert war die Oper sehr beliebt.   10. Das ist eine Mode aus den vierziger Jahren.   11. Vor einem Jahr wußte man noch nichts davon.   12. Am Sonntag schlafe ich immer lange.   13. Abends lese ich zuerst die Zeitung (*newspaper*).   14. Er kommt immer gegen drei Uhr nachts nach Hause.   15. Es ist jetzt genau fünf nach halb drei.

23

Subjunctive: Formation;

Indirect Discourse

Die Anfänge der Psychoanalyse

In den neunziger Jahren arbeiteten an einer Wiener Klinik für Geisteskranke zwei junge Ärzte, Dr. Josef Breuer und Dr. Sigmund Freud. Wir verdanken der Zusammenarbeit dieser beiden bedeutenden Männer die Anfänge der Psychoanalyse. Dr. Breuer hatte nämlich eine Patientin, deren Krankheits-
5 symptome wichen, wenn sie in der Hypnose frei und ungehemmt sprechen konnte. Sie selbst nannte dies ihre „talking cure", denn ein Symptom ihrer Geistesstörung war, daß sie während ihrer Krankheit nur Englisch sprach. Eines Tages nun, so berichtet Dr. Breuer, sei etwas sehr Eigentümliches geschehen.
10 Die Patientin habe sechs Wochen lang nichts trinken können, obwohl der Sommer sehr heiß gewesen war. Sie hätte daher furchtbar unter Durst gelitten, den sie nur mit Früchten und besonders mit Melonen hätte löschen können. Wenn ihr ein Glas Wasser angeboten worden wäre, habe sie es heftig weggestoßen. Dr. Breuer hypnotisierte sie, und in der Hypnose erzählte sie,
15 sie teile ein Zimmer mit einer Engländerin, gegen die sie eine tiefe Abneigung fühle. Diese Engländerin besitze einen Hund, der ihr genauso unangenehm wäre wie seine Herrin. Sie sei nämlich eines Tages ins Zimmer gekommen und habe gesehen, wie dieser Hund auf den Tisch gesprungen wäre und aus

einem Glas getrunken hätte. Aus Höflichkeit habe sie aber der Engländerin gegenüber von dem Vorfall geschwiegen. Erst in der Hypnose sprach sie nun 20 ohne Hemmung darüber und verlangte dabei etwas zu trinken. Man goß ihr Wasser in ein Glas und sie wachte mit dem Glas am Mund auf. Ihre „talking cure" hatte ihr wieder geholfen.

Aus diesem und ähnlichen Fällen entwickelte Freud seine Theorie des Unbewußten und bewies, daß viele Störungen und andere psychische Sym- 25 ptome durch irgendein frühes Erlebnis verursacht seien, das der Patient verdrängt habe und das nun im Unterbewußtsein weiterlebe. Es sei die Aufgabe des Arztes, behauptete er, durch psychoanalytische Behandlung ein solches Erlebnis ins Bewußtsein zurückzurufen und den Patienten dadurch von seiner Hemmung zu befreien.   30

FRAGEN

1. Wann arbeiteten zwei junge Ärzte an einer Wiener Klinik für Geisteskranke? 2. Wo arbeiteten diese beiden jungen Ärzte? 3. Was verdanken wir diesen beiden jungen Ärzten? 4. Was für eine Patientin hatte Dr. Breuer? 5. Was geschah mit ihr in der Hypnose? 6. Was war ein Symptom ihrer Geistesstörung? 7. Was war eines Tages geschehen? 8. Was hat die Patientin sechs Wochen lang nicht tun können? 9. Wie hatte sie versucht, ihren Durst zu löschen? 10. Was kann man außer Durst „löschen"? 11. Was hat sie getan, wenn ihr ein Glas Wasser angeboten wurde? 12. Was erzählte sie in der Hypnose? 13. Wie war ihr der Hund der Engländerin? 14. Warum war er ihr unangenehm? 15. Warum hatte sie von diesem Vorfall geschwiegen? 16. Was verlangte sie bei der Hypnose? 17. Was tat sie und was gab man ihr? 18. Woraus entwickelte Freud seine Theorie des Unbewußten? 19. Was bewies er? 20. Was, sagte er, sei die Aufgabe des Arztes?

WORTSCHATZ

die **Abneigung, –en**	aversion	der **Durst**	thirst
angenehm	pleasant	**unter Durst**	to suffer from
die **Aufgabe, –n**	task; lesson	**leiden (i, i)**	thirst
sich **auf /regen**	to get (be) excited	**eigentümlich**	strange
befreien	to free	**frech**	insolent, "fresh"
berichten	to report	die **Frechheit, –en**	insolence
bewußt	conscious	**im Grunde**	really
das **Bewußtsein**	consciousness	**hemmen**	to inhibit

die **Hemmung, –en**	inhibition	(*noun:* **das Unterbewußt-sein**)
höflich	polite	
die **Höflichkeit, –en**	politeness	**verdrängen** — to push aside; to suppress
irgendein	(just) any	
löschen	to quench; to extinguish	**verursachen** — to cause (*from* die **Ursache, –n** cause)
das **Mehl**	flour	
die **Störung, –en**	disturbance	der **Vorfall, ꞏe** — occurrence
teilen	to share	das **Wetter, –** — weather
das **Unbewußte**	unconscious	die **Zusammen-arbeit, –en** — collaboration
ungehemmt	uninhibited	
unterbewußt	subconscious	

STRONG VERBS

(an)/bieten	to offer		**bot (an)**	**(an)geboten**
backen	to bake		**buk** (also: **backte**)	**gebacken**
empfehlen	to recommend	**empfiehlt**	**empfahl**	**empfohlen**
gießen	to pour		**goß**	**gegossen**
messen	to measure	**mißt**	**maß**	**gemessen**
schließen	to close, shut, conclude		**schloß**	**geschlossen**
stoßen	to push	**stößt**	**stieß**	**gestoßen**
weichen	to yield; to subside		**wich**	**ist gewichen**

GRAMMATICAL TERMS

1. The *subjunctive*, like the indicative, is a mood. But while the indicative states facts (I *am* rich), the subjunctive expresses thoughts, wishes, doubts, or conditions which are contrary-to-fact[1] (I wish I *were* rich).

2. The subjunctive is used in indirect discourse, that is, in a form of speech that is not quoted directly but in which what has been said is reported in the words of someone else:

> Direct discourse: "I can do it."
> Indirect discourse: He said he could do it.

3. While subjunctive forms differing from the indicative are relatively rare in English (if I *were* king; I asked that he *send* me the money; *be* it ever so humble), the subjunctive as a mood is quite common even in everyday speech. Aside from forms like *might, could, would, should*, the past indicative may function as a subjunctive in clauses like: If I *had* a million dollars . . .

[1] To be discussed in Lesson 24.

SUBJUNCTIVE IN GERMAN

Subjunctive forms have but one set of endings for all tenses:

(ich)	**–e**	(wir)	**–en**
(du)	**–est**	(ihr)	**–et**
(er)	**–e**	(sie)	**–en**

These endings are added to the stems (present and past) of a verb or its auxiliary to form the only four tenses that exist in the subjunctive: *present*, *past*, *future*, and *future perfect*. There are two sets of forms for each tense in the subjunctive: the *general subjunctive* and the *special subjunctive*.

GENERAL SUBJUNCTIVE

1. The present tense of the general subjunctive is formed by adding the subjunctive endings to the *past stem* of the verb. For weak verbs, the forms of the present tense of the general subjunctive are identical with those of the indicative:

ich lebte	wir lebten
du lebtest	ihr lebtet
er lebte	sie lebten

The following verb groups take the Umlaut in the present tense of the general subjunctive:

a. Strong verbs,[1] including the auxiliaries **sein (wäre)** and **werden (würde):**

ich **tränke**	wir **tränken**
du **tränkest**	ihr **tränket**
er **tränke**	sie **tränken**

b. The (weak) auxiliary **haben (hätte);**
c. Modal auxiliaries with an Umlaut in the infinitive (**könnte, dürfte, möchte, müßte);**
d. The irregular weak verbs **wissen, denken, bringen (wüßte, dächte, brächte).**[2]

---

[1] Some strong verbs have two present tense forms of the general subjunctive, of which the one cited below right (with the stem vowel differing from that of the past indicative) is the older and still the more colloquial:

er **stände**	er **stünde**
er **hälfe**	er **hülfe**

[2] The irregular weak verbs **brennen, kennen, nennen, rennen** form the present subjunctive by changing the **a** of their past stem to **e (brennte, kennte, nennte, rennte); senden** and **wenden** form it like regular weak verbs **(sendete, wendete).**

2. The past tense of the general subjunctive is formed by adding the subjunctive endings to **hätt-** or, if the verb is constructed with **sein,** to **wär-** and then combining these forms with the past participle of the main verb:

<table>
<tr><td>ich hätte getrunken</td><td>ich wäre gekommen</td></tr>
<tr><td>du hättest getrunken</td><td>du wärest gekommen</td></tr>
<tr><td>er hätte getrunken</td><td>er wäre gekommen</td></tr>
<tr><td>wir hätten getrunken</td><td>wir wären gekommen</td></tr>
<tr><td>ihr hättet getrunken</td><td>ihr wäret gekommen</td></tr>
<tr><td>sie hätten getrunken</td><td>sie wären gekommen</td></tr>
</table>

3. The future and future perfect of the general subjunctive are formed by adding the subjunctive endings to **würd-** and combining these forms with the present or perfect infinitives, respectively; these **würde-**forms are commonly called the "conditional":

FUTURE SUBJUNCTIVE (Present Conditional or **würde-**Form)

<table>
<tr><td>ich würde trinken</td><td>wir würden trinken</td></tr>
<tr><td>du würdest trinken</td><td>ihr würdet trinken</td></tr>
<tr><td>er würde trinken</td><td>sie würden trinken</td></tr>
</table>

FUTURE PERFECT SUBJUNCTIVE (Past Conditional or **würde-**Form)

<table>
<tr><td>ich würde getrunken haben</td><td>ich würde gekommen sein</td></tr>
<tr><td>du würdest getrunken haben</td><td>du würdest gekommen sein</td></tr>
<tr><td>er würde getrunken haben</td><td>er würde gekommen sein</td></tr>
<tr><td>etc.</td><td>etc.</td></tr>
</table>

As can be seen from the headings of the two tables above, the German future subjunctive also functions as the present conditional (or **würde-**form) and is equivalent to the English *would* + infinitive. In most instances, the use of the present subjunctive (er **tränke,** er **käme**) or of the present conditional (er **würde trinken,** er **würde kommen**) is a matter of style, since both forms mean the same:

Er **käme** heute.
Er **würde** heute **kommen.** } *He would come today.*

SPECIAL SUBJUNCTIVE

Compared with the general subjunctive, the special subjunctive has an incomplete set of forms.

1. The present tense of the special subjunctive is formed by adding the subjunctive endings to the infinitive stem·

(ich trinke)	(wir trinken)
du trink**est**	ihr trink**et**
er trink**e**	(sie trink**en**)

Since the forms in parentheses are indistinguishable from the indicative, they must be replaced by corresponding forms from the general subjunctive: ich **tränke**, wir **tränken**, sie **tränken.**

Strong verbs with the stem vowels **e** and **a** do not have the irregularities in the subjunctive which they have in the indicative; for example, **geben** and **tragen** are conjugated in the present of the special subjunctive as follows:

INDICATIVE	SPECIAL SUBJUNCTIVE	INDICATIVE	SPECIAL SUBJUNCTIVE
ich **gebe**	(ich **gebe**)	ich **trage**	(ich **trage**)
du **gibst**	du **gebest**	du **trägst**	du **tragest**
er **gibt**	er **gebe**	er **trägt**	er **trage**
etc.	etc.	etc.	etc.

The present tense of the special subjunctive of **sein** is slightly irregular and, therefore, complete:

ich **sei**	wir **seien**
du **sei(e)st**	ihr **seiet**
er **sei**	sie **seien**

2. The past tense of the special subjunctive is formed by adding the subjunctive endings to **hab-** or, if the verb is conjugated with **sein,** by using the present tense of the special subjunctive of **sein,** and combining these forms with the past participle of the main verb:

(ich habe getrunken)	ich **sei gekommen**
du **habest getrunken**	du **sei(e)st gekommen**
er **habe getrunken**	er **sei gekommen**
(wir haben getrunken)	wir **seien gekommen**
ihr **habet getrunken**	ihr **seiet gekommen**
(sie haben getrunken)	sie **seien gekommen**

3. The future and future perfect of the special subjunctive are formed by adding the subjunctive endings to **werd-** and combining these forms with the present and perfect infinitives, respectively:

FUTURE SPECIAL SUBJUNCTIVE

(ich werde trinken)	(wir werden trinken)
du **werdest trinken**	ihr **werdet trinken**
er **werde trinken**	(sie werden trinken)

FUTURE PERFECT SPECIAL SUBJUNCTIVE

(ich werde getrunken haben)	(wir werden getrunken haben)
du **werdest getrunken haben**	ihr **werdet getrunken haben**
er **werde getrunken haben**	(sie werden getrunken haben)

Similarly for a verb taking the auxiliary **sein:**

(ich werde gekommen sein)
du **werdest gekommen sein,** etc.

INDIRECT DISCOURSE

1. In indirect discourse, German uses the indicative if the speaker or writer can vouch for what has been said or identifies himself with it:

DIRECT: „Es hat geregnet!" *It rained!*
INDIRECT: Er sagt, **es hat geregnet.**

2. If the writer or speaker does not or cannot vouch for what has been said, or wishes to disassociate himself from it, either the general or the special subjunctive is used:

Er sagt, **es hätte (habe) geregnet.**
He says it rained.
Er behauptet, daß diese Theorie bloße Spekulation **wäre (sei).**
He asserts that this theory is mere speculation.

Note that English normally uses the indicative in indirect discourse where German uses the general or special subjunctive.

3. Of the two subjunctives, the general subjunctive is commonly used in everyday speech or informal writing:

Er sagt, sie **wären** sehr schön.
He says they are very beautiful.

In formal or literary usage, the special subjunctive predominates, but the general subjunctive must be used if the special subjunctive is identical with the indicative. (This is always the case in the third person plural except with the auxiliary **sein.**):

Es heißt, daß sie nicht genug zu essen **habe.**
They say that she doesn't have enough to eat.
But: Es heißt, daß sie nicht genug zu essen **hätten.**
They say that they don't have enough to eat.

4. Indirect discourse generally retains the tenses of direct discourse, but note that in indirect discourse the past subjunctive is equivalent to the past, present perfect, and past perfect indicative of direct discourse:

DIRECT DISCOURSE (Indicative)	INDIRECT DISCOURSE (Subjunctive)

Er sagt,

PRESENT:	Er **hat** kein Geld.	er **hätte (habe)** kein Geld.
PAST:	Er **hatte** kein Geld.	
PRES. PERF.:	Er **hat** kein Geld **gehabt.**	er **hätte (habe)** kein Geld **gehabt.**
PAST PERF.:	Er **hatte** kein Geld **gehabt.**	
FUTURE:	Er **wird** kein Geld **haben.**	er **würde (werde)** kein Geld **haben.**
FUT. PERF.:	Er **wird** kein Geld **gehabt haben.**	er **würde (werde)** kein Geld **gehabt haben.**

5. The conjunction **daß** may be omitted, but normal word order must then be used:

> Er sagt, **daß** Deutschland kleiner als Texas **wäre (sei).**
> Er sagt, **Deutschland wäre (sei)** kleiner als Texas.

OTHER USES OF THE SPECIAL AND THE GENERAL SUBJUNCTIVES

1. The special subjunctive is also used:

a. to form the imperative of the auxiliary **sein** (which is really a wish!):

> **Sei** nicht so dumm!
> *Don't be so stupid.*
> **Seien Sie so gut und . . .**
> *Kindly* (lit.: be so good and) . . .

b. in impersonal wishes:

> **Es lebe die Freiheit!**
> *Long live freedom!*

c. in recipes and instructions, with the subject **man:**

> **Man nehme drei Eier und schlage sie . . .**
> *Take three eggs and beat them . . .*

d. in concessive statements:

> **Wie dem auch sei . . .**
> *However that may be . . .*

Note that this construction is followed by the normal word order in the principal clause (no inversion!):

> **Wie dem auch sei, ich kann** es nicht glauben.
> *However that may be, I cannot believe it.*

  e. to introduce additional remarks:

> **Erwähnt sei noch, daß** . . .
> *It should also be mentioned that* . . .

2. The general subjunctive is also used:[1]

  a. to express potentiality (English: *would be* . . .):

> **Das wäre schön. (Das würde schön sein.)**
> *That would be nice.*

  b. to express probability (with modal auxiliary **dürfen** or **können**):

> **Das dürfte (könnte) wahr sein.**
> *That might (could) be true.*

  c. in expressions of politeness:

> **Dürfte ich (wohl)** . . .   *May I (perhaps)* . . .
> **Ich möchte (gerne)** . . .   *I would like to* . . .
> **Könnte ich (vielleicht)** . . .   *Could I (perhaps)* . . .
> **Würden Sie wohl** . . .   *Would you perhaps* . . .

RECAPITULATION OF MAIN POINTS

1. The subjunctive has four tenses: present, past, future, future perfect.

2. Each tense has two forms:

  a. The special subjunctive (the endings are added to the infinitive stem or to **hab-** or **werd-**). The forms of **sein** are irregular:

  er **sage**, er **habe gesagt**, er **werde sagen**, er **werde gesagt haben.**
  er **komme**, er **sei gekommen**, er **werde kommen**, er **werde gekommen sein.**

  b. The general subjunctive (endings are added to the past stem of the verb or to **hätt-, wär-, würd-**):

  er **sagte**, er **hätte gesagt**, er **würde sagen**, er **würde gesagt haben.**
  er **käme**, er **wäre gekommen**, er **würde kommen**, er **würde gekommen sein.**

3. Indirect discourse uses either subjunctive; the general subjunctive is preferred in informal usage:

> **Man sagt, er wäre (sei)** der größte Psychologe des Jahrhunderts.

[1] Its use in contrary-to-fact conditions will be treated separately in the next lesson.

General subjunctive forms must be used if the special subjunctive forms are identical with the indicative! This is always the case in the third person plural, except with the auxiliary **sein**.

4. The most common additional uses of the special subjunctive are:

In impersonal wishes: **Es lebe die Freiheit!**   *Long live freedom!*
In instructions: **Man nehme . . .**   *Take . . .*

5. The most common additional uses of the general subjunctive are:

Expressions of politeness: **Ich möchte (gerne) . . .**   *I should like to . . .*
                               Dürfte ich (wohl) . . .   *May I perhaps . . .*
                               Könnte ich . . .   *Could I . . .*
To express probability: **Das könnte sein.**   *That could be.*
                               Das dürfte so sein.   *That might be so.*

ÜBUNGEN

Practice in Reading and Writing

A. *Read aloud and translate:*

Metternich bei Napoleon

1. Der österreichische Kanzler Metternich pflegte zu erzählen, daß er in jüngeren Jahren einmal eine Audienz bei Napoleon gehabt habe. 2. Er habe im Vorzimmer gewartet, und da sei plötzlich die Tür aufgerissen worden. 3. Ein junger Mann sei herausgeflogen, und dann sei Napoleon selbst in der Tür erschienen. 4. Er habe furchtbar auf den jungen Mann geschimpft. 5. Schließlich sei er, Metternich, Napoleon ins Zimmer gefolgt, und dann habe dieser sich bei ihm entschuldigt, daß er ihn habe warten lassen. 6. Bald sei Napoleon wieder ruhiger geworden und habe dann gemeint, jetzt könne er über die Sache schon lachen. 7. Aber im Grunde habe er sich doch immer noch sehr aufgeregt. 8. Solche Frechheiten, habe er gesagt, könnten ihn immer sehr aufregen. 9. Was es denn eigentlich gegeben habe, hätte Metternich wissen wollen. 10. Da habe ihm Napoleon dann erzählt, der amerikanische Gesandte Livingstone in Paris hätte ihm einen richtigen Idioten mit einem Empfehlungsbrief geschickt. 11. Dieser vollkommene Idiot habe ihm, Napoleon, gesagt, er habe eine Erfindung gemacht, mit der er, Napoleon, unabhängig von Wind und Wetter, Truppen

2	**das Vorzimmer, –** *antechamber*	**der Empfehlungs-**	*letter of recommen-*
	auf/reißen (i, i) *to tear (throw) open*	**brief, –e**	*dation*
10	**der Gesandte,–n,–n** *ambassador*	11 **unabhängig**	*independent*

in England landen könne, und zwar mit Hilfe von kochendem Wasser.
12. Das sei ihm, Napoleon, denn doch zuviel gewesen! 13. Und so habe er
ihn also an die Luft gesetzt. 14. Dieser Mann aber, schloß Metternich, sei
der Amerikaner Robert Fulton gewesen, der Erfinder des Dampfschiffes.
15. Was würde wohl geschehen sein, wenn Napoleon damals die Bedeutung
dieser Erfindung verstanden hätte?

12	**denn doch**	*after all*	14	**das Dampfschiff,** *steamship*
13	**an die Luft setzen**	(lit., to put out into the air) *to throw out*		**–e**

B. *Identify the verb forms in italics:*

1. *Möchten* Sie wissen, wie man Pfannkuchen backt? 2. Das *könnte* ich
Ihnen sagen. 3. Oder *möchten* Sie, daß ich Ihnen das Rezept (*recipe*) lieber
aufschreibe? 4. Man *nehme* vier Eier und *schlage* sie. 5. Dann *nehme* man
etwas Mehl und *rühre* (rühren *to stir*) es unter die Eier. 6. Den Rest des
Rezeptes *sollten* Sie lieber im Kochbuch nachlesen. 7. *Nehmen* wir für
morgen die nächste Aufgabe! 8. Ich *möchte* wissen, wie er das meint.
9. *Sei* dem, wie ihm *wolle*. 10. Es *lebe* die Republik! 11. Auch die anderen
Werke des Dichters *seien* noch kurz genannt. 12. Er findet, sie *lache* zuviel.
13. Er behauptet, wir *lachten* zuviel. 14. Er sagte, das *wisse* er nicht.
15. Er erklärte, er *könne* nicht kommen. 16. Er glaubt, wir *könnten* nicht
kommen. 17. Er glaubte, das Feuer *brennte* noch. 18. *Hätten* Sie das von
ihm gedacht? 19. Was *dächten* Sie davon? 20. Das *dürfte* gelogen sein.

C. *Give the two subjunctive forms corresponding to the indicative forms which
follow.* (*First review paragraph 4 on page 273.*):

1. er hat. 2. er ist 3. sie wird 4. du stößt 5. er schließt 6. du gießt
7. wir gewannen 8. sie haben geteilt 9. ich hatte versucht 10. du wirst
entwickeln 11. er hat befreit 12. ich bin aufgestanden 13. ihr werdet
berichten 14. sie haben geschwiegen 15. wir sind gewichen.

D. *Translate:*

1. He claims he understands the spirit of his work. 2. He told us that he
has seen *Hamlet* in Berlin. 3. Let's avoid this danger. 4. Would you like
to share this bottle with us? 5. Could you give me another chair? 6. We
would like to own such a nice house. 7. However that may be, I don't believe
it. 8. He told us that he was not interested in modern art. 9. It would be
nice if you could have these pictures developed soon. 10. A woman who
says she cannot understand a man should not marry him. 11. Some of
them, he said, discovered that only too late. 12. Would you know a better
treatment for her? 13. Let's assume that we have understood this lesson.
14. Take some water and stir it slowly into the flour. 15. Would you be so

good and explain the subjunctive to me once more? 16. I thought they had brought their books along. 17. He said the train arrived at 9:15. 18. I should add that we also have to review the last five lessons.

Oral Exercises

E. *Preliminary exercise. Change the sentences to past indicative:*

EXAMPLE: Die Patientin kann nichts trinken.
Die Patientin konnte nichts trinken.

1. Man gießt Wasser in ein Glas.   2. Der Arzt bietet ihr das Glas Wasser an. 3. Die Patientin stößt es weg.   4. Der Arzt muß das Symptom untersuchen. 5. Sie teilt ihr Zimmer mit einer Engländerin.   6. Die Engländerin besitzt einen Hund.   7. Der Hund trinkt aus dem Glas.   8. Sie schweigt darüber aus Höflichkeit.   9. Der Arzt weiß jetzt genug.

F. *Indirect discourse. Change the direct quotes to indirect quotes. Use the present tense of the general subjunctive, and begin each sentence with* **Er sagte:**

EXAMPLE: „Die Patientin kann nicht trinken."
Er sagte, die Patientin könnte nicht trinken.

1. „Man gießt Wasser in ein Glas."   2. „Der Arzt bietet ihr das Glas Wasser an."   3. „Die Patientin stößt es weg."   4. „Der Arzt muß das Symptom untersuchen."   5. „Sie teilt ihr Zimmer mit einer Engländerin."   6. „Die Engländerin besitzt einen Hund."   7. „Der Hund trinkt aus dem Glas." 8. „Sie schweigt darüber aus Höflichkeit."   9. „Der Arzt weiß jetzt genug."

G. *Continue in the same manner. Use the past tense of the general subjunctive. Begin each sentence with* **Er sagt:**

EXAMPLES: „Freud hat eine neue Theorie entwickelt."
Er sagt, Freud hätte eine neue Theorie entwickelt.

„Freud entwickelte die Psychoanalyse."
Er sagt, Freud hätte die Psychoanalyse entwickelt.

1. „Er hat viele Patienten gehabt."   2. „Er hatte auch einmal eine amerikanische Patientin."   3. „Sie ist nach Wien gekommen."   4. „Sie kam in seine Klinik."   5. „Sie hat nicht schlafen können."   6. „Sie konnte auch nichts trinken."   7. „Sie hat nichts erzählen wollen."   8. „Sie wollte ihre Geschichte nicht erzählen."   9. „Sie ist hypnotisiert worden."   10. „Sie war dann frei und ungehemmt."

H. *Continue in the same manner. This time use the present tense of the special* *subjunctive for the 3rd person singular and the present tense of the general subjunctive for the 3rd person plural. Begin each sentence with* **Er sagte:**

EXAMPLES: „Ich fahre diesen Sommer nach Wien."
   Er sagte, er fahre diesen Sommer nach Wien.

   „Die meisten Leute fahren nach Paris."
   Er sagte, die meisten Leute führen nach Paris.

1. „Ich habe genug Geld." 2. „Viele Leute haben dafür kein Geld."
3. „Ich kann den Psychoanalytiker bezahlen." 4. „Manche Leute können den Psychiater nicht bezahlen." 5. „Man muß mit den jungen Damen immer höflich sein." 6. „Viele Leute müssen lange Zeit warten." 7. „Ich bleibe ein halbes Jahr in Wien." 8. „Die Leute bleiben oft länger dort." 9. „Man weiß das vorher nie." 10. „Die Ärzte wissen es auch nicht."

I. *Continue in the same manner. Use the past tense of the special subjunctive where possible and the past tense of the general subjunctive where necessary. Begin each sentence with* **Er erzählte:**

EXAMPLES: „Ich habe eine Erfindung gemacht."
   Er erzählte, er habe eine Erfindung gemacht.

   „Die Amerikaner haben schon davon gehört."
   Er erzählte, die Amerikaner hätten schon davon gehört.

   „Ich bin deswegen an die Luft gesetzt worden."
   Er erzählte, er sei deswegen an die Luft gesetzt worden.

   „Alle sind sehr aufgeregt gewesen."
   Er erzählte, alle seien sehr aufgeregt gewesen.

1. „Ich habe das nicht wissen können." 2. „Die Leute haben die Erfindung nicht verstanden." 3. „Das ist mir zuviel gewesen." 4. „Die Leute sind immer eigentümlich frech." 5. „Ich habe eine Abneigung dagegen gehabt."
6. „Die Amerikaner haben eine große Aufgabe gehabt." 7. „Ich bin kein Idiot gewesen." 8. „Die andern sind die Idioten gewesen."

24

Subjunctive in

Contrary-to-Fact Conditions

Geschichtliche Spekulationen

Die Frage, was geschehen wäre, wenn eine geschichtliche Tatsache anders gekommen wäre, als sie wirklich gekommen ist, hat die Köpfe immer wieder beschäftigt. Nehmen wir nur ein Beispiel: wie sähe Deutschland und wie sähe die deutsche Sprache heute aus, wenn die Römer im Teutoburger Wald[1] über die Germanen gesiegt hätten und nicht die Germanen über die Römer? 5
Würde man heute in Deutschland Deutsch sprechen oder eine Sprache, die sich aus dem Lateinischen entwickelt hätte, wie das moderne Französisch oder das moderne Spanisch?

Auf[2] solche Fragen schweigt die Geschichte. Tatsache ist und bleibt, daß die Römer im Jahre 9 n.Chr.[3] eine entscheidende Niederlage erlitten haben. 10
Varus, der römische Feldherr, war mit drei Legionen durch den Teutoburger Wald gezogen. Da kam ein furchtbares Gewitter auf. Bäume, die von den Germanen angeschlagen[4] worden waren, stürzten nieder, und die Germanen, die sich in den Wäldern verborgen hatten, griffen an. In drei Tagen wurden die Legionen fast vollkommen vernichtet, und Varus nahm sich mit seinem 15
eigenen Schwert das Leben. Nur ein paar römische Soldaten entflohen; sie

1. **Teutoburger Wald** *Teutoburg Forest* (range of hills in Western Germany). 2. **auf** (here:) *to*. 3. **n.Chr.** (read: **nach Christus**) *A.D., after Christ*. 4. **angeschlagen** *cut into*.

schlichen sich durch die Wälder zurück und brachten die Nachricht von der furchtbaren Niederlage nach Rom.

In Rom selbst brach eine Panik aus. Kaiser Augustus fürchtete, die Ger-
20 manen würden nun in Italien einfallen und Rom belagern. Die meisten römischen Legionen waren im Osten. Es wäre viel Zeit vergangen, wenn man versucht hätte, sie zurückzubringen. Diese Furcht aber war zunächst grund-los, denn Arminius, der germanische Fürst, hatte sein Ziel erreicht, Ger-manien von den Römern zu befreien. Weitere Versuche der Römer, Ger-
25 manien zu erobern, blieben erfolglos.

Die Schlacht im Teutoburger Wald ist schon damals viel erörtert worden. Manche schworen, die Niederlage sei ein Urteil der Götter gewesen. Andere behaupteten, die Armee des Varus würde nicht vernichtet worden sein, wenn dieser dem Arminius, seinem Freund, weniger getraut hätte, und wenn er mit
30 seinen Legionen in einem feindlichen Lande vorsichtiger gewesen wäre. Als ob Varus die Zukunft hätte voraussehen können!

Hätten aber die Römer gesiegt und das ganze Land vom Rhein bis zur Elbe erobert, dann wären hier sicher eine gemeinsame Sprache und Kultur[5] ent-standen, die bis an die östlichen Grenzen Germaniens gereicht hätten. Das
35 würde die Geschichte Europas bis in unsere Tage vollkommen geändert haben.

5. **Kultur** (here:) *civilization.*

FRAGEN

1. Was hat die Köpfe immer wieder beschäftigt? 2. Welches Beispiel können wir nehmen? 3. Was würde man heute in Deutschland sprechen, wenn die Römer über die Germanen gesiegt hätten? 4. Worauf schweigt die Ge-schichte? 5. Was ist und bleibt Tatsache? 6. Was hatte Varus getan? 7. Was war da geschehen? 8. Was hatten die Germanen getan, bevor sie angriffen? 9. Was geschah in drei Tagen? 10. Was taten ein paar römische Soldaten? 11. Was fürchtete Kaiser Augustus? 12. Womit wäre viel Zeit vergangen? 13. Wollte Arminius in Italien einfallen? 14. Was blieb er-folglos? 15. Was schworen manche? 16. Was behaupteten andere? 17. Was würde die Geschichte Europas bis in unsere Tage vollkommen geändert haben?

WORTSCHATZ

der **Baum,** ⸗e	tree	**erfolglos**	unsuccessful, with-out success

	erörtern	to discuss	das **Schwert, –er**	sword
	feindlich	hostile, enemy (*adj.*)	**siegen**	to win, be victorious
die	**Furcht**	fear	**stimmen**	to be correct
	fürchten	to fear	**stürzen**	to dash; to fall head-
der	**Fürst, –en, –en**	(ruling) prince		long
	gemeinsam	common	die **Tatsache, –n**	fact
der	**Germane, –n, -n**	Teuton	**trauen**	to trust
	geschichtlich	historical	**(so) tun, als ob**	to act (do) as if
	sich handeln um	to be a matter of,	der **Umstand, ⁼e**	circumstance
		concern	**unter diesen**	under these cir-
	jedenfalls	in any case	**Umständen**	cumstances
die	**Nachricht, –en**	news	**vernichten**	to annihilate,
	nieder- (*prefix*)	down		destroy
die	**Niederlage, –n**	defeat	**vorsichtig**	careful
der	**Nutzen**	use(fulness)	der **Wald, ⁼er**	forest
	reichen (bis an,	to teach (to)	**weiter** (*adj.*)	further
	w. acc.)		das **Ziel, –e**	goal
			zunächst	for the time being

STRONG VERBS

an /greifen	to attack		**griff an**		**angegriffen**
aus /brechen	to break out	**bricht aus**	**brach aus**	ist	**ausgebrochen**
befehlen	to command	**befiehlt**	**befahl**		**befohlen**
ein /fallen[1] **(in)**	to invade	**fällt ein**	**fiel ein**	ist	**eingefallen**
entfliehen	to escape		**entfloh**	ist	**entflohen**
erleiden (trans.)[2]	to suffer		**erlitt**		**erlitten**
schleichen	to sneak; to creep		**schlich**	ist	**geschlichen**
schwören	to swear		**schwor**		**geschworen**
vergehen	to pass, elapse		**verging**	ist	**vergangen**
voraus /sehen	to foresee, anticipate	**sieht voraus**	**sah voraus**		**vorausgesehen**

GRAMMATICAL TERMS

1. Conditions may be true to fact or contrary to fact. True-to-fact conditions are based on reality:

> If he *takes* the medicine, he will get well.
> If he *saw* him, he gave him the letter.

2. Contrary-to-fact conditions are based on unfulfilled possibility or probability:

> If he *took* the medicine, he would get well.
> If he *had* seen him, he would have given him the letter.

---

[1] impersonal verb: *to occur to* (see Aufgabe 13).
[2] intransitive: **leiden** (see Aufgabe 10).

CONTRARY-TO-FACT CONDITIONS IN GERMAN

1. True-to-fact conditions are expressed in the indicative:

> Wenn ich Zeit **habe, komme** ich.
> *If I have time, I'll come.*

2. Contrary-to-fact conditions in the present use the present of the general subjunctive in both the **wenn-**clause and the conclusion:

> Wenn ich Zeit **hätte, käme** ich.
> *If I had time, I would come.*

In the conclusion, the future subjunctive (present conditional, **würde-**form) may also be used and is preferred in colloquial German:

> Wenn ich Zeit hätte, **würde** ich **kommen.**

3. Contrary-to-fact conditions in the past use the past subjunctive in both the **wenn-**clause and the conclusion:

> Wenn ich Zeit **gehabt hätte, wäre** ich **gekommen.**
> *If I had had time, I would have come.*

As in the present, there is an alternate (and colloquially preferred) form for the conclusion: the future perfect subjunctive (past conditional, **würde-**form):

> Wenn ich Zeit gehabt hätte, **würde** ich **gekommen sein.**

4. If the **wenn-**clause and the conclusion refer to different times, the times to be expressed have to be in the appropriate tense forms, as in English:

> Wenn ich Zeit **gehabt hätte** (past), **wäre** (present) ich jetzt fertig.
> *If I had had time, I would be ready now.*

5. Wenn (*if*) may be omitted in German; if it is, the verb comes first in the clause (inverted word order):

> **Hätte ich** Zeit, so würde ich kommen.

Rule: If the verb comes first and the clause is neither a question nor a command, begin the translation with *if:*

> QUESTION: **Haben Sie** eine gute Brille?
> *Do you have good glasses?*
> CONDITION: **Haben Sie** eine gute Brille, **dann** können Sie dies lesen.
> *If you have good glasses, you can read this.*

The conclusion of a conditional sentence is often introduced by **so** or **dann,** especially if **wenn** is omitted; this **so** or **dann** is a signal by which to recognize a conditional sentence. In most cases, **so** and **dann** have no equivalent in English; sometimes they may be rendered by *then*.

6. To express an anxious wish in the present, German (like English) uses the **wenn**-clause of a contrary-to-fact condition in the present, sometimes adding **doch, nur,** or **doch nur** for emphasis; in such constructions, **nur** has the function of English *only:*

> **Wenn er (doch) nur käme!**   *If he would only come!*

Similarly, a wish that something should have happened in the past (but didn't) is expressed as a **wenn**-clause of a contrary-to-fact-condition in the past:

> **Wenn er (doch) nur gekommen wäre!**   *If he had only come!*

Here, too, **wenn** can be omitted:

> **Käme er doch (nur)! Wäre er doch (nur) gekommen!**

7. **Als ob** or **als wenn** (*as if*) are usually followed by the verb in the general subjunctive, although modern writers frequently favor the special subjunctive forms:[1]

> Es sieht aus, **als ob es regnete (geregnet hätte, regnen würde).**
> *It looks as if it is (were) raining (had rained, would rain).*

> Es schien, **als ob er** noch nicht **angekommen wäre.**[2]
> *It seemed as if he had not yet arrived.*

Ob or **wenn** may be omitted, in which case the finite verb follows **als:**

> Es sieht aus, **als regnete es (als hätte es geregnet, als würde es regnen).**

Therefore: If a verb (usually in the subjunctive) immediately follows **als,** translate **als** by *as if:*

> Er tat, **als hätte** er sie nicht gesehen.
> *He acted as if he hadn't seen her.*

RECAPITULATION OF MAIN POINTS

1. For contrary-to-fact conditions, use the general subjunctive:

---

[1] In colloquial, and even in written German, the indicative is increasingly used: Er tut, als ob er es **weiß.** *He acts as if he knows it.*
[2] **Als ob** constructions are common after: **aus**/**sehen** (*to look*), **scheinen** (*to seem*), **tun** (*to act*), **es ist mir (dir, ihm,** etc.) or **mir (dir,** etc.) **ist** (*I, you, he, etc. feel[s]*):

> **Mir ist (Es ist mir), als ob ich das Buch kennte.**
> *I feel (It seems to me) as if I knew the book.*

PRESENT CONDITION: Wenn ich Zeit **hätte, käme** ich (**würde** ich **kommen**).
PAST CONDITION: Wenn ich Zeit **gehabt hätte, wäre** ich **gekommen**
                                                     (**würde** ich **gekommen sein**).

2. If the verb comes first in a sentence which is neither a question nor a command, begin the translation with *if:*

> **Hätte ich** das gewußt, dann hätte ich nichts gesagt.
> *If I had (had I) known that I wouldn't have said anything.*

3. If the verb (in the subjunctive) immediately follows **als,** translate **als** by *as if:*

> Es sieht aus, **als hätte** er drei Tage nichts gegessen.
> *He looks as if he had not eaten anything for three days.*

ÜBUNGEN

Practice in Reading and Writing

A. *Read aloud and translate:*

Tilly und der Soldat

1. Die Geschichte berichtet, ein Soldat Tillys habe bei der Plünderung Magdeburgs eine reiche Beute gemacht. 2. Ihm seien mehr als 30 000 Dukaten in die Hände gefallen. 3. Ob das stimmt, wissen wir nicht, aber die Sache dürfte kaum übertrieben sein. 4. Natürlich könnte es sich auch genauso gut um nichts als eine Anekdote handeln. 5. Wenn die Akten der Armee Tillys noch existierten, könnten wir den Fall untersuchen. 6. Diese Akten aber existieren nicht mehr, wenn sie überhaupt jemals existiert haben. 7. Jedenfalls sagt man, Tilly habe davon gehört und den Soldaten vor sich bringen lassen. 8. Wo er denn das ganze Geld gelassen habe, hätte er den Soldaten gefragt, 9. Das Geld habe er noch am selben Tag am Spieltisch wieder verloren, sei die Antwort gewesen. 10. Da hätte Tilly befohlen, der Soldat solle sofort aufgehängt werden. 11. „Du hättest mit deinem Geld wie ein Herr leben können, wenn etwas in dem Kopf wäre, an dem du jetzt hängen wirst", habe Tilly erklärt. 12. „Es sieht aus, als ob du nicht einmal dir selbst helfen kannst. Ich sehe nicht, wie du unter diesen Umständen deinem Kaiser noch von Nutzen sein könntest."

| 1 | **die Plünderung** | *sack* | 10 | **auf/hängen** | *to hang* |
| 5 | **die Akten** | *files, documents* | | | |

B. *Read aloud and translate:*

Diogenes und der Tyrann

1. Man sagt, der Philosoph Aristippus sei reich geworden, weil er dem Tyrannen geschmeichelt habe.   2. Diogenes aber sei arm geblieben, weil er das nicht getan hätte.   3. Eines Tages nun sei Aristippus zu Diogenes gekommen, während dieser Linsen wusch, weil er sich daraus eine Suppe machen wollte.   4. Da habe Aristippus ironisch gemeint: „Wenn du, o Diogenes, dem Tyrannen geschmeichelt hättest wie ich, dann brauchtest du jetzt nicht mit einer Linsensuppe zufrieden zu sein."   5. „Und wenn du, o Aristippus", habe Diogenes geantwortet, „mit einer Linsensuppe zufrieden wärest wie ich, dann brauchtest du dem Tyrannen nicht zu schmeicheln."   6. Dächten alle wie Diogenes, dann gäbe es weniger Tyrannen auf der Welt.

	der Tyrạnn, –en, –en	*tyrant*	3	die Linse, –n	*lentil*
1	schmeicheln	*to flatter*		die Suppe, –n	*soup*

C. *Translate:*

1. Ein junger Komponist hatte auf Franz Liszts Tod einen Trauermarsch (*funeral march*) komponiert und spielte ihn Brahms vor: „Wenn Liszt den Trauermarsch auf Ihren Tod komponiert hätte", soll Brahms gesagt haben, „dann wäre er sicher besser geworden."   2. Es war ihr, als hätte er sie gar nicht verstanden.   3. Fritz aß, als ob er drei Tage lang nichts gegessen hätte.   4. Er tut wirklich, als wäre er allein auf der Welt.   5. Warum tun Sie immer, als ob Sie alles besser wüßten?   6. Heinrich Heine hat einmal von seiner Heimatstadt gesagt: „Düsseldorf ist eine schöne Stadt, und wenn ich in der Ferne (*from afar*) an sie denke, so ist es mir, als müßte ich gleich nach Hause gehen."

D. *Translate:*

1. He looks as if he were an artist.   2. If only the news were better!   3. When it gets dark, we'll sneak into the house.   4. If they had sneaked into the city, they could have conquered it easily.   5. Don't act as if this matter were so easy.   6. If they had only fled into the woods!   7. The trees looked as if the children had played in them.   8. If he had only trusted his family a little more!   9. They declared that they could defend their city.   10. If we had a goal we could make an attempt now.   11. Don't always act as if you did not see me.   12. They went home and acted as if they knew nothing.   13. When all the facts are known we'll try a new experiment.   14. Be careful! In any case, don't trust these people!   15. It would be easy to form (**sich bilden**) an opinion if one knew all the facts.   16. They could have worked together, had they known what they wanted to do.   17. Kant must have thought: if only these ladies would keep their mouths shut!   18. He swore he had not done it.

Oral Exercises

E. *Respond with a contrary-to-fact wish. Use* **wenn** *and the present subjunctive:*

EXAMPLE: Er nimmt das Beispiel nicht.
        Wenn er das Beispiel doch nähme!

1. Du bringst ihm die Nachricht nicht.   2. Sie versteht das nicht.   3. Wir
können ihm nicht entfliehen.   4. Ihr seid nicht vorsichtig.   5. Sie sprechen
nicht darüber.   6. Er sieht das nicht voraus.   7. Er weiß das nicht.

F. *Do exercise* **E** *again, this time omitting* **wenn:**

EXAMPLE: Er nimmt das Beispiel nicht.
        Nähme er doch das Beispiel!

G. *The following conditions are stated in the indicative. Make them contrary
to fact; use the present subjunctive and change the conditions and conclusions
from negative to positive:*

EXAMPLE: Wenn die Geschichte nicht richtig ist, glaube ich sie Ihnen nicht.
        (Aber) wenn die Geschichte richtig wäre, glaubte ich sie Ihnen.

1. Wenn du nicht schweigst, traue ich dir nicht.
2. Wenn Tilly die Stadt nicht belagert, werden sie sie nicht verteidigen.
3. Sie werden sich nicht in den Häusern verbergen, wenn er die Stadt nicht
   erobert.
4. Wenn sie sich nicht in die Stadt schleichen, können sie sie nicht vernichten.
5. Wir sind oft nicht vorsichtig, wenn wir den Tatsachen nicht trauen können.
6. Er gewinnt die Schlacht nicht, wenn er die Stadt nicht erobert.
7. Wenn wir den Konjunktiv (*subjunctive*) nicht können, sprechen wir nicht
   gut Deutsch.

H. *Respond with a contrary-to-fact wish. Use* **wenn** *and the past subjunctive:*

EXAMPLES:
Er hat das Ziel nicht erreicht.   Wenn er das Ziel doch erreicht hätte!
Ich erreichte das Ziel nicht.   Wenn ich das Ziel doch erreicht hätte!

1. Sie hat diese Situation nicht geändert.   2. Sie änderten diese Situation
nicht.   3. Wir haben kein Beispiel gefunden.   4. Er fand kein Beispiel.
5. Sie haben die Gefahr nicht gesehen.   6. Ich sah die Gefahr nicht.   7. Er
hat nicht Englisch gesprochen.   8. Wir sprachen nicht Deutsch.   9. Du
hast ihm keine Nachricht geschickt.   10. Er entwickelte seine Theorie nicht.

I. *The following contrary-to-fact conditions refer to the present; change them
to refer to the past:*

EXAMPLE: Wenn er sich entschiede, erreichte er sein Ziel.

Wenn er sich entschieden hätte, hätte er sein Ziel erreicht.

1. Weniger Zeit würde vergehen, wenn wir die Nachricht schneller bekämen.
2. Siegte er, so würde er die Stadt vernichten.
3. Kennten wir die Tatsachen, dann könnten wir den Fall gemeinsam entscheiden.
4. Sie würden die Niederlage nicht erleiden, wenn sie ihren Freunden trauten.
5. Sie würden sich im Walde verbergen, wenn er die Stadt eroberte.
6. Nordamerika spräche vielleicht nicht Englisch, wenn die amerikanische Geschichte anders aussähe.
7. Die Zeit verginge erfolglos, hätten wir nicht immer unser Ziel vor Augen.

J. *Respond with an as-if clause:*

EXAMPLE: Er versteht die Geschichte nicht. Aber er tut, ...

Aber er tut, als ob er die Geschichte verstünde.

1. Sie kennen uns nicht. Aber sie tun, ...
2. Die Sache ist nicht interessant. Aber sie tut, ...
3. Das Gewitter hat nicht den ganzen Wald vernichtet. Aber es schien, ...
4. Er hat keine wichtige Nachricht gebracht. Aber er scheint, ...

25

Special Constructions

Goethe und die Naturwissenschaften

Johann Wolfgang von Goethe (1749–1832) stammte aus einer in Frankfurt sehr angesehenen Familie. Der Vater war streng, aber doch auch stolz auf den hoffnungsvollen Sohn. So verdankte der Sohn dem Vater vor allem jene geistige Disziplin, ohne die so manches seiner Werke kaum geschrieben,
5 wenigstens nicht beendet worden wäre.

Goethe gilt heute vor allem als der Dichter des „Faust". Man hat gemeint, es lohne sich, die deutsche Sprache zu lernen, nur um diese große, im Grunde unübersetzbare Dichtung im Original lesen zu können. Aber Goethe war ja nicht nur der Dichter des „Faust". Es gibt kaum eine literarische Gattung,
10 die er nicht bewältigt hätte—aber man wird ihm nicht gerecht, wenn man nicht auch seiner wissenschaftlichen Leistungen gedenkt.

Schon der Student Goethe hatte sich für Medizin interessiert und an der Straßburger Universität medizinische Vorlesungen gehört, anstatt an seiner juristischen[1] Dissertation zu arbeiten. In späteren Jahren hat er dann unter
15 anderem Geologie, Physik, Botanik und Mineralogie getrieben. Wenn er von einer Reise zurückkehrte, hatte er seine Kutsche mit Steinen aller Art

1. **juristischen** *legal.*

beladen, die er dann in seine Sammlungen einordnete. In der Physik entwickelte er eine gegen Newton gerichtete Farbenlehre,[2] und wenn es ihm auch
nicht gelungen ist, sich gegen Newton durchzusetzen, so hat er doch Wesentliches zur physiologischen Optik beigetragen. Der Physiologe Johannes 20
Müller erklärte 1826 in seiner „Physiologie des Gesichtssinnes",[3] er hätte
sein Werk nicht schreiben können, ohne sich zuerst mit Goethes Arbeiten
auseinandergesetzt zu haben.

In der Botanik legte Goethe den Grund für eine vergleichende Morphologie, und in seinem 1790 erschienenen „Versuch, die Metamorphose der 25
Pflanzen zu erklären", befinden sich bereits sehr an Darwin erinnernde Gedanken. Er glaubte, die verschiedenen Organe der Pflanze als umgebildete[4]
Blätter erkennen zu können. Alle heute existierenden Pflanzen schienen ihm
auf eine Urpflanze[5] zurückzugehen.

Schon früh hatte Goethe sich auch mit dem Problem des Zwischenkiefer- 30
knochens[6] beschäftigt. Dieser angeblich im menschlichen Schädel nicht vorkommende Knochen im Oberkiefer[7] ist in manchen Säugetieren[8] sehr entwickelt, wächst aber beim[9] Menschen schon nach der Geburt mit dem Oberkiefer zusammen. Man hat Jahrhunderte lang geglaubt, das Fehlen des
Zwischenkieferknochens unterscheide den Menschen von den anderen Säuge- 35
tieren. Von der Einheit allen organischen Lebens fest überzeugt, glaubte und
bewies Goethe, daß dieser Knochen auch beim Menschen zu finden sei.

Typisch für Goethes Art zu denken und wissenschaftlich zu arbeiten ist die
Episode mit dem Schafskelett.[10] Auf seiner Reise nach Venedig[11] sah er ein
solches Skelett eines Tages auf dem Lido[12] liegen. Er untersuchte es und 40
fand, daß der Schädel sich aus einigen Wirbeln[13] entwickelt habe. Auch
dieser für seine Zeit sehr radikale Gedanke weist schon auf die von Darwin
später entwickelten Theorien voraus.

2. **Farbenlehre** *theory of colors.* 3. **Gesichtssinn** *visual sense.* 4. **umgebildete** *transmuted.*
5. **Urpflanze** *original plant.* 6. **Zwischenkieferknochen** *intermaxillary bone.* 7. **Oberkiefer**
upper jaw. 8. **Säugetiere** *mammals.* 9. **beim** (here:) *in the case of.* 10. **Schafskelett** *sheep
skeleton.* 11. **Venedig** *Venice.* 12. **Lido** *famous beach near Venice.* 13. **Wirbel** *ver-
tebrae.*

FRAGEN

1. Aus was für einer Familie stammte Goethe? 2. Wie war der Vater?
3. Was verdankte der Sohn dem Vater vor allem? 4. Warum lohnt es sich,
die deutsche Sprache zu lernen? 5. Welche literarischen Gattungen hat
Goethe bewältigt? 6. Wann wird man Goethe nicht gerecht? 7. Was hatte
schon der Student Goethe in Straßburg getan? 8. Was hat er in späteren

Jahren unter anderem getrieben?   9. Wie war seine Kutsche, wenn er von einer Reise zurückkehrte?   10. Was hat er in der Physik entwickelt?   11. Waren seine Arbeiten für die Farbenlehre ganz wertlos?   12. Was hat der Physiologe Johannes Müller erklärt?   13. Was hat er in dem „Versuch, die Metamorphose der Pflanze zu erklären", getan?   14. Was ist der Zwischenkieferknochen?   15. Was hatte man Jahrhunderte lang geglaubt?   16. Wovon war Goethe fest überzeugt?   17. Was ist typisch für Goethes Art, wissenschaftlich zu denken und zu arbeiten?   18. Wo und wann fand er das Schafskelett?   19. Was fand er, als er es untersuchte?   20. Worauf weist dieser Gedanke schon voraus?

WORTSCHATZ

unter anderem	among other things	das Gesicht, –er (*also* *pl.* –e)	face; vision
angeblich	supposedly	im Grunde	essentially, basically
aller Art	of all kinds	hoffnungsvoll	promising
sich auseinan- der /setzen (mit)	to come to grips (with)	der Knochen, –	bone
beobachten	to observe	die Kutsche, –n	coach
beruhen (auf, *w. dat.*)	to rest (on)	sich lohnen	to be worthwhile
bewältigen	to master	die Pflanze, –n	plant
das Blatt, ⸗er	leaf	richten	to direct
die Dichtung, –en	work of fiction	der Schädel, –	skull
sich durch /setzen (gegen)	to prevail (over)	die Spur, –en	trace, track
die Einheit, –en	unity, unit	der Stein, –e	stone, rock
ein /ordnen	to arrange (into)	stolz (auf, *w. acc.*)	proud (of)
erinnern	to remind	streng	strict
fest	firm(ly)	treiben (ie, ie)	to engage in (*also* to drive)
sich finden (a, u)	to be (found)	überzeugen	to convince
die Gattung, –en	genre, species	unübersetzbar	untranslatable
gedenken (*w. gen.*)	to remember	vergleichend	comparative
geistig	intellectual, spiritual	verschwenden	to waste
		voraus- (*prefix*)	ahead
gerecht (jemandem)	just	weh tun (*w. dat. of person*)	to hurt
gerecht werden (*w. dat. of person*)	to do justice (to a person)	wenigstens	at least
		wesentlich	essential
		zurück /kehren	to return

STRONG VERBS

bei /tragen	to contribute	trägt bei	trug bei	beigetragen
beladen	to load (up)	belädt	belud	beladen
gelten (als)	to be considered (as)	gilt	galt	gegolten
unterscheiden	to distinguish		unterschied	unterschieden

MODIFIED-ADJECTIVE CONSTRUCTION

1. Typical of German prose is its ability to modify a noun not only by a simple adjective (or adverb-adjective combination like **sehr gut**) but also by a whole phrase: a so-called modified-adjective phrase, which lends to the language its peculiar density. This construction is widely used, but favored especially by writers on scientific and technical subjects. In English, such constructions are impossible without violating the language. English cannot construct phrases like: *This in-the-year-1790-written-and-by-everybody-read book.* . . .

2. The German construction that amounts to exactly the hypothetical example just given is readily recognized because the article (or its equivalent, any **der-** or **ein**-word) is not followed directly by the noun it modifies but by a phrase which ends, and is anchored, in an adjective. This adjective may be a participle, so that the construction may also be a "modified-participle construction":

> Die **von dem berühmten Charles Darwin aufgestellte** Theorie . . . .
> (lit., *The [by-the-famous-Charles-Darwin-formulated] theory* . . . .)
> *The theory* (*which was*) *formulated by the famous Charles Darwin* . . . .

3. It is easy to translate such a construction once it has been recognized. Here are two clues: (a) the **der-** or **ein**-word is in most instances followed by a preposition,[1] and (b) the noun dependent on the **der-** or **ein**-word is not the next noun in the sentence, but follows later and is preceded by an adjective or participle:

> Diese **von allen anderen so verschiedene** Pflanze . . .
> *This plant* (*which is*) *so different from all others* . . .

> Der[2] **an die Einheit allen organischen Lebens unbedingt glaubende** Goethe . . .
> *Goethe, who firmly believed in the unity of all organic life* . . .

A participial modifier, however, frequently appears without a **der-** or **ein**-word:

> **Im Tal angepflanzte** Bäume . . .
> *Trees planted in the valley* . . .

---

[1] Occasionally, the modified-adjective construction will not contain a prepositional object but only adjectives (or a participle) and adverbs:

> Der Großvater des **später so berühmt gewordenen** Charles Darwin . . .
> *The grandfather of Charles Darwin, who later became so famous* . . .

[2] Names preceded by a modifier require an article in German: **der junge Goethe** *young Goethe;* in English this is only the case if the modifier is to be stressed: *the young Goethe.*

4. To translate a phrase containing a modified-adjective construction, proceed as follows:

FIRST STEP: Go from the article (or other **der-** or **ein**-word) to the noun with which it agrees in case, number, and gender. Taking the example in paragraph 3 above:

Der . . . Goethe   *Goethe*

SECOND STEP: Translate the adjective (or participle) preceding the noun, together with its immediate modifiers (if any), such as an adverb or **nicht;** the adjective (or participle) may be translated either as it is or as a relative clause:

unbedingt glaubende   *firmly (absolutely) believing*

Thus, we have:

Der . . . unbedingt glaubende Goethe . . .
Goethe, firmly believing . . . or *Goethe, who firmly believed . . .*

THIRD STEP: Translate the preposition with its object(s):

an die Einheit allen organischen Lebens
in the unity of all organic life

and combine the different parts for a translation of the whole sentence:

Der an die Einheit allen organischen Lebens unbedingt glaubende
  Goethe . . .
Goethe, who firmly believed in the unity of all organic life . . .

5. Modified-adjective constructions may consist of two or more modified adjectives or participles (in heavy type in the example below) and be combined, within the construction, with unmodified adjectives. In such a case, take care to translate unmodified adjectives together with the noun *before* going to the prepositional object(s):

Die von Goethe begründete und **von Johannes Müller weiterentwickelte** physiologische Optik . . .
Physiological optics (which was) founded by Goethe and further developed by Johannes Müller . . .

Similarly, genitive objects placed after the noun ending a modified-adjective construction (in heavy type below) should be translated before the adjective construction itself:

Das von so vielen Leuten gelesene Buch dieser Dichterin . . . .
The book of this poetess, read by so many people . . . .

PARTICIPIAL CONSTRUCTIONS

1. In literary German, present-participle constructions occur as follows:

> Er ging die Straße entlang, **leise vor sich hin singend.**
> *He went down the street, softly singing to himself.*

In everyday German a new principal clause would be preferred:

> Er ging die Straße entlang **und sang leise vor sich hin.**

2. Past-participle constructions occur without auxiliary verbs. Translate such constructions by beginning with the participle:

> **In Berlin angekommen,** ging er sofort in ein Hotel.
> *Having arrived in Berlin,*
> *After he had arrived in Berlin,* } *he immediately went to a hotel.*
> *On arriving in Berlin,*

INFINITIVE CONSTRUCTIONS

1. An infinitive which is in any way modified (if only by one word) is considered a dependent clause in German and, therefore, set off by a comma:

> Ich habe keine Lust, **nach Hause zu gehen.**
> *I have no desire to go home.*

2. **Um . . . zu** (*in order to*) is used in clauses which express a purpose. **Um** introduces the clause and is preceded by a comma; **zu** stands immediately before the infinitive at the end of the clause. English *to* frequently translates **um . . . zu** adequately:

> Er ging nach Straßburg, **um** dort **zu studieren.**
> *He went to Strasbourg (in order) to study there.*

An **um . . . zu** construction must be used if the idea of "in order to" is to be expressed or merely implied.

3. **Ohne . . . zu** (*without* plus present participle) and **anstatt . . . zu** (*instead of*) with the infinitive are constructed in the same way; note how in both instances English uses a present participle instead of the infinitive:

> Er hätte sein Buch nicht schreiben können, **ohne** zuerst die Goetheschen Arbeiten genau **studiert zu haben.**
> *He could not have written his book without first having studied closely Goethe's works.*

Er besuchte medizinische Vorlesungen, **anstatt** an seiner Dissertation **zu arbeiten.**
He attended medical lectures instead of working on his dissertation.

4. The English infinitive constructions *what to . . .*, *how to . . .*, *where to . . .*, etc. normally require in German a dependent clause with a modal auxiliary, commonly **sollen:**

Ich weiß nicht, **was ich sagen soll.**
I don't know what to say.

RECAPITULATION OF MAIN POINTS

1. The modified-adjective construction is best translated by a relative clause or a participial construction placed after the noun thus modified:

Eine **im Urwald wachsende** Pflanze . . . .
A plant which grows in the primeval forest . . . .
A plant growing in the primeval forest . . . .

2. In translating past-participial clauses, begin your translation with the participle:

Zu Hause angekommen, ging er gleich zu Bett.
Having arrived at home, he went straight to bed.

3. **Um . . . zu** (*in order to*, *to*) expresses purpose:

Er kam, **um** sie **abzuholen.**   *He came to call for her.*

4. **Ohne . . . zu** (*without*) and **anstatt . . . zu** (*instead of*) are translated by changing the German infinitive to a present participle in English:

Ohne etwas **zu sagen,** . . . .   *Without saying anything,* . . . .
Anstatt mir **zu danken,** . . . .   *Instead of thanking me,* . . . .

ÜBUNGEN

Practice in Reading and Writing

A. *Read aloud and translate:*

1. Der Goethit ist ein von einem Freunde Goethes nach ihm benanntes Mineral.   2. Der im Deutschen als Zwischenkieferknochen bezeichnete Inter-

maxillarknochen wird auch der Goetheknochen genannt.   3. Aber man kann nicht sagen: mir tut der Goetheknochen weh, denn den unter diesem Namen bekannten Knochen gibt es beim Schaf, aber nicht beim Menschen.   4. Goethes gegen Newton gerichtete Theorie über die Natur des Lichtes wird von der heutigen Wissenschaft nicht akzeptiert.   5. Die an Darwin erinnernde Schrift Goethes über die Metamorphose der Pflanze war noch nicht im Geiste der modernen Evolutionstheorie geschrieben.   6. Die damals nur von wenigen geglaubte und auch heute noch von vielen einfach als Erfindung betrachtete Theorie beruht auf Tatsachen.   7. Er hat Spuren von einem heute in Europa nicht mehr vorkommenden Säugetier gefunden.   8. Wir studieren diese komplizierte Konstruktion, um sie besser erkennen und übersetzen zu können.   9. Ohne diese Konstruktion zu verstehen, kann man wissenschaftliche Arbeiten nicht lesen.   10. Mit dieser Arbeit Jahre lang beschäftigt, hat er für nichts anderes Zeit gehabt.   11. Viele meinen, Goethe hätte sich nur mit literarischen Dingen beschäftigen sollen, anstatt seine Zeit unnötig mit wissenschaftlichen Arbeiten zu verschwenden.

B. *Infinitives with* **zu.** *Translate:*

1. Er schrieb das Buch nur, um seine Theorien zu beweisen.   2. Sie schrieb ihm, um ihn zu bitten, zu ihr zurückzukommen.   3. Anstatt in Italien einzufallen, feierten (*celebrated*) die Germanen ihren Sieg.   4. Er hatte einen erstaunlichen Scharfsinn (*acumen*), ohne doch wirklich wissenschaftlich arbeiten zu können.   5. Er plant, um sein Haus Bäume zu pflanzen.   6. Um fünf Uhr gehe ich nach Hause, um noch etwas Klavier zu spielen.   7. Um das Haus kaufen zu können, müßte man Millionär sein.   8. Er glaubt, mit seiner Erfindung viel Geld verdienen zu können.   9. Er arbeitet an einer Erfindung, um damit eines Tages viel Geld verdienen zu können.   10. Lerne zu leiden, ohne zu klagen (*complain*).

C. *Translate:*

1. He told (**sagen**) the truth without convincing his listeners.   2. Instead of writing a good story he wasted his time on (**mit**) nonsense.   3. Above all, Goethe surely was a great poet, and we can enjoy his poetry without knowing anything (**etwas**) about his scientific works.   4. This novel, once much discussed, is now forgotten (use a modified-adjective construction).   5. Goethe investigated the phenomenon of light in order to disprove (**widerlegen**) Newton's theories, which he considered to be wrong.   6. We must avoid all distraction in order to finish this lesson tonight.   7. I did not know where to find the money to buy a new car.   8. She could not distinguish the different leaves, and so she claimed they were the leaves of the original plant invented by Goethe (use a modified-adjective construction).   9. The skeleton discovered by Goethe on the Lido (modified-adjective construction) was the skeleton of a sheep.   10. If you call somebody a "sheep," that is no reason to assume that he has a Goethe bone.

Oral Exercises

D. *Change the following sentence parts into modified-adjective constructions:*

EXAMPLES:
Die Leute, die um ihn sitzen . . . .   Die um ihn sitzenden Leute.
Die Arbeit, die heute angefangen wurde . . . .   Die heute angefangene Arbeit.

1. Die Theorie, die von der Wissenschaft nicht anerkannt wird . . . .
2. Das Kind, das im Garten spielt . . . .
3. Diese Geschichte, die von vielen geglaubt wird . . . .
4. Die Arbeit, die endlich von ihm begonnen wurde . . . .
5. Das Skelett, das er (= von ihm) am Lido gefunden hat . . . .
6. Er verglich seine Theorie mit den Arbeiten, die andere vor ihm veröffentlicht hatten.

E. *Change the second sentence to an infinitive construction using* **um . . . zu** *or*
ohne . . . zu.

EXAMPLES: Er kam. Er wollte das Geld von mir holen.
           Er kam, um das Geld von mir zu holen.

           Er redete lange. Er konnte uns nicht überzeugen.
           Er redete lange, ohne uns überzeugen zu können.

1. Er schrieb den Roman. Er wollte Geld verdienen.
2. Er untersuchte die Blätter. Er verstand nicht viel von Botanik.
3. Er unterschied die beiden genau. Er konnte sie im Dunkeln nicht sehen.
4. Wir gingen in die Oper. Wir wollten ihn singen hören.
5. Er sagt das. Er will mich ärgern.
6. Er hatte nicht genug Geld. Er wollte sich ein Auto kaufen.
7. Er redete lange. Er wollte uns überzeugen.
8. Er überzeugte uns. Er brauchte nicht lange zu reden.

Appendix 1

Lesson Readings in

German Type

1. Hans lernt etwas

Hans und Fritz sind Freunde und besuchen dieselbe Universität. Sie studieren nicht dasselbe, aber sie beide lernen Deutsch. Und man lernt manchmal mehr, als man studiert!

Nach der Deutschstunde stehen sie noch eine Weile im Korridor der Universität und reden miteinander. Eine Studentin kommt, und Fritz zwinkert mit den Augen.

„Nett, hm?" sagt er zu Hans.

„Sehr nett", antwortet Hans. Gute Freunde verstehen einander ohne viele Worte.

„Guten Tag!" sagt Hans zu dem Mädchen. Aber das Mädchen antwortet nicht und geht weiter.

„Hübsch", sagt Hans, „aber nicht sehr freundlich."

„Und du bist freundlich, aber nicht sehr intelligent", sagt Fritz. „Man macht das anders. Warte, ich zeige dir, wie man das macht!"

Eine zweite Studentin kommt. Fritz macht jetzt den zweiten Versuch.

„Entschuldigen Sie", sagt er zu dem Mädchen. „Ist das Ihr Bleistift? Ich glaube, Sie haben ihn eben verloren."

„Oh, danke schön", antwortet das Mädchen und lächelt freundlich. „Das ist sehr nett von Ihnen", und geht weiter, aber sehr langsam.

„Donnerwetter!" sagt Hans. „Wer ist das?"

„Keine Ahnung", antwortet Fritz, „ich kenne sie nicht. Und das war mein Bleistift. So macht man das!"

„Das war dein Bleistift? Gute Idee! Jetzt verstehe ich alles. Also, auf Wiedersehen."

„Gehst du in die Bibliothek?"

„Sei nicht so dumm", antwortet Hans, „ich kaufe mir ein Dutzend Bleistifte."

2. Die Damen

Zwei Damen fahren mit der Eisenbahn nach Berlin. Die eine Dame ist sehr dick, die andere ist sehr dünn. Der dicken Dame ist es sehr heiß, und der dünnen Dame ist es kalt. In der Ecke des Abteils sitzt ein Mann und raucht eine Zigarre, denn das Abteil ist ein Abteil für Raucher.

Alle drei sitzen und schweigen. Plötzlich schreit die dicke Dame: „Diese Hitze ist ja furchtbar! Und dann der Rauch dieser Zigarre!" Sie öffnet das Fenster.

Kalte Luft strömt ins Abteil. Die dünne Dame zittert und ruft: „Ich friere furchtbar!" und schließt das Fenster wieder.

Jetzt ist die dicke Dame böse. „Kein Mensch erträgt das!" ruft sie empört. „Ich ersticke hier." Und sie öffnet das Fenster wieder.

Aber die dünne Dame jammert jetzt laut: „Ich hole mir hier noch den Tod, o Gott"! Und sie schließt schnell das Fenster. Der Mann in der Ecke raucht ruhig seine Zigarre.

In diesem Augenblick kommt der Schaffner. „Was wünschen Sie, meine Damen?" fragt er freundlich.

„Ach, Herr Schaffner", sagt die dicke Dame, „helfen Sie mir. Ich ersticke in diesem Abteil. Diese Leute schließen immer wieder das Fenster."

„Und ich sterbe in der Kälte!" erklärt die dünne Dame.

Der Schaffner betrachtet ratlos das Fenster, dann die dicke Dame und schließlich die dünne Dame. Endlich fragt er den Mann in der Ecke: „Was tun wir denn nun?"

„Ganz einfach", antwortet dieser. „Wir öffnen das Fenster weit, dann stirbt die eine Dame. Dann schließen wir das Fenster wieder, und die andere Dame erstickt. Und dann haben wir endlich Ruhe."

3. Ein Besuch beim Psychiater

Eine junge Dame besucht ihren Psychiater. Sie ist hübsch, elegant und kommt aus einer guten Familie. Die Sekretärin des Psychiaters öffnet die Tür und stellt ihr einige Fragen: „Ihr Name? Ihre Adresse? Ihr Alter?"

Die junge Dame ist erstaunt. „Mein Alter?" fragt sie. „Was für eine Frage! Ich bin nicht verheiratet."

Nun lacht die Sekretärin. „Ihr Alter, meine ich, nicht Ihren Alten. Bitte, nehmen Sie Platz, der Herr Doktor kommt gleich."

Nach einer Weile kommt der Arzt wirklich und bittet die junge Dame in sein Zimmer. Auch er hat manche Frage. „Haben Sie Angst vor Gewitter? Was sind Ihre Interessen? Tanzen Sie gern? Sind Sie verliebt? Seit wann? In wen? Warum?"

Die junge Dame beantwortet seine Fragen kurz und klar. „Nun", sagt der Psychiater schließlich, „Sie sind ja wunderbar gesund und ganz normal. Aber warum sind Sie eigentlich hier?"

Die junge Dame hat auch jetzt eine Antwort. „Das war der Wunsch meiner Eltern. Meine Eltern behaupten, Pfannkuchen sind ungesund. Und ich weiß genau, das ist nicht wahr."

„Was sagen Sie?" sagt der Arzt, „Ich verstehe Sie nicht ganz. Pfann= kuchen sind ungesund? Ich esse auch gerne Pfannkuchen."

„Wirklich?" ruft die junge Dame erfreut. „Dann kommen Sie nur einmal in unser Haus. In meinem Zimmer sind viele Pfannkuchen. Ganze Koffer voll."

4. Der Kaufmann und der Tod

Nürnberg ist schon im Mittelalter eine Reichsstadt, eine Stadt des Handels und des Gewerbes, aber auch der Kunst. Es ist ebenso reich an Geschichte wie an Sage. Von keiner anderen erzählt man in Deutschland so viele Geschichten. Eine solche ist die vom Kaufmann und dem Tod.

Die Kaufleute in Nürnberg führen alle ein gutes Leben, aber einer ist besonders reich, und seine junge Frau besonders schön. Sie leben wie im Paradies. Junge Leute tun das nämlich. Der Kaufmann hat viel Erfolg, denn er ist schlau, und manchmal sogar ein wenig zu schlau, wie wir sehen werden. Viele in der Stadt sind seine Freunde, und keiner ist wirklich sein Feind. So hat er keine Sorgen, bis auf eine: er lebt in Angst vor dem Tod.

Eines Tages nun muß er nach Rothenburg. Da packt ihn wieder die Angst: Was wartet auf ihn in Rothenburg? Er ist diesmal ganz sicher: der Tod kommt! Vielleicht steht er schon vor der Tür. Der Kaufmann ruft in der Angst seinen Diener: „Schnell", sagt er zu diesem, „hole mir mein Pferd! Der Tod kommt. Ich reite nach Rothenburg. Da habe ich viele Freunde, und die helfen sicher. Wenn der Tod kommt, sage ihm, ich bin in München. Da findet er mich nicht. Grüße meine Frau und sage ihr, ich bin bald wieder zurück!" Dann besteigt er sein Pferd und reitet fort.

Wenig später kommt der Tod wirklich. Er klopft an die Tür wie jeder andere und der Diener ruft: „Herein!" Der Tod öffnet und sieht nur den Diener.

„Suchen Sie meinen Herrn?" fragt der Diener. „Er ist nicht hier. Er ist gerade auf dem Weg nach München."

„Nein", antwortet jener. „Ich suche heute einen anderen, den kranken Bürgermeister. Sage mir, wo der wohnt!"

Der Diener zeigt dem Tod das Haus des Bürgermeisters. Der Tod dankt und meint: „Gut. Das ist also der eine, und morgen hole ich mir dann den anderen. Aber warum sagst du: mein Herr ist in München? Das verstehe ich nicht. Ich treffe ihn nämlich morgen in Rothenburg."

5. Der ehrliche Mann und sein Hemd

In einem fernen, fernen Land lebt ein König. Er hat nur eine Tochter. Sie ist wunderschön und er liebt sie mehr als sein Land und alle seine Schätze. Er erfüllt ihr jeden ihrer Wünsche und lebt nur für sie. So vergeht manches Jahr in Glück und Frieden. Aber plötzlich wird das Mädchen krank. Sie redet kein Wort, spielt nicht mit ihren Puppen und ihren Freundinnen, hat keine Wünsche und weint viel. Die Feste im Schloß ihres Vaters, Kleider und Speisen machen auf sie keinen Eindruck. Der König schickt in seiner Verzweiflung nach allen Ärzten seines Reiches, aber deren Weisheit ist bald am Ende. Die Krankheit bleibt ein Rätsel. Da ruft der König die Weisen seines Landes in den Palast und sagt zu ihnen: „Meine Tochter ist sehr krank. Sagt mir, wie findet sie ihre Gesundheit wieder?"

Die Weisen überlegen eine lange Zeit. Sie sitzen da im Kreise und denken. Schließlich finden sie die Antwort: „Deine Tochter bekommt ihre Gesundheit wieder, o König, wenn sie das Hemd eines ehrlichen Mannes trägt."

Nun schickt der König seine Boten in das Land mit dem Befehl, einen ehrlichen Mann zu suchen. Diesem verspricht er Gold, Silber und alle Ehren seines Landes. Die Boten wandern viele Jahre über Berg und Tal, von Stadt zu Stadt und von Dorf zu Dorf. Endlich kehren sie zum König zurück.

Der merkt sofort, daß sie kein Hemd in der Hand haben und fragt: „Ist denn in meinem ganzen Land kein einziger ehrlicher Mann?"

„Doch, Majestät", antworten die Boten. „Ganz am Ende deines Reiches, in einem kleinen Dorf, lebt ein ehrlicher Mann. Aber er ist leider so arm, daß er kein Hemd hat."

6. Bertolt Brecht

In vielen Theatern aller Länder spielt man heute die Dramen von Bertolt Brecht. Das Publikum schätzt besonders die „Dreigroschenoper", schon wegen der Musik von Kurt Weill, und dann vor allem die Geschichtsdramen, wie „Leben des Galilei" und „Mutter Courage". In allen seinen Stücken ist Brecht Dichter, selbst dort, wo er den Lehrer spielt — und er spielt gern den Lehrer. Einige dieser Stücke heißen daher „Lehrstücke".

Auch im Privatleben war Brecht gern Erzieher. So hatte einmal einer seiner Freunde im Ersten Weltkrieg den Gedanken, freiwillig Soldat zu werden. Brecht war gegen den Krieg und reagierte daher auf seine Weise: „Gut", sagte er zu ihm, „du wirst Soldat. Aber im Falle deines Heldentodes komme ich nicht zum Begräbnis." Eine Woche später änderte er seine Meinung. „Ich komme doch zu deinem Begräbnis", erklärte er nun. Da änderte auch der Freund die seine: er verzichtete auf den Heldentod und wurde nicht Soldat.

Immer wieder haben Freunde und Bekannte Brecht um seinen Rat gefragt. Der eine beabsichtigte, Literaturwissenschaft zu studieren, ein anderer eine Schauspielerin zu heiraten. Was hatte Brecht dazu zu sagen? Dem Liebhaber der Literatur antwortete er: „Literaturwissenschaft? Was für eine Wissenschaft ist das? Nur die exakten Wissenschaften sind Wissenschaften. Ein Pfund Eisen ist ein Pfund Eisen. Aber was ist ein Pfund Meinung?" Dem Liebhaber der Frauen: „Sie wollen heiraten? Warum fragen Sie mich, ob Sie schwimmen können, wenn Sie ins Wasser springen?"

Aber Brecht war gar nicht gegen das Heiraten und noch weniger gegen die Frauen. Er hat sogar mehr als einmal geheiratet. Schon der junge Brecht hatte Freundinnen in vielen Städten — oder, wie man sagt, in allen Häfen. Und was verspricht man Freundinnen nicht alles? Zum Beispiel die Ehe. Zwei solche Freundinnen hörten voneinander. Die eine besuchte die andere, und sie diskutierten den Fall auf ihre Weise. Jede behauptete: Brecht ist mein Bräutigam! Aber das war vielleicht auch wieder nur eine Meinung. Sie fragten daher Brecht selbst nach seiner exakten Meinung: „Wen beabsichtigst du nun zu heiraten?" Brecht zögerte keinen Augenblick und sagte: „Beide!"

Schüler imitieren oft ihre Lehrer. Auch Brechts Schüler imitierten ihn: seinen Stil, seine Technik, seine Kleidung, seine Frisur — und das tat auch der Komponist Paul Dessau. Brecht merkte das und meinte: „Dessau ist so gesund, der überlebt mich sicher. Aber ich frage mich: wozu?"

7. Friedrich Nietzsche

Goethe hat einmal gesagt: „Genie ist Fleiß." Genie ist vielleicht nicht nur Fleiß, aber es ist sicher auch Fleiß. Nehmen wir Friedrich Nietzsche, den Philosophen des „Übermenschen", als Beispiel: Schon als Kind war er wirklich fleißig, nicht nur in der Schule, auch zu Hause. Seine Interessen gingen in viele Richtungen. Bereits im Alter von zehn Jahren schrieb er eine Motette

und fünfzig Gedichte, vier Jahre später seine erste Autobiographie. Da liest
man den Satz: „Überhaupt war es stets mein Vorhaben, ein kleines Buch zu
schreiben und es selbst zu lesen. Diese kleine Eitelkeit habe ich immer noch."

Sein Vater, ein Pastor, starb früh, und das Kind lebte seitdem mit fünf
Frauen: der Mutter, der Großmutter, zwei Tanten und der Schwester. Diese
Schwester spielte später überhaupt die Rolle der Frau in seinem Leben —
einer sehr unweiblichen Frau allerdings. Nach seinem Tode veröffentlichte sie
seine Schriften, aber sie unterdrückte alles, was ihr nicht gefiel, und ihr gefiel
vieles nicht: vor allem nicht sein Radikalismus. Außer dieser Schwester gab
es nur noch eine andere Frau in seinem Leben: die Russin Lou Andreas Salomé,
Tochter eines russischen Generals und später Frau eines deutschen Professors.
Sie wurde dann auch die Freundin des Dichters Rilke, und später arbeitete
sie mit Sigmund Freud. Die Eifersucht der Schwester zerstörte sehr bald ihre
Freundschaft mit Nietzsche.

Nietzsche hatte als Philologe begonnen. Aber auch Geschichte interessierte
ihn, sowie die Naturwissenschaften und die Philosophie, und in der Philosophie
besonders die des großen Pessimisten Schopenhauer. Bekannt sind die Worte
Nietzsches: „Gott ist tot" — aber nicht so bekannt ist das Ende dieses Zitats:
„Gott bleibt tot! Und wir haben ihn getötet! Wie trösten wir uns, die Mörder
aller Mörder?"

Auch die Künste beschäftigten ihn sein Leben lang, die Literatur und vor
allem die Musik. Nietzsche wurde einer der großen Meister der deutschen
Sprache und in der Musik für einige Jahre ein Verehrer Richard Wagners.

Das junge Genie war schon im Alter von 24 Jahren Professor an der
Universität Basel. Da schrieb er nun nicht nur kleine, sondern viele große
Bücher. Auch seine Eitelkeit verlor er nicht. Er vergaß nie, wer er war: „der
erste Geist des Zeitalters". Aus Marienbad schrieb er einmal: „Seit Goethe
hier war, hat niemand hier so viel gedacht."

Aber Nietzsches Gesundheit war immer schon schwach, und mit 34 Jahren
verließ er die Universität wieder. Er reiste seitdem viel, besonders in der
Schweiz und in Italien. Überall suchte er einen Ort mit gutem Klima. Die
Krankheit ergriff nicht nur seinen Körper, sondern auch seinen Geist. Im
Jahre 1889, elf Jahre vor seinem Tode, kam die unheilbare Geisteskrankheit.
Kurz vorher las er noch einmal seine Bücher. Diese „kleine Eitelkeit" hatte
er immer noch. „Ich verstehe seit vier Wochen meine eigenen Schriften", sagte
er, „mehr noch, ich schätze sie."

8. Nietzsche und Wagner

Friedrich Nietzsche war schon in seiner Jugend für Richard Wagner begei=

stert. Noch in der Schule gründete er mit zwei Freunden die „Literarische Vereinigung Germania" und kaufte mit ihnen die Noten zu Wagners Oper „Tristan". Zu Weihnachten schrieb er seiner Mutter: „Ich wünsche mir die Fotografie eines berühmten Mannes, vielleicht die von Richard Wagner."

Später wurden Nietzsche und Wagner Freunde. Nietzsche bewunderte Wagner grenzenlos, und dieser wieder genoß die Bewunderung eines solchen Freundes. Nietzsche war damals Professor an der Universität Basel. Er lebte in der Nähe Wagners und besuchte ihn in drei Jahren 23 Mal. Wagners Frau Cosima und ihre Kinder verlangten, Nietzsche jedes Wochenende zu sehen. „Wie geht es Ihnen, wir erwarten Sie . . . besuchen Sie uns . . . wann kommen Sie zu uns . . . der Meister spricht täglich von Ihnen", schrieb Frau Cosima immer wieder an den Freund in Basel.

Es war eine glückliche Zeit für sie alle. Nietzsche sah in Wagners Musik die Bestätigung seiner Philosophie, und Wagner fand in Nietzsches Philosophie die Bestätigung seiner Musik. Nietzsche war nicht nur sein junger Freund, er war fast sein Sohn, und Wagner gab ihm oft gute Ratschläge. Einmal schrieb er ihm: „Komponieren Sie eine Oper oder heiraten Sie!" Nietzsche tat beides nicht. Ja, sein Verhältnis zu Wagner wurde bald kühl und kritisch. Bei einem seiner Besuche brachte er ihm ein Werk seines Rivalen Brahms. Wagner war gekränkt und machte ihm eine Szene. Nietzsche erklärte später: „In diesem Augenblick war er nicht groß."

Warum gingen sie von nun an verschiedene Wege? Wagner war für Nietz= sche nicht mehr der Seher der Zukunft wie in seiner Jugend. Er sah in ihm jetzt einen Mann der Vergangenheit. Er fand die Festspiele in Bayreuth furchtbar, denn man machte hier die Kunst zu einem Geschäft. Und dann er= zählte ihm Wagner eines Tages von seiner neuen Oper „Parsifal", einem Kunstwerk mit christlichen Ideen. „Die Leute verlangen etwas Christliches", erklärte Wagner. Das ertrug Nietzsche nicht und verließ ihn. Der Freund Wagners wurde nun dessen größter Feind. Er erklärte ihn und den Philosophen Schopenhauer für seine „Antipoden" und Wagners Musik für eine „Musik ohne Zukunft". 1888 veröffentlichte er seine Schrift „Nietzsche contra Wagner". Da stehen die Sätze: „Auf wen wirkt Wagners Musik? Auf etwas, worauf ein vornehmer Künstler niemals wirkt — auf die Masse! auf die Unreifen! auf die Blasierten! auf die Krankhaften! auf die Idioten! auf Wagnerianer!"

9. Heinrich Heine

Heinrich Heine wurde im Jahre 1797 in Düsseldorf geboren und ist 1856 in Paris gestorben. Er war wegen seines Witzes in ganz Europa berühmt, und Matthew Arnold sagte einmal in einem Essay über den Dichter: „Der Welt=

geist sieht die Dummheiten der Menschheit und lächelt. Dieses Lächeln ist Heine."

Heine hat von sich selbst gern als von dem letzten Romantiker gesprochen, und das sicher mit Recht. Er hat romantisch gelebt und romantisch geliebt — nicht nur die Frauen, sondern das Leben überhaupt. In vielen Liedern und Gedichten hat er von dem Leben und der Liebe gesungen, aber in seiner Prosa lebt ein anderer Heine: da hat er mit Leidenschaft für die Freiheit, für ein liberales und demokratisches Deutschland gekämpft. Schon als junger Mann hat er daher seine Heimat verlassen und ist nach Frankreich gegangen, und hier ist er viele Jahre später nach langer Krankheit gestorben.

Heine hatte immer viele Freundinnen, auch in Paris, unter ihnen die dicke Mathilde. Sie hat er schließlich geheiratet. „Morgen", schrieb er einem Freund, „begehe ich mit meiner Mathilde Monogamie."

Seine Mathilde war ein einfaches Mädchen aus dem Volk und sprach kein Deutsch. Heine sprach zwar Französisch, aber schon in der Schule hatte er die Sprachen schwer gefunden, besonders das Latein. „Die Römer haben Glück gehabt", meinte er, „sie sprachen schon als Kinder Latein. Man hat keine Zeit, erst Latein zu lernen und dann die Welt zu erobern." Im Deutschen fand der Junge den Unterschied zwischen dem Dativ und dem Akkusativ schwer. Später meinte er einmal: „Mein Onkel in Hamburg, der Millionär, hat es leicht: er hat einen Diener für den Dativ und einen für den Akkusativ."

Im Exil leben ist eine schreckliche Sache, schrieb er aus Paris. „Komme ich einst in den Himmel, werde ich sicher auch unter den Engeln unglücklich sein. Sie singen so schön und riechen so gut, aber sie sprechen ja kein Deutsch und rauchen keinen Kanaster. Nur im Vaterland ist mir wohl".

Heine kämpfte mit der Feder in der Hand gegen Intoleranz und Unge= rechtigkeit. Sein Lächeln ist nicht immer das Lächeln des Weltgeistes, es ist manchmal sehr bitter. Bekannt sind seine Worte über den Staat der Zukunft. Sie klingen heute fast prophetisch: „Nur e i n Vaterland wird es geben, näm= lich die Erde, und nur e i n e n Glauben, nämlich das Glück auf Erden. Es wird vielleicht nur e i n e n Hirten und e i n e Herde geben — ein freier Hirte mit einem eisernen Hirtenstab und eine gleichgeschorene, gleichblökende Menschenherde! . . . Die Zukunft riecht nach Blut, nach Gottlosigkeit und nach sehr viel Prügeln. Ich rate unsern Enkeln, mit einer dicken Rückenhaut zur Welt zu kommen."

10. Albert Einstein

Die Relativitätstheorie ist etwas, wovon die meisten Leute nicht viel verstehen. Man hört zwar schon in der Schule davon — zum Beispiel, daß

Albert Einstein ihr „Vater" ist. Das ist nicht viel, aber für die meisten ist es genug.

Wer war Albert Einstein? Ohne jede Frage einer der großen Geister unserer Zeit. Man nennt ihn gerne den Newton unseres Jahrhunderts, womit aber noch nicht alles gesagt ist, denn wir bewundern in Einstein ja nicht nur den Wissenschaftler, sondern auch und vielleicht sogar vor allem den Menschen. Als solcher stand er in der Tradition des deutschen Humanismus wie Heine, denn er war, wie dieser, ein Feind aller Intoleranz und Ungerechtigkeit, worunter er selbst fast sein ganzes Leben lang zu leiden hatte.

Die Geburtsstadt Einsteins ist Ulm an der Donau, wo einige Jahrhunderte früher auch der berühmte Astronom Johannes Kepler, der Erfinder des Fern= rohrs, gelebt hatte. Schon früh beschäftigte den jungen Einstein die Mathematik, besonders die Algebra. „Die Algebra ist wunderbar", sagte er. „Wenn man etwas nicht weiß, nennt man es ,X' und sucht danach." Auch die Geometrie faszinierte ihn schon in jungen Jahren. Ein Freund schenkte ihm einmal ein Buch darüber, und er las darin so begeistert wie andere seines Alters in Detektivgeschichten.

Aber nicht nur die Wissenschaft, auch Kunst, Musik und Literatur interes= sierten ihn sein Leben lang. Er spielte die Geige und liebte es, mit seinen Freunden zu musizieren. Er las gerne, aber er hatte nur wenig Zeit dafür. Als Wissenschaftler wollte er nicht experimentieren, sondern denken. Eines Tages besuchte ihn ein Freund und bemerkte ein Fernrohr in seinem Zimmer. „Ah", sagte er, „das ist also das Instrument, mit dem Sie das Universum durchdringen!"

„Ach nein", antwortete dieser, „das Fernrohr gehörte dem früheren Besitzer des Hauses", womit er Kepler meinte.

„Ja, aber womit arbeiten Sie denn?" fragte der Freund.

„Damit!" antwortete Einstein und wies mit dem Finger auf die Stirn.

Aber auch ein großer Mathematiker rechnet nicht immer so schnell wie eine Hausfrau. Darüber gibt es eine hübsche Anekdote. Während der Inflation fuhr Einstein eines Tages mit der Straßenbahn. Es war die Zeit nach dem ersten Weltkrieg, als das Geld rapide im Wert sank. Von Tag zu Tag fiel die Mark im Kurs, und die Preise stiegen astronomisch. Schließlich hatte jeder die Taschen voll von wertlosem Papiergeld. Einstein also gab dem Schaffner in der Straßenbahn ein Bündel Geld. Es waren mehrere Milliarden Mark. Er erhielt einige Millionen zurück und begann, sie nachzurechnen. Aber wer rechnet so schnell! Der Schaffner wurde ungeduldig, nahm ihm die Scheine aus der Hand und zählte sie selbst noch einmal. „Richtig!" sagte er dann und schüttelte den Kopf. „Ich weiß nicht, womit Sie Ihr Geld verdienen, aber ein Mathematiker sind Sie bestimmt nicht!"

Einstein hatte sogar für das Glück eine mathematische Formel. Ein Künstler malte ihn einmal und fragte dabei: „Haben Sie auch für das Glück eine Formel?" — „Jawohl", antwortete Einstein. „Sie lautet: $A = X + Y + Z$".

„Und wofür stehen A, X, Y und Z?"

„A für das Glück, X für die Arbeit und Z für das Spiel."

„Und wofür steht Y?" fragte der Künstler zurück.

„Y steht für: den Mund halten!"

11. Gerhart Hauptmann und Thomas Mann

Es gibt in der modernen deutschen Literatur nicht viele so klare und scharfe Gegensätze wie den Schlesier Gerhart Hauptmann und den Norddeutschen Thomas Mann. Hauptmann hatte sich schon in jungen Jahren mit seinem sozialen Drama „Die Weber" einen Namen gemacht. Zwar hatte auch Thomas Mann schon früh seine ersten Erfolge als Schriftsteller gehabt, aber er wurde doch erst viel später durch seine großen Romane in der ganzen Welt bekannt. Für die Kunst Thomas Manns ist die Klarheit des Intellekts das Entscheidende, für die Hauptmanns „die Seele des Volkes".

Hauptmann hatte vielleicht keinen sehr klaren, aber dafür einen sehr auffallenden Kopf, besonders seit er sich auf Goethe frisierte. Er hielt sich für den wiedergeborenen Goethe. Man hat sich oft darüber lustig gemacht, wie etwa die ziemlich respektlose Dichterin Else Lasker-Schüler, denn sie begrüßte ihn einmal mit den Worten: „Sie sehen ja aus wie die Großmutter von Goethe!"

Man fragt sich natürlich, wie Hauptmann sich bei einer solchen Gelegenheit verhielt. Hat er sich geärgert? Gefreut hat er sich sicher nicht.

Gegensätze ziehen sich an, sagt ein deutsches Sprichwort. Thomas Mann und Gerhart Hauptmann sind dafür ein gutes Beispiel. Sie kannten sich gut und sind einander auch oft begegnet. Vor allem aber: sie schätzten sich nicht nur als Dichter, sondern auch als Menschen. Thomas Mann hat Hauptmann in einer Rede einmal als den „König des Volkes" bezeichnet, und das bestimmt nicht nur wegen seiner großen Popularität. In den Jahren der Weimarer Republik gab man den beiden gerne den Titel „Hofdichter der deutschen Republik". „Hofdichter" in einer Republik gibt es wohl nur in Deutschland.

Dann aber kam das „Dritte Reich". Thomas Mann begab sich, wie viele andere deutsche Schriftsteller, in die Schweiz, aber Hauptmann hatte sich gegen die Emigration entschieden. In Zürich haben sie sich dann noch einmal getroffen — man kann auch sagen: sie haben sich verfehlt. Thomas Mann befand sich nämlich eines Tages in einem Geschäft. Er kaufte sich irgendetwas —

sagen wir: eine Krawatte. Da sagte der Verkäufer zu ihm: "Wir haben gerade noch einen anderen deutschen Dichter im Haus, Gerhart Hauptmann. Möchten Sie ihn sprechen?"

"Nein", antwortete Thomas Mann, "damit warten wir besser bis nach dem Ende des Dritten Reiches."

"Genau dasselbe hat Herr Hauptmann auch gesagt", meinte der Verkäufer.

12. Der Wissenschaftler als Schriftsteller: Georg Christoph Lichtenberg

Lichtenberg war für seine Zeitgenossen vor allem der kleine, verwachsene Professor der Physik und Astronomie in Göttingen, Lehrer einer ganzen Generation von Naturwissenschaftlern. Seine eigene wissenschaftliche Leistung aber war gering und ist heute überhaupt vergessen. Nur die Leistung des Schriftstellers Lichtenberg hat die Zeiten überlebt. Durch die genaue Beobachtung und Beschreibung des Menschen und seiner Verhältnisse ist er ein Vorläufer Nietzsches und der modernen Psychologie geworden.

In einem Jahrhundert der philosophischen Spekulation war er einer der ersten, die als Wissenschaftler wirklich experimentierten. Er besaß eine berühmte Sammlung physikalischer Apparate und liebte es, seinen Studenten während der Vorlesung die physikalischen Phänomene zu demonstrieren. Das ist gut, meinte er, damit die Studenten nicht einschlafen. Und sie sind, wie wir hören, bei ihm nicht eingeschlafen. Es waren vor allem elektrochemische Experimente, oft auch Experimente mit Gasen. Besonders lebendig waren seine Vorlesungen offenbar, wenn er Ballons mit Gas füllte und explodieren ließ. Die Bürger Göttingens waren daran gewöhnt, daß es im Hause des Professors donnerte und krachte. Und noch an etwas anderes hatten sie sich zu gewöhnen: an den Blitzableiter auf seinem Haus, den ersten Blitzableiter in Deutschland. Sie waren darüber zuerst sehr erschrocken. War das nicht gegen den Willen Gottes? Hören wir Lichtenberg selbst: "Daß in den Kirchen gepredigt wird, macht deswegen die Blitzableiter auf ihnen nicht unnötig." Das sind die Worte eines freien Geistes in einer dogmatischen Zeit.

Als Astronom hat Lichtenberg sich besonders mit dem Mond beschäftigt und eine erste Mondkarte hergestellt. Dafür hat man später einen Mondkrater nach ihm genannt.

Lichtenberg ist im Jahre 1742 als siebzehntes Kind eines Pastors in der Nähe von Darmstadt geboren. Der Vater liebte es, seine Predigten durch Betrachtungen über Physik und Astronomie zu beleben. Auch bei ihm ist man bei der Predigt offenbar nicht eingeschlafen. Er unterrichtete seine Kinder selbst in Mathematik und Physik. Das große Erlebnis für den jungen Lichtenberg waren seine beiden Reisen nach England. In London haben sich ihm die Augen für die große Welt geöffnet, im Gegensatz zu den kleinen Verhältnissen zu Hause in Deutschland. In England aber ist er vor allem zum deutschen Schriftsteller geworden. „Ich bin eigentlich nach England gegangen“, schreibt er, „um deutsch schreiben zu lernen.“ Seine Beschreibungen Englands und englischer Verhältnisse sind immer noch Meisterwerke der deutschen Literatur. Er ist nicht nur tief in den Geist Englands, sondern auch in den der englischen Literatur eingedrungen. Der Satiriker Sterne ist immer sein Vorbild geblieben. Die Resultate seiner Beobachtungen und Erfahrungen liegen heute in den Tausenden von Aphorismen vor uns, als sein eigentliches Lebenswerk.

13. Else Lasker-Schüler

Else Lasker-Schüler war nicht nur eine der wirklich bedeutenden Dichterinnen zu Beginn unseres Jahrhunderts, sie war überhaupt ein menschliches und soziales Phänomen. Mitten in der Großstadt Berlin führte sie ein Leben der Phantasie wie in einem Märchen. „Ich bin in Theben geboren“, erklärte sie, „auch wenn ich in Elberfeld zur Welt kam, im Rheinland.“ Sie gab sich exotische Namen: „Jussuf von Theben“ oder „Tino von Bagdad“, und ihre Freunde redeten sie gerne als „Prinz von Theben“ an. Das klingt vielleicht amüsant, aber es ist auch tragisch. Einer ihrer Freunde, selbst ein Schriftsteller, erinnerte sich später: keiner nahm ihr ihr metaphysisches Flirten mit einer breiten, fluktuierenden Menge übel, besonders da es Frucht abwarf: Liebesgedichte oft hohen Ranges. Zwei andere Freunde haben sich einmal im Café geohrfeigt, denn der eine hatte erklärt: ihren Gedichten fehlte das „Mentale“. Diese Szene spielte sich in dem berühmten „Café des Westens“ ab, wo die jungen Genies jeden Tag zusammenkamen, diskutierten, Zeitschriften gründeten und sich aus ihren Werken vorlasen. Im Volksmund hieß es „Café Größenwahn“.

Gottfried Benn, der führende Lyriker dieser expressionistischen Generation, hat die Erscheinung der Lasker-Schüler einmal so beschrieben: Rote Samtjacke mit Goldknöpfen und schwarze Jockeymütze, dazu seidene Hosen, Sandalen mit kleinen Glöckchen, die bei jedem Schritt klingelten, und eine Menge unechten Schmucks an Armen und Hals. Zu Beginn des Ersten Weltkrieges lief sie mit einer schwarz-weiß-roten Fahne um den Hals in den Straßen von München herum. „Lieber Prinz von Theben,“ redete eine Freundin sie an, „sind Sie denn so patriotisch?“ — „Nein,“ war die Antwort, „aber ohne meine Schärpe halten mich die Leute für eine Spionin.“ Das alles kommt uns heute sehr bekannt vor. Wir übertreiben sicher nicht, wenn wir Else Lasker-Schüler als eins der ersten Blumenkinder bezeichnen.

Hinter ihrer Exotik aber verbarg sich bei ihr ein warmes Herz. Einmal begegnete ihr eine andere junge Dichterin auf der Straße. Das Mädchen war gerade sehr unglücklich. „Mein liebes Kind," tröstete Else Lasker-Schüler sie, „schreiben Sie ein schönes Gedicht. Aus jedem Leid muß ein Gedicht erblühen, das dazu da ist, eines anderen Leid zu mildern." Besonders hübsch ist die Episode mit dem Dramatiker Carl Zuckmayer. Zuckmayers erstes Stück hatte seine Uraufführung, aber es fiel durch. Er saß selbst im Theater, Else Lasker-Schüler neben ihm. Sie wollte auch ihn trösten und begann, ihm Schokolade in den Mund zu schieben, ein Stück nach dem andern. Zuckmayer aber haßte Süßigkeiten. Ihm wurde ganz übel davon, aber er war, wie er sich ausdrückte, ihrer „Caritas" hoffnungslos ausgeliefert. „Ein einziger Schnaps wäre mir lieber gewesen", erklärte er in seiner Autobiographie.

14. Till Eulenspiegel

Wenn in Deutschland einer gerne Streiche spielt, nennt man ihn einen „Eulenspiegel", und jedes Kind weiß, daß Till Eulenspiegel ein großer Spaßmacher war. Vielen ist er durch Richard Strauß' Tondichtung „Till Eulenspiegels lustige Streiche" bekannt.

Till Eulenspiegel war der Sohn eines Bauern aus Braunschweig in Norddeutschland. Er war zu seiner Zeit so berühmt wie die Braunschweiger Wurst. Ein Volksbuch aus dem 16. Jahrhundert erzählt von seinen vielen lustigen Streichen. Es war ein gutes Buch für lange Winterabende, wenn — wie es im Vorwort heißt — die Mäuse unter die Bänke rennen, das Feuer im Ofen lustig brennt und die gebratenen Birnen gut schmecken. Das Buch war sehr beliebt und findet sich in vielen Übersetzungen, denn man kannte Till nicht nur in Deutschland, sondern auch in Holland, Frankreich, Italien, Dänemark und Polen. In Polen war Till sogar der Freund und Hofnarr König Kasimirs. Auch in England war er berühmt. Man nannte ihn da „Owl-Glass", denn man meinte, daß Eule „owl" bedeutet und Spiegel „looking glass". Aber der Name „Eulenspiegel" kommt wahrscheinlich von dem französischen Wort für „Schelm".

Aber wenden wir uns Till selbst zu! Auf dem Markt einer Stadt traf er einmal einen Bauern mit einem schönen grünen Tuch. Er fragte ihn, wo er wohnte. Der Bauer nannte ihm den Namen eines Dorfes, und Till behauptete darauf, aus derselben Gegend zu sein. „Warte hier auf mich", sagte er zu ihm, „wir haben denselben Weg und können zusammen nach Hause gehen." Dann rannte er zu zwei Freunden; der eine von ihnen war Advokat. Till dachte sich mit ihnen einen Plan aus, dem Bauern das Tuch abzuschwindeln. Dann ging er zum Markt zurück und machte sich mit dem Bauern auf den Weg. Sie waren noch nicht weit gekommen, da wollte Till wissen, wieviel der Bauer für das schöne blaue Tuch bezahlt hatte. Der antwortete: „Zwei Taler, aber das Tuch ist nicht blau, sondern grün, wie jeder Dummkopf sehen kann."

„Nun, ich bin aber kein Dummkopf", wandte Till ein, „und ich behaupte immer noch, daß das Tuch blau ist."

„Hast du denn keine Augen im Kopf?" rief der Bauer. „Das Tuch ist grün!"

„Wenn das Tuch grün ist", erwiderte Till, „dann gebe ich dir fünf Taler. Aber wenn es blau ist, dann gibst du mir das Tuch."

„Gut", meinte der Bauer nach einigem Bedenken, „wenn das Tuch nicht grün ist wie Gras, gebe ich es dir."

Nun trafen sie den ersten der Freunde Tills und fragten ihn nach der Farbe des Tuches. Tills Freund sagte natürlich blau, aber der Bauer wollte die Entscheidung nicht anerkennen und das Tuch nicht hergeben. „Ihr steckt beide unter einer Decke", erklärte er.

„Nun", meinte Till, „da kommt ein Advokat. Wenden wir uns an den!"

„Geehrter Herr Advokat", begann der Bauer, „ich habe eine große Bitte. Ich weiß natürlich, daß dieses Tuch grün ist, grün wie Gras, aber die beiden hier behaupten, es ist blau. Sagen Sie uns bitte, ob es blau oder grün ist!"

Der Advokat bedachte sich nicht lange. „Ich habe zwar Besseres zu tun, als meine Zeit mit Dummheiten zu verbringen. Aber ich will euch helfen, und so erkläre ich denn, daß das Tuch selbstverständlich blau ist, wie jeder Dumm= kopf sehen kann."

Der Bauer dankte dem Advokaten und wandte sich dann wieder an Till: „Das ist nun ein Advokat", sagte er, „und ich sehe daher ein, daß ihr doch nicht unter einer Decke steckt." Und so bekam Till das Tuch.

15. Günter Grass

Durch Günter Grass hat die deutsche Literatur nach dem Zweiten Welt= krieg ihren alten guten Namen wiedergewonnen. Sein erster, ziemlich langer, sehr origineller Roman, „Die Blechtrommel", hat die Leser in aller Welt fasziniert.

Grass ist jedoch nicht nur ein ausgezeichneter Schriftsteller. Man kann sich sogar mit gutem Grund fragen: in welcher Kunst hat er eigentlich nicht gear= beitet? Mit zwanzig Jahren erlernte er zunächst das Handwerk eines Stein=

metzen. Dann besuchte er die Düsseldorfer Kunstakademie und lernte da zeichnen und modellieren. Gleichzeitig war er Mitglied einer Jazzkapelle und spielte in Düsseldorfer Lokalen. Damals schrieb er auch seine ersten Gedichte und kurze Theaterszenen sowie Ballette.

Heute sind seine epischen, lyrischen, dramatischen und graphischen Arbeiten den Lesern moderner deutscher Literatur gut bekannt. Grass hat nämlich noch jedes seiner Bücher mit einer eigenen Zeichnung für den Schutzumschlag versehen. Der kleine Oskar mit seiner großen Blechtrommel, dem spitzen Papierhelm und dem runden, offenen Mündchen trommelt durch die ganze Welt. Auch die Bände seiner Gedichte enthalten Illustrationen von ihm selbst.

Heute spielt Günter Grass nicht mehr auf dem Waschbrett. Er macht auch keine Skulpturen mehr. „Das ist so anstrengend wie Romanschreiben", sagt er. „Man arbeitet acht Stunden am Tag und hat dann erst eine Kniescheibe fertig."

Dafür hat Grass sich in den letzten Jahren politisch sehr engagiert. Er arbeitet für die Sozialdemokratische Partei, schreibt für ihre Kandidaten Wahlreden und nimmt auch selbst an den Wahlkämpfen teil. Er hat sogar katholische Nonnen aufgefordert, sozialdemokratisch zu wählen! Das war für deutsche Nonnen etwas ganz Neues.

Auch in den Zeiten zwischen den Wahlen in der Bundesrepublik ist Grass politisch aktiv. Er schickt nicht nur seine Bücher in die Welt, sondern reist auch selbst gern in alle Himmelsrichtungen. Einige Zeit hat er in Paris gelebt, und dort ist auch seine „Blechtrommel" entstanden.

Eine seiner ersten Reisen führte den noch unbekannten Autor nach Polen. Dafür brauchte er aber ein offizielles Dokument, und so bat er einen bekannten polnischen Kritiker um eine Einladung. Zum Beweis für sein Dichtertum schickte er ihm in seinem Brief zwei seiner Gedichte mit. Er bekam seine Einladung und sandte seinem Gastgeber darauf folgendes Telegramm: „Komme Sonntag mittag stop Trage blaues Hemd stop Günter Grass."

Aber am Sonntag mittag kommen in Warschau zwei Züge an verschiedenen Bahnhöfen und zwei Flugzeuge verschiedener Gesellschaften aus Berlin an. Der polnische Kritiker war in einiger Verlegenheit. Er konnte nicht gut an vier Stellen zur selben Zeit sein. Schließlich entschied er sich für den Hauptbahnhof. Aber seine Verlegenheit wuchs, als mehr als zweihundert blaue Hemden aus dem Berliner Zug sprangen. Eine ostdeutsche Studentenorganisation machte an diesem Tag einen Ausflug nach Polen, und alle ihre Mitglieder trugen blaue Hemden als Uniform. Den zahllosen Hemden aber folgte ganz zuletzt noch ein einzelnes blaues Hemd. Der Wartende fühlte sich erleichtert: „Herr Grass! Sie sind wirklich ein Dichter! Das hat mir Ihr Telegramm bewiesen."

16. Franz Kafka

Franz Kafka verbrachte fast die ganzen einundvierzig Jahre seines Lebens in seiner Heimatstadt Prag. Damals war er noch ein ziemlich unbekannter Autor. Er las manchmal einigen Freunden aus seinen Manuskripten vor, aber er veröffentlichte wenig und nur kleinere Werke. Er verlangte sogar, daß man nach seinem Tod alle seine Manuskripte verbrannte.

Heute sehen wir in Kafka einen der größten Dichter unseres Jahrhunderts. Seine Romane, die längeren und die kürzeren Erzählungen, seine Tagebücher und sogar viele seiner zahllosen Briefe sind Kunstwerke höchsten Ranges.

Kafka war ein äußerst liebenswürdiger Mensch. Einmal traf er in einem Park ein weinendes kleines Mädchen und fragte es freundlich: „Warum weinst du denn?"

„Ich habe meine liebste Puppe verloren", antwortete das Mädchen unter fließenden Tränen. Kafka aber fand sofort den richtigen Trost: „Du hast deine Puppe gar nicht verloren", sagte er. „Sie macht nur gerade eine größere Reise. Ich weiß das, denn ich habe eben einen Brief von ihr bekommen."

„Hast du den Brief bei dir?" fragte das Kind.

„Nein", sagte Kafka, „ich habe ihn zu Hause gelassen, aber ich werde ihn dir morgen mitbringen." Kafka ging nach Hause und schrieb den Brief. Und er schrieb in den folgenden Tagen noch mehrere Briefe im Namen der Puppe. Er arbeitete sie so genau und mit derselben Konzentration aus wie seine Erzählungen und Romane. Dann brachte er sie mit in den Park und las sie dem kleinen Mädchen vor, denn es ging noch nicht in die Schule. In den Briefen erzählte die Puppe, daß sie jetzt lieber eine Zeitlang woanders lebte. Sie wurde nämlich rasch größer, sie hatte Wichtigeres zu tun, und zuletzt heiratete sie sogar. Das kleine Mädchen war über diese Briefe äußerst glücklich und vergaß seinen Schmerz.

Kafka hatte überhaupt viel Sinn für Humor. Natürlich waren ihm die Stunden des Schreibens die liebsten, aber er war auch ein sehr genauer Beamter. Er arbeitete in einer Versicherungsgesellschaft. Nach einigen Jahren beförderte man ihn und zwei andere Kollegen in eine höhere Stellung mit besserer Bezahlung. Das verlangte aber einen Besuch der drei Angestellten beim Präsidenten der Gesellschaft. Einer der beiden Kollegen Kafkas hielt die Dankrede. Der Präsident saß würdig an seinem Schreibtisch, mit seinem weißen Bart und einem etwas dicken Bauch, fast würdiger noch als der Kaiser selbst. Kafka mußte lachen, und er lachte immer mehr und immer heftiger, so daß der Besuch fast in einer Katastrophe endete. Die drei flohen zuletzt aus dem Zimmer.

Am lustigsten war Kafka in der Gesellschaft seiner Freunde. Er reiste gern mit ihnen, aber sie hatten nie genug Urlaub und noch weniger Geld. Dadurch bekam Kafka die Idee für eine neue Art von Reiseführern mit dem Titel „Billig durch die Schweiz" oder „Billig in Paris". Er machte aus dem Adjektiv einen Mann und für diesen Mann die verschiedensten Pläne. Mit „Billig" brauchte der Reisende weniger Zeit und Geld, er hatte mit ihm überhaupt nicht die geringsten Probleme, denn „Billig" wußte alles: er kannte das beste Hotel zum niedrigsten Preis, das einfachste Transportmittel, er wußte, wo man das kleinste Trinkgeld gab und am leichtesten Freikarten für das Theater bekam. „Billig" gab sogar Sprachunterricht, und er gab ihn nach folgendem Prinzip: es ist unmöglich, eine fremde Sprache richtig zu lernen, daher lehren wir sie lieber gleich falsch.

Leider fand sich für diesen „Billig" kein Verleger.

17. Georg Friedrich Händel

Die deutsche Musik ist weltberühmt. In beinahe jedem Konzert kann man Werke von Bach, Beethoven, Brahms, Mozart, Haydn, Schubert, Strauß, Wagner oder anderen großen Komponisten hören. Wagner war lange einer der beliebtesten unter ihnen, besonders bei der Jugend. Viele aber mögen Wagner nicht, und man kann sicher sagen, daß Wagners Musik noch heute eine Sache des persönlichen Geschmacks ist. Dagegen dürfte es nur wenige Menschen geben, die wirklich kein Ohr für Mozart oder Haydn haben. Auch Händel, den man allerdings zur englischen Musikgeschichte rechnen kann, war Deutscher. Er war in Halle geboren, ist aber schon als junger Mann nach London gegangen, wo er in hohem Alter gestorben ist und in der Westminster Abbey begraben liegt. Trotzdem hat er nie gut Englisch gekonnt, und wenn er wütend wurde, soll er in vier oder fünf Sprachen geschimpft haben.

Wir dürfen uns mit Recht über die Energie wundern, mit der einige der großen Meister der Musik gearbeitet haben. Händel vermochte, sein großes Oratorium „Messias" in ungefähr drei Wochen zu beenden. Er hat es zum ersten Mal in Dublin aufführen lassen, und zwar als Wohltätigkeitskonzert für Krankenhäuser und Gefängnisse. Wie groß das Interesse an diesem Konzert war, läßt sich daran erkennen, daß die Damen an diesem Abend keine Reifröcke tragen durften, denn so viele Leute wie möglich sollten Platz finden können.

Später führte man den „Messias" auch in London auf, wo König Georg II. (der Zweite) beim Halleluja=Chor aufgestanden sein soll. Seitdem pflegt man während dieses Chores zu stehen.

Händel war eine sehr imposante Figur. Er konnte sehr liebenswürdig sein, ließ sich aber auch leicht aufbringen. Er soll einmal so wütend geworden sein,

daß er eine Pauke ergriff und sie nach dem Dirigenten warf. Ein anderes Mal
mochte eine italienische Sängerin eine Arie nicht, die Händel für sie geschrieben
hatte. Da rief er ihr zu: „Madame, ich weiß, daß Sie ein Teufel sind, aber
ich bin Beelzebub, der Herr der Teufel", und wollte sie aus dem Fenster werfen.
Andere Zeiten, andere Sitten! Ein englischer Sänger wollte sich Händels
Behandlung nicht gefallen lassen und drohte, auf das Klavier zu springen. „Tun
Sie das", erklärte Händel, „ich kann es dann in allen Zeitungen bekannt=
machen lassen. Sicher kommen mehr Leute, Sie springen zu sehen als singen
zu hören."

Trotzdem war Händel sehr beliebt und ein großer Künstler. Beethoven soll
ihn sogar für den größten Musiker aller Zeiten gehalten haben. Wir fragen
uns freilich: was will ein so extravagantes Urteil wirklich besagen? Wahr=
scheinlich nicht mehr als: ich mag Händel.

18. Der Freiherr von Münchhausen

Hieronymus Karl Friedrich Freiherr von Münchhausen wird heute gerne
als einer der größten Lügner aller Zeiten bezeichnet. Und doch war dieser
lustige Jäger und tapfere Soldat kein gewöhnlicher Schwindler. Denn wenn
wirklich gut gelogen wird, wird das Lügen zur Kunst. Münchhausen war im
Russisch=Türkischen Krieg gewesen, und nach seiner Rückkehr pflegte er die
unglaublichsten Geschichten über seine Abenteuer in Rußland und in der
Türkei zu erzählen. Natürlich mußten seine Freunde recht gut, daß diese
Geschichten mehr oder weniger frei erfunden waren. Das machte aber nichts,
denn es kam ja nur darauf an, daß man sich bei einer Flasche Wein gut unter=
hielt. Münchhausens Geschichten wurden dann mit anderen zusammen in
einem Buch unter dem Titel „Vademecum für lustige Leute" veröffentlicht.

Aber wirklich berühmt wurde der Freiherr erst in England. Dort erschien
nämlich ein Buch unter dem Titel „The Original Adventures of Baron
Münchhausen". Es war von einem deutschen Professor Raspe aus Kassel
herausgegeben worden, denn der Herr Professor brauchte Geld. Daß ein
Professor Geld brauchte, war natürlich nichts Neues. Dieser Professor aber
hatte eine etwas originelle Art, sich Geld zu verdienen. So originell war seine
Methode, daß die Polizei ein Auge auf ihn warf und er Deutschland verlassen
mußte. Übrigens hat er auch England später wieder verlassen und ist nach
Irland gegangen, wo er dann gestorben ist und begraben wurde.

Raspes Buch kam dann nach Deutschland und wurde von dem Dichter
Gottfried August Bürger frei übersetzt. Es erfreute sich bei den deutschen
Lesern einer großen Beliebtheit, trotz seines langen Titels: „Wunderbare

Reisen zu Wasser und zu Lande, Feldzüge und lustige Abenteuer des Freiherrn von Münchhausen, wie er dieselben bei einer Flasche Wein im Zirkel seiner Freunde zu erzählen pflegt".

Ein solches Abenteuer sah ungefähr folgendermaßen aus: Der Freiherr wurde einmal von den Türken gefangen und als Sklave an den Sultan verkauft. Er mußte nun jeden Tag die Bienen des Sultans auf die Weide treiben. Einmal aber wurde eine Biene plötzlich von zwei Bären angefallen. Münchhausen warf seine Axt nach den Bären, aber sie flog an den Bären vorbei bis auf den Mond. Er pflanzte daher schnell eine türkische Bohne, und diese wuchs sofort bis zum Mond hinauf. Er kletterte daran auf den Mond und holte sich seine Axt wieder. Aber als er wieder herunterklettern wollte, war die Bohne verdorrt. Er nahm daher Stroh und machte sich daraus einen Strick, und den band er an einem Horn des Mondes fest. Aber der Strick war nicht lang genug, und jedes Mal, wenn Münchhausen ans Ende kam, mußte er ihn oben abschneiden und unten wieder anbinden. So kam er beinahe bis zur Erde, aber nur beinahe — denn als er noch in den Wolken war, riß der Strick. Da war nun nichts mehr zu machen: Münchhausen fiel und fiel, tief in die Erde hinein. Das Loch, das er im Fallen machte, war so tief, daß er nicht herausklettern konnte. Glücklicherweise aber waren ihm in der langen Zeit die Fingernägel so lang gewachsen, daß er damit eine Treppe graben konnte. Und so kam er schließlich wieder auf die Erde zurück.

19. Immanuel Kant

Kant, mit dem ein Zeitalter in der Geschichte der Philosophie zu Ende ging und ein neues begann, ist in Königsberg in Ostpreußen geboren, einer Stadt, die er sein ganzes Leben lang nicht verlassen hat. Die Familie des Vaters stammte aus Schottland, wo sie sich „Cant" geschrieben hatte. Kant selbst war das vierte von elf Kindern, von denen aber sechs schon in jungen Jahren gestorben sind.

Im 18. Jahrhundert, das wir das Zeitalter der „Aufklärung" nennen, hatte man bis zu Kant geglaubt, mit dem Verstand alles erklären zu können. Für diese Zeit war alles vernünftig, was der Mensch mit seinem Kopf fassen konnte, aber niemand hatte bisher gefragt, wie es denn in diesem Kopf selbst aussah. Kant war der erste, der das Denken selbst kritisch untersuchte und damit nicht nur dessen Gesetze, sondern auch die Grenzen, denen es unterlag, fand, was ihn mehr als einmal mit den herrschenden Ideen, besonders auf dem Gebiete der Religion, in Konflikt brachte. Sein Hauptwerk, in dem er sein kritisches System entwickelte, ist die „Kritik der reinen Vernunft" aus dem Jahre 1781.

Die Genauigkeit bestimmte aber nicht nur sein Denken, sondern auch sein ganzes Leben, was uns von vielen seiner Zeitgenossen bezeugt wird. Er ging abends pünktlich um zehn Uhr zu Bett und stand ebenso pünktlich morgens um fünf Uhr auf. Auch der Einrichtung des Bettes stand er kritisch gegenüber. „Das Bett ist das Nest einer Menge von Krankheiten", erklärte er einmal. Nach dem Aufstehen nahm er ein leichtes Frühstück zu sich, welches aus einer Tasse Kaffee und einer Pfeife Tabak bestand, was wir kaum als besonders gesund empfinden werden. Den Vormittag verbrachte er arbeitend hinter seinem Schreibtisch. Um ein Uhr ging er zum Essen, in jüngeren Jahren in einem Restaurant, später bei sich zu Hause, und dazu lud er sich dann gerne einige Freunde ein, mit denen er sich lange, bis vier oder gar fünf Uhr, unter=hielt. Über alles durfte dabei gesprochen werden, sogar über die Küche und das Kochen — nur nicht über die Philosophie. Kant, der nicht nur das Gespräch liebte, sondern auch gerne gut aß, interessierte sich sehr für die Geheimnisse der Kochkunst, besonders in der Gegenwart von Frauen. Einer seiner Freunde schlug ihm einmal vor, auch eine „Kritik der Kochkunst" zu schreiben.

Nach dem Essen machte er dann seinen täglichen Spaziergang, bei dem er immer denselben Weg nahm. Er soll aus diesem Grunde seine Schwester, die in einem Teil der Stadt wohnte, der nicht an seinem Weg lag, vierundzwanzig Jahre nicht gesehen haben. So pünktlich erschien er in den Straßen der Stadt, daß die Königsberger ihre Uhren nach ihm stellen konnten.

Kant hat nie geheiratet. Er war kein Weiberfeind, aber er stand doch auch den Frauen recht kritisch gegenüber. „Die Damen kommen nicht in den Himmel", erklärte er einmal kategorisch, „denn schon in der Offenbarung Johannis heißt es an einer Stelle: es war eine Stille von einer halben Stunde. So etwas läßt sich aber, wo Frauenzimmer sind, gar nicht als möglich denken." Zweimal soll er trotzdem ans Heiraten gedacht haben, aber dafür brauchte er so viel Zeit, daß die Frauen schon verheiratet oder weggezogen waren, als er seinen Entschluß endlich gefaßt hatte. So lebte er denn allein, nur mit seinem Diener, dessen Name Lampe war. Wie Diogenes seine Laterne, so hatte Kant seinen Lampe. Lampe war ziemlich dumm, aber offenbar sehr arrogant. Kant mußte ihn schließlich gehen lassen, aber er konnte ihn doch nicht vergessen. Er war nun auch schon etwas alt und zerstreut geworden und schrieb sich daher ein Memorandum, das er auf seinen Schreibtisch stellte, und das lautete: „Lampe muß vergessen werden!"

20. Der Dreißigjährige Krieg

Der Dreißigjährige Krieg (1618 bis 1648) hat als Religionskrieg begon=nen, als das letzte Kapitel in der Geschichte der Reformation. Die beiden

Parteien, die protestantische und die katholische, mußten erst, wie es scheint, miteinander um die Macht ringen, ehe sie in Frieden zusammenleben konnten. Aber schon früh hatten die politischen Fragen die religiösen immer mehr verdrängt. Obwohl nämlich Gustav Adolf mit seinen Schweden im Namen der Reformation in Deutschland erschienen war, war er in Wirklichkeit gekommen, weil er sein kleines Schweden zu einer europäischen Großmacht zu machen beabsichtigte. Aber nicht nur Deutschland, Österreich und Schweden waren miteinander im Krieg, sondern auch Frankreich, Spanien, England, Dänemark und Holland. Wir haben wirklich jeden Grund, den Dreißigjährigen Krieg als den ersten Weltkrieg zu bezeichnen.

Deutschland war durch seine Lage, in der Mitte Europas, zum Schlachtfeld besonders geeignet. Immer wieder drangen die Armeen von allen Seiten durch das Land, von Norden nach Süden, von Westen nach Osten. Wie Heuschrecken stürzten sie sich auf alles und fraßen es auf. Wenn auch einige Teile Deutschlands, wie etwa die Stadt Hamburg, in diesen langen Krieg, der eigentlich aus vier oder fünf verschiedenen Kriegen bestand, nicht hineingezogen wurden, so sind andere fast vollkommen zerstört worden. Zu Beginn des Krieges hatte Deutschland achtzehn Millionen Einwohner, nach dessen Ende jedoch nur noch vier. Aber nicht nur Menschen waren gemordet, Städte zerstört, Felder verwüstet, sondern auch das Leben selbst war verwildert, die kulturelle Entwicklung des Landes unterbrochen. Der Landsknecht war der Herr im Land, und Soldatsein war sein Beruf. Außerdem hat man geschätzt, daß einer Armee von 40 000 Mann ein Troß von 140 000 Männern, Frauen und Kindern folgte, die von dem Sold und der Beute der Soldaten lebten. Hans Jakob Christoffel von Grimmelshausen hat uns in seinem großen Roman vom „Abenteuerlichen Simplizissimus", einer Geschichte seiner eigenen Kindheit und Jugend während des Krieges, ein lebendiges Bild von den Zuständen der Zeit gegeben.

Das Schicksal der Stadt Magdeburg ist besonders interessant, indem es uns zeigt, wie wenig das menschliche Leben damals wert war. Tilly, der Feldherr Kaiser Ferdinands, hatte die Stadt belagert, während die Magdeburger auf die Hilfe der Schweden warteten. Als Tilly die Stadt schließlich nahm, hatten seine Soldaten freie Hand, denn eine eroberte Stadt war nach damaligem Kriegsrecht die Beute des Siegers. Nachdem aber die Soldaten in die Stadt eingedrungen waren, fingen einige Häuser bei der Plünderung Feuer, und niemand war da, es zu löschen. Vor ihren Augen sahen die Soldaten ihre Beute verbrennen, und damit begann ein Morden und Brennen ohne Beispiel. Am Ende blieb von der Stadt nichts als die Kathedrale und ein großer, glimmender Aschenhaufen.

21. Shakespeare und die Deutschen

Eine Theatersaison in den deutschsprechenden Ländern, also in Deutschland, Österreich und der Schweiz, bringt etwa 2 000 Schauspielpremieren an ungefähr 200 Theatern. An den hundert wichtigsten Bühnen werden in einem Jahr allein 50 Dramen Shakespeares neu einstudiert.

Das ist die Folge einer langen kulturhistorischen Entwicklung, die um das Jahr 1600 begann. Schon vor seinem Tode wurde Shakespeare durch die sogenannten „englischen Komödianten" (d.h. Schauspieler) in Deutschland eingeführt. Sie waren aus England gekommen und zogen nun mit ihren Stücken, vor allem mit Shakespeare-Dramen, von Hof zu Hof und von Stadt zu Stadt. Zuerst spielten sie Shakespeare noch auf englisch, später in schlechten deutschen Übersetzungen, bis die englischen Schauspieler nach dem Dreißigjährigen Krieg mehr und mehr durch deutsche ersetzt wurden und schließlich ganz aus den Truppen verschwanden.

Bis in die Mitte des 18. Jahrhunderts und zum Teil noch länger war es Sitte, Shakespeare in solchen Bearbeitungen auf die Bühne zu bringen. Der gute Geschmack der Zeit duldete das Grausame und Schreckliche bei Shakespeare nicht. So wurde noch in den neunziger Jahren in Weimar ein „Macbeth" gespielt, in dem die Rolle des Königs Duncan ganz gestrichen war.

Die erste vollständige und erstaunlich genaue Übersetzung Shakespeares erschien in 13 Bänden während der zweiten Hälfte des 18. Jahrhunderts, und zwar in den Jahren 1775 bis 1782. Sie wurde dann noch einmal bearbeitet und 16 Jahre später, von 1798 bis 1806, in 12 Bänden neu herausgebracht. Ihr Verfasser war Johann Joachim Eschenburg (1743-1820), ein höchst belesener und angesehener Professor der Literatur in Braunschweig. Wie ernst Eschenburg seine Arbeit nahm, geht daraus hervor, daß man nach seinem Tode 400 Bände zum Thema Shakespeare in seiner Bibliothek fand. Eschenburg konnte sich allerdings auf wichtige Vorarbeiten stützen. Zwischen 1762 und 1766 hatte nämlich der große Dichter und Schriftsteller der Aufklärung, Christoph Martin Wieland (1733-1813), seine berühmte Übersetzung von 22 Stücken Shakespeares in 8 Bänden veröffentlicht.

Wielands Übersetzungen waren, wie Eschenburgs, in Prosa, und hatten sich bemüht, den Geist Shakespeares dem des eleganten 18. Jahrhunderts anzupassen. Sie haben einen großen Einfluß auf die Generation von jungen Dichtern gehabt, mit der zu Ende des Jahrhunderts eine neue Zeit begann, die wir als europäische Frühromantik bezeichnen können, und die in Deutschland den Namen „Sturm und Drang" trägt. Zu diesen Dichtern gehörten auch der junge Goethe und der junge Schiller. Ihnen genügte der Aufklärungs-Shakespeare Wielands und Eschenburgs nicht mehr: sie wollten den richtigen, historischen Shakespeare wiederentdecken. Der Student Goethe hielt 1771 eine enthusiastische Rede „Zum Shakespeare=Tag" und folgte in seinem eigenen ersten Schauspiel, „Götz von Berlichingen" (1771), ganz dem Vorbild Shakespeares.

D i e Form aber, in der Shakespeare den heutigen Deutschen bekannt ist, ist die der sog. Schlegelschen Übersetzung. Sie ist von den Romantikern August Wilhelm Schlegel (1767=1845), Ludwig Tieck (1773=1853) und einigen anderen gegen Ende des 18. und zu Beginn des 19. Jahrhunderts in Blank= versen geschaffen worden. Der vollständige Text der Übersetzung erschien zum ersten Mal in neun Bänden in den zwanziger und dreißiger Jahren des vorigen Jahrhunderts und ist seitdem immer wieder nachgedruckt worden. Wenn die Helden und Heldinnen Shakespearescher Dramen den Deutschen augenschein= lich ebenso bekannt sind wie den Engländern, verdanken sie das zum großen Teil dieser Übersetzung, die man eine der größten Leistungen in der Über= setzungsliteratur aller Völker genannt hat.

Vergleichen Sie die folgenden Zitate aus der Schlegelschen Shakespeare= Übersetzung mit den englischen Texten:

Sein oder nicht sein, das ist hier die Frage.

Dies war der beste Römer unter allen.

Nicht durch die Schuld der Sterne, lieber Brutus,
Durch eigne Schuld nur sind wir Schwächlinge.

Nimm vor des Märzen Jdus dich in acht!

Was ist ein Name? Was uns Rose heißt,
wie es auch hieße, würde lieblich duften.

22. Wieviel Uhr ist es?

In der deutschen Übersetzung von „Julius Cäsar" sagt Brutus: „Still! Zählt die Glocke!", und Cassius antwortet: „Sie hat drei geschlagen." Das ist natürlich ein Anachronismus, denn die Römer hatten zwar Sonnenuhren, Sanduhren, ja sogar Wasseruhren, aber es hat in Rom niemals drei „ge= schlagen". Wir können uns heute die Welt ohne Uhren und Uhrenschlagen kaum noch vorstellen. Unzählige Male am Tage hören, sagen oder denken wir: wieviel Uhr ist es? Und dann wollen wir nicht wissen, wo die Sonne am Himmel steht, denn wir sind ja keine Pfadfinder, sondern ob es schon zehn Minuten vor halb drei oder erst zehn nach zwei ist. Deshalb sehen wir auf die Uhr. Das können wir fast überall, denn Uhren befinden sich auf Kirchtürmen,

an Rathäusern und Straßenecken, in Büros, in Kinos, in Küchen, in Wohn=
zimmern und am Arm.

Schon am frühen Morgen werden wir von Uhren tyrannisiert, wenn neben
unserem Bett der Wecker rasselt, und wir möchten noch gerne ein Viertel=
stündchen länger schlafen. Von diesem Augenblick an geht es Minute um
Minute und Stunde um Stunde mit der Uhr durch den Tag. Um wieviel
Uhr muß ich auf dem Bahnhof sein? Der Autobus geht alle zehn Minuten. Ich
komme drei Minuten zu spät zum Bahnhof, und der Zug, der sonst immer
Verspätung hat, ist gerade heute einmal pünktlich abgefahren. Der nächste
geht erst in dreiviertel Stunden. Mittags wollen wir uns — wieder pünkt=
lich! — um zwölf oder halb eins zum Essen treffen, das Abendbrot steht um
Viertel nach sechs oder Viertel vor sieben auf dem Tisch, und den „Fünf=Uhr=
Tee" gibt es — wie den Nachmittagskaffee — manchmal schon um vier. Für
das, was ich gerne tun möchte, habe ich „keine Zeit".

Was schenken wir einem Mädchen, das wir gern haben? Einen Ring oder
eine Armbanduhr. Was erben wir vom Großvater? Eine dicke goldene Taschen=
uhr. Die Taschenuhr ist übrigens eine deutsche Erfindung, die aus Nürnberg
stammt. Weil sie ursprünglich die Form eines Eis hatte, hieß sie früher das
„Nürnberger Ei".

Seit der Erfindung des elektrischen Lichts hat die Nacht an Bedeutung
gewonnen: wir arbeiten tagsüber, damit wir des Abends und des Nachts das
Leben genießen können. In früheren Zeiten war das Stadtleben von der Dauer
des Tageslichts bestimmt. Man stand früh auf. Friedrich der Große zum
Beispiel stand im Sommer morgens um vier und im Winter um fünf Uhr
auf, und Lichtenberg verhielt sich ähnlich, wie wir gesehen haben. Abends um
neun war fast alles dunkel. Nachts gab es keine Straßenbeleuchtung, nur in
ein paar Wirtshäusern brannten vor Mitternacht noch trüb die Kerzen. Der
Nachtwächter wanderte dann durch die Straßen und rief die Stunden aus.
Das war „die gute alte Zeit" — eine Zeit, in der Schiller noch schreiben
konnte: „Die Uhr schlägt keinem Glücklichen".

23. Die Anfänge der Psychoanalyse

In den neunziger Jahren arbeiteten an einer Wiener Klinik für Geistes=
kranke zwei junge Ärzte, Dr. Josef Breuer und Dr. Sigmund Freud. Wir
verdanken der Zusammenarbeit dieser beiden bedeutenden Männer die Anfänge
der Psychoanalyse. Dr. Breuer hatte nämlich eine Patientin, deren Krank=
heitssymptome wichen, wenn sie in der Hypnose frei und ungehemmt sprechen
konnte. Sie selbst nannte dies ihre „talking cure", denn ein Symptom ihrer
Geistesstörung war, daß sie während ihrer Krankheit nur Englisch sprach.

Eines Tages nun, so berichtet Dr. Breuer, sei etwas sehr Eigentümliches geschehen.

Die Patientin habe sechs Wochen lang nichts trinken können, obwohl der Sommer sehr heiß gewesen war. Sie hätte daher furchtbar unter Durst gelitten, den sie nur mit Früchten und besonders mit Melonen hätte löschen können. Wenn ihr ein Glas Wasser angeboten worden wäre, habe sie es heftig weggestoßen. Dr. Breuer hypnotisierte sie, und in der Hypnose erzählte sie, sie teile ein Zimmer mit einer Engländerin, gegen die sie eine tiefe Abneigung fühle. Diese Engländerin besitze einen Hund, der ihr genauso unangenehm wäre wie seine Herrin. Sie sei nämlich eines Tages ins Zimmer gekommen und habe gesehen, wie dieser Hund auf den Tisch gesprungen wäre und aus einem Glas getrunken hätte. Aus Höflichkeit habe sie aber der Engländerin gegenüber von dem Vorfall geschwiegen. Erst in der Hypnose sprach sie nun ohne Hemmung darüber und verlangte dabei etwas zu trinken. Man goß ihr Wasser in ein Glas und sie wachte mit dem Glas am Mund auf. Ihre „talking cure" hatte ihr wieder geholfen.

Aus diesem und ähnlichen Fällen entwickelte Freud seine Theorie des Unbewußten und bewies, daß viele Störungen und andere psychische Symptome durch irgendein frühes Erlebnis verursacht seien, das der Patient verdrängt habe und das nun im Unterbewußtsein weiterlebe. Es sei die Aufgabe des Arztes, behauptete er, durch psychoanalytische Behandlung ein solches Erlebnis ins Bewußtsein zurückzurufen und den Patienten dadurch von seiner Hemmung zu befreien.

24. Geschichtliche Spekulationen

Die Frage, was geschehen wäre, wenn eine geschichtliche Tatsache anders gekommen wäre, als sie wirklich gekommen ist, hat die Köpfe immer wieder beschäftigt. Nehmen wir nur ein Beispiel: wie sähe Deutschland und wie sähe die deutsche Sprache heute aus, wenn die Römer im Teutoburger Wald über die Germanen gesiegt hätten und nicht die Germanen über die Römer? Würde man heute in Deutschland Deutsch sprechen oder eine Sprache, die sich aus dem Lateinischen entwickelt hätte, wie das moderne Französisch oder das moderne Spanisch?

Auf solche Fragen schweigt die Geschichte. Tatsache ist und bleibt, daß die Römer im Jahre 9 n. Chr. eine entscheidende Niederlage erlitten haben. Varus, der römische Feldherr, war mit drei Legionen durch den Teutoburger Wald gezogen. Da kam ein furchtbares Gewitter auf. Bäume, die von den Germanen angeschlagen worden waren, stürzten nieder, und die Germanen, die sich in den Wäldern verborgen hatten, griffen an. In drei Tagen wurden die Legionen fast vollkommen vernichtet, und Varus nahm sich mit seinem eigenen Schwert das Leben. Nur ein paar römische Soldaten entflohen; sie schlichen sich durch die Wälder zurück und brachten die Nachricht von der furchtbaren Niederlage nach Rom.

In Rom selbst brach eine Panik aus. Kaiser Augustus fürchtete, die Germanen würden nun in Italien einfallen und Rom belagern. Die meisten römischen Legionen waren im Osten. Es wäre viel Zeit vergangen, wenn man versucht hätte, sie zurückzubringen. Diese Furcht aber war zunächst grundlos, denn Arminius, der germanische Fürst, hatte sein Ziel erreicht, Germanien von den Römern zu befreien. Weitere Versuche der Römer, Germanien zu erobern, blieben erfolglos.

Die Schlacht im Teutoburger Wald ist schon damals viel erörtert worden. Manche schworen, die Niederlage sei ein Urteil der Götter gewesen. Andere behaupteten, die Armee des Varus würde nicht vernichtet worden sein, wenn dieser dem Arminius, seinem Freund, weniger getraut hätte, und wenn er mit seinen Legionen in einem feindlichen Lande vorsichtiger gewesen wäre. Als ob Varus die Zukunft hätte voraussehen können!

Hätten aber die Römer gesiegt und das ganze Land vom Rhein bis zur Elbe erobert, dann wären hier sicher eine gemeinsame Sprache und Kultur entstanden, die bis an die östlichen Grenzen Germaniens gereicht hätten. Das würde die Geschichte Europas bis in unsere Tage vollkommen geändert haben.

25. Goethe und die Naturwissenschaften

Johann Wolfgang von Goethe (1749-1832) stammte aus einer in Frankfurt sehr angesehenen Familie. Der Vater war streng, aber doch auch stolz auf den hoffnungsvollen Sohn. So verdankte der Sohn dem Vater vor allem jene geistige Disziplin, ohne die so manches seiner Werke kaum geschrieben, wenigstens nicht beendet worden wäre.

Goethe gilt heute vor allem als der Dichter des „Faust". Man hat gemeint, es lohne sich, die deutsche Sprache zu lernen, nur um diese große, im Grunde unübersetzbare Dichtung im Original lesen zu können. Aber Goethe war ja nicht nur der Dichter des „Faust". Es gibt kaum eine literarische Gattung, die er nicht bewältigt hätte — aber man wird ihm nicht gerecht, wenn man nicht auch seiner wissenschaftlichen Leistungen gedenkt.

Schon der Student Goethe hatte sich für Medizin interessiert und an der Straßburger Universität medizinische Vorlesungen gehört, anstatt an seiner juristischen Dissertation zu arbeiten. In späteren Jahren hat er dann unter anderem Geologie, Physik, Botanik und Mineralogie getrieben. Wenn er von einer Reise zurückkehrte, hatte er seine Kutsche mit Steinen aller Art beladen, die er dann in seine Sammlungen einordnete. In der Physik entwickelte er eine gegen Newton gerichtete Farbenlehre, und wenn es ihm auch nicht gelungen ist, sich gegen Newton durchzusetzen, so hat er doch Wesentliches zur physiologischen Optik beigetragen. Der Physiologe Johannes Müller erklärte 1826 in seiner „Physiologie des Gesichtssinnes", er hätte sein Werk nicht schreiben können, ohne sich zuerst mit Goethes Arbeiten auseinandergesetzt zu haben.

In der Botanik legte Goethe den Grund für eine vergleichende Morphologie, und in seinem 1790 erschienenen „Versuch, die Metamorphose der Pflanzen zu erklären", befinden sich bereits sehr an Darwin erinnernde Gedanken. Er glaubte, die verschiedenen Organe der Pflanze als umgebildete Blätter erkennen zu können. Alle heute existierenden Pflanzen schienen ihm auf eine Urpflanze zurückzugehen.

Schon früh hatte Goethe sich auch mit dem Problem des Zwischenkieferknochens beschäftigt. Dieser angeblich im menschlichen Schädel nicht vorkommende Knochen im Oberkiefer ist in manchen Säugetieren sehr entwickelt, wächst aber beim Menschen schon nach der Geburt mit dem Oberkiefer zusammen. Man hat Jahrhunderte lang geglaubt, das Fehlen des Zwischenkieferknochens unterscheide den Menschen von den anderen Säugetieren. Von der Einheit allen organischen Lebens fest überzeugt, glaubte und bewies Goethe, daß dieser Knochen auch beim Menschen zu finden sei.

Typisch für Goethes Art zu denken und wissenschaftlich zu arbeiten ist die Episode mit dem Schafskelett. Auf seiner Reise nach Venedig sah er ein solches Skelett eines Tages auf dem Lido liegen. Er untersuchte es und fand, daß der Schädel sich aus einigen Wirbeln entwickelt habe. Auch dieser für seine Zeit sehr radikale Gedanke weist schon auf die von Darwin später entwickelten Theorien voraus.

Appendix 2

Condensed Summary of

German Grammar

1. Auxiliary Verbs

INFINITIVE

haben *to have*   **sein** *to be*   **werden** *to become*

PRESENT PARTICIPLE

habend   **seiend**   **werdend**

PAST PARTICIPLE

gehabt   **gewesen**   **geworden**

PRESENT INDICATIVE

ich habe	ich bin	ich werde
du hast	du bist	du wirst
er hat	er ist	er wird
wir haben	wir sind	wir werden
ihr habt	ihr seid	ihr werdet
sie haben	sie sind	sie werden
Sie haben	Sie sind	Sie werden

PAST INDICATIVE

ich hatte	ich war	ich wurde
du hattest	du warst	du wurdest
er hatte	er war	er wurde
wir hatten	wir waren	wir wurden
ihr hattet	ihr wart	ihr wurdet
sie hatten	sie waren	sie wurden
Sie hatten	Sie waren	Sie wurden

FUTURE INDICATIVE

ich werde haben	ich werde sein	ich werde werden
du wirst haben	du wirst sein	du wirst werden
er wird haben	er wird sein	er wird werden
wir werden haben	wir werden sein	wir werden werden
ihr werdet haben	ihr werdet sein	ihr werdet werden
sie werden haben	sie werden sein	sie werden werden
Sie werden haben	Sie werden sein	Sie werden werden

PRESENT PERFECT

ich habe gehabt	ich bin gewesen	ich bin geworden
du hast gehabt	du bist gewesen	du bist geworden
er hat gehabt	er ist gewesen	er ist geworden
wir haben gehabt	wir sind gewesen	wir sind geworden
ihr habt gehabt	ihr seid gewesen	ihr seid geworden
sie haben gehabt	sie sind gewesen	sie sind geworden
Sie haben gehabt	Sie sind gewesen	Sie sind geworden

PAST PERFECT

ich hatte gehabt	ich war gewesen	ich war geworden
du hattest gehabt	du warst gewesen	du warst geworden
er hatte gehabt	er war gewesen	er war geworden
wir hatten gehabt	wir waren gewesen	wir waren geworden
ihr hattet gehabt	ihr wart gewesen	ihr wart geworden
sie hatten gehabt	sie waren gewesen	sie waren geworden
Sie hatten gehabt	Sie waren gewesen	Sie waren geworden

FUTURE PERFECT INDICATIVE

ich werde gehabt haben	ich werde gewesen sein
du wirst gehabt haben	du wirst gewesen sein
er wird gehabt haben	er wird gewesen sein
wir werden gehabt haben	wir werden gewesen sein
ihr werdet gehabt haben	ihr werdet gewesen sein
sie werden gehabt haben	sie werden gewesen sein
Sie werden gehabt haben	Sie werden gewesen sein

ich werde geworden sein
du wirst geworden sein
er wird geworden sein
wir werden geworden sein
ihr werdet geworden sein
sie werden geworden sein
Sie werden geworden sein

PRESENT SPECIAL SUBJUNCTIVE

ich habe	ich sei	ich werde
du habest	du sei(e)st	du werdest
er habe	er sei	er werde

wir haben	wir seien	wir werden
ihr habet	ihr seiet	ihr werdet
sie haben	sie seien	sie werden
Sie haben	Sie seien	Sie werden

PRESENT GENERAL SUBJUNCTIVE

ich hätte	ich wäre	ich würde
du hättest	du wärest	du würdest
er hätte	er wäre	er würde
wir hätten	wir wären	wir würden
ihr hättet	ihr wäret	ihr würdet
sie hätten	sie wären	sie würden
Sie hätten	Sie wären	Sie würden

PAST SPECIAL SUBJUNCTIVE

ich habe gehabt	ich sei gewesen	ich sei geworden
du habest gehabt	du sei(e)st gewesen	du sei(e)st geworden
er habe gehabt	er sei gewesen	er sei geworden
wir haben gehabt	wir seien gewesen	wir seien geworden
ihr habet gehabt	ihr seiet gewesen	ihr seiet geworden
sie haben gehabt	sie seien gewesen	sie seien geworden
Sie haben gehabt	Sie seien gewesen	Sie seien geworden

PAST GENERAL SUBJUNCTIVE

ich hätte gehabt	ich wäre gewesen	ich wäre geworden
du hättest gehabt	du wärest gewesen	du wärest geworden
er hätte gehabt	er wäre gewesen	er wäre geworden
wir hätten gehabt	wir wären gewesen	wir wären geworden
ihr hättet gehabt	ihr wäret gewesen	ihr wäret geworden
sie hätten gehabt	sie wären gewesen	sie wären geworden
Sie hätten gehabt	Sie wären gewesen	Sie wären geworden

FUTURE SPECIAL SUBJUNCTIVE

ich werde haben	ich werde sein	ich werde werden
du werdest haben	du werdest sein	du werdest werden
er werde haben	er werde sein	er werde werden
wir werden haben	wir werden sein	wir werden werden
ihr werdet haben	ihr werdet sein	ihr werdet werden
sie werden haben	sie werden sein	sie werden werden
Sie werden haben	Sie werden sein	Sie werden werden

FUTURE GENERAL SUBJUNCTIVE (CONDITIONAL)

ich würde haben	ich würde sein	ich würde werden
du würdest haben	du würdest sein	du würdest werden
er würde haben	er würde sein	er würde werden
wir würden haben	wir würden sein	wir würden werden
ihr würdet haben	ihr würdet sein	ihr würdet werden
sie würden haben	sie würden sein	sie würden werden
Sie würden haben	Sie würden sein	Sie würden werden

FUTURE PERFECT SPECIAL SUBJUNCTIVE

ich werde gehabt haben   **ich werde gewesen sein**
etc.   etc.

ich werde geworden sein etc.

FUTURE PERFECT GENERAL SUBJUNCTIVE (PAST CONDITIONAL)

ich würde gehabt haben   **ich würde gewesen sein**
etc.   etc.

ich würde geworden sein etc.

IMPERATIVE

habe!	**sei!**	**werde!**
habt!	**seid!**	**werdet!**
haben Sie!	**seien Sie!**	**werden Sie!**

2. Modal Auxiliaries

PRESENT INDICATIVE

dürfen	**können**	**mögen**
(may)	*(can)*	*(like to)*
ich darf	**ich kann**	**ich mag**
du darfst	**du kannst**	**du magst**
er darf	**er kann**	**er mag**
wir dürfen	**wir können**	**wir mögen**
ihr dürft	**ihr könnt**	**ihr mögt**
sie dürfen	**sie können**	**sie mögen**
Sie dürfen	**Sie können**	**Sie mögen**

müssen	**sollen**	**wollen**
(must)	*(be to)*	*(want to)*
ich muß	**ich soll**	**ich will**
du mußt	**du sollst**	**du willst**
er muß	**er soll**	**er will**
wir müssen	**wir sollen**	**wir wollen**
ihr müßt	**ihr sollt**	**ihr wollt**
sie müssen	**sie sollen**	**sie wollen**
Sie müssen	**Sie sollen**	**Sie wollen**

PAST INDICATIVE

ich durfte	**ich konnte**	**ich mochte**
du durftest	**du konntest**	**du mochtest**
er durfte	**er konnte**	**er mochte**
wir durften	**wir konnten**	**wir mochten**
ihr durftet	**ihr konntet**	**ihr mochtet**
sie durften	**sie konnten**	**sie mochten**
Sie durften	**Sie konnten**	**Sie mochten**

ich mußte	ich sollte	ich wollte
du mußtest	du solltest	du wolltest
er mußte	er sollte	er wollte
wir mußten	wir sollten	wir wollten
ihr mußtet	ihr solltet	ihr wolltet
sie mußten	sie sollten	sie wollten
Sie mußten	Sie sollten	Sie wollten

FUTURE INDICATIVE

ich werde dürfen (können, mögen, müssen, sollen, wollen)

PRESENT PERFECT

ich habe gedurft (gekonnt, gemocht, gemußt, gesollt, gewollt)

PAST PERFECT

ich hatte gedurft (gekonnt, gemocht, gemußt, gesollt, gewollt)

FUTURE PERFECT INDICATIVE

ich werde gedurft (gekonnt, gemocht, gemußt, gesollt, gewollt) haben

PRESENT SPECIAL SUBJUNCTIVE

ich dürfe   ich könne   ich möge   ich müsse   ich solle   ich wolle

PRESENT GENERAL SUBJUNCTIVE

ich dürfte   ich könnte   ich möchte   ich müßte   ich sollte   ich wollte

PAST SPECIAL SUBJUNCTIVE

ich habe gedurft (gekonnt, gemocht, gemußt, gesollt, gewollt)

PAST GENERAL SUBJUNCTIVE

ich hätte gedurft (gekonnt, gemocht, gemußt, gesollt, gewollt)

FUTURE SPECIAL SUBJUNCTIVE

ich werde dürfen (können, mögen, müssen, sollen, wollen)

FUTURE GENERAL SUBJUNCTIVE (CONDITIONAL)

ich würde dürfen (können, mögen, müssen, sollen, wollen)

FUTURE SPECIAL PERFECT SUBJUNCTIVE

ich werde gedurft (gekonnt, gemocht, gemußt, gesollt, gewollt) haben

FUTURE PERFECT GENERAL SUBJUNCTIVE (PAST CONDITIONAL)

ich würde gedurft (gekonnt, gemocht, gemußt, gesollt, gewollt) haben

Semimodal Auxiliaries

heißen	*to bid, ask*	lassen	*to let, cause*	lernen	*to learn*
helfen	*to help*	lehren	*to teach*	sehen	*to see*
hören	*to hear*				

Wissen (*to know*) is conjugated like a modal auxiliary in the present tense:

ich weiß	wir wissen
du weißt	ihr wißt
er weiß	sie wissen

3. Summary of a Weak and a Strong Verb

a. Active

INFINITIVE

lieben   *to love*   **fahren**   *to drive*

PRESENT PARTICIPLE

liebend   **fahrend**

PAST PARTICIPLE

geliebt   **gefahren**

PRESENT INDICATIVE

I love	*I drive*
ich liebe	ich fahre
du liebst	du fährst
er liebt	er fährt
wir lieben	wir fahren
ihr liebt	ihr fahrt
sie lieben	sie fahren
Sie lieben	Sie fahren

PAST INDICATIVE

I loved	*I drove*
ich liebte	ich fuhr
du liebtest	du fuhrst
er liebte	er fuhr
wir liebten	wir fuhren
ihr liebtet	ihr fuhrt
sie liebten	sie fuhren
Sie liebten	Sie fuhren

FUTURE INDICATIVE

I will love	*I will drive*
ich werde lieben	ich werde fahren
du wirst lieben	du wirst fahren
er wird lieben	er wird fahren

wir werden lieben	wir werden fahren
ihr werdet lieben	ihr werdet fahren
sie werden lieben	sie werden fahren
Sie werden lieben	Sie werden fahren

PRESENT PERFECT

I loved, I have loved	*I drove, I have driven*
ich habe geliebt	ich bin gefahren[1]
du hast geliebt	du bist gefahren
er hat geliebt	er ist gefahren
wir haben geliebt	wir sind gefahren
ihr habt geliebt	ihr seid gefahren
sie haben geliebt	sie sind gefahren
Sie haben geliebt	Sie sind gefahren

PAST PERFECT

I had loved	*I had driven*
ich hatte geliebt	ich war gefahren[1]
du hattest geliebt	du warst gefahren
er hatte geliebt	er war gefahren
wir hatten geliebt	wir waren gefahren
ihr hattet geliebt	ihr wart gefahren
sie hatten geliebt	sie waren gefahren
Sie hatten geliebt	Sie waren gefahren

FUTURE PERFECT INDICATIVE

I will have loved	*I will have driven*
ich werde geliebt haben	ich werde gefahren sein[1]
du wirst geliebt haben	du wirst gefahren sein
er wird geliebt haben	er wird gefahren sein
wir werden geliebt haben	wir werden gefahren sein
ihr werdet geliebt haben	ihr werdet gefahren sein
sie werden geliebt haben	sie werden gefahren sein
Sie werden geliebt haben	Sie werden gefahren sein

IMPERATIVE

liebe!	fahre!
liebt!	fahrt!
lieben Sie!	fahren Sie!

PRESENT SPECIAL SUBJUNCTIVE

I love	*I drive*
ich liebe	ich fahre
du liebest	du fahrest
er liebe	er fahre

[1] For intransitive verbs conjugated with **sein,** see Aufgabe 12.

wir lieben	wir fahren
ihr liebet	ihr fahret
sie lieben	sie fahren
Sie lieben	Sie fahren

PRESENT GENERAL SUBJUNCTIVE

I loved, I love	*I drove, I drive*
ich liebte	ich führe
du liebtest	du führest
er liebte	er führe
wir liebten	wir führen
ihr liebtet	ihr führet
sie liebten	sie führen
Sie liebten	Sie führen

Note: In the Present General Subjunctive, irregular weak verbs change their stem vowel to **e**, except **bringen** and **denken: ich brennte, ich kennte, ich nennte, ich rennte; ich sendete, ich wendete,** but: **ich brächte, ich dächte.**

PAST SPECIAL SUBJUNCTIVE

I have loved, I loved	*I have driven, I drove*
ich habe geliebt	ich sei gefahren[1]
du habest geliebt	du sei(e)st gefahren
er habe geliebt	er sei gefahren
wir haben geliebt	wir seien gefahren
ihr habet geliebt	ihr seiet gefahren
sie haben geliebt	sie seien gefahren
Sie haben geliebt	Sie seien gefahren

PAST GENERAL SUBJUNCTIVE

I had loved	*I had driven*
ich hätte geliebt	ich wäre gefahren[1]
du hättest geliebt	du wärest gefahren
er hätte geliebt	er wäre gefahren
wir hätten geliebt	wir wären gefahren
ihr hättet geliebt	ihr wäret gefahren
sie hätten geliebt	sie wären gefahren
Sie hätten geliebt	Sie wären gefahren

FUTURE SPECIAL SUBJUNCTIVE

I will love	*I will drive*
ich werde lieben	ich werde fahren
du werdest lieben	du werdest fahren
er werde lieben	er werde fahren

[1] For intransitive verbs conjugated with **sein**, see Aufgabe 12.

wir werden lieben	wir werden fahren
ihr werdet lieben	ihr werdet fahren
sie werden lieben	sie werden fahren
Sie werden lieben	Sie werden fahren

FUTURE GENERAL SUBJUNCTIVE (CONDITIONAL)

I would love	*I would drive*
ich würde lieben	ich würde fahren
du würdest lieben	du würdest fahren
er würde lieben	er würde fahren
wir würden lieben	wir würden fahren
ihr würdet lieben	ihr würdet fahren
sie würden lieben	sie würden fahren
Sie würden lieben	Sie würden fahren

FUTURE PERFECT SPECIAL SUBJUNCTIVE

I will have loved	*I will have driven*
ich werde geliebt haben	ich werde gefahren sein[1]
du werdest geliebt haben	du werdest gefahren sein
er werde geliebt haben	er werde gefahren sein
wir werden geliebt haben	wir werden gefahren sein
ihr werdet geliebt haben	ihr werdet gefahren sein
sie werden geliebt haben	sie werden gefahren sein
Sie werden geliebt haben	Sie werden gefahren sein

FUTURE PERFECT GENERAL SUBJUNCTIVE (PAST CONDITIONAL)

I would have loved	*I would have driven*
ich würde geliebt haben	ich würde gefahren sein[1]
du würdest geliebt haben	du würdest gefahren sein
er würde geliebt haben	er würde gefahren sein
wir würden geliebt haben	wir würden gefahren sein
ihr würdet geliebt haben	ihr würdet gefahren sein
sie würden geliebt haben	sie würden gefahren sein
Sie würden geliebt haben	Sie würden gefahren sein

b. Passive

INFINITIVE

geliebt werden *to be loved*   **gefahren werden** *to be driven*

PRESENT INDICATIVE

I am (being) loved	*I am (being) driven*
ich werde geliebt	ich werde gefahren
du wirst geliebt	du wirst gefahren
er wird geliebt	er wird gefahren

[1] For intransitive verbs conjugated with **sein,** see Aufgabe 12.

wir werden geliebt	wir werden gefahren
ihr werdet geliebt	ihr werdet gefahren
sie werden geliebt	sie werden gefahren
Sie werden geliebt	Sie werden gefahren

PAST INDICATIVE

I was loved	*I was driven*
ich wurde geliebt	ich wurde gefahren
du wurdest geliebt	du wurdest gefahren
er wurde geliebt	er wurde gefahren
wir wurden geliebt	wir wurden gefahren
ihr wurdet geliebt	ihr wurdet gefahren
sie wurden geliebt	sie wurden gefahren
Sie wurden geliebt	Sie wurden gefahren

FUTURE INDICATIVE

I will be loved	*I will be driven*
ich werde geliebt werden	ich werde gefahren werden
du wirst geliebt werden	du wirst gefahren werden
er wird geliebt werden	er wird gefahren werden
wir werden geliebt werden	wir werden gefahren werden
ihr werdet geliebt werden	ihr werdet gefahren werden
sie werden geliebt werden	sie werden gefahren werden
Sie werden geliebt werden	Sie werden gefahren werden

PRESENT PERFECT

I was loved, I have been loved	*I was driven, I have been driven*
ich bin geliebt worden	ich bin gefahren worden
du bist geliebt worden	du bist gefahren worden
er ist geliebt worden	er ist gefahren worden
wir sind geliebt worden	wir sind gefahren worden
ihr seid geliebt worden	ihr seid gefahren worden
sie sind geliebt worden	sie sind gefahren worden
Sie sind geliebt worden	Sie sind gefahren worden

PAST PERFECT

I had been loved	*I had been driven*
ich war geliebt worden	ich war gefahren worden
du warst geliebt worden	du warst gefahren worden
er war geliebt worden	er war gefahren worden
wir waren geliebt worden	wir waren gefahren worden
ihr wart geliebt worden	ihr wart gefahren worden
sie waren geliebt worden	sie waren gefahren worden
Sie waren geliebt worden	Sie waren gefahren worden

FUTURE PERFECT INDICATIVE

I will have been loved	*I will have been driven*
ich werde geliebt worden sein	ich werde gefahren worden sein
du wirst geliebt worden sein	du wirst gefahren worden sein
er wird geliebt worden sein	er wird gefahren worden sein
wir werden geliebt worden sein	wir werden gefahren worden sein
ihr werdet geliebt worden sein	ihr werdet gefahren worden sein
sie werden geliebt worden sein	sie werden gefahren worden sein
Sie werden geliebt worden sein	Sie werden gefahren worden sein

PRESENT SPECIAL SUBJUNCTIVE

I am being loved	*I am being driven*
ich werde geliebt	ich werde gefahren
du werdest geliebt etc.[1]	du werdest gefahren etc.[1]

PRESENT GENERAL SUBJUNCTIVE

I am loved, I would be loved	*I am driven, I would be driven*
ich würde geliebt	ich würde gefahren
du würdest geliebt etc.[1]	du würdest gefahren etc.[1]

PAST SPECIAL SUBJUNCTIVE

I was loved, I have been loved	*I was driven, I have been driven*
ich sei geliebt worden	ich sei gefahren worden
du sei(e)st geliebt worden etc.[1]	du sei(e)st gefahren worden etc.[1]

PAST GENERAL SUBJUNCTIVE

I was loved, I had been loved	*I was driven, I had been driven*
ich wäre geliebt worden	ich wäre gefahren worden
du wärest geliebt worden etc.[1]	du wärest gefahren worden etc.[1]

FUTURE SPECIAL SUBJUNCTIVE

I will be loved	*I will be driven*
ich werde geliebt werden	ich werde gefahren werden
du werdest geliebt werden etc.[1]	du werdest gefahren werden etc.[1]

FUTURE GENERAL SUBJUNCTIVE (CONDITIONAL)

I would be loved	*I would be driven*
ich würde geliebt werden	ich würde gefahren werden
du würdest geliebt werden etc.[1]	du würdest gefahren werden etc.[1]

FUTURE PERFECT SPECIAL SUBJUNCTIVE

I will have been loved	*I will have been driven*
ich werde geliebt worden sein	ich werde gefahren worden sein
du werdest geliebt worden sein etc.[1]	du werdest gefahren worden sein etc.[1]

[1] For full conjugation, see **werden,** pages 325–327. Remember that the passive past participle **geworden** becomes **worden.**

FUTURE PERFECT GENERAL SUBJUNCTIVE (PAST CONDITIONAL)

I would have been loved	*I would have been driven*
ich würde geliebt worden sein	ich würde gefahren worden sein
du würdest geliebt worden sein etc.	du würdest gefahren worden sein etc.

4. Reflexive Verbs

sich freuen *to be glad*	**sich helfen** *to help oneself*

PRESENT INDICATIVE

I am glad	*I help myself*
ich freue mich	ich helfe mir
du freust dich	du hilfst dir
er freut sich	er hilft sich
wir freuen uns	wir helfen uns
ihr freut euch	ihr helft euch
sie freuen sich	sie helfen sich
Sie freuen sich	Sie helfen sich

For the formation of other tenses, see Section 3.

5. Verbs Governing the Dative

antworten	*to answer*	folgen (ist)	*to follow*
begegnen	*to meet*	gefallen (ä; ie, a)	*to please*
danken	*to thank*	gehorchen	*to obey*
dienen	*to serve*	gehören	*to belong to*
entgegnen } erwidern }	*to answer*	geschehen (ie; a, e) (ist)	*to happen*
fehlen	*to be missing, lacking; to be the matter with*	glauben	*to believe*
		helfen (i; a, o)	*to help*
		scheinen (ie, ie)	*to seem*

6. Irregular Verbs

INFINITIVE	SIMPLE PAST	PAST PART.	3RD SG. PRES.
backen (*bake*)	(buk) backte	gebacken	bäckt
befehlen (*command*)	befahl	befohlen	befiehlt
befleißen, sich (*apply oneself*)	befliß	beflissen	
beginnen (*begin*)	begann	begonnen	
beißen (*bite*)	biß	gebissen	

INFINITIVE	SIMPLE PAST	PAST PART.	3RD SG. PRES.
bergen (hide)	barg	geborgen	birgt
bersten (burst)	barst	ist geborsten	birst
betrügen (deceive)	betrog	betrogen	
beweisen (prove)	bewies	bewiesen	
biegen (bend)	bog	gebogen	
bieten (offer)	bot	geboten	
binden (bind)	band	gebunden	
bitten (beg, request)	bat	gebeten	
blasen (blow)	blies	geblasen	bläst
bleiben (remain, stay)	blieb	ist geblieben	
bleichen (bleach)	blich	geblichen	
braten (roast)	briet	gebraten	brät
brechen (break)	brach	gebrochen	bricht
brennen (burn)	brannte	gebrannt	
bringen (bring, take)	brachte	gebracht	
denken (think)	dachte	gedacht	
dreschen (thrash)	drosch	gedroschen	drischt
dringen (penetrate)	drang	ist gedrungen	
empfangen (receive)	empfing	empfangen	empfängt
erlöschen (go out, become extinct [light, flame])	erlosch	ist erloschen	
erscheinen (appear)	erschien	ist erschienen	
erschrecken (be startled)	erschrak	ist erschrocken	erschrickt
essen (eat)	aß	gegessen	ißt
fahren (drive, travel)	fuhr	(ist) gefahren	fährt
fallen (fall)	fiel	ist gefallen	fällt
fangen (catch)	fing	gefangen	fängt
fechten (fence; fight)	focht	gefochten	ficht
finden (find)	fand	gefunden	
flechten (plait, braid)	flocht	geflochten	flicht
fliegen (fly)	flog	(ist) geflogen	
fliehen (flee)	floh	ist geflohen	
fließen (flow)	floß	ist geflossen	
fressen (eat)	fraß	gefressen	frißt
frieren (be cold; freeze)	fror	(ist) gefroren	
gären (ferment)	gor / gärte	ist gegoren / (gegärt)	
gebären (give birth to)	gebar	geboren	gebiert
geben (give)	gab	gegeben	gibt
gedeihen (thrive)	gedieh	ist gediehen	
gefallen (please)	gefiel	gefallen	gefällt
gehen (go)	ging	ist gegangen	
gelingen (succeed)	gelang	ist gelungen	
gelten (be worth, be considered)	galt	gegolten	gilt
genesen (recover)	genas	ist genesen	
genießen (enjoy)	genoß	genossen	

INFINITIVE	SIMPLE PAST	PAST PART.	3RD SG. PRES.
geschehen (*happen*)	geschah	ist geschehen	geschieht
gestehen (*confess*)	gestand	gestanden	
gewinnen (*win*)	gewann	gewonnen	
gießen (*pour*)	goß	gegossen	
gleichen (*resemble*)	glich	geglichen	
gleiten (*slide, slip*)	glitt	ist geglitten	
glimmen (*glow*)	glomm	geglommen	
graben (*dig*)	grub	gegraben	gräbt
greifen (*grasp, grip*)	griff	gegriffen	
haben (*have*)	hatte	gehabt	hat
halten (*hold; stop*)	hielt	gehalten	hält
hängen (*hang*)	hing	gehangen	hängt
hauen (*beat; hew*)	hieb	gehauen	
heben (*lift, raise*)	hob	gehoben	
heißen (*be called*)	hieß	geheißen	
helfen (*help*)	half	geholfen	hilft
kennen (*know*)	kannte	gekannt	
klimmen (*climb*)	klomm	ist geklommen	
klingen (*sound, tinkle*)	klang	geklungen	
kneifen (*pinch*)	kniff	gekniffen	
kommen (*come*)	kam	ist gekommen	
kriechen (*creep, crawl*)	kroch	ist gekrochen	
laden (*load*)	lud	geladen	lädt
lassen (*let; cause*)	ließ	gelassen	läßt
laufen (*run*)	lief	ist gelaufen	läuft
leiden (*suffer*)	litt	gelitten	
leihen (*lend*)	lieh	geliehen	
lesen (*read*)	las	gelesen	liest
liegen (*lie, be lying*)	lag	gelegen	
lügen (*tell a lie*)	log	gelogen	
mahlen (*grind*)	mahlte	gemahlen	
meiden (*avoid*)	mied	gemieden	
melken (*milk*)	molk	gemolken	
	(melkte)	(gemelkt)	
messen (*measure*)	maß	gemessen	mißt
nehmen (*take*)	nahm	genommen	nimmt
nennen (*name, call*)	nannte	genannt	
pfeifen (*whistle*)	pfiff	gepfiffen	
preisen (*praise*)	pries	gepriesen	
quellen (*gush forth*)	quoll	ist gequollen	quillt
raten (*advise; guess*)	riet	geraten	rät
reiben (*rub*)	rieb	gerieben	
reißen (*tear, rend*)	riß	gerissen	
reiten (*ride horseback*)	ritt	(ist) geritten	
rennen (*run*)	rannte	ist gerannt	
riechen (*smell*)	roch	gerochen	

INFINITIVE	SIMPLE PAST	PAST PART.	3RD SG. PRES.
ringen (*struggle, wrestle*)	rang	gerungen	
rinnen (*trickle*)	rann	ist geronnen	
rufen (*call*)	rief	gerufen	
salzen (*salt*)	salzte	gesalzen (gesalzt)	
saufen (*drink*)	soff	gesoffen	säuft
saugen (*suck*)	sog (saugte)	gesogen (gesaugt)	
schaffen (*create*)	schuf	geschaffen	
scheiden (*part*)	schied	geschieden	
scheinen (*shine; seem*)	schien	geschienen	
schelten (*scold*)	schalt	gescholten	schilt
scheren (*shear*)	schor	geschoren	
schieben (*push*)	schob	geschoben	
schießen (*shoot*)	schoß	geschossen	
schlafen (*sleep*)	schlief	geschlafen	schläft
schlagen (*beat, hit, strike*)	schlug	geschlagen	schlägt
schleichen (*sneak*)	schlich	ist geschlichen	
schleifen (*sharpen*)	schliff	geschliffen	
schließen (*close*)	schloß	geschlossen	
schlingen (*sling*)	schlang	geschlungen	
schmeißen (*throw*)	schmiß	geschmissen	
schmelzen (*melt*)	schmolz	(ist) geschmolzen	schmilzt
schneiden (*cut*)	schnitt	geschnitten	
schreiben (*write*)	schrieb	geschrieben	
schreien (*shout; scream*)	schrie	geschrie(e)n	
schreiten (*stride*)	schritt	ist geschritten	
schweigen (*be silent*)	schwieg	geschwiegen	
schwellen (*swell*)	schwoll	ist geschwollen	schwillt
schwimmen (*swim*)	schwamm	(ist) geschwommen	
schwinden (*dwindle*)	schwand	ist geschwunden	
schwingen (*swing*)	schwang	geschwungen	
schwören (*swear*)	schwor (schwörte)	geschworen (geschwört)	
sehen (*see*)	sah	gesehen	sieht
sein (*be*)	war	ist gewesen	ist
senden (*send*)	sandte (sendete)	gesandt (gesendet)	
sieden (*boil, seethe*)	sott (siedete)	gesotten (gesiedet)	
singen (*sing*)	sang	gesungen	
sinken (*sink*)	sank	ist gesunken	
sinnen (*meditate*)	sann	gesonnen	
sitzen (*sit*)	saß	gesessen	
speien (*spit*)	spie	gespie(e)n	
spinnen (*spin*)	spann	gesponnen	

INFINITIVE	SIMPLE PAST	PAST PART.	3RD SG. PRES.
sprechen (*speak*)	sprach	gesprochen	spricht
sprießen (*sprout*)	sproß	ist gesprossen	
springen (*jump*)	sprang	ist gesprungen	
stechen (*prick, sting*)	stach	gestochen	sticht
stehen (*stand*)	stand	gestanden	
stehlen (*steal*)	stahl	gestohlen	stiehlt
steigen (*climb, ascend*)	stieg	ist gestiegen	
sterben (*die*)	starb	ist gestorben	stirbt
stinken (*stink*)	stank	gestunken	
stoßen (*push*)	stieß	gestoßen	stößt
streichen (*stroke; paint*)	strich	gestrichen	
streiten (*fight, quarrel*)	stritt	gestritten	
tragen (*carry; wear*)	trug	getragen	trägt
treffen (*meet; hit*)	traf	getroffen	trifft
treiben (*drive*)	trieb	getrieben	
treten (*kick; step*)	trat	(ist) getreten	tritt
trinken (*drink*)	trank	getrunken	
tun (*do*)	tat	getan	
verbergen (*hide*)	verbarg	verborgen	verbirgt
verbieten (*forbid*)	verbot	verboten	
verderben (*spoil*)	verdarb	verdorben	verdirbt
vergessen (*forget*)	vergaß	vergessen	vergißt
verlieren (*lose*)	verlor	verloren	
vermeiden (*avoid*)	vermied	vermieden	
vermögen (*be able*)	vermochte	vermocht	vermag
verzeihen (*forgive; excuse*)	verzieh	verziehen	
wachsen (*grow*)	wuchs	ist gewachsen	wächst
waschen (*wash*)	wusch	gewaschen	wäscht
weben (*weave*)	wob	gewoben	
	(webte)	(gewebt)	
weisen (*show, point to*)	wies	gewiesen	
wenden (*turn*)	wandte	gewandt	
	(wendete)	(gewendet)	
werben (*vie, compete*)	warb	geworben	wirbt
werden (*become, get*)	wurde	ist geworden	wird
werfen (*throw*)	warf	geworfen	wirft
wiegen (*weigh*)	wog	gewogen	
winden (*wind*)	wand	gewunden	
wissen (*know*)	wußte	gewußt	weiß
ziehen (*pull; go, march*)	zog	(ist) gezogen	
zwingen (*force*)	zwang	gezwungen	

7. Declension of der and dieser

SINGULAR

NOM.	der	die	das	dieser	diese	dieses (dies)
ACC.	den	die	das	diesen	diese	dieses (dies)
DAT.	dem	der	dem	diesem	dieser	diesem
GEN.	des	der	des	dieses	dieser	dieses

PLURAL (all genders)

NOM.	die	diese
ACC.	die	diese
DAT.	den	diesen
GEN.	der	dieser

8. Der-Words

dieser	*this*	**mancher**	*many a* (pl. *some*)
jeder	*each, every*	**solcher**	*such a*
(plural: **alle**)		**welcher**	*which, what*
jener	*that*		

9. Der and welcher as Relative Pronouns

SINGULAR

NOM.	der	die	das	welcher	welche	welches
ACC.	den	die	das	welchen	welche	welches
DAT.	dem	der	dem	welchem	welcher	welchem
GEN.	dessen	deren	dessen	(dessen)	(deren)	(dessen)

PLURAL (all genders)

NOM.	die	welche
ACC.	die	welche
DAT.	denen	welchen
GEN.	deren	(deren)

10. Interrogative Pronouns wer and was

NOM.	wer?	was?
ACC.	wen?	was?
DAT.	wem?	—
GEN.	wessen?	—

11. Declension of Ein-Words (ein, mein, unser)

SINGULAR

NOM.	ein	eine	ein	mein	meine	mein
ACC.	einen	eine	ein	meinen	meine	mein
DAT.	einem	einer	einem	meinem	meiner	meinem
GEN.	eines	einer	eines	meines	meiner	meines

NOM.	unser	unsere	unser
ACC.	unseren	unsere	unser
DAT.	unserem	unserer	unserem
GEN.	unseres	unserer	unseres

PLURAL (all genders)

NOM.	meine	unsere
ACC.	meine	unsere
DAT.	meinen	unseren
GEN.	meiner	unserer

12. Ein-Words

ein	*a, an*			kein	*no*
mein	*my*			unser	*our*
dein	*your*	**Ihr**	*your*	euer	*your*
sein	*his*			ihr	*their*
ihr	*her*				
sein	*its*				

13. Ein-Words used as Pronouns are declined like der

	SINGULAR			PLURAL (all genders)
NOM.	keiner	keine	keines (keins)	keine
ACC.	keinen	keine	keines (keins)	keine
DAT.	keinem	keiner	keinem	keinen
GEN.	keines	keiner	keines	keiner

14. Personal Pronouns

NOM.	ich	du	er	sie	es	man
ACC.	mich	dich	ihn	sie	es	einen
DAT.	mir	dir	ihm	ihr	ihm	einem
GEN.	(meiner)	(deiner)	(seiner)	(ihrer)	(seiner)	

NOM.	wir	ihr	sie	Sie
ACC.	uns	euch	sie	Sie
DAT.	uns	euch	ihnen	Ihnen
GEN.	(unserer)	(euerer)	(ihrer)	(Ihrer)

15. Weak Adjective Endings (after der-words)

NOM.	e	der gute Mann		e	die arme Frau
ACC.	en	den guten Mann		e	die arme Frau
DAT.	en	dem guten Mann		en	der armen Frau
GEN.	en	des guten Mannes		en	der armen Frau

NOM.			e	das kleine Kind
ACC.			e	das kleine Kind
DAT.			en	dem kleinen Kind
GEN.			en	des kleinen Kindes

NOM.	en	die armen Männer (Frauen, Kinder)
ACC.	en	die armen Männer (Frauen, Kinder)
DAT.	en	den armen Männern (Frauen, Kindern)
GEN.	en	der armen Männer (Frauen, Kinder)

16. Strong Adjective Endings (not preceded by a der-word)

SINGULAR

NOM.	er	e	es	heißer Tee	süße Butter	grünes Gras
ACC.	en	e	es	heißen Tee	süße Butter	grünes Gras
DAT.	em	er	em	heißem Tee	süßer Butter	grünem Gras
GEN.	en	er	en	heißen Tees	süßer Butter	grünen Grases

PLURAL (all genders)

NOM.	e	rote Äpfel
ACC.	e	rote Äpfel
DAT.	en	roten Äpfeln
GEN.	er	roter Äpfel

17. Mixed Adjective Endings (after ein-words)

NOM.	er	kein guter Mann	e	keine arme Frau
ACC.	en	keinen guten Mann	e	keine arme Frau
DAT.	en	keinem guten Mann	en	keiner armen Frau
GEN.	en	keines guten Mannes	en	keiner armen Frau

NOM.		es	kein kleines Kind
ACC.		es	kein kleines Kind
DAT.		en	keinem kleinen Kind
GEN.		en	keines kleinen Kindes

PLURAL (all genders)

NOM.	en	keine guten Männer (Frauen, Kinder)
ACC.	en	keine guten Männer (Frauen, Kinder)
DAT.	en	keinen guten Männern (Frauen, Kindern)
GEN.	en	keiner guten Männer (Frauen, Kinder)

18. Declension of derselbe (*the same*) and derjenige (*the one*)

SINGULAR

NOM.	derselbe	dieselbe	dasselbe
ACC.	denselben	dieselbe	dasselbe
DAT.	demselben	derselben	demselben
GEN.	desselben	derselben	desselben
NOM.	derjenige	diejenige	dasjenige
ACC.	denjenigen	diejenige	dasjenige
DAT.	demjenigen	derjenigen	demjenigen
GEN.	desjenigen	derjenigen	desjenigen

PLURAL (all genders)

NOM.	dieselben	diejenigen
ACC.	dieselben	diejenigen
DAT.	denselben	denjenigen
GEN.	derselben	derjenigen

19. Class I Nouns (strong)

(No ending in plural; umlaut: masculines sometimes, feminines always, neuters never.)

SINGULAR			PLURAL		
-	der Vater		(ꞏ)-	die Väter
-	den Vater		(ꞏ)-	die Väter
-	dem Vater		(ꞏ)n	den Vätern
-s	des Vaters		(ꞏ)-	der Väter

To Class I belong:

a. masculine and neuter nouns ending in **-el, -en, -er;**

b. nouns with the suffixes **-chen** and **-lein** (always neuter);

c. neuter nouns with the prefix **Ge-** and the ending **-e** (**das Gebirge** *mountain range*);

d. the two feminines **die Mutter, die Tochter.**

20. Class II Nouns (strong)

(Plural in **-e;** umlaut: masculines often, feminines always, neuters never.)

SINGULAR	-	der Baum	PLURAL	(≐)e	die Bäume
	-	den Baum		(≐)e	die Bäume
	-(e)	dem Baum(e)		(≐)en	den Bäumen
	-(e)s	des Baumes		(≐)e	der Bäume

To Class II belong:

a. most masculine, feminine, and some common neuter monosyllabic nouns;
b. masculine nouns ending in **-ich, -ig, -ling;**
c. feminine and neuter nouns ending in **-nis** and **-sal;**
d. some neuter nouns of non-German origin with the word accent on the last syllable **(das Pakęt).**

21. Class III Nouns (strong)

(Plural in **-er;** umlaut: wherever possible.)

SINGULAR	-	das Buch	PLURAL	≐er	die Bücher
	-	das Buch		≐er	die Bücher
	-(e)	dem Buch(e)		≐ern	den Büchern
	-(e)s	des Buches		≐er	der Bücher

To Class III belong:

a. a few monosyllabic masculine nouns;
b. most monosyllabic neuter nouns;
c. nouns ending in **-tum;**
d. no feminine nouns.

22. Class IV Nouns (weak)

(Singular and plural in **-en;** umlaut: never.)

SINGULAR	-	der Mensch	PLURAL	-en	die Menschen
	-en	den Menschen		-en	die Menschen
	-en	dem Menschen		-en	den Menschen
	-en	des Menschen		-en	der Menschen

To Class IV belong:

a. masculine nouns ending in **-e** and denoting male beings;

b. masculine nouns of non-German origin with the accent on the last syllable;

c. a few monosyllabic nouns (**der Mensch, der Fürst, der Herr** [**-n** in the singular, **-en** in the plural], and others);

d. feminine nouns of more than one syllable (except **die Mutter, die Tochter**);

e. a few monosyllabic feminines not in Class II (**die Frau, die Tür, die Uhr, die Zeit,** and others);

f. No neuter nouns.

23. A few masculine and neuter nouns have strong forms in the singular and weak forms in the plural; they never have umlaut:

SINGULAR			PLURAL	
-	der Staat		-en	die Staaten
-	den Staat		-en	die Staaten
-(e)	dem Staat(e)		-en	den Staaten
-(e)s	des Staates		-en	der Staaten

24. The following nouns in -en are nouns of Class I, but normally occur without a final n in the nominative singular:

der Name	der Glaube
der Gedanke	der Friede

Herz is declined as follows:

das Herz	die Herzen
das Herz	die Herzen
dem Herzen	den Herzen
des Herzens	der Herzen

25. Prepositions governing the Genitive

anstatt, statt	*instead of*		diesseits	*this side of*
trotz	*in spite of*		jenseits	*that side of*
während	*during*		oberhalb	*above*
wegen	*on account of*		unterhalb	*below*
um . . . willen	*for the sake of*		innerhalb	*within*
			außerhalb	*outside of*

(rare)

infolge	*because of*		mittels	*by means of*
längs	*alongside of*		zwecks	*for the purpose of*

26. Prepositions governing the Dative only

aus	*out of*		nach	*after, to, according to*
außer	*besides, except*		seit	*since, for* (temporal)
bei	*near, at* (*someone's*) *house*		von	*from, by*
mit	*with*		zu	*to*

Also (rare): **gegenüber** (*opposite, toward*), **gemäß** (*according to*), **nebst** (*together with*).

27. Prepositions governing the Accusative only

durch	*through, by means of*		ohne	*without*
für	*for*		um	*around, at* (time)
gegen	*against*		wider	*against*

28. Prepositions governing the Dative (location: wo?) or the Accusative (motion toward, direction: wohin?):

an	*on, at, to*		über	*over, above*
auf	*on, upon*		unter	*under, among*
hinter	*behind*		vor	*before, in front of*
in	*in, into*		zwischen	*between*
neben	*beside, next to*			

29. Inseparable Prefixes

be-, emp-, ent-, er-, ge-, hinter-, miß-, ver-, zer-

30. Separable Prefixes

Adverbs, prepositions, verbs

31. Variable Prefixes

durch-, über-, um-, unter-, voll-, wieder-

Vocabularies

ABBREVIATIONS

acc.	accusative
adj.	adjective
adv.	adverb
arch.	archaic
aux.	auxiliary
conj.	conjunction
coord.	coordinating
dat.	dative
excl.	exclamation
gen.	genitive
impers.	impersonal
interr.	interrogative
intrans.	intransitive
irr.	irregular
mod.	modal
pl.	plural
poss.	possessive
p.p.	past participle
prep.	preposition
pref.	prefix
reg.	regular
rel.	relative
subord.	subordinating
trans.	transitive
w.	with
wk.	weak

For easy identification of words in the text, the number of the lesson in which a word occurs for the first time is given in either brackets or parentheses. Parentheses indicate that a word occurs in the active vocabulary of that lesson; brackets indicate recognition vocabulary, much of which consists of cognates.

Irregular verbs have two parentheses if they have been used in their regular forms before the verbs as such are discussed.

The plural of nouns is indicated as follows: **der Mann,** **⸗er.** The genitive ending is given only for masculine and neuter nouns forming the genitive in **-(e)n** or **-(e)ns: der Advokat, -en, -en; das Herz, -ens, -en.**

Principal parts are listed for strong and irregular verbs. A separable prefix is indicated by a slash: **ab /brennen.**

Words not stressed on the first or root syllable are marked as follows: a dot to indicate a stressed short vowel **(amüsạnt),** a dash to indicate a stressed long vowel or diphthong **(Amerikạner, Polizẹi).**

ab- (*pref.*) off (18)
ab /brennen (*irr. wk.*) to burn down [18]
ab /decken to clear (a table) [20]
der **Abend, –e** evening (7); **den ganzen Abend** *all evening* [7]; **des Abends** *in the evening* [22]
das **Abendbrot, –e** supper (22)
abend: heute abend tonight [22], **gestern abend** last night [11]
abends in the evening (19)
das **Abenteuer, –** adventure [5] (18)
abenteuerlich adventurous [20]
ab /fahren, fährt ab, fuhr ab, ist abgefahren to depart (22)
ab /küssen to cover with kisses [17]
die **Abneigung, –en** aversion [19] (23)
ab /schneiden, schnitt ab, abgeschnitten to cut off [18]
ab /senden, sandte ab, abgesandt (*irr. wk.*) to send off [14]
s. ab /spielen to take place (13)
das **Abteil, –e** compartment (2)
ab /werfen, wirft ab, warf ab, abgeworfen to yield; to throw off (13)
ach! (*excl.*) oh! [10]
acht eight (8)
acht: s. in acht nehmen (vor *w. dat.*), **nimmt s. in acht, nahm s. in acht, s. in acht genommen** to beware (of) (21)
achtzehn eighteen [18]
das **Adjektiv, –e** adjective [16]
der **Admirạl, –e** admiral [21]

die **Adrẹsse, –n** address (3)
der **Advokạt, –en, –en** (*arch.*) lawyer [14]
die **Affạire, –n** affair [13]
der **Affe, –n, –n** ape, monkey (5)
ähnlich similar (22)
die **Ahnung, –en** inkling (1); **keine Ahnung** no idea (1)
der **Akkusativ, –e** accusative [9]
die **Akten** (*pl.*) files, documents [24]
aktịv active [13]
akzeptierẹn to accept [25]
die **Algebra** algebra [10]
alle (*pl.*) all (4); **vor allem** above all, especially (6); **alles** all (1)
allẹin (*adj.*) alone [6]; (*conj.*) yet [20]
allerdings to be sure (7)
als (*prep.*) as (a) (7); (*after comparative and* **anders**) than [12]; (*conj.*) when [11]; **als ob** as if [24]
also therefore, then [6]; that is [21]; (*followed by comma*) well then (1)
alt old [15]
der **Alte, –n, –n** the old man (3); **ein Alter** an old man (3)
das **Alter, –** age (3); old age [20]
der **Amerikạner, –** American [9]
amerikạnisch American [23]
das **Amt, ⸗er** office, department [5]
amüsạnt amusing [13]
s. (gut) amüsierẹn to have a good time [11]
an- (*pref.*) on (18)

der **Anachronismus** anachronism [22]
an/bieten, bot an, angeboten to offer
(somebody something) (23)
an/binden, band an, angebunden to tie
on [18]
an/brennen, brannte an, angebrannt (*irr.
wk.*) to burn (*of food*) [14]
ander- other, else (2); **etwas anderes**
something else [7] (12); **unter anderem** among other things (25)
ändern to change (6)
anders different(ly) (1); **anders als** other
than (12)
anderthalb one and a half [21]
die **Anekdote, –n** anecdote [10]
an/erkennen, erkannte an, anerkannt
(*irr. wk.*) to recognize, accept [14]
an/fallen, fällt an, fiel an, angefallen to
attack (18)
der **Anfang, ⸗e** beginning (22)
an/fangen, fängt an, fing an, angefangen
to begin (13)
angeblich supposedly (25)
angenehm pleasant (23)
angesehen respected (21)
der **Angestellte, –n, –n** employee (16)
die **Angewohnheit, –en** habit [19]
an/greifen, griff an, angegriffen to attack (24)
die **Angst, ⸗e** fear (3); **Angst haben vor** to
be afraid of (3)
an/kommen, kam an, ist angekommen to
arrive (15); **ankommen auf** (*w. acc.*)
to matter (18)
an/passen to adapt (21)
an/reden to address (13)
an/regen to stimulate (13)
**an/schlagen, schlägt an, schlug an, ange-
schlagen** to cut into (24)
anstatt . . . zu instead of (25)
anstrengend strenuous (15)
der **Anthropologe, –n, –n** anthropologist [14]
der **Antipode, –n, –n** antipode [8]
die **Antwort, –en** answer (3)
antworten (**auf** *w. acc.*) to answer (to)
(1)
an/wenden, wandte an, angewandt (*irr.
wk.*) to use, apply [14]
der **Anzug, ⸗e** suit [17]
der **Apfel, ⸗** apple [15]
der **Aphorismus, Aphorismen** aphorism [12]
der **Apparat, –e** apparatus [12]
die **Arbeit, –en** work (10); **bei der Arbeit** at
work [10]
arbeiten to work (7)
die **Architektur, –en** architecture [19]
ärgern to annoy [25]; **s. ärgern** to get
angry (11)

die **Arie, –n** aria [17]
arm poor
der **Arm, –e** arm [13]
die **Armbanduhr, –en** wrist watch (22)
die **Armee, –n** army [2]
arrogant arrogant [19]
die **Art, –en** kind, manner (16); **aller Art** of
all kinds (25)
der **Arzt, ⸗e** doctor, physician (3)
(das) **Aschenbrötel** Cinderella [20]
der **Aschenhaufen, –** pile of ashes [20]
der **Aschermittwoch, –e** Ash Wednesday [22]
ästhetisch aesthetic, very refined [9]
der **Astronaut, –en, –en** astronaut [12]
der **Astronom, –en, –en** astronomer [10]
die **Astronomie** astronomy [12]
astronomisch astronomical [10]
das **Atom, –e** atom [5]
auch also (1); **auch wenn** (*conj.*) even
though (13)
die **Audienz, –en** audience (*in the sense of:*
reception) [23]
auf . . . zu toward [20]
auf/bringen, brachte auf, aufgebracht
(*irr. wk.*) to excite, upset (17)
auffallend striking (11)
auf/fordern to exhort (15)
**auf/fressen, frißt auf, fraß auf, aufge-
fressen** to eat up [20]
auf/führen to perform (17)
die **Aufführung, –en** performance (17)
die **Aufgabe, –n** lesson (1); task (23)
auf/greifen, griff auf, aufgegriffen to
pick up [25]
auf/hängen to hang [24]
auf/heben, hob auf, aufgehoben to pick
up [17]
die **Aufklärung** Enlightenment [19]
auf/kommen, kam auf, ist aufgekommen
to come up [24]
die **Auflage, –n** edition [19] (21)
die **Aufmerksamkeit** attention (11)
**auf/nehmen, nimmt auf, nahm auf, aufge-
nommen** to receive [18]
auf/regen to get excited (23)
auf/reißen, riß auf, aufgerissen to tear
(throw) open [23]
**auf/schreiben, schrieb auf, aufgeschrie-
ben** to write down [23]
auf/stehen, stand auf, ist aufgestanden
to get up [17]
auf/wachen to wake up (22)
das **Auge, –n** eye (1)
der **Augenblick, –e** moment (2); **einen Augenblick** (for) a moment (9)
augenscheinlich apparently (21)
der **August** August [22]

aus (*prep. w. dat.*) from, out of [15]; **aus sein** to be over [22]
aus/arbeiten to work out [16]
aus/brechen, bricht aus, brach aus, ist ausgebrochen to break out [24]
aus/denken, dachte aus, ausgedacht (*irr. wk.*) to think up [14]
der **Ausdruck, ⸗e** expression [14]
s. aus/drücken to express oneself [13]
s. auseinander/setzen (mit) to come to grips with (25)
der **Ausflug, ⸗e** excursion (15)
aus/gehen, ging aus, ist ausgegangen to go out [22]
ausgezeichnet excellent (15)
aus/liefern to deliver (13)
aus/rufen, rief aus, ausgerufen to call out [22]
aus/sehen, sieht aus, sah aus, ausgesehen to look (like) (18) [24]
außer (*prep. w. gen.*) besides, except for [7]
außerdem besides [20]
äußerst extremely (16)
ausstehen können to be able to stand [19]
die **Auster, –n** oyster [2]
aus/wandern to emigrate [13]
das **Auto, –s** auto, car [12]
die **Autobiographie, –n** autobiography (7)
der **Autobus, –se** bus [22]
der **Autor, Autoren** author [2]
die **Authorität, –en** authority [13]
die **Axt, ⸗e** axe [18]

backen, backte (buk), gebacken to bake (23)
der **Bahnhof, ⸗e** railroad station (15)
bald soon (4)
der **Balkon, –e** balcony [13]
der **Ball, ⸗e** ball [2]
das **Ballett, –e** ballet [15]
der **Ballon, –s** balloon [12]
der **Band, ⸗e** volume (of books) (15)
die **Bank, ⸗e** bench (14)
die **Bank, –en** bank [14]
der **Bär, –en** bear (18)
die **Barkarole, –n** barcarole [18]
der **Baron, –e** baron [9]
der **Bart, ⸗e** beard (16)
der **Bauch, ⸗e** stomach, belly (16)
der **Bauer, –s** *or* **–n, –n** peasant [5], farmer (14)
der **Baum, ⸗e** tree (24)
beabsichtigen to intend (6)
der **Beamte, –n, –n (ein Beamter)** official, civil servant (16)
beantworten to answer (3)
bearbeiten to rework, revise (21)

die **Bearbeitung, –en** adaptation (21)
bedenken, bedachte, bedacht (*irr. wk.*) to reflect (14); **das Bedenken** reflection (14); **s. bedenken** to hesitate, ponder (14)
bedeuten to mean (14)
bedeutend significant, important, distinguished (13)
die **Bedeutung, –en** significance, meaning (22)
s. beeilen to hurry (up) [11]
beenden to finish (something) (17)
der **Befehl, –e** order, command (5)
befehlen, befiehlt, befahl, befohlen to order, command (24)
s. befinden, befand s., s. befunden to be, to feel (11)
befördern to promote (16)
befreien to free (23)
s. begeben, begibt s., begab s., s. begeben to go (11)
s. begegnen (*w. sein*) to meet (11)
begeistert enthusiastic(ally) (8)
der **Beginn** beginning [13]; **zu Beginn** at the beginning (11)
beginnen, begann, begonnen to begin (7)
begraben, begräbt, begrub, begraben to bury (17)
das **Begräbnis, –se** funeral (6)
begrüßen to greet (11)
behandeln to treat [20]
die **Behandlung, –en** treatment [13] (17)
behaupten to claim, assert (3)
bei (*prep. w. dat.*) at the house of, with [9]
bei/bringen, brachte bei, beigebracht (*irr. wk.*) to teach [14]
beide, beides both (1); **die beiden** the two [11]
beinahe almost (17)
beiseite aside [19]
das **Beispiel, –e** example (6); **zum Beispiel** for example (6)
bei/tragen, trägt bei, trug bei, beigetragen to contribute (25)
bei/wohnen (*w. dat.*) to attend [19]
bekannt well known (7); **bekannt sein mit** to be familiar with [14]
der **Bekannte, –n, –n** acquaintance (6)
bekannt/machen to announce (17)
bekennen (*irr. wk.*) to confess [14]; **s. bekennen zu** to profess, espouse [14]
bekommen, bekam, bekommen to get, receive (5, 7)
beladen, belädt, belud, beladen to load (up) (25)
belagern to besiege, lay siege to (20)
beleben to enliven (12)

belesen well read (21)
beliebt popular (14)
die **Beliebtheit** popularity [18]
bemerken to notice (10)
die **Bemerkung, –en** remark [14]
s. **bemühen** to make an effort, attempt (21)
benennen (*irr. wk.*) to name [25]
das **Benzin** gasoline [12]
beobachten to observe (25)
die **Beobachtung, –en** observation (12)
bereit ready [19]
bereits already (7)
der **Berg, –e** mountain (5)
berichten to report (23)
der **Beruf, –e** profession (20)
beruhen (auf *w. dat.*) to rest (on) (25)
berühmt famous (8)
besagen to mean, signify (17)
beschäftigen to occupy (one's time) (7); s. **beschäftigen mit** to occupy oneself with [12]
beschreiben, beschrieb, beschrieben to describe (12)
die **Beschreibung, –en** description (12)
besitzen, besaß, besessen to possess, own (12)
der **Besitzer, –** owner (12)
besonders especially (4)
besser better [10]
best– best [12]
die **Bestätigung, –en** confirmation (8)
bestehen, bestand, bestanden (aus) to consist of (19)
besteigen, bestieg, bestiegen to climb on; to mount (4)
bestimmen to determine (19)
bestimmt certainly, definitely (10)
der **Besuch, –e (bei)** visit (to, with) (3)
besuchen to visit (1); to attend [15]
betrachten to look at, watch (2); to view [19]
die **Betrachtung, –en** reflection [12]
betrügen, betrog, betrogen to deceive [7] (8)
das **Bett, –en** bed [14]; **zu Bett** to bed [19]
die **Beute** booty (20)
bewältigen to master (25)
s. **bewegen** to move [11]
der **Beweis, –e** proof (15); **zum Beweis** as proof (15)
beweisen, bewies, bewiesen to prove (15)
bewundern to admire (8)
die **Bewunderung** admiration (8)
bewußt conscious (23)
das **Bewußtsein** consciousness (23)
bezahlen to pay (14)
die **Bezahlung, –en** pay(ment) (16)

bezeichnen to characterize (11)
bezeugen to attest (19)
die **Bibliothek, –en** library (1)
biegen, bog, gebogen to bend (22)
die **Biene, –n** bee [14] (18)
das **Bier, –e** beer [6]
bieten, bot, geboten to offer (23)
das **Bild, –er** picture (20)
billig cheap (16)
binden, band, gebunden to bind (18)
die **Biologie** biology (1)
die **Biologieklasse, –n** biology class (1)
die **Birne, –n** pear (14)
bis (*prep.*) until [7] (11) (*usually in comb. with other prepositions:* **bis zu** *etc.*); **bis auf** down to [18]
bisher until now (19)
bist (*see:* **sein**) [1]
die **Bitte, –n** request (14)
bitte! please! (3)
bitten, bat, gebeten (um) to ask for (a favor) (3, 12)
bitter bitter [9]
das **Blatt, ⸗er** sheet [20]; leaf (25)
blau blue (14)
das **Blech, –e** tin [15]
die **Blechtrommel, –n** tin drum [15]
bleiben, blieb, ist geblieben to remain (5, 7)
der **Bleistift, –e** pencil (1)
der **Blitzableiter, –** lightning rod [12]
blitzen to be lightening [11]
die **Blume, –n** flower (13)
das **Blumenkind, –er** flower child [13]
das **Blut** blood [9]
die **Bohne, –n** bean (18)
Bord: an Bord aboard [21]
böse angry (2); evil [15]
Bostoner (*adj.*) of Boston, Boston [18]
die **Botanik** botany [25]
der **Bote, –n, –n** messenger (5)
braten, brät, briet, gebraten to roast (14)
der **Braten, –** roast [19]
brauchen to need (12); to use [18]
der **Bräutigam, –e** fiancé (6)
brav kind [17]
brechen, bricht, brach, gebrochen to break (7)
breit broad, wide, large (13)
brennen, brannte, gebrannt (*irr. wk.*) to burn (14)
der **Brief, –e** letter [7] (15)
bringen, brachte, gebracht (*irr. wk.*) to bring (14)
der **Bruder, ⸗** brother [11]
das **Buch, ⸗er** book [2] (7)
die **Bühne, –n** stage [18] (21)
das **Bündel, –** bundle [10]

der **Bürger,** – citizen (12)
der **Bürgermeister,** – mayor (4)
das **Büro,** –s bureau, office [10]
   bürsten to brush [11]
die **Butter** butter [2]

das **Café,** –s Café [13] (19)
das **Chaos** chaos [12]
(das) **China** China [18]
   chinesisch Chinese [18]
der **Chor,** ⸗e chorus, choir [17]
   christlich Christian [8]

   da (*adv.*) there (4); (*subord. conj.*) since
      [13]
   dabei in so doing [16]
   dagegen on the other hand (11)
   daher therefore (6)
   damalig (*adj.*) at (of) that time (20)
   damals (*adv.*) at that time (8)
die **Dame,** –n lady (2); **meine Damen!** la-
      dies! (2)
   damit (*subord. conj.*) so that (12)
das **Dampfschiff,** –e steamship [23]
(das) **Dänemark** Denmark [14]
   danke (schön)! thanks (very much)! (1)
   danken (*w. dat.*) to thank (4); to owe
      [21]
   dann then (2)
   darauf thereupon [16]
   daß (*subord. conj.*) that (5)
der **Dativ,** –e dative [9]
die **Dauer** duration (22)
   dein, deine, dein your (1)
der **Demokrat,** –en democrat [5]
   demokratisch democratic [9]
   demonstrieren to demonstrate [12]
   denken, dachte, gedacht (*irr. wk.*) **an** (*w.*
      acc.) to think (of) (5, 14); **s. denken**
      to imagine [11]
   denn (*coord. conj.*) for, because (2); (*in*
      a question, untranslated) [10] (*or*
      rendered by) but [16]; **denn doch** after
      all [23]
   derselbe, dieselbe, dasselbe the same (1)
   deshalb therefore [9]
   deswegen for that reason (12)
die **Detektivgeschichte,** –n detective story
      [10]
   deutsch German [11]; **auf deutsch** in
      German [9]
(das) **Deutsch** German (*language*) (1)
der **Deutsche,** –n, –n (the) German [11]
(das) **Deutschland** Germany (4)
die **Deutschstunde,** –n German lesson (class)
      (1)
der **Diamant,** –en diamond (5)
der **Dichter,** – poet (6)

die **Dichterin,** –nen poetess [11]
die **Dichtung,** –en work of fiction (25)
   dick fat (2)
der **Diener,** – servant (4)
   diesmal this time (4)
der **Diktator, Diktatoren** dictator [14]
das **Ding,** –e thing [25]
   dir (*dat.*) (to) you (1)
   direkt direct(ly) [10]
der **Direktor, Direktoren** director [2]
der **Dirigent,** –en, –en conductor (17)
   diskutieren to discuss [5] (6)
die **Dissertation,** –en dissertation [25]
die **Disziplin** discipline [25]
   doch yet (11); after all (14); anyway
      [17]; (*after a negative question*) yes,
      indeed (5); (*in a question: emphasis*)
      don't you? [19]
   dogmatisch dogmatic [12]
der **Doktor, Doktoren** doctor, physician
      [16]; **Herr Doktor!** Doctor! [16]
das **Dokument,** –e document [15]
die **Donau** Danube [10]
   donnern to thunder [11]
   Donnerwetter! Gosh! (1)
das **Dorf,** ⸗er village (5)
   dort there (6); **dort, wo,** where (6)
das **Drama, Dramen** play, drama (6)
der **Dramatiker,** – dramatist [11]
   dramatisch dramatic [15]
   drei three (2)
   dreißig thirty [20]; **die dreißiger Jahre**
      the thirties [21]
   dreiviertel three quarters [22]
   dreizehn thirteen [13]
   dringen, drang, ist gedrungen to push,
      penetrate (20)
   dritt- third [15]
   drohen to threaten (17)
   duften to smell [21]
der **Dukat,** –en ducate (*old gold coin*) [24]
   dulden to tolerate (21)
   dumm dumb, stupid (1)
   dummerweise stupidly enough [16]
die **Dummheit,** –en stupidity (14)
der **Dummkopf,** ⸗e dumbbell, blockhead
      (14)
   dunkel dark (22)
   dünn thin (2)
   durch (*prep. w. acc.*) through [15]
   durch/brennen, brannte durch, durchge-
      brannt (*irr. wk.*) to run away [14]
   durchdringen, durchdrang, durchdrungen
      to penetrate (10)
   durch/fallen, fällt durch, fiel durch, ist
      durchgefallen to fail, "flunk" (13)
   s. durch/setzen (gegen) to prevail (over)
      (25)

dürfen, darf, durfte, gedurft (*modal aux.*) to be permitted to (17)

der **Durst** thirst (23); **unter Durst leiden** to suffer from thirst (23)

das **Dutzend, –e** dozen (1); **ein Dutzend Bleistifte** a dozen pencils (1)

eben just now (1)

ebenso . . . wie just as . . . as (4)

die **Ecke, –n** corner (2)

ehe (*subord. conj.*) before [20]

die **Ehe, –n** marriage, wedlock (6)

die **Ehre, –n** honor (5)

der **Ehrgeiz** ambition [18]

ehrlich honest (5)

das **Ei, –er** egg (22)

die **Eifersucht** jealousy (7)

eigen own (*adj.*) (7); of one's own [15]

eigentlich anyway, really, properly speaking (3)

eigentümlich strange (23)

s. eignen (für, zu) to be suited (for) (20)

ein, eine, ein a, an (1); **ein(s)** one (1)

einander one another (1)

ein/dringen, drang ein, ist eingedrungen to enter into, penetrate into (12)

der **Eindruck, ⁼e** impression (5)

einfach simple, simply (2)

ein/fallen, fällt ein, fiel ein, ist eingefallen (in *w. acc.*) to invade (24); (*impers.*) to occur to [13]

der **Einfluß, Einflüsse** influence (21)

ein/führen to introduce (21)

die **Einheit, –en** unity, unit (25)

einig- some (14); **einige Zeit** for some time [15]; **einige** (*pl.*) a few (3)

das **Einkommen, –** income [5]

ein/laden, lädt ein, lud ein, eingeladen to invite (15)

die **Einladung, –en** invitation (15)

einmal once (3); **nicht einmal** not even (5); **noch einmal** once more (6)

ein/ordnen to arrange (25)

die **Einrichtung, –en** setup, provision, institution [19]

ein/schlafen, schläft ein, schlief ein, ist eingeschlafen to go to sleep (12)

ein/sehen, sieht ein, sah ein, eingesehen to come to realize, understand (14)

einst some day (in the future) (9)

ein/studieren to rehearse (21)

ein/wenden, wandte ein, eingewandt (*irr. wk.*) to object, interject, argue (14)

der **Einwohner, –** inhabitant (20)

einzeln single (individual) (15)

einzig single (only) (5)

das **Eisen** iron (6)

die **Eisenbahn, –en** railroad (2)

eisern (of) iron (9)

die **Eitelkeit, –en** vanity (7)

die **Elbe** Elbe River [24]

elegant elegant (3)

elektrisch electrical [22]

elektrochemisch electrochemical [12]

elf eleven (7)

die **Eltern** (*pl.*) parents (3)

die **Emigration, –en** emigration [11]

empfehlen, empfiehlt, empfahl, empfohlen to recommend (23)

der **Empfehlungsbrief, –e** letter of recommendation [23]

empört outraged (2)

das **Ende, –n** end (5); **am Ende** in the end [20]; **zu Ende gehen** to come to an end (19)

enden to end [12]

endlich in the end, finally (2)

die **Energie, –n** energy [17]

s. engagieren to get involved [15]

der **Engel, –** angel (9)

(das) **England** England [12]

der **Engländer, –** Englishman [7]

die **Engländerin, –nen** English woman [23]

englisch English [12]; (**das**) **Englisch(e)** English (language) [7]

der **Enkel, –** grandchild (9)

entdecken to discover (21)

entfliehen, entfloh, ist entflohen to escape (24)

entgegen/lächeln to smile at [13]

enthalten, enthält, enthielt, enthalten to contain (15)

enthusiastisch enthusiastic [21]

entlang: an . . . entlang along [11]

s. entscheiden, entschied s., s. entschieden to decide (11); **sich entscheiden für** to decide in favor of [15]

entscheidend decisive (11); **das Entscheidende** the decisive thing (11)

die **Entscheidung, –en** decision (14)

der **Entschluß, Entschlüsse** decision (19); **einen Entschluß fassen** to make a decision (19)

entschuldigen to excuse (1); **s. entschuldigen** to apologize [11] (23)

entstehen, entstand, ist entstanden to originate, be caused (12); to be created [15]

entweder . . . oder (*conj.*) either . . . or [20]

entwickeln to develop (19)

die **Entwicklung, –en** development [5] (20)

episch epic (*adj.*) [15]; **das Epische** the epic, fiction [15]

die **Episode, –n** episode [13]

erben to inherit (22)

die **Erde** earth (9); **auf Erden** (*arch.*) on earth (9)

erfahren, erfährt, erfuhr, erfahren to find out, experience (19)

die **Erfahrung, –en** experience (*from which one learns*) (12)

erfinden, erfand, erfunden to invent (18)

der **Erfinder, –** inventor (10)

die **Erfindung, –en** invention (22)

der **Erfolg, –e** success (4)

erfolglos unsuccessful, without success (24)

s. erfreuen (*w. gen.*) to enjoy (18)

erfreut pleased (3)

erfüllen to fulfill (5)

ergreifen, ergriff, ergriffen to seize (7)

erhalten to receive (10)

erinnern to remind (25); **s. erinnern (an** *w. acc.*) to remember [11] (13)

s. erkälten to catch a cold [11]

erkennen, erkannte, erkannt (*irr. wk.*) **an** (*w. dat.*) to recognize (from) [14] (17)

erklären to declare (2); to explain (8); **erklären für** to declare to be (8)

s. erkundigen to enquire [11]

erlauben to permit [13]

die **Erlaubnis** permission, permit (12)

erleben to experience, live to see [18]

das **Erlebnis, –se** experience (*as a chance happening*) (12)

erleichtern to relieve (15)

erleiden, erlitt, erlitten to suffer (24)

erlernen (*trans.*) to learn [15]

ermorden to kill [20]

ernennen, ernannte, ernannt (*irr. wk.*) to name, elect [14]

ernst serious (21)

ernsthaft serious(-minded) [18]

erobern to conquer (9)

erörtern to discuss (24)

erreichen to reach (4)

erscheinen, erschien, ist erschienen to appear (16)

die **Erscheinung, –en** appearance (13)

erschrecken, erschrak, ist erschrocken to be shocked, frightened, startled (12)

ersetzen to replace (21)

erst first (6); (*as adv. of time*) only (11)

erstaunlich amazing(ly), astonishing(ly) [17] (21)

erstaunt surprised (3)

erstens in the first place [21]

ersticken to suffocate (2)

ertragen, erträgt, ertrug, ertragen to bear, tolerate (8); **nicht ertragen** not to be able to bear (8)

erwachen to wake up [12]

erwarten to await, expect [8]

erwidern to answer [14]

erzählen to tell [4]

die **Erzählung, –en** story, tale [16]

der **Erzieher, –** educator, pedagogue (6)

der **Essay, –s** essay [9]

essen, ißt, aß, gegessen to eat (3, 19)

das **Essen, –** dinner, lunch [7], food [14]; **zum Essen** for dinner (lunch) [14]

etwa for instance (11)

etwas something (1), somewhat, a little [16]; **etwas anderes** something else [7] (19); **noch etwas** something else [21]

die **Eule, –n** owl [14]

(das) **Europa** Europe [9]

der **Europäer, –** (the) European [19]

europäisch European [18]

die **Evolutionstheorie, –n** theory of evolution [25]

die **Ewigkeit** eternity [19]

exakt exact (6)

das **Examen, –** exam(ination) [9]

exerzieren to exercise, practice [17]

das **Exil, –e** exile [9]

existieren to exist [24]

die **Exotik** exoticism [13]

exotisch exotic [13]

das **Experiment, –e** experiment [12]

experimentieren to experiment [10]

explodieren to explode [12]

expressionistisch expressionist [13]

extravagant extravagant [17]

der **Fächer, –** fan [14]

die **Fahne, –n** flag (13)

fahren, fährt, fuhr, ist gefahren to travel [2] (9); (*of trains*) to depart [22]

die **Fahrt, –en** trip (9)

der **Fall, ⸗e** case (6)

fallen, fällt, fiel, ist gefallen to fall (10)

falsch wrong, incorrect (16)

die **Familie, –n** family [2] (3)

fangen, fängt, fing, ist gefangen to catch, capture (15)

die **Farbe, –n** color (14)

die **Farbenlehre, –n** theory of colors [25]

fassen to grasp (19)

fast almost (8)

faszinieren to fascinate [10]

faul lazy, rotten [15]

die **Feder, –n** pen (9)

fehlen to be lacking (13); **ihren Gedichten fehlt** her poems are lacking in (13); **das Fehlen** absence [25]

der **Feiertag, –e** holiday (22)

fein fine; delicately [6]

der **Feind, –e** enemy (4)

feindlich hostile, enemy (*adj.*) (24)

das **Feld, –er** field [14]
der **Feldherr, –n, –en** general (20)
der **Feldzug, ≃e** campaign (18)
das **Fenster, –** window (2)
die **Ferien** (*pl.*) vacation [10] (22)
    fern distant (5); **in der Ferne** from afar
    [24]
das **Fernrohr, –e** telescope (10)
    fertig ready, finished (15)
    fest firm(ly) (25); **fest-** (*pref.*) on, fast
    (18)
das **Fest, –e** festival, celebration, party (5)
    fest/binden, band fest, festgebunden to
    attach to; to fasten (18)
das **Feuer, –** fire (14)
die **Figur, –en** figure [17]
der **Finanzminister, –** minister (secretary) of
    finance [6]
    finden, fand, gefunden to find (1, 8); **s.**
    finden to be found; to be [25]
der **Finger, –** finger [2]
die **Firma, Firmen** firm, company [2]
der **Fisch, –e** fish [14]
    fischen to fish [15]
die **Flasche, –n** bottle (18)
der **Fleiß** diligence, industriousness (7)
    fleißig diligent, industrious (7)
    fliegen, flog, ist geflogen to fly (12)
    fliehen, floh, ist geflohen to flee (16)
    fließen, floß, ist geflossen to flow (16)
das **Flirten** flirting, flirtation [13]
das **Flugzeug, –e** airplane (15)
    fluktuieren to fluctuate [13]
    flüstern to whisper [19]
die **Folge, –n** consequence (21)
    folgen to follow [6] (15); **folgendes** the
    following [7]
    folgendermaßen as follows (18)
    folglich consequently [11]
die **Form, –en** form [21]
die **Formel, –n** formula; equation [10]
    formell formal [11]
der **Fortschritt, –e** progress [13]
die **Fotografie, –n** photograph [8]
die **Frage, –n** question (3); **eine Frage stellen**
    to ask a question (3)
    fragen (nach) to ask (about) (2); to ask
    for [17]; **s. fragen** to ask oneself [11];
    to be a question [20]
(das) **Frankreich** France (9)
(das) **Französisch** French (language) (9)
die **Frau, –en** wife, woman (4)
das **Frauenzimmer, –** woman, female(s) (4)
das **Fräulein, –** miss, young lady (5)
    frech insolent, "fresh" (23)
die **Frechheit, –en** insolence (23)
    frei free [9]
die **Freiheit, –en** freedom (9)

die **Freikarte, –n** free ticket [16]
    freilich to be sure, however (17)
    fremd foreign, strange (16)
die **Fremdsprache, –n** foreign language [14]
    fressen, frißt, fraß, gefressen to eat (*of*
    animals) (20)
die **Freude, –n** joy [20]
    s. freuen to be glad, happy (11); **s.**
    freuen auf (*w. acc.*) to look forward
    to [11]; **sich freuen über** (*w. acc.*) to
    be happy about [11], enjoy [20]; **es**
    freut mich it pleases me, I am glad
    [11]
der **Freund, –e** friend (1); **die Freundin, –nen**
    girl friend (5)
    freundlich (*adv.*) in a friendly manner
    (1)
die **Freundschaft, –en** friendship [7]
der **Friede(n)** peace (5)
    frieren, fror, gefroren to freeze (2); **mich**
    friert I am cold [11]
    s. frisieren (auf *w. acc.*) to do one's hair
    (in the manner of) (11)
die **Frisur, –en** hairdo [6]
die **Frucht, ≃e** fruit (13)
    früh early (7)
    früher earlier (10)
der **Frühling, –e** spring (22)
die **Frühromantik** Early Romanticism [21]
das **Frühstück, –e** breakfast (19)
    fühlen to feel (15)
    führen to lead (4)
    füllen to fill (12)
    fünf five [2]
    fünfzehn fifteen [15]
    fünfzig fifty [7]
    für (*prep. w. acc.*) for (2)
die **Furcht** fear (24)
    furchtbar terrible (2)
    fürchten to fear (24); to be afraid [11]
der **Fürst, –en, –en** (ruling) prince (24)
der **Fuß, ≃e** foot [11]
der **Fußboden, ≃** floor [17]
das **Futter** fodder [2]

    ganz (*adj.*) whole (3); **in ganz Europa** in
    all of Europe [9]; (*adv.*) quite (2),
    entirely [15], completely [21]; **das**
    Ganze the whole [21]
    gar even (19)
    gar nicht not at all (6)
der **Garten, ≃** garden [2]
die **Gartentür, –en** garden door [11]
das **Gas, –e** gas [12]
der **Gast, ≃e** guest (7)
der **Gastgeber, –** host (15)
die **Gattung, –en** genre (25)
    gebären, gebiert, gebar, geboren to give

birth to (9); **geboren werden** to be born (9); **geboren sein** to be born [13]

das **Gebäude, –** building [5]

geben, gibt, gab, gegeben to give (7); (*in the theater*) to play [22]; **Was gibt's?** What's the matter? (11)

das **Gebiet, –e** realm, region (19)

geboren born

die **Geburt, –en** birth (10)

die **Geburtsstadt, ⸗e** native city (10)

der **Geburtstag, –e** birthday [21]

der **Gedanke, –ns, –n** thought (6)

gedenken (*w. gen.*) to remember (25)

das **Gedicht, –e** poem (7)

die **Geduld** patience (10)

geduldig patient (10)

geeignet suited (for) (20)

die **Gefahr, –en** danger [13]

gefallen, gefällt, gefiel, gefallen (*impers.*) to please (7); **was ihr gefiel** what she liked [11]); **s. gefallen lassen (ä, ie, a)** to put up with (17)

das **Gefängnis, –se** prison (17)

das **Gefühl, –e** feeling (11)

gegen (*prep. w. acc.*) against (6)

die **Gegend, –en** region (14)

der **Gegensatz, ⸗e** opposite, contrast (11)

der **Gegenstand, ⸗e** object [5]

gegenüber (*w. dat.*) toward [9]

die **Gegenwart** presence, present (tense) (19)

das **Geheimnis, –se** secret (5)

gehen, ging, ist gegangen to go on foot; to walk (1, 7); to work, do, suit [11]; **wie geht es Ihnen?** how are you? [8]; **gut gehen** (*impers.*) to feel well [11]; **es geht** it can be done (16); (*of trains, etc.*) to leave [22]

das **Gehör** hearing [17]

gehören (*w. dat. or* **zu**) to belong to (10)

die **Geige, –n** violin (10)

der **Geist, –er** mind, spirit, intellect [5] (7)

der **Geisteskranke, –n, –n** mental patient [15]

die **Geisteskrankheit, –en** mental illness (7)

die **Geistesstörung, –en** mental disturbance [23]

geistig intellectual, spiritual (25)

das **Geld, –er** money [6] (10)

die **Gelegenheit, –en** opportunity, occasion (11)

gelingen, gelang, ist gelungen (*impers.*) to succeed (11); **es gelingt mir** I succeed (11)

gelten, gilt, galt, gegolten (als) to be considered (as) (25)

gemeinsam common (24)

gemütlich comfortable [15]

genau exact (3)

die **Genauigkeit** exactness [19]

genauso (. . . wie) just as (. . . as) [14]

der **General, ⸗e** general (7)

die **Generation, –en** generation [12]

das **Genie, –s** genius (7)

genießen, genoß, genossen to enjoy (8)

genug enough [3] (10)

genügen (*w. dat.*) to satisfy (21)

die **Geologie** geology [25]

die **Geometrie** geometry [10]

gerade just now (4); just then [13]; **gerade heute** of all days today; **gerade er** he of all people (22)

gerecht just (25); **(jemandem) gerecht werden** to do justice to (25)

gering slight, small (12); **der, die, das geringste** the least (16)

der **Germane, –n, –n** Teuton (24)

(das) **Germanien** Germany [24]

gern(e) gladly; (*combined with a verb*) to like to (3); to be happy to (8); **gern haben (mögen)** to like, be fond of [11]

der **Gesandte, –n, –n** ambassador [23]

das **Geschäft, –e** business (8), shop (11)

geschehen, geschieht, geschah, ist geschehen (*impers.*) to happen (10)

das **Geschenk, –e** present [11]

die **Geschichte, –n** history; story (4); affair (10)

geschichtlich historical (24)

der **Geschmack, ⸗er** taste (7)

die **Geschwindigkeit, –en** speed [16]

die **Geschwister** (*pl.*) brothers and sisters (19)

das **Gesetz, –e** law (19)

das **Gesicht, –er** face; vision (25)

der **Gesichtssinn, –e** visual sense [25]

das **Gespräch, –e** conversation (19)

die **Gestalt, –en** figure [5]

gestern yesterday [11]; **gestern abend** last night [11]; **gestern nachmittag** yesterday afternoon [22]

gesund healthy, well (3)

die **Gesundheit** health (5)

gewinnen, gewann, gewonnen (an) to win (15), obtain [18], gain (in) [22]

gewiß certainly (11)

das **Gewitter, –** (thunder)storm (3)

s. gewöhnen (an *w. acc.***)** to get used to, accustom oneself to (12)

gewöhnlich ordinary, ordinarily (18)

gewöhnt sein (an) to be accustomed (to) (12)

es gibt there is, are [7]; **Was gibt's?** What is the matter? (11)

gießen, goß, gegossen to pour (23)

glänzen to glitter [11]

das **Glas, ⸗er** glass [6]

glatt smooth, slippery [17]
glauben to believe (1)
der Glaube(n) belief [9]
gleich in a minute, presently (3); equal
  even(ly) (9); same [15]; right away
  (16)
gleichblökend bleating the same way (9)
gleichgeschoren shorn the same way [9]
gleichzeitig at the same time (15)
gleiten, glitt, geglitten to slide (22)
glimmen, glomm, geglommen to glow
  (20)
die Glocke, –n bell (13), clock [22]
das Glück happiness (5); good luck [7];
  Glück haben to be lucky (11)
glücklich happy (8)
glücklicherweise fortunately [16]
der Goetheknochen, – Goethe bone [25]
der Goethit, –e Goethite [25]
das Gold gold (5)
golden golden [22]
der Gott, =er God (2)
die Gottlosigkeit godlessness, atheism [9]
Gottseidank thank goodness [22]
graben, gräbt, grub, gegraben to dig (13)
die Grammatik, –en grammar [15]
die Graphik, –en graphics [15]
graphisch graphic [15]
das Gras, =er grass [14]
grausam cruel (21)
die Grenze, –n limit, boundary, frontier (8)
grenzenlos boundless(ly), immensely (8)
der Grieche, –n, –n Greek [15]
groß great (7)
die Großmacht, =e big (world) power [20]
die Großmutter, = grandmother (7)
der Großvater, = grandfather [22]
grün green (14)
der Grund, =e ground, reason (15); ground-
  work [25]; aus diesem Grunde for this
  reason [19]; im Grunde essentially,
  basically (25)
gründen to found (8)
grundlos groundless [24]
grüßen to greet, send regards to (4)
gut good (1); well (9)

das Haar, –e hair [11]
der Hafen, = harbor, port (6)
halb half [6]
die Hälfte, –n half (21)
der Hals, =e neck (13)
halten, hält, hielt, gehalten to hold (7);
  to keep (7); s. halten für to consider
  oneself (to be) [9] (11); halten von to
  think of [9]
die Hand, =e hand [2] (5)

handeln to act [16]; s. handeln um to
  deal with, concern (24)
das Handwerk, –e craft (15)
hängen, hing, gehangen to hang (be
  hanging); (as trans. verb, reg.) to hang
  up [11]
hassen to hate (13)
das Haupt, =er head (15); (as prefix) main
  (15)
der Hauptbahnhof, =e central railway station [15]
die Hauptfigur, –en main figure [11]
das Hauptwerk, –e principal work [19]
das Haus, =er house [2] (3); nach Hause
  home [10] (7); zu Hause at home (7)
die Hausfrau, –en housewife [10]
das Hauskonzert, –e private concert [17]
das Hausmärchen, – family fairy tale [20]
die Haustür, –en front door [16]
heben, hob, gehoben to lift, pick up (17)
heftig violent (16)
heilig holy (22)
die Heimat native land (9)
die Heimatstadt, =e native city [16]
heiraten to marry (6)
heiß hot (2)
heißen, hieß, geheißen to be called (1,
  13); to call [5]; das heißt that means
  [7]; es heißt (in) it says (in print) (14);
  Wie heißt das Mädchen? What's the
  girl's name? (1)
der Held, –en, –en hero (6); die Heldin, –nen
  heroine [21]
der Heldentod, –e hero's death (6)
helfen, hilft, half, geholfen to help (2, 14)
das Hemd, –en shirt (5)
hemmen to inhibit (23)
die Hemmung, –en inhibition (23)
heraus- (pref.) out [15] (18)
heraus/bringen, brachte heraus, herausgebracht (irr. wk.) to bring out, publish (14)
heraus/fliegen, flog heraus, ist herausgeflogen to come flying out; to be
  thrown out [23]
heraus/geben, gibt heraus, gab heraus,
  herausgegeben to edit, publish (18)
heraus/kommen, kam heraus, ist heraus-
  gekommen to come out [15]
heraus/laufen, läuft heraus, lief heraus,
  ist herausgelaufen to run out [20]
die Herde, –n herd [9]
herein! come in! (4)
herein/lassen, läßt herein, ließ herein,
  hereingelassen to let in [20]
her/geben, gibt her, gab her, hergegeben
  to hand over (14)
der Herr, –n, –en master, gentleman; (in ad-

dress) Mr. (4); **die Herrin, –nen** mistress [23]
herrschen to prevail (19)
her/stellen to manufacture, produce (12)
herum- (*pref.*) around (13)
herum/laufen, läuft herum, lief herum, ist herumgelaufen to run around (13)
herunter- (*pref.*) down (18)
hervor/bringen, brachte hervor, hervorgebracht (*irr. wk.*) to produce (14)
das **Herz, –ens, –en** heart (5)
die **Heuschrecke, –n** locust [20]
heute (*adv.*) today (4); **heute abend** tonight [11]; **heute morgen** this morning [22]
heutig (*adj.*) today's (21)
heutzutage nowadays [18]
hier here (2)
die **Hilfe** help [16] (20); **mit Hilfe** with the help [23]
der **Himmel, –** heaven (9); sky (15)
die **Himmelsrichtung, –en** direction of the sky (15)
die **Himmelstür, –en** gate to heaven [20]
hinauf- (*pref.*) up (18)
hinein- (*pref.*) into (18)
hinein/ziehen, zieht hinein, zog hinein, hineingezogen to draw into [20]
hin/fallen, fällt hin, fiel hin, ist hingefallen to fall down [. .]
s. hin/setzen to sit down [17]
hinter (*prep. w. dat. or acc.*) behind [13]
hinunter- (*pref.*) down [18]
der **Hirt, –en, –en** shepherd (9)
historisch historical [11]
die **Hitze** heat (2)
hoch high (16)
höchst highest [16]; most [16]
der **Hof, ⸗e** court (11)
der **Hofdichter, –** court poet [11]
die **Hoffnung, –en** hope (13)
hoffnungslos hopeless(ly) (13)
hoffnungsvoll promising (25)
der **Hofgarten, ⸗** "Court Park" (*public park in Munich*) [11]
höflich polite [15] (23)
die **Höflichkeit, –en** politeness (23)
holen to fetch, get (2)
(das) **Holland** Holland [14]
hören to hear (6)
das **Horn, ⸗er** horn [18]
die **Hose, –n** (*often used in pl.*) pants (13)
das **Hotel, –s** hotel [5]
hübsch pretty (1); nice [10]
der **Humanismus** Humanism [10]
der **Humor** humor, sense of humor [16]
der **Hund, –e** dog (7)

der **Hundebraten, –** roast dog [19]
die **Hypnose, –n** hypnosis [23]
hypnotisieren to hypnotize [23]

idealisieren to idealize [15]
die **Idee, –n** idea (1)
der **Idiot, –en, –en** idiot [8]
ihm (*dat. of* er) him, to him, for him (4)
ihn (*acc. of* er) him (4)
ihnen (*dat. pl. of* sie) them (5)
Ihnen (*dat. pl. of* Sie) you, to you (1)
ihr (*poss. adj.*) her (3)
Ihr (*poss. adj.*) your (1)
die **Illustration, –en** illustration [15]
imitieren to imitate (6)
immer always (2); **noch immer** still (7); **immer wieder** again and again (2)
imposant imposing, impressive (17)
indem (*conj.*) in that, by, while [20]
der **Indianer, –** American Indian [14]
die **Inflation, –en** inflation [10]
der **Inhalt, –e** content [5]
inspirieren to inspire [18]
das **Instrument, –e** instrument [10]
der **Intellekt, –e** intellect [11]
intelligent intelligent (1)
interessant interesting [11]
das **Interesse, –n** interest (3)
interessieren to interest (7); **s. interessieren (für** *w. acc.*) to be interested (in) [11]
die **Intoleranz** intolerance [9]
irgendein (just) any (23)
irgendetwas just anything (11)
(das) **Irland** Ireland [18]
ironisch ironical(ly) [9]
s. irren to be mistaken [11]
(das) **Italien** Italy (7)
italienisch Italian [17]

ja yes (8); (*exclamation, followed by comma*) indeed (8); (*in a clause, emphasis*) you know! [9]; (*in a question*) you know [13]
der **Jäger, –** hunter (18)
das **Jahr, –e** year (5)
das **Jahrhundert, –e** century (10)
jammern to wail, complain (2)
japanfreundlich pro-Japanese [21]
japanisch Japanese [21]
jawohl yes, indeed (10)
die **Jazzkapelle, –n** jazz band [15]
je each (22)
jedenfalls in any case (24)
jeder, jede, jedes each, every (4)
jedesmal each time [16]
jedoch however (15)

jemals ever [20]; **überhaupt jemals** ever
. . . at all [24]
jemand someone [20]
jenseits (*prep. w. gen.*) the other side of,
beyond [15]
jetzt now (1)
die **Jugend** youth (8)
jung young (3)
der **Junge, –n, –n** boy, son (5)
der **Jurist, –en, –en** lawyer [18]
juristisch legal, law (*adj.*) [25]

der **Kaffee** coffee (19)
der **Kaiser, –** emperor (16); **die Kaiserin,
–nen** empress [17]
kaiserlich imperial [17]
kalt cold (2)
die **Kälte** cold (2)
kämmen to comb [11]
kämpfen to fight (9)
der **Kandidat, –en, –en** candidate [5]
kann can (10)
der **Kanzler, –** chancellor [21]
der **Kapitän, –e** captain [21]
das **Kapitel, –** chapter (20)
der **Karikaturist, –en, –en** cartoonist [18]
der **Karneval** carnival (period preceding
Lent) [22]
die **Katastrophe, –n** catastrophe [16]
kategorisch categorical [16]
die **Kathedrale, –n** cathedral [20]
katholisch catholic [15]
der **Katholizismus** Catholicism, Catholic
Church [14]
die **Katze, –n** cat [2]
kaufen to buy (1)
der **Kaufmann, Kaufleute** merchant (4)
kaum hardly (9)
kein, keine, kein no, not a (1)
keinmal never [21]
kennen (*irr. wk.*) to know, be acquainted with (1, 14)
kennen/lernen to meet; to get to know
[11]
der **Kerl, –e** fellow [11]
die **Kerze, –n** candle (22)
der **Kilometer, –** kilometer [16]
das **Kind, –er** child (1)
die **Kinderjahre** (*pl.*) childhood years [13]
das **Kinderzimmer, –** playroom [3]
die **Kindheit** childhood (13)
das **Kino, –s** movie house (22)
die **Kirche, –n** church (12)
der **Kirchturm, ⸗e** church tower, steeple
(22)
klagen to complain [25]
klar clear(ly) (3)
die **Klarheit, –en** clarity [11]

die **Klasse, –n** classroom (7)
das **Klavier, –e** piano (17)
das **Klavierkonzert, –e** piano concerto [17]
die **Klaviermusik** piano music [17]
das **Kleid, –er** dress (5)
die **Kleidung, –en** clothing (6)
klein small, little (5)
klettern to climb (18)
das **Klima, –s** climate (7)
klingeln to ring (a bell) [11]
klingen to ring, sound (9)
die **Klinik, –en** clinic [23]
klopfen (**an** *w. acc.*) to knock (on) (4);
to beat [11]
klug clever (16)
der **Knochen, –** bone (25)
das **Kochbuch, ⸗er** cookbook [23]
kochen to cook, boil (19)
die **Kochkunst, ⸗e** art of cooking [19]
der **Koffer, –** suitcase (3)
der **Kollege, –n, –n** colleague [16]
komisch funny [8]
kommen, kam, ist gekommen to come
(1, 11)
der **Komödiant, –en, –en** comedian, actor [21]
kompliziert complicated [25]
komponieren to compose [8]
der **Komponist, –en, –en** composer (6)
der **Konflikt, –e** conflict [11]
der **Kongreß, –sse** congress [20]
der **König, –e** king (5); **die Königin, –nen**
queen [17]
der **Konjunktiv, –e** subjunctive [24]
können, kann, konnte, gekonnt (*mod.
aux.*) to be able to (6, 17); **Sie können**
you can (6)
die **Konstruktion, –en** construction [25]
die **Konzentration** concentration [16]
das **Konzert, –e** concert; concerto [17]
der **Kopf, ⸗e** head [10]; head, mind (11);
das Köpfchen, – little head [13]
köpfen to behead [18]
der **Körper, –** body (7)
die **Körpersprache, –n** body language [14]
der **Korridor, –e** corridor, hallway (1)
kosten to cost [21]
der **Krach** (thundering) noise (12)
krachen (*impers.*) to bang (12)
krank sick, ill (4)
der **Kranke, –n, –n** sick man, patient [15]
kränken to hurt, insult (8)
das **Krankenhaus, ⸗er** hospital [15] (17)
krankhaft sickly, morbid (8)
die **Krankheit, –en** illness, disease (5)
das **Krankheitssymptom, –e** symptom of disease [23]
die **Krawatte, –n** tie (11)
der **Kreis, –e** circle (5)

der **Krieg, –e** war (6)
das **Kriegsrecht** law of war [20]
das **Kriegsschiff, –e** war ship [21]
die **Kritik** criticism [19]
der **Kritiker, –** critic [15]
   kritisch critical [8]; **kritisch gegenüber /
   stehen** to be critical toward (19)
die **Küche, –n** kitchen [13] (19)
die **Kuh, ⸗e** cow [2]
   kühl cool (8)
die **Kultur, –en** culture, civilization [24]
   kulturell cultural [20]
   kulturhistorisch cultural-historical [21]
die **Kunst, ⸗e** art (4)
die **Kunstakademie, –n** art academy [15]
der **Künstler, –** artist (8)
das **Kunstwerk, –e** work of art (8)
der **Kurs, –e** rate of exchange [10]
   kurz brief (3), short (15)
   küssen to kiss (5)
die **Kutsche, –n** coach (25)

   lächeln to smile (1)
   lachen to laugh (3)
der **Laden, ⸗** shop (7)
die **Lage** situation, location (20)
die **Lampe, –n** lamp [19]
das **Land, ⸗er** land, country (5)
   landen to land [20]
der **Landsknecht, –e** mercenary [20]
   lang(e) (*adj.*) long (5); (*adv.*) for a long
   time [9] (14)
   langsam slow(ly) (1)
   längst long ago, for a long time [20]
   lassen, läßt, ließ, gelassen to let (12); **es
   läßt sich, ließ sich** (*impers.*) can be,
   could be (17); to have (something)
   done [17]
das **Latein, das Lateinische** Latin [9] [24]
die **Laterne, –n** lantern [19]
   laufen to run (13)
   laut loud (2)
der **Laut, –e** sound [14]
   lauten to sound, run (*of a text*) (10)
die **Lautsprache, –n** sound language [14]
   leben to live (4)
das **Leben, –** life [2] (4); **s. das Leben nehmen**
   to commit suicide [24]
   lebendig lively, alive (12)
das **Lebenswerk** life's work [12]
   legen to lay (7); to put [9]
die **Legion, –en** legion [24]
   lehren to teach (16)
der **Lehrer, –** teacher (6)
   leicht easy [7] (9); easily [11]; light [19];
   es leicht haben to have an easy time
   of it; to be lucky (9)
das **Leid, –en** sorrow [13]

   leid tun to be sorry about [11]; **es tut
   mir leid** I am sorry about it [11]
   leiden, litt, gelitten (**unter** *w. dat.*) to
   suffer (from) (10)
die **Leidenschaft, –en** passion (9)
   leider (*adv.*) unfortunately (5)
   leihen, lieh, geliehen to lend (17)
die **Leistung, –en** achievement (12)
   lernen to learn (1)
   lesen, liest, las, gelesen to read (7)
der **Leser, –** reader [15]
   letzt last (9)
die **Leute** (*pl.*) people (2)
   liberal liberal [9]
das **Licht, –er** light [22]
   lieb dear (13)
   lieblich lovely, sweet [24]
das **Liebchen, –** sweetheart [9]
die **Liebe** love [5] (9)
   lieben to love (5)
   liebenswürdig charming (16)
   lieber rather (16); **lieber + verb** to prefer (16)
das **Liebesgedicht, –e** love poem [13]
der **Liebhaber, –** lover, connoisseur (6)
das **Lied, –er** song (9)
   liegen, lag, gelegen to lie (12)
die **Linse, –n** lentil [24]
der **Liter, –** liter [21]
   literarisch literary [8]
die **Literatur, –en** literature (7)
die **Literaturgeschichte, –n** history of literature [13]
das **Loch, ⸗er** hole [18]
die **Logik** logic [5]
   s. lohnen to be worthwhile (25)
das **Lokal, –e** public place (of entertain-
   ment) (15)
   löschen to extinguish (20); to quench
   (23)
die **Luft, ⸗e** air (2); **an die Luft setzen** to
   throw out [23]
   lügen, log, gelogen to (tell a) lie (18)
der **Lügner, –** liar (18)
   lustig merry, gay (14); **s. lustig machen
   (über)** to poke fun at (11)
der **Lyriker, –** lyrical poet [13]
   lyrisch lyrical [15]
das **Lyrische** the lyrical, poetry [15]

   machen to make, do (1); **s. machen** to
   make for oneself [11]; **das macht
   nichts** that makes no difference (18)
die **Macht, ⸗e** power (20)
das **Mädchen, –** girl (1)
die **Mahlzeit, –en** meal [19]
die **Majestät, –en** majesty (5); **Majestät!**
   Your Majesty! (6)

das **Mal, –e** time (*in an enumerative sense*) (17); **zum ersten Mal** for the first time (17)

mal (*in multiplication*) times (22)

malen to paint (10)

man (*impers. pron.*) one, you (1)

manch ein many a (4)

mancher, manche, manches many a, several (3)

manchmal sometimes (1)

der **Mann, ⸗er** man (2), husband [3]

das **Manuskript, –e** manuscript [16]

das **Märchen, –** fairy tale [12] (13)

die **Mark** Mark (*German monetary unit, equivalent to about 27 U.S. cents*) [10]

der **Markt, ⸗e** market (place) (14)

marschieren to march [20]

der **März** (*arch. gen.* **–en**) March [21]

die **Maschine, –n** machine [2] (8)

die **Masse, –n** mass(es) (8)

die **Mathematik** math(ematics) (1)

der **Mathematiker, –** mathematician [10]

die **Mathematikklasse, –n** mathematics class (1)

mathematisch mathematical (10)

die **Maus, ⸗e** mouse [14]

die **Medizin, –en** medicine [7]

medizinisch medical [25]

das **Mehl** flour (23)

mehr (als) more (than) (1)

mehrere several (10)

mein, meine, mein my (1)

meinen to mean (3); to say (4, 6); to express an opinion, suggest (25)

meinetwegen(!) for my sake; for all I care! (7)

die **Meinung, –en** opinion, mind (6); **seine Meinung ändern** to change one's mind (6)

meist most (10); **die meisten** most of (12); **die meisten Leute** most people (10)

der **Meister, –** master (7)

das **Meisterwerk, –e** masterpiece (12)

die **Melodie, –n** melody [18]

die **Melone, –n** melon [23]

das **Memorandum, Memoranden** memo(randum) [19]

die **Menge, –n** great number (*of people or things*), multitude, mass (13)

der **Mensch, –en, –en** human being (2); man [11]; **kein Mensch** nobody [3]

die **Menschenherde, –n** herd of humans [9]

die **Menschheit** humanity (9)

menschlich human [13]

mental mental, intellectual [31]

merken to notice, perceive (5)

messen, mißt, maß, gemessen to measure (23)

das **Messer, –** knife [16]

die **Metamorphose, –n** metamorphosis [25]

die **Metapher, –n** metaphor [10]

metaphysisch metaphysical [31]

die **Methode, –n** method [18]

die **Milch** milk [2]

mildern to lessen (13)

die **Milliarde, –n** billion [10]

die **Million, –en** million [10]

der **Millionär, –e** millionaire [5]

das **Mineral, –e** mineral [25]

die **Mineralogie** mineralogy [25]

mineralogisch mineralogical [25]

der **Minister, –** minister, secretary (*in government*) (6)

die **Minute, –n** minute [16]

mir (*dat. of* **ich**) me, to me (2)

mit (*prep. w. dat.*) with (1)

mit/bringen, brachte mit, mitgebracht (*irr. wk.*) to bring along [14]

miteinander with one another [11]

das **Mitglied, –er** member (15)

der **Mittag, –e** noon [19]; **zu Mittag essen** to have lunch [19]

mittag (at) noon (15)

mittags at noon [22]

die **Mitte** middle, center (20)

das **Mittelalter** Middle Ages (4)

der **Mittelpunkt, –e** center [25]

mitten in (*w. dat.*) in the middle of (13)

die **Mitternacht, ⸗e** midnight (22)

möchten Sie? would you like to? (11)

modellieren to model [15]

modern modern [11]

mögen, mag, mochte, gemocht (*mod. aux.*) to like to (17)

möglich possible (12)

möglicherweise possibly [16]

der **Mohammedaner, –** Mohammedan, Moslem [21]

der **Mond, –e** moon (12)

die **Mondkarte, –n** moon chart (12)

der **Mondkrater, –** crater of the moon [12]

die **Monogamie** monogamy [9]

der **Montag, –e** Monday [22]

morden to murder (20)

der **Mörder, –** murderer (7)

der **Morgen, –** morning [21]

morgen tomorrow [2] (4); **morgen früh** tomorrow morning [22]; **heute morgen** this morning [22]

morgens in the morning (19)

das **Morphium** morphium, morphine [13]

die **Morphologie** morphology [25]

(das) **Moskau** Moscow [12]

s. Mühe geben to take pains [11]

(das) **München** Munich (4)

der **Mund, ⸗er** mouth (10); **den Mund halten** to keep quiet, shut up (10); **das Mündchen,** – little mouth [15]

murmeln to murmur [21]

die **Musik (von)** music (by) (6)

der **Musikant, –en, –en** musician [18]

der **Musiker,** – musician [17]

die **Musikgeschichte** history of music [17]

der **Musikkenner,** – musical expert, music connoisseur [17]

musizieren to make music, play [10]

muß (*pres. of* müssen) must (9)

müssen, muß, mußte, gemußt (*mod. aux.*) to have to (17)

die **Mutter, ⸗** mother [2]

nach (*prep. w. dat.*) after (1); (*going to cities*) to (2); according to [16]

der **Nachbar, –n** neighbor [5]

nachdem (*conj.*) after [20]

nach /denken, dachte nach, nachgedacht (*irr. wk.*) **über** (*w. acc.*) to reflect, think about, ponder [14]

nach /drucken to reprint (21)

nach /gehen, ging nach, ist nachgegangen to be slow (of clocks) [22]

nach /lesen, liest nach, las nach, nachgelesen to read up (on), check [23]

der **Nachmittag, –e** afternoon [22]; **am Nachmittag** in the afternoon [22]

nachmittags in the afternoon (22)

der **Nachmittagskaffee** afternoon coffee [22]

die **Nachricht, –en** news [16] (24)

nach /sehen, sieht nach, sah nach, nachgesehen to have a look; to check [20]

nächst- next [16]

die **Nacht, ⸗e** night (22); **eines Nachts** one night [16]; **des Nachts** at night (22); **heute nacht** tonight, during the night [22]

der **Nachtbesuch, –e** nightly visit [16]

die **Nachtmusik** "night music" [15]

nachts at night [22]

der **Nachtwächter,** – night watchman [22]

der **Nagel, ⸗** nail [11] (18)

nah(e) near [16]; **am nächsten** nearest [16]; **in der Nähe (von)** near (8)

der **Name, –ns, –n** name (3)

nämlich namely; that is to say (4)

die **Nation, –en** nation [2]

die **Natur, –en** nature [14]

natürlich natural(ly) (11)

die **Naturwissenschaft, –en** (natural) science [7]

der **Naturwissenschaftler,** – (natural) scientist [12]

neben (*prep. w. dat. /acc.*) next to, at the side of [13]

der **Neffe, –n, –n** nephew (5)

nehmen, nimmt, nahm, genommen to take (7)

nein no (*in answers*) (4)

nennen, nannte, genannt (*irr. wk.*) to call (10, 14); **den Namen nennen** to give one's name [14]

das **Nest, –er** nest [19]

nett nice (1)

neu new (8)

das **Neujahr** New Year's Day [22]

neun nine [2]

neunzehn nineteen [19]

neunzig ninety; **die neunziger Jahre** the Nineties [21]

nicht not (1); **nicht mehr** no longer (7)

nichts (als) nothing (but) [6] (10)

nieder- (*pref.*) down (24)

die **Niederlage, –n** defeat (24)

nieder /stürzen to collapse [24]

niedrig low (16)

niemals never (8)

niemand nobody (7)

noch still (1), yet (2); **noch ein** one more, another (7); **noch einmal** once more [6] (7); **noch etwas** something else [21]; **noch nicht** not yet (16)

die **Nonne, –n** nun (15)

der **Norden** North [14]

der **Norddeutsche, –n** North German [11]

(das) **Norddeutschland** Northern Germany [12]

normal normal (3)

die **Not** need [16]

die **Noten** (*pl.*) (musical) notes, score (8)

nötig necessary (12)

null zero [22]

nun now (2); **von nun an** from now on (8); **nun** (*followed by a comma*) well [10]

nur only (1)

der **Nutzen** use(fulness) (24)

ob (*conj.*) whether (14); I (etc.) wonder whether [20]

oben above, upstairs (18); **oberst-** uppermost [16]

der **Oberkiefer,** – upper jaw [25]

obgleich (*conj.*) although [20]

obwohl (*conj.*) although [20]

der **Ochse, –n, –n** ox, oxen (5)

oder (*conj.*) or (6)

der **Ofen, ⸗** stove, oven (14)

offen open (15)

offenbar apparently (12)

die **Offenbarung, –en** revelation [19]

offiziell official [15]

der **Offizier, –e** officer [21]

öffnen to open (2); **s. öffnen** to be
  opened [12]
oft often (6)
ohne (*prep. w. acc.*) without (1)
das Ohr, –en ear (17)
die Ohrfeige, –n box on the ear (13)
  s. ohrfeigen to box one another's ears
    (13)
der Onkel, – uncle (9)
die Oper, –n opera [8]
die Operette, –n operetta, light opera [18]
der Opernkomponist, –en, –en opera composer [18]
die Optik optics [25]
der Optimist, –en, –en optimist [6]
das Oratorium, Oratorien oratorio [17]
das Organ, –e organ [25]
  organisch organic [25]
der Orientale, –n, –n Oriental [21]
das Original, –e original [25]
  originell original [15]
der Ort, –e place (17)
  ostdeutsch East German [15]
der Osten East [15]
(das) Ostern Easter [21]
(das) Österreich Austria (20)
der Österreicher, – Austrian [20]
  österreichisch Austrian [23]
  östlich Eastern [24]

ein paar a few (22)
  packen to seize; to pack (*a suitcase*) (4)
der Page, –n, –n page (*at a court, hotel*) [6]
der Palast, ⸗e palace (5)
die Panik panic [24]
der Papagei, –en parrot [14]
das Papier, –e paper [10]
das Papiergeld, –er paper money [10]
das Paradies, –e paradise (4)
der Paragraph, –en, –en paragraph[5]
der Park, –s park [6]
die Parodie, –n parody [11]
  parodieren to parody [11]
die Partei, –en (*political*) party [15]
die Passion, –en passion (9)
der Pastor, Pastoren pastor (7)
der Patient, –en, –en patient [16]; **die
    Patientin, –nen** woman patient [23]
  patriotisch patriotic [13]
  persönlich personal(ly) [2]
der Pessimismus pessimism [7]
der Pessimist, –en, –en pessimist (7)
der Pfadfinder, – boy scout [22]
der Pfannkuchen, – pancake (3)
die Pfeife, –n pipe (19)
das Pferd, –e horse (4)
(das) Pfingsten Whitsun(tide) [22]
die Pflanze, –n plant (25)
  pflanzen to plant (18)

pflegen (zu) to be accustomed (used) to
  (17)
das Phänomen, –e phenomenon [12]
die Phantasie, –n fancy, imagination [13]
der Philologe, –n, –n philologist (7)
der Philosoph, –en, –en philosopher [5] (7)
die Philosophie, –n philosophy (7)
  philosophieren to philosophize [6]
  philosophisch philosophical [12]
die Physik physics [12]
  physikalisch physical [12]
der Physiologe, –n, –n physiologist [25]
die Physiologie physiology [25]
  physiologisch physiological [25]
der Plan, ⸗e plan [14]
  planen to plan [19]
  platonisch Platonic [9]
der Platz, ⸗e place, seat (3); **Platz nehmen**
    to sit down (3)
  plötzlich suddenly (2)
  plündern to sack, plunder, ravage [20]
die Plünderung, –en sack [24]
(das) Polen Poland [14]
die Politik politics [10]
  politisch political [15]
die Polizei police (18)
  polnisch Polish [15]
die Popularität popularity [11]
  präsentieren to hand, present [9]
der Präsident, –en, –en president [3]
  predigen to preach (12)
die Predigt, –en sermon (12)
der Preis, –e price [2]; prize [10]
der Prinz, –en, –en prince [13]; **die Prinzes-
    sin, –nen** princess [6]
das Prinzip, –ien principle [10]
das Privatleben private life (6)
das Problem, –e problem (1)
das Produkt, –e product [2]
  produktiv productive [16]
der Professor, Professoren professor [3] (7)
  prophetisch prophetic [9]
die Prosa prose [9]
  protestantisch Protestant [20]
die Prügel (*pl.*) thrashing [9]
der Psychiater, – psychiatrist (3)
  psychisch psychic [23]
die Psychoanalyse, –n psychoanalysis (7)
  psychoanalytisch psychoanalytical [23]
der Psychologe, –n, –n psychologist [12]
die Psychologie psychology [5]
das Publikum public, audience (6)
  pünktlich punctual [5]
die Puppe, –n doll (5)
  putzen to clean [11]

der Rabe, –n, –n raven [14]
  radikal radical [25]

der **Radikalismus** radicalism (7)
der **Rang,** ⸗e rank, quality [13]
   rapide rapid [10]
   rasch quick(ly) (16)
   rasseln to rattle (22)
der **Rat, Ratschläge** advice (6); **um Rat fragen** to ask (someone's) advice (6)
   raten, rät, riet, geraten to advise (9)
das **Rathaus,** ⸗er city hall (22)
die **Rathausuhr, –en** city hall clock [22]
   ratlos perplexed (2)
der **Ratschlag,** ⸗e (bit of) advice (8)
das **Rätsel, –** puzzle, riddle (5)
der **Rauch** smoke (2)
   rauchen to smoke (2)
der **Raucher, –** smoker (2)
   reagieren (auf w. acc.) to react (to) (6)
   rechnen to count; to calculate (10)
das **Recht, –e** right; **mit Recht** rightly (so) (9)
   recht quite (18)
die **Rede, –n** speech (11); **eine Rede halten** to make a speech (21)
   reden to talk (1)
die **Redensart, –en** figure of speech [10]
die **Reformation, –en** Reformation [20]
die **Regierung, –en** government [5]
   regnen to rain [11]
der **Rehbraten, –** roast venison [19]
   reiben, rieb, gerieben to rub (22)
   reich (an) rich (in) (4)
das **Reich, –e** realm, empire (5)
   reichen (bis an) to reach (up to) (24)
   reif ripe, mature (8); **unreif** unripe, immature (8)
   rein pure, clean (19)
die **Reise, –n** trip, journey (12); **eine Reise machen** to take a trip [16]
der **Reiseführer, –** (travel) guide [16]
   reisen to travel (7)
der **Reisende, –n, –n** traveler [16]
   reißen, riß, gerissen to tear (18)
   reiten, ritt, ist geritten to ride (on horseback) (4)
die **Relativitätstheorie, –n** theory of relativity [10]
das **Relativpronomen, –** relative pronoun [19]
die **Religion, –en** religion [19]
der **Religionskrieg, –e** religious war [20]
   religiös religious [20]
   rennen, rannte, gerannt (irr. wk.) to run (14)
die **Republik, –en** republic [5]
der **Republikaner, –** Republican [5]
   respektlos (lacking respect), irreverent [11]
der **Rest, –e** rest, remainder [23]
das **Restaurant, –s** restaurant [2]

das **Resultat, –e** result [12]
   revolutionieren to revolutionize [6]
das **Rezept, –e** recipe [5]
der **Rhein** Rhine River [9]
das **Rheinland** Rhineland [13]
   richten to direct (25)
   richtig correct(ly) (10); right [16]; real [23]
die **Richtung, –en** direction (7)
   riechen, roch, gerochen (nach) to smell (of) (9)
der **Ring, –e** ring [22]
   ringen, rang, gerungen (um) to fight (for); to wrestle (20)
der **Rivale, –n** rival [8]
die **Rolle, –n** role (7)
der **Roman, –e** novel [5] (11)
das **Romanschreiben** writing of novels [15]
der **Romantiker, –** romanticist [9]
   romantisch romantic [5]
der **Römer, –** Roman [9]
   römisch Roman [24]
die **Rose, –n** rose [5]
   rot red (13)
(das) **Rotkäppchen** Red Ridinghood [20]
die **Rückkehr** return (18)
   rufen, rief, gerufen to call (2, 14)
die **Ruhe** quiet, peace (2)
   ruhig quiet (2)
   rühren to stir [23]
   rund round [15]
der **Russe, –n, –n** Russian (7); **die Russin, –nen** Russian woman (7)
   russisch Russian (7)
(das) **Rußland** Russia [18]

die **Sache, –n** thing, matter (9)
(das) **Sachsen** Saxony [15]
die **Sage, –n** legend (4)
   sagen to say (1)
   sammeln to collect [20]
die **Sammlung, –en** collection (12)
die **Sandale, –n** sandal [13]
die **Sanduhr, –en** hour glass [22]
der **Sänger, –** singer; **die Sängerin, –nen** (woman) singer [17]
der **Satiriker, –** satirist [12]
der **Satz,** ⸗e sentence (7)
   säubern to clean [11]
das **Säugetier, –e** mammal [25]
der **Schädel, –** skull (25)
das **Schaf, –e** sheep [25]
   schaffen, schuf, geschaffen to create (21)
der **Schaffner, –** conductor (2)
das **Schafskelett, –e** sheep skeleton [25]
   s. schämen (für) to feel ashamed (of) [11]
   scharf sharp [11]

der **Scharfsinn** acumen [25]
der **Schatz,** ≃e treasure, sweetheart (5)
　schätzen to value (6); to estimate (20)
das **Schauspiel,** –e play (21)
der **Schauspieler,** – actor [6]; die **Schau-spielerin,** –nen actress
die **Schauspielpremiere,** –n first perform-ance [2]
der **Schein,** –e bill (10)
　scheinen, schien, geschienen to seem, appear [7]; to shine [7] (12)
der **Schelm,** –e rascal (14)
　schenken to give (*as a present*) [2] (10)
　scheren, schor, geschoren to shear (9)
　schicken to send (5)
das **Schicksal,** –e fate [18] (20)
　schieben, schob, geschoben to shove, push (13)
der **Schimpanse,** –n, –n chimpanzee [14]
　schimpfen (auf *w. acc.*) to scold (17); to rail (against) [23]
die **Schlacht,** –en battle (20)
das **Schlachtfeld,** –er battlefield (20)
der **Schlaf** sleep [16]
　schlafen, schläft, schlief, geschlafen to sleep [7] (12)
　schlagen, schlägt, schlug, geschlagen to strike, hit [7]; to beat (22)
　schlau "sly," clever, smart (4)
　schlecht bad, poor [13] (21)
　schleichen, schlich, ist geschlichen to sneak, creep (24)
　schließen, schloß, geschlossen to close, to shut (2); to conclude (23)
　schließlich finally (*after a string of events*) (2)
das **Schloß, Schlösser** castle (5)
　schmecken to taste (14)
　schmeicheln to flatter [24]
der **Schmerz,** –ens, –en pain, sorrow (16)
der **Schnaps,** ≃e (cheap) liquor (13)
　schneiden, schnitt, geschnitten to cut [7] (8)
　schnell quick(ly), fast (2)
die **Schokolade,** –n chocolate [13]
　schon already (4)
　schön beautiful (4)
der **Schoß,** ≃e lap [17]
(das) **Schottland** Scotland [19]
　schrecklich terrible (9)
　schreiben, schrieb, geschrieben to write (7)
der **Schreibtisch,** –e desk (16)
　schreien, schrie, geschrien to scream (2, 14)
die **Schrift,** –en writing (7)
der **Schriftsteller,** – writer (11)
der **Schritt,** –e step (13)

der **Schuh,** –e shoe [11]
die **Schuld,** (–en) guilt; debt (21)
die **Schule,** –n school (7); **in die Schule** to school (16); **in der Schule** in school (16); **nach der Schule** after school [14]
der **Schüler,** – pupil (6)
　schütteln to shake (10); **den Kopf schütteln** to shake one's head (10); **s. die Hand schütteln** to shake hands [11]
　schwach weak (7)
　schwarz black (13)
der **Schwede,** –n, –n Swede [20]
(das) **Schweden** Sweden [20]
　schweigen, schwieg, geschwiegen to be silent (2, 13); **das Schweigen** silence [23]
die **Schweiz** Switzerland (7); **in der Schweiz** in Switzerland (7)
　schwer hard, difficult, heavy (9)
das **Schwert,** –er sword (24)
die **Schwester,** –n sister (7)
　schwimmen, schwamm, ist geschwommen to swim [6]
der **Schwindler,** – swindler [18]
　schwören, schwor, geschworen to swear (24)
　sechs six (6)
　sechstel sixth (21)
　sechzehn sixteen (16)
die **Seele,** –n soul (11)
　sehen, sieht, sah, gesehen to see [7] (8)
der **Seher,** – seer (8)
　sehr very (1)
die **Seide** silk (13)
　seiden silken (13)
　sein, ist, war, ist gewesen to be (1); **es ist mir als (ob),** I feel as if (24)
　sein, seine, sein his (2)
　seit (*conj.*) since, for (7); (*prep. w. dat.*) since (3)
　seitdem since then (7)
die **Seite,** –n side, page (2)
die **Sekretärin,** –nen (woman) secretary (3)
　selb- same (1)
　selber (*after a noun or pronoun*) himself, themselves
　selbstverständlich of course, naturally (14)
　selten seldom [15]
　senden, sandte (sendete), gesandt (gesendet) (*irr. wk.*) **(nach)** to send (for) (14)
　sentimental sentimental [19]
der **September** September [21]
　s. setzen to sit down [11]
　sicher (*adv.*) certainly (4); (*adj.*) sure (4)
　sie (*acc. of* **sie**) her (1)
　sieben seven (7)

siebzehnt- seventeenth [12]
der **Siedler, –** settler [14]
siegen to win, be victorious (24)
der **Sieger, –** victor (20)
sieht (*from* **sehen**) sees (4)
das **Silber** silver (5)
der **Silvester** New Year's Eve [22]
sind (*from* **sein**) (they) are (1)
singen, sang, gesungen to sing [6] (9)
sinken, sank, gesunken to sink (10)
der **Sinn, –e (für)** sense (of) (16)
die **Sitte, –n** custom (17)
die **Situation, –en** situation [11]
sitzen, saß, gesessen to sit (2, 8)
das **Skelett, –e** skeleton [25]
der **Sklave, –n, –n** slave [18]
die **Skulptur, –en** sculpture [15]
so so, thus, like this (1); (*followed by a comma*) well [16]
so daß (*conj.*) so that [16]
sofort immediately (5)
sogar even (4)
sogenannt (*abbr.:* **sog.**) so-called (21)
der **Sohn, –e** son (8)
ein solcher, eine solche, ein solches such a (4)
der **Sold** (army) pay (20)
der **Soldat, –en, –en** soldier (5)
das **Soldatsein** being a soldier (21)
sollen, soll, sollte, gesollt (*mod. aux.*) to be said to, be obliged to (17); **wir sollten** we should (4)
der **Sommer, –** summer [21]
sonderbar strange [19]
sondern (*subord. conj.*) but, but rather [6] (7)
die **Sonne, –n** sun (7)
die **Sonnenuhr, –en** sun dial [22]
der **Sonntag, –e** Sunday [12]
sonst otherwise, at other times (22)
die **Sorge, –n** worry (4)
soviel as far as (21)
sowie as well as (7)
sozial social [11]
sozialdemokratisch social-democratic [15]
sozialistisch socialistic (11)
(das) **Spanien** Spain [20]
(das) **Spanisch** Spanish [24]
der **Spaßmacher, –** joker, prankster [14]
spät late (9); **zu spät kommen** to be late [22]
später later (4)
spazieren/gehen, ging spazieren, ist spazierengegangen to go for a walk (14)
der **Spaziergang, –e** walk (19)
die **Speise, –n** food (5)

die **Speisekarte, –n** menu (5)
die **Spekulation, –en** speculation [12]
die **Spezialität, –en** specialty [2]
der **Spiegel, –** mirror (14)
das **Spiel, –e** play (10)
spielen to play (5)
der **Spieltisch, –e** gambling table [24]
der **Spion, –e** spy; **die Spionin, –nen** spy (*fem.*) (13)
spitz pointed (15)
die **Sprache, –n** language (7)
der **Sprachunterricht** language instruction (16)
sprechen, spricht, sprach, gesprochen to speak [7] (9); (*w. acc.*) to talk to [11]
das **Sprichwort, –er** proverb (11)
springen, sprang, ist gesprungen to jump (6, 15)
die **Spur, –en** trace, track (25)
der **Staat, –en** state (9)
die **Stadt, –e** city (4)
das **Stadtleben** city life [22]
stammen (aus) to come (hail) from (19)
stark strong [2]
statt/finden, findet statt, stattgefunden to take place [13]
stehen, stand, gestanden to stand (1, 8)
stehlen, stiehlt, stahl, gestohlen to steal [1] (15)
steigen, stieg, ist gestiegen to climb (10)
der **Stein, –e** stone, rock (25)
die **Stelle, –n** place (15)
stellen to place (19); (*of clocks*) to set (19); **eine Frage stellen** to ask a question (3)
die **Stellung, –en** position (16)
sterben, stirbt, starb, ist gestorben (vor) to die (of) (2, 7)
der **Stern, –e** star [21]
stets always (7)
die **Steuer, –n** tax [5]
der **Stil, –e** style (6)
still quiet (19); **die Stille** stillness, quiet (19)
die **Stimme, –n** voice [16]
stimmen to tune [17]; to be correct (24)
stimulieren to stimulate [13]
stirbt (*from* **sterben**) (he, she, it) dies (2)
die **Stirn, –en** forehead (10)
der **Stoff, –e** material, subject [18]
stolz (auf) proud (of) [17] (25)
die **Störung, –en** disturbance (23)
stoßen, stößt, stieß, gestoßen to push (23)
die **Straße, –n** street (12)
die **Straßenbahn, –en** streetcar (10)
die **Straßenbeleuchtung, –en** street lighting [22]

die **Straßenecke, –n** street corner [22]
der **Streich, –e** prank (14)
   streichen, strich, gestrichen to cut; to stroke; to paint (21)
   streng strict [20] (25)
der **Strick, –e** rope (18)
das **Stroh** straw (18)
   strömen to stream (2)
das **Stück, –e** play, piece (6)
der **Student, –en** student (9); die **Studentin, –nen** (girl) student, coed (1)
die **Studentenorganisation, –en** student organization [15]
   studieren to study (1)
   stumm silent [14]
die **Stunde, –n** hour (15)
   stürzen to dash, fall headlong (24); **s. stürzen (auf** *w. acc.***)** to descend (violently) (upon) (20)
   stützen to support [20]; **s. stützen (auf** *w. acc.***)** to lean (rely) on; to base on (21)
   suchen (nach) to look (for) (4)
der **Süden** South [20]
der **Sultan, –e** sultan [18]
die **Suppe, –n** soup (24)
   süß sweet (13)
die **Süßigkeiten** (*pl.*) sweets (13)
das **Symptom, –e** symptom [23]
das **System, –e** system [19]
die **Szene, –n** scene [8]

der **Tabak, –e** tobacco [19]
die **Tafel, –n** blackboard (9)
der **Tag, –e** day (1); **Guten Tag!** hello!, good morning, good afternoon, etc. (*according to time of day*) (1); **am Tag** a day [15]; **eines Tages** one day (4); **eines schönen Tages** one fine day [15]; **alle Tage** every day [20]
das **Tagebuch, =er** diary (16)
das **Tageslicht** daylight [22]
   täglich daily [8]
   tagsüber during the day (22)
das **Tal, =er** dale, valley (5)
die **Tante, –n** aunt (7)
der **Tanz, =e** dance [14]
   tanzen to dance (3)
   tapfer brave [16] (18)
die **Tasche, –n** pocket [7] (10)
die **Taschenuhr, –en** pocket watch [22]
die **Tasse, –n** cup (19)
die **Tatsache, –n** fact (24)
   tausend thousand [12]; **das Tausend** the thousand [12]
   tausendstel thousandth [21]
das **Taxi, –s** taxi [16]
die **Technik, –en** technique, technology [6]
der **Tee** tea [22]; **zum Tee** for tea [22]

der **Teil, –e** part (19); **zum Teil** in part, partly (21); **zum großen Teil** to a large extent [21]
   teilen to share (23)
   teil/nehmen, nimmt teil, nahm teil, teilgenommen to participate [13] (15)
das **Telefon, –e** telephone [2]
das **Telefonbuch, =er** telephone book [9]
   telefonieren to phone [6]
die **Telefonnummer, –n** telephone number [2]
das **Telegramm, –e** telegram [15]
das **Temperament, –e** temperament [6]
die **Temperatur, –en** temperature [Rev. II]
das **Testament** testament, (last) will [15]
   teuer dear, expensive [16]
der **Teufel, –** devil (17)
der **Text, –e** text [21]
das **Theater, –** theater (6)
das **Theaterpublikum** theater public [18]
die **Theatersaison, –s** theater season [21]
die **Theaterszene, –n** scene for the theater [15]
das **Thema, Themen** theme, subject [10]
der **Theologe, –n, –n** theologian [9]
die **Theorie, –n** theory [10]
   tief deep(ly) (12)
das **Tier, –e** animal (14)
die **Tiersprache, –n** animal language [14]
der **Tisch, –e** table [7] (22)
die **Tischdecke, –n** table cloth [20]
der **Titel, –** title [11]
die **Tochter, =** daughter (5)
der **Tod** death (2)
die **Tondichtung, –en** tone poem (14)
   tot dead (7)
   töten to kill (7)
die **Tradition, –en** tradition [10]
   tragen, trägt, trug, getragen to wear, carry (15)
   tragisch tragic [13]
die **Träne, –n** tear (16)
   trauen to trust (24)
der **Trauermarsch, =e** funeral march [24]
   traurig sad [20]
   treffen, trifft, traf, getroffen to meet (4); hit, strike [17]; **s. treffen** to meet (11)
   treiben, trieb, getrieben to drive (18); to engage in (25)
die **Treppe, –n** stairs, staircase (18)
   treten, tritt, trat, ist getreten to step (9)
   trinken, trank, getrunken to drink [9] (11)
das **Trinkgeld, –er** tip (16)
   trommeln to drum (15)
der **Troß** camp following [20]
der **Trost** comfort (16)
   trösten to comfort (13)

trotz (*prep. w. gen.*) in spite of (9)
trotzdem (*adv.*) nevertheless (17)
trüb dim(ly) (22)
die Truppe, –n troupe [21]
das Tuch, ⸗er cloth (14)
tüchtig capable [16]
tun, tat, getan to do [1] (4, 8); so tun als
    ob to act as if (24)
die Tür, –en door (3)
der Türke, –n, –n Turk [18]
die Türkei Turkey [18]
türkisch Turkish [18]
typisch typical [25]
der Tyrann, –en, –en tyrant [24]
tyrannisieren to tyrannize [22]

übel /nehmen, nimmt übel, nahm übel,
    übelgenommen to take amiss, hold
    against (13)
übel werden (*impers.*) to get sick [11]
    (13)
über (*prep. w. dat./acc.*) over, across (5)
überall everywhere (7)
überhaupt altogether, anyway (7); in
    general (9); überhaupt nicht not at all
    (16)
überlegen to reflect, ponder (5)
übermorgen day after tomorrow [22]
übersetzen to translate (18)
die Übersetzung, –en translation (14)
die Übersetzungsliteratur literature in trans-
    lation [21]
übertreiben, übertrieb, übertrieben to
    exaggerate (13)
überzeugen to convince (25)
übrigens by the way (18)
die Uhr, –en clock (19); um . . . Uhr at . . .
    o'clock (19)
das Uhrenschlagen the striking of clocks
    [22]
um /bilden to transmute [25]
um /bringen, brachte um, umgebracht
    (*irr. wk.*) to kill [14]
um /kippen to turn upside-down [20]
der Umstand, ⸗e circumstance (24); unter
    diesen Umständen under these cir-
    cumstances (24)
s. umwenden, wandte sich um, s. umge-
    wandt (*irr. wk.*) to turn around [14]
unabhängig independent [23]
unangenehm unpleasant [23]
unbedingt absolutely [19]
unbekannt unknown [15]
unbewußt unconscious, subconscious
    (23)
und (*coord. conj.*) and (1)
uneingeladen uninvited [19]
ungeduldig impatient (10)

ungefähr approximately (17)
ungehemmt uninhibited (23)
die Ungerechtigkeit, –en injustice (9)
ungesund unhealthy
unglaublich unbelievable [17] (18)
das Unglück misfortune [18]
unglücklich unhappy [9]; unlucky, ill-
    fated [17]
die Uniform, –en uniform [11]
die Universität, –en university (1)
das Universum universe [10]
unmöglich impossible [16]
unnatürlich unnatural [13]
unnötig unnecessary (12)
unreif unripe; immature (8)
unser, unsere, unser (*poss. adj.*) our (3)
unsicher unsure of (oneself), discon-
    certed [19]
unten (down) below, downstairs [16]
    (18)
unter (*prep. w. dat./acc.*) under, below,
    among (9)
unterbewußt subconscious (23)
unterbrechen, unterbricht, unterbrach,
    unterbrochen to interrupt (20)
unter /bringen, brachte unter, unterge-
    bracht (*irr. wk.*) to put up at [14]
unterdrücken to suppress (7)
untergraben, untergräbt, untergrub, un-
    tergraben to undermine (13)
s. unterhalten, unterhält s., unterhielt s.,
    s. unterhalten (mit) to talk to, con-
    verse, engage in conversation (19);
    s. (gut) unterhalten to have a good
    time (18)
unterliegen, unterlag, unterlegen to un-
    derlie, be subjected to (19)
unterrichten to instruct, teach (12)
unterscheiden, unterschied, unterschieden
    to distinguish (25)
der Unterschied, –e difference (9)
untersuchen to investigate (19); to ex-
    amine [25]
unübersetzbar untranslatable (25)
unweiblich unfeminine (7)
unzählig innumerable (22)
uraufführen to perform for the first time
    [13]
die Uraufführung, –en premiere, first per-
    formance (13)
der Urlaub leave, furlough (16)
die Urpflanze, –n original plant [25]
ursprünglich original(ly) [18] (22)
das Urteil, –e judgement, verdict [16] (17)

die Variation, –en variation [10]
der Vater, ⸗er father [3] (5)

das **Vaterland, ⁼er** fatherland, home (native) country [9]
Venedig Venice [25]
veraltet outdated [20]
s. **verabschieden** to take leave, depart [19]
das **Verb, –en** verb [14]
s. **verbergen, verbirgt s., verbarg s., s. verborgen** to hide (13)
die **Verbeugung, –en** bow [21]
verbieten, verbat, verboten to forbid (19)
verbrennen, verbrannte, verbrannt (*irr. wk.*) to burn (down) [16]
verbringen, verbrachte, verbracht (*irr. wk.*) to spend (14)
verdanken to owe (21)
verdienen to earn (10)
verdorren to dry up, wither (18)
verdrängen to supplant, displace (20); to push aside, suppress (23)
der **Verehrer, –** admirer (7)
die **Vereinigten Staaten** United States [15]
die **Vereinigung, –en** society (8)
der **Verfasser, –** author (21)
s. **verfehlen** to miss one another (11)
verfolgen to pursue [18]
die **Vergangenheit** past (8)
vergehen, verging, ist vergangen to pass; to elapse (5, 24)
vergessen, vergißt, vergaß, vergessen to forget [7] (13)
vergleichen, verglich, verglichen to compare (21); **vergleichend** comparative (25)
s. **verhalten, verhält s., verhielt s., s. verhalten** to behave, act (11)
das **Verhältnis, –se** relationship (8); condition (12)
verheiratet married (3)
verhexen to bewitch [18]
verhindern to prevent [19]
verkaufen to sell (18)
der **Verkäufer, –** salesman (11)
verkennen, verkannte, verkannt (*irr. wk.*) to misjudge [14]
verlangen to demand (8)
verlassen, verläßt, verließ, verlassen to leave (*something*) (7)
verleben to spend one's life (or time) [13]
die **Verlegenheit, –en** embarrassment (15)
der **Verleger, –** publisher (16)
s. **verlieben (in)** to fall in love (with) [11]
verliebt sein to be in love (3)
verlieren, verlor, verloren to lose (7)
s. **verloben** to get engaged [11]
s. **vermehren** to increase [21]

vermögen, vermag, vermochte, vermocht to be able to (17)
vernichten to annihilate, destroy (24)
die **Vernunft** (critical) reason (19)
vernünftig reasonable [17] (19)
veröffentlichen to publish (7)
verrückt crazy [11]
der **Vers, –e** verse [9]
verschieden different (8)
verschlafen sleepy [16]
verschonen to spare [20]
verschwenden to waste (25)
verschwinden, verschwand, ist verschwunden to disappear (21)
versehen, versieht, versah, versehen (mit) to provide (with) (15)
die **Versicherung, –en** insurance (16)
die **Versicherungsgesellschaft, –en** insurance company [16]
Verspätung haben to be late (22)
versprechen, verspricht, versprach, versprochen to promise (6, 8)
der **Verstand** reason, intelligence (19)
verstehen, verstand, verstanden to understand (1, 7)
der **Versuch, –e** attempt, experiment (1)
versuchen to try (10)
verursachen to cause (23)
verwachsen (*p.p.*) deformed, hunchbacked [21]
der **Verwandte, –n, –n** relative [18]
verwenden, verwandte, verwandt (*irr. wk.*) to use [14]
verwildern to lay bare [20]
verwöhnen to spoil [18]
verwüsten to devastate (20)
das **Verzeichnis, –se** table, index, listing [5]
verzichten (auf, *w. acc.*) to renounce (*something*), do without (6)
die **Verzweiflung** despair (5)
der **Veteran, –en, –en** veteran [5]
viel much (4); **viele** many (1)
vielleicht perhaps (4)
vielmehr rather [14]
vier four [4]
vierte fourth [19]
Viertel (vor) quarter . . . (of) [22]
die **Viertelstunde, –n** quarter of an hour (22); **ein Viertelstündchen** a little quarter of an hour [22]
der **Viertelton, ⁼e** quarter tone [17]
vierundzwanzig twenty-four [19]
vierzehn fourteen [14]
die **Violine, –n** violin [17]
der **Vogel, ⁼** bird (22)
das **Volk, ⁼er** people [6] (9)
voll full (of) (3)
vollkommen complete(ly) (20)

vollständig complete (21)

von . . . an (*prep.*) from . . .on (22)

vor (*prep. w. dat./acc.*) in front of (4)

vor allem above all, especially (6)

die Vorarbeit, –en spade work [21]

voraus- (*pref.*) ahead (25)

voraus/sehen, sieht voraus, sah voraus, vorausgesehen to foresee, anticipate (24)

vorbei- (*pref.*) past (18)

das Vorbild, –er model, ideal (12)

der Vorfall, ⸗e occurrence (23)

vor/gehen, ging vor, ist vorgegangen (*of clocks*) to be fast [22]

vorgestern day before yesterday [22]

vorher (*adv.*) before (7)

vorig (*adj. derived from prep.* vor) last, previous (21)

vor/kommen, kam vor, ist vorgekommen to occur; to seem; to strike as (13)

der Vorläufer, – precursor (4)

vor/lesen, liest vor, las vor, vorgelesen (aus) to read out loud (from) (13)

die Vorlesung, –en (university) lecture (12)

der Vormittag, –e forenoon, morning (19)

vormittags in the morning [22]

vornehm refined (8)

vor/schlagen, schlägt vor, schlug vor, vorgeschlagen to suggest (19)

vorsichtig careful [17] (24)

vor/spielen to play to (24)

s. vor/stellen to imagine [13] (22)

das Vorwort, –e foreword, introduction (14)

das Vorzimmer, – antechamber [23]

wachsen, wächst, wuchs, ist gewachsen to grow (12)

der Wagen, – car (12)

der Wagnerianer, – Wagnerian [8]

die Wahl, –en election (15)

wählen to vote, elect (15)

der Wahlkampf, ⸗e election campaign (15)

die Wahlrede, –n election speech [15]

wahr true (3); nicht wahr?, isn't that so?, aren't we (etc.)? [11]

während (*prep. w. gen.*) during [9]; (*conj.*), while [20]

wahrscheinlich probably (14)

der Wald, ⸗er forest (24)

wandern to wander, hike (5)

wann when (3)

war (*from* sein) (he, she, it) was (1)

warm warm (1)

(das) Warschau Warsaw [15]

warten to wait (1); warten auf (w. acc.) to wait for [9]

warum? why? (3)

was für ein what a (3)

waschen, wäscht, wusch, gewaschen to wash (11)

das Wasser, – water (6); zu Wasser by water [18]

die Wasseruhr, –en water clock [22]

wecken to waken, awaken (22)

der Wecker, – alarm (clock) (22)

der Weg, –e way; auf dem Weg on the way (4)

weg- (*pref.*) away (19)

wegen (*prep. w. gen.*) on account of, because of (9)

weg/stoßen, stößt weg, stieß weg, weggestoßen to push away [23]

weg/ziehen, zog weg, ist weggezogen to move away (19)

weh tun (w. dat. of person) to hurt (25)

der Weiberfeind, –e antifeminist [19]

weiblich feminine (7); unweiblich unfeminine (7)

weichen, wich, ist gewichen to yield, subside (23)

(die) Weihnachten (*pl.*) Christmas (8); zu Weihnachten for Christmas (8)

weil (*subord. conj.*) because [20]

Weile: eine Weile a while (1)

der Wein, –e wine [18]

weinen to cry (5)

weise wise [11]

der Weise, –n, –n wise man (5)

die Weise, –n manner (6); auf seine (ihre, *etc.*) Weise in his (her, *etc.*) manner (6)

weisen, wies, gewiesen to point (10)

die Weisheit, –en wisdom (5)

weiß white [13]

weiß (*from* wissen) I, he know(s) (*for a fact*) (3)

weit wide (2); far (14)

weiter (*adj.*) further (24); (*pref.*) on, to go on doing; weiter/fischen to go on fishing [15], weiter/leben to live on [23]

welcher, welche, welches which (2)

die Welt, –en world (9)

weltberühmt world-famous [17]

die Weltgeschichte world history [13]

der Weltkrieg, –e world war (6)

s. wenden, wandte (wendete), gewandt (gewendet) (*irr. wk.*) (an w. acc.) to turn to (14)

wenig little (*in quantity*) (4); ein wenig a little (4)

wenigstens at least (25)

wenn (*subord. conj.*) if (6); wenn . . . auch even if [20]

wer? who? (1)

werden, wird, wurde, ist geworden (zu) to become (12)

werfen, wirft, warf, geworfen (nach) to throw (at) (13), cast [18]

das **Werk, –e** work [8]

wert worth (20)

der **Wert, –e** value (10)

wertlos worthless (10)

wesentlich essential (25)

der **Westen** West [13]

die **Wette, –n** wager, bet [7]

das **Wetter** weather (23)

wichtig important (16)

der **Widerspruch, ≈e** contradiction (11)

wie(?) how (1); like, as (4); (*in questions*) isn't it? [15]

wieder again, back (2); (*pref.*) back (18)

wieder /entdecken to rediscover [21]

wieder /gewinnen, gewann wieder, wieder-gewonnen to win back [15]

auf Wiedersehen good-by (1)

wiegen to weigh (22)

(das) **Wien** Vienna [12]

der **Wiener, –** Viennese [23]

wieviel how much [14]; **(um) wieviel Uhr** (at) what time [22]; **wie viele** how many [15]; **am wievielten?** on what day [21]

will (*from* wollen) (I, he) want(s) (6)

der **Wille, (gen.) –ns** will [12]

der **Wind, –e** wind [23]

der **Winter, –** winter [14]

der **Winterabend, –e** winter evening [14]

der **Wirbel, –** vertebra [25]

wirken to have an effect (8)

wirklich really (3)

die **Wirklichkeit** reality [13] (20)

der **Wirt, –e** host (15)

das **Wirtshaus, ≈er** inn (22)

wissen, weiß, wußte, gewußt to know (10, 14)

die **Wissenschaft, –en** (natural) science (6)

der **Wissenschaftler, –** scientist (10)

wissenschaftlich scientific [12]

die **Witwe, –n** widow [5]

der **Witz, –e** wit, humor (9)

wo where (1)

woanders somewhere else (16)

die **Woche, –n** week (6)

das **Wochenende, –n** weekend [8]

wohl well (9); probably (11)

wohnen to live (4)

das **Wohnzimmer, –** living room (22)

die **Wolke, –n** cloud (18)

wollen, will, wollte, gewollt (*mod. aux.*) to want to (6, 17); **er wollte** he wanted to (10)

das **Wort, –e** (*also* **Wörter**) word (1)

das **Wörterbuch, ≈er** dictionary [20]

der **Wortschatz** vocabulary (1)

wunderbar wonderful(ly) (3)

das **Wunderkind, –er** child prodigy [17]

wundern to surprise [11]; **s. wundern** (**über** *w. acc.*) to be surprised (about) (11), marvel at (17)

der **Wunsch, ≈e** wish (3)

wünschen to wish (2)

würdig worthy, dignified (16)

die **Wurst, ≈e** sausage (14)

wütend furious, angry (17)

die **Zahl, –en** number (15)

zählen to count (10)

zahllos innumerable (15)

zehn ten (7)

das **Zeichen, –** sign [14]

die **Zeichensprache, –n** sign language [14]

zeichnen to draw (15)

die **Zeichnung, –en** drawing (15)

zeigen to show (1); point (10); **s. zeigen** to appear [11]

die **Zeit, –en** time (5); **die ganze Zeit** the whole time (7); **zur Zeit** at the moment [10]; **eine Zeitlang** for a while (16)

das **Zeitalter, –** age (7)

der **Zeitgenosse, –n, –n** contemporary (12)

die **Zeitschrift, –en** periodical (13)

die **Zeitung, –en** newspaper [15] (17)

zerstören to destroy (7)

zerstreut absent-minded (19)

die **Zertrümmerung, –en** smashing [5]

ziehen, zog, (ist) gezogen (*trans.*) to pull (2); (*intrans.*) to move (19)

das **Ziel, –e** goal (24)

ziemlich rather (11)

die **Zigarre, –n** cigar (2)

das **Zimmer, –** room (3)

der **Zirkel, –** circle [18]

das **Zitat, –e** quote, quotation (7)

zittern to tremble (2)

zögern to hesitate (6)

zu (*prep. w. dat.*) to (1); (*adv.*) too (4); **zu sich nehmen** to partake (of) (19)

zu /bringen, brachte zu, zugebracht (*irr. wk.*) to spend [14]

zuerst (at) first (12)

zufrieden satisfied (10)

der **Zug, ≈e** train (15)

zu /geben, gibt zu, gab zu, zugegeben to admit [13]

zu /hören to listen (to) [17]

zu /kommen (auf *w. acc.***), kam zu, ist zugekommen** to come toward, walk up]15[

die **Zukunft** future (8)

zuletzt finally, in the end, last (15); **bis zuletzt** to the end [18]

zunächst first (of all) (15); for the time being (24)

zu /rechnen to count among (to) [18]

zurück back (4)

zurück /bringen, **brachte zurück, zurückgebracht** (*irr. wk.*) to bring back [24]

zurück /gehen (**auf** *w. acc.*), **ging zurück, ist zurückgegangen** to go back to [25]

zurück /halten, **hält zurück, hielt zurück, zurückgehalten** to hold back

zurück /kehren to return (25)

zurück /rufen, **rief zurück, zurückgerufen** to call back; to recall [23]

zurück /schleichen, **schlich zurück, ist zurückgeschlichen** to sneak back [24]

zusammen together (10)

die **Zusammenarbeit** collaboration (23)

zusammen /kommen, **kam zusammen, ist zusammengekommen** to get together, gather [13]

zusammen /leben to live together [20]

zusammen /wachsen, **wächst zusammen, ist zusammengewachsen** to grow together [25]

der **Zustand,** ⸗e condition (20)

s. zu /wenden, **wandte s. zu, s. zugewandt** (*irr. wk.*) to turn to [14]

zwanzig twenty (15); **die zwanziger Jahre** the twenties [21]

zwar to be sure (9); to be specific (17)

der **Zweck, –e** purpose (14)

zwei two (2)

zweihundert two hundred [15]

zweimal twice [19]

zweite second (1)

zweitens in the second place, secondly [21]

zwinkern to wink (1)

zwischen (*prep. w. dat. /acc.*) between (9)

der **Zwischenkieferknochen,** – intermaxillary bone [25]

zwölf twelve [12]

Numbers given in brackets indicate the lesson in which the English word occurs for the first time.

able: to be able to können (*mod. aux.*) (17)
about über (*prep. w. dat. or acc.*) (9)
above all vor allem (25)
act handeln (19); **act (as if)** tun (als ob) (24)
add hinzufügen (23)
address die Adresse, –n (3)
admire bewundern (8)
advice der Rat; der Ratschlag, ⁼e (8)
afraid: be afraid of sich fürchten vor (*w. dat.*) (12)
after nach (*prep. w. dat.*) (13); nachdem (*conj.*) (20)
again wieder (2)
against gegen (*prep. w. acc.*) (10)
ago vor (*prep. w. dat.*) (22)
air die Luft, ⁼e (2)
all (the) alle (5)
along mit (*pref.*) (23)
already schon (21)
also auch (4)
although obgleich (*conj.*) (20)
always immer (2)
America (das) Amerika (15)
American amerikanisch (21); (*noun*) der Amerikaner, – (11)
among unter (*prep. w. dat. or acc.*) (9)
angry böse (3); **get angry** s. ärgern (11)
announce an/kündigen (17)
another ein anderer; noch einer (23)
answer die Antwort, –en (1)
answer antworten (1); (*a question*) (eine Frage) beantworten (3)
any: (not) . . . any kein, keine, kein (4)
anybody: (not) . . . anybody keiner, keine, kein (8)
anymore: not . . . anymore nicht mehr (12)
anything: not . . . anything nichts (6)
appearance die Erscheinung, –en (13)
aria die Arie, –n (17)
around (*approximately*) gegen (22)
arrive an/kommen, kam an, ist angekommen (13)
art die Kunst, ⁼e (5)
artist der Künstler, – (8)
as wie (22)
as . . . as so . . . wie (4)
ask fragen (1); **ask for** bitten, bat, gebeten (um) (9)
assume an/nehmen, nimmt an, nahm an, angenommen (23)
at (*time*) um (22)
attack angreifen, griff an, angegriffen (18)
attempt der Versuch, –e (24)

August der August (21)
aunt die Tante, –n (7)
Austria (das) Österreich (20)
avoid vermeiden (ie, ie) (25)
away weg (*pref.*) (22)

bee die Biene, –n (18)
bean die Bohne, –n (18)
bear der Bär, –en (18)
beautiful schön (8)
because denn (*coord. conj.*), weil (*subord. conj.*) (20)
become (of) werden, wird, wurde, ist geworden (aus) (6)
bed das Bett, –en (5)
before bevor (*conj.*) (22)
begin beginnen (a, o); an/fangen, fängt an fing an, angefangen (21)
behind hinter (*prep. w. dat. or acc.*) (9)
believe (in) glauben (an, *w. acc.*) (1)
bell (*see:* **ring a bell**)
belong gehören (*w. dat.*) (13)
best der, die, das beste (16)
better besser (16)
between zwischen (*prep. w. dat. or acc.*) (9)
birthday der Geburtstag, –e (7)
blue blau (14)
bone der Knochen, – (25)
book das Buch, ⁼er (7)
both beide (4)
bottle die Flasche, –n (23)
boy der Junge, –n (18)
breakfast das Frühstück, –e (15)
bring bringen (*irr. wk.*) (18); **bring along** mit/bringen, brachte mit, mitgebracht (14)
brother der Bruder, ⁼ (15)
burn (*something*) verbrennen (*irr. wk.*) (13); **burn oneself** s. verbrennen (*irr. wk.*) (14)
business das Geschäft, –e (7)
but aber (*coord. conj.*) (1)
buy kaufen (3)
by (*authorship*) von (*prep. w. dat.*) (9); (*agency*) durch (*prep. w. acc.*) (18)

cake der Kuchen, – (7)
call rufen (ie, u) (3); (*to name*) nennen (irr. wk.) (25); **to be called** heißen (ie, ei) (2)
can *see:* **be able to**
candidate der Kandidat, –en, –en (16)
car das Auto, –s (5)
careful vorsichtig (24)
case: in any case auf jeden Fall (24)

castle das Schloß, Schlösser (5)
catch fangen (ä, i, a) (18); **catch cold** s.
  erkälten (15)
celebrate feiern (22)
center der Mittelpunkt, –e (20)
chair der Stuhl, ⸗e (23)
change ändern (6)
cheap billig (16)
child das Kind, –er (1)
Christmas die Weihnachten (*pl.*) (22)
church die Kirche, –n (12)
cigar die Zigarre, –n (2)
citizen der Bürger, – (12)
city die Stadt, ⸗e (10)
claim behaupten (25)
clearly klar (13)
climb klettern (18)
close schließen, schloß, geschlossen (2)
closely genau (13)
cloth das Tuch, ⸗er (14)
cold kalt (7)
collect sammeln (19)
collection die Sammlung, –en (12)
color die Farbe, –n (14)
come kommen, kam, ist gekommen (1);
  come back zurück /kommen, kam zurück,
  ist zurückgekommen (13)
compartment das Abteil, –e (2)
compose komponieren (17)
concert das Konzert, –e (17)
conductor der Schaffner, – (2)
conjunction die Konjunktion, –en (20)
conquer erobern (24)
consider halten (ä, ie, a) für (25)
convince überzeugen (25)
corner die Ecke, –n (2)
correct(ly) richtig (13)
country das Land, ⸗er (5)
cry weinen (17)
cultural kulturell (20)
cut schneiden, schnitt, geschnitten (7)

danger die Gefahr, –en (22)
dark dunkel (22)
daughter die Tochter, ⸗ (5)
day der Tag, –e (9); **one day** eines Tages (13)
declare erklären (24)
defend verteidigen (24)
demand verlangen (16)
describe beschreiben (ie, ie) (13)
description die Beschreibung, –en (12)
desk der Schreibtisch, –e (18)
destroy zerstören (20)
devastate zerstören (20)
develop entwickeln (23)
development die Entwicklung, –en (20)
die sterben (i, a, o, ist) (12)
difference der Unterschied, –e (9)

different verschieden (25)
difficult schwer (15)
discover entdecken (23)
discuss diskutieren (6)
displace verdrängen (20)
distinguish unterscheiden (ie, ie) (25)
distraction die Ablenkung, –en (25)
do machen, tun (tat, getan) (1)
doctor der Arzt, ⸗e (14)
doll die Puppe, –n (5)
door die Tür, –en (5)
dress das Kleid, –er (5)
drink trinken (a, u) (18)
during während (*prep. w. gen.*) (9)

ear das Ohr, –en (5)
early früh (13)
earn verdienen (10)
Easter (das) Ostern (22)
easy, easily leicht (11)
eat essen, ißt, aß, gegessen (3)
either . . . or entweder . . . oder (20)
end das Ende, –n (5); (*verb*) zu Ende gehen
  (20)
enemy der Feind, –e (10)
enjoy genießen, genoß, genossen (25)
enough genug (10)
especially besonders (6)
estimate schätzen (20)
Europe (das) Europa (12)
even selbst, sogar (11)
evening der Abend, –e (21)
every jeder, jede, jedes (2)
everybody jeder (7)
everyone jeder (4)
everything alles (17)
everywhere überall (11)
exact genau (12)
example das Beispiel, –e (6)
excuse entschuldigen (1)
exist (*construction with* geben): es gibt (11)
expect erwarten (8)
expensive teuer (16)
experience das Erlebnis, –se (12)
experiment das Experiment, –e (24)
explain erklären (6)
express oneself sich ausdrücken (13)
extremely äußerst (16)
eye das Auge, –n (5)

fact die Tatsache, –n (24)
fairy tale das Märchen, – (20)
fall hin /fallen, fällt hin, fiel hin, ist hingefallen (13)
family die Familie, –n (3)
famous berühmt (12)
farmer der Bauer, –n (14)

fast schnell (7); **to be fast** (*of a clock*) vor/gehen, ging vor, ist vorgegangen (22)
fat dick (15)
father der Vater, = (4)
fetch holen (4); **fetch back** wieder/holen (13)
few: a few (*not many*) wenige (11); (*more than one*) einige (13)
find finden (a, u) (5)
finish beenden, fertig machen (25)
first zuerst (6); **in the first place** erstens
five fünf (21)
flee fliehen (o, o) (ist) (24)
flour das Mehl (23)
fly fliegen (o, o) (ist) (12)
follow folgen (*w. dat.*) (19)
for für (*prep. w. acc.*) (4)
forest der Wald, =er (5)
forget vergessen, vergißt, vergaß, vergessen (7)
formerly früher (14)
freedom die Freiheit, –en (9)
freeze frieren (o, o) (7)
French französisch; **in French** auf französisch (9)
Frenchman der Franzose, –n (9)
Friday der Freitag, –e (21)
friend der Freund, –e (4)
frightened: get frightened erschrecken, erschrickt, erschrak, ist erschrocken (12)
from von (*prep. w. dat.*) (5)
front: in front of vor (*prep. w. dat. or acc.*) (9)
full voll (21)

garage die Garage, –n (16)
garden der Garten, = (14)
gay lustig (21)
gentleman der Herr, –n, –en (5)
German Deutsch (1); **the German** der Deutsche, –n, –n (9)
Germany (das) Deutschland (12)
get (*become*) werden, wird, wurde, ist geworden (1); (*receive*) bekommen, bekam, bekommen (5); **get frightened** erschrecken, erschrickt, erschrak, ist erschrocken (12); **get to know** kennen/lernen (9); **get used to** s. gewöhnen an (12); **get up** auf/stehen, stand auf, ist aufgestanden (14); (*fetch*) holen (4)
girl das Mädchen, – (1)
girl friend die Freundin, –nen (5)
give geben (i, a, e) (10); (*as a present*) schenken (10)
go gehen, ging, ist gegangen (1); reisen (9); **go to sleep** ein/schlafen, schläft ein, schlief ein, ist eingeschlafen (12)
goal das Ziel, –e (24)

Goethe bone der Goetheknochen, – (25)
good gut (4)
grammar die Grammatik, –en (21)
grandmother die Großmutter, = (13)
greet grüßen (8)
grow wachsen (ä, u, a) (ist) (7)

half die Hälfte, –n (7)
hand die Hand, =e (3)
happen geschehen (ie, a, e) (ist) (11)
happy glücklich; **to be happy about** sich freuen über (11)
have haben (3); **have** (*something done*) lassen, läßt, ließ, gelassen (23); **have to** müssen (17)
healthy gesund (3)
hear hören (4); **(of)** (von) (19)
heat die Hitze (3)
her ihr, ihre, ihr (3)
here hier (4)
high hoch (15)
him ihm (*dat.*) (6); ihn (*acc.*) (6)
his sein, seine, sein (3)
history die Geschichte (19)
home nach Hause (14); **at home** zu Hause (8)
honest ehrlich (5)
hope hoffen (20)
hotel das Hotel, –s (5)
hour die Stunde, –n (19)
house das Haus, =er (3)
hospital das Krankenhaus, =er (17)
how? wie? (7); **how are you?** wie gehts? wie geht es Ihnen? (8)
however wie auch immer (23)
human being der Mensch, –en, –en (3)

if wenn (*conj.*) (24)
illness die Krankheit, –en (14)
imitate imitieren (6)
immediately sofort (14)
impossible unmöglich (17)
impression der Eindruck, =e (5)
inhabitant der Einwohner, – (20)
instead of anstatt (*prep. w. gen.*) (25)
intelligent intelligent (16)
intend beabsichtigen (6)
interested: be interested in s. interessieren für (*w. acc.*) (12)
interesting interessant (9)
interrupt unter/brechen, unterbricht, unterbrach, unterbrochen (20)
into in (*prep. w. acc.*) (6)
invent erfinden, erfand, erfunden (18)
investigate untersuchen (25)
invite ein/laden, lädt ein, lud ein, eingeladen (19)

jump springen (a, u) (ist) (6)
just gerade (16)

kill ermorden (13)
kind: what kind of? was für (ein) (8)
king der König, –e (6)
kitchen die Küche, –n (22)
kitchen clock die Küchenuhr, –en (22)
knock (on) klopfen (an, *w. acc.*) (5); **there is a knock on the door** es klopft (11)
know (*be acquainted with*) kennen (*irr. wk.*) (22); (*a fact*) (**of**) wissen, weiß, wußte, gewußt (über) (25); **I know** (*a thing*) ich weiß; **he knows** (*a thing*) er weiß (4); **to get to know** kennen /lernen (13)

lady die Dame, –n (2)
landlady die Wirtin, –nen (5)
language die Sprache, –n (15)
large groß (15)
last letzt (19)
last (*verb*) dauern (19)
late spät (19)
laugh lachen (3)
lead führen (5)
leaf das Blatt, ⸗er (25)
learn lernen (6)
leave weg/gehen, ging weg, ist weggegangen (17)
lecture die Vorlesung, –en (12)
less weniger (16)
lesson die Aufgabe, –n (25)
letter der Brief, –e (7)
library die Bibliothek, –en (2)
Lido der Lido (*beach near Venice*) (25)
lie liegen, lag, gelegen (5)
life das Leben (9)
light das Licht, –er (25)
lightning der Blitz, –e (18)
lightning rod der Blitzableiter, – (12)
like gefallen, gefällt, gefiel, gefallen (*impers.*) (7); mögen, mag, mochte, gemocht (17); **I would like to** ich möchte (23); **like to** (*w. verb*): **like to eat** gern essen (3); **like best** am liebsten (*w. verb*) (16)
liquor der Schnaps, ⸗e (13)
listener der Zuhörer, – (25)
little (*in size*) klein (15); (*in quantity*) (ein) wenig (10)
live leben (5); wohnen (2)
living room das Wohnzimmer, – (5)
long (*adj.*) lang (15); **all day long** den ganzen Tag (22); (*adv.*) lange (12)
look (as if) aus /sehen, sieht aus, sah aus, ausgesehen (als ob) (24); **be looking for** suchen (9)
look forward to s. freuen auf (*w. acc.*) (11)
love die Liebe (9); **to love** lieben (8); **to fall in love** s. verlieben (16)

man der Mann, ⸗er (2)
manner: in the manner of aufs . . . (*w. superlative*) (16)
many viele (4); **many a** mancher, manch ein (2)
March der März (21)
marry; get married heiraten (6)
matter die Sache, –n (24)
may *see:* mögen (*mod. aux.*) (23); dürfen (*mod. aux.*) (17)
me mich (*acc.*) (1)
mean meinen (4)
meet s. treffen, trifft sich, traf sich, sich getroffen (11)
merchant der Kaufmann, Kaufleute (5)
messenger der Bote, –n (6)
method die Methode, –n (18)
Middle Ages das Mittelalter (5)
milk die Milch (11)
million die Million, –en (20)
mind die Meinung, –en (6)
minute die Minute, –n (22)
model das Vorbild, –er (12)
modern modern (15)
moment der Augenblick, –e (2)
money das Geld, –er (10)
moon der Mond, –e (12); **moon chart** die Mondkarte, –n (12)
more mehr (20)
most die meisten (16)
mother die Mutter, ⸗ (3)
mountain der Berg, –e (16)
mouth: keep one's mouth shut den Mund halten (10)
movies das Kino, –s (21)
Mr. Herr (1)
much viel (9)
museum das Museum, Museen (5)
music die Musik (6)
must *see:* müssen (*mod. aux.*) (19)
my mein, meine, mein (3)

name der Name, –ns, –n (3)
nearby in der Nähe (8)
necktie die Krawatte, –n (11)
never nie, niemals (20)
new neu (5)
news die Nachrichten (*pl.*) (24)
next der, die, das nächste (16)
nice nett (4)
night: at night abends (22)
no (*adj.*) kein, keine, kein (3)
nobody keiner, keine, keins; kein Mensch; niemand (4)
noise das Geräusch, –e (12)
nonsense der Unsinn (25)
not nicht (1); **not a** kein, keine, kein (3)
nothing nichts (10)

novel der Roman, –e (11)
now nun, jetzt (1)

object (against) ein /wenden (gegen), wandte
  ein, eingewandt (eingewendet) (*irr. wk.*)
  (14)
observation die Beobachtung, –en (12)
o'clock um (gegen) . . . Uhr (22)
office das Büro, –s (17)
often oft (6)
old alt; **the old man** der Alte, –n, –n (15)
once (*enumerative*) einmal; (*in the past*) einst
  (25); **once again** noch einmal (13); **once
  more** noch einmal (25)
one (*adj.*) ein, eine, ein (4) (*pronoun*) einer
  eine, eins (4); (*impers. pronoun*) man (15);
  one's sein, seine, sein (3)
only nur (2)
open offen (15); **to open** öffnen (2)
opinion die Meinung, –en (6)
order der Befehl, –e (5); **in order to** um . . .
  zu (25)
original plant die Urpflanze, –n (25)
originate entstehen, entstand, ist entstanden
  (12)
other ander– (16)
our unser, unsere, unser (3)
oven der Ofen, = (14)
own eigen (15); **to own** besitzen, besaß,
  besessen (23)

pack packen (4)
page die Seite, –n (21)
palace der Palast, =e (5)
pancake der Pfannkuchen, – (23)
paper (*news*) die Zeitung, –en (17)
parents die Eltern (3)
part der Teil, –e (21)
peace der Friede(n) (5)
peasant der Bauer, –n (14)
pencil der Bleistift, –e (1)
people (*collective*) die Leute (5)
performance die Aufführung, –en; **first performance** die Uraufführung, –en (13)
periodical die Zeitschrift, –en (13)
personal(ly) persönlich (13)
phenomenon das Phänomen, –e (25)
philosopher der Philosoph, –en, –en (19)
photograph fotografieren (6)
physician der Arzt, =e (11)
piano das Klavier, –e (17)
picture das Bild, –er (23)
place: in the first place erstens (21)
plan der Plan, =e (19)
plant pflanzen (18)
play (*drama*) das Stück, –e (9); (*verb*) spielen (4)
please gefallen (ä, ie, a) (*impers.*) (13);
  please! bitte! (3)

plunder plündern (20)
poem das Gedicht, –e (9)
poet der Dichter, – (13)
poetry die Dichtung, –en (25)
poke fun at s. lustig machen über (11)
police die Polizei (18)
polite höflich (16)
poor arm (10)
popular beliebt (16)
position die Stellung, –en (16)
pound das Pfund, –e (21)
preach predigen (12)
precursor der Vorläufer, – (12)
prefer to lieber (*w. verb*) (16)
pretty hübsch (4)
problem das Problem, –e (5)
produce herstellen (13)
properly richtig (20)
prove beweisen (ie, ie) (12)
public: in public öffentlich (18)
punctual pünktlich (20)
put up unter /bringen, brachte unter, untergebracht (*irr. wk.*) (14); **put up with** s.
  gefallen lassen (ä, ie, a) (17)

question die Frage, –n (1)

radio das Radio, –s (18)
read lesen (ie, a, e) (7); **read out loud**
  vor /lesen (ie, a, e) (13)
really wirklich (3)
reason der Grund, =e (25)
reasonable vernünftig (19)
receive erhalten, erhält, erhielt, erhalten
  (10); bekommen, bekam, bekommen (15)
recognize erkennen, erkannte, erkannt (*irr.
  wk.*) (13)
region die Gegend, –en (16)
relative pronoun das Relativpronomen, –
  (19)
remain bleiben, blieb, ist geblieben (5)
remember s. erinnern (11)
remind of erinnern an (*w. acc.*) (22)
repeat wiederholen (13)
request die Bitte, –n (14)
restaurant das Restaurant, –s (7)
review wiederholen (23)
rich reich (15)
right: all right with me meinetwegen (8)
ring (*a bell*) klingeln (*impers.*) (13)
rock der Stein, –e (19)
room das Zimmer, – (4)
run laufen (äu, ie, au) (ist) (7); **run away**
  weg /laufen, läuft weg, lief weg, ist weg-
  gelaufen (14)

sake: for . . . sake . . . wegen; **for her sake**
  ihretwegen (8)

same derselbe, dieselbe, dasselbe (1)
satisfied zufrieden (10)
say sagen (1); **be said to** sollen
school die Schule, –n (19); **in school** in der
  Schule (19); **school year** das Schuljahr, –e
  (22)
science die Wissenschaft, –en (10)
scientific wissenschaftlich (25)
scientist der Wissenschaftler, – (12)
scream schreien (ie, ie) (2)
seat der Platz, ≈e (4)
second der, die, das zweite (21); **secondly**
  zweitens (21)
secret das Geheimnis, –se (5)
see sehen (ie, a, e) (5)
send schicken (6); **send for** schicken nach,
  senden nach (14)
sentence der Satz, ≈e (20)
September der September (21)
set (*a watch*) stellen (20)
to shake schütteln; **shake someone's hand**
  jemandem die Hand schütteln (10)
share teilen (23)
she sie (1)
sheep das Schaf, –e (25)
shirt das Hemd, –en (5)
shop das Geschäft, –e (11)
short kurz (5)
should *see:* sollen (*mod. aux.*) (19)
similar ähnlich (19)
simple einfach (16)
sing singen (a, u) (17)
sit sitzen, saß, gesessen (3); **sit down** s.
  setzen (11)
situation die Situation, –en, die Lage, –n
  (20)
skeleton das Skelett, –e (25)
sleep: go to sleep ein/schlafen (ä, ie, a) (12)
slow(ly) langsam (1); **to be slow** (*of a watch*)
  nach/gehen (i, a) (ist) (22)
small klein (5)
smile lächeln (1)
smoke rauchen (2)
smoker der Raucher, – (4)
sneak schleichen (i, i) ist (24)
society die Gesellschaft, –en (19)
soldier der Soldat, –en, –en (5)
solve lösen (18)
some (*w. noun in sing.*) etwas; (*w. noun in pl.*)
  einige (6)
somebody jemand (25)
something etwas (12); **something else** etwas
  anderes
sometimes manchmal (6)
song das Lied, –er (9)
soon bald (23)
so that so daß (20)
speak sprechen (i, a, o) (7)

spend verbringen, verbrachte, verbracht (*irr.*
  wk.) (13)
spirit der Geist, –er (23)
spoil verwöhnen (18)
spring der Frühling, –e (21)
stand stehen, stand, gestanden (9)
stay bleiben (ie, ie) ist (7)
stir rühren (23)
stop auf/hören (13)
storm der Sturm, ≈e; das Gewitter, – (24)
story die Geschichte, –n (4)
strange sonderbar (15)
street die Straße, –n (13)
strong stark (16)
student der Student, –en, –en (2)
study studieren (1)
subjunctive der Konjunktiv, –e (23)
succeed gelingen (a, u) ist (*impers.*); **I suc-**
  ceed es gelingt mir (11)
such a solcher, solche, solches; ein solcher,
  eine solche, ein solches (3)
suffer leiden, litt, gelitten (10)
suffocate ersticken (2)
suitcase der Koffer, – (4)
summer der Sommer, – (22)
Sunday der Sonntag, –e (12)
sure of sicher (*w. gen.*) (8); **surely** sicher (25)
surprised erstaunt (3)
swear schwören (o, o) (24)

take nehmen, nimmt, nahm, genommen
  (19); **take amiss** übel/nehmen, nimmt
  übel, nahm übel, übelgenommen (13);
  take a trip eine Reise machen (19)
talk about reden (3); sprechen (i, a, o)
  (über *w. acc.*) (19)
technique die Technik (6)
telephone telefonieren (6)
telescope das Fernrohr, –e (10)
tell (about) erzählen (von) (4); (*make a*
  statement) sagen (17)
ten zehn (22)
terrible schrecklich, furchtbar (3)
than als (16)
thank you! danke (schön)! (1)
that das (1)
the . . . the je . . . desto (16)
theater das Theater, – (6)
theory die Theorie, –n (25)
there dort (7); da (14); **– is (are)** es gibt (15)
thing: one thing ein(e)s (4)
think denken, dachte, gedacht (*irr. wk.*);
  glauben (23); **think about** nach/denken
  (über *w. acc.*) (*irr. wk.*) (14)
third der, die, das dritte (21); (*noun*) das
  Drittel, – (21)
Thirty Years War der Dreißigjährige Krieg
  (21)

this dieser, diese, dieses (*pl.* diese) (2)
thought der Gedanke, –ns, –n (5)
three drei (21)
thrive gedeihen (ie, ie) ist (7)
through durch (*prep. w. acc.*) (10)
time die Zeit, –en (5); (*enumerative*) das Mal,
    –e; **three times** dreimal (21); **for a long**
    time lange (12); **on time** pünktlich (13);
    at that time zu der Zeit, damals (11);
    this time diesmal (18)
to zu (*prep. w. dat.*) (5)
today heute (4)
together zusammen (10)
tomorrow morgen (11); **tomorrow morning**
    morgen früh (22)
tonight heute abend (25)
too zu; **too much** zuviel (7)
town die Stadt, ⸗e (11); **in town** in der Stadt
    (17)
train der Zug, ⸗e (22)
translate übersetzen (18)
treatment die Behandlung, –en (23)
tree der Baum, ⸗e (24)
trip die Reise, –n (12)
trust (ver)trauen (*with dat.*) (24)
truth die Wahrheit, –en (25)
try versuchen (24)
turn around s. umwenden, wandte sich um,
    sich umgewandt (*irr. wk.*) (14)
twelve zwölf (22)
two zwei (5)

unbelievable unglaublich (18)
uncle der Onkel, – (9)
understand verstehen (a, a) (1)
university die Universität, –en (2)
unrest die Unruhe, –n (11)
until bis (20)
upstairs oben (18)
us uns (6)
use gebrauchen (20); **get used to** s. ge-
    wöhnen an (12)
usually gewöhnlich (15)

valley das Tal, ⸗er (5)
value (as) schätzen (als) (6)
very sehr (1)
Vienna (das) Wien (20)
village das Dorf, ⸗er (5)
visit der Besuch, –e (11); (*verb*) besuchen (2)

wait (for) warten (auf, *w. acc.*) (1)
walk gehen, ging, ist gegangen (1)
wander wandern (5)

want to wollen (*mod. aux.*) (17)
war der Krieg, –e (20)
warm warm (1)
wash waschen (ä, u, a); **wash one's hands**
    s. die Hände waschen (11)
waste verschwenden (25)
watch die Uhr, –en (20)
water das Wasser, – (6)
way der Weg, –e (5)
we wir (1)
weather das Wetter, – (7)
week die Woche, –n (9); **for a week now**
    seit einer Woche (9)
well gut (6); **be well** gesund sein, s. gut
    fühlen (20)
what was? (1); **what a** was für ein (3); **what**
    for? wofür?, warum? (6)
where wo? (1)
whether ob (14)
which (*rel.*) der, die, das; welcher, welche,
    welches (25); (*interr.*) welcher? welche?
    welches? (2)
while: for a while eine Weile (14)
who wer (2)
whoever wer (19)
why warum (3)
wife die Frau, –en (17)
window das Fenster, – (2)
wise man der Weise, –n, –n (5)
wish der Wunsch, ⸗e (3)
witch die Hexe, –n (13)
with mit (*prep. w. dat.*) (5)
without ohne (*prep. w. acc.*) (9)
woman die Frau, –en (16)
wonder s. fragen (20)
wonderful wunderbar (3)
woods der Wald, ⸗er (24)
word das Wort, –e *or* ⸗er (6)
work die Arbeit, –en (13); (*as an accom-*
    plished piece) das Werk,–e (23); **work of**
    art das Kunstwerk, –e (8); (*verb*) arbeiten
    (8)
would be wäre (23)
would like to möchte (23)
wrist watch die Armbanduhr, –en (22)
write schreiben (ie, ie) (9)
writer der Schriftsteller, – (12)
wrong falsch (25)

year das Jahr, –e (7)
yesterday gestern (21)
you Sie (1)
young jung (15)
your Ihr (3)

Index

(Numbers refer to pages. No reference has been made to Recapitulations of Main Points and to Reviews.)

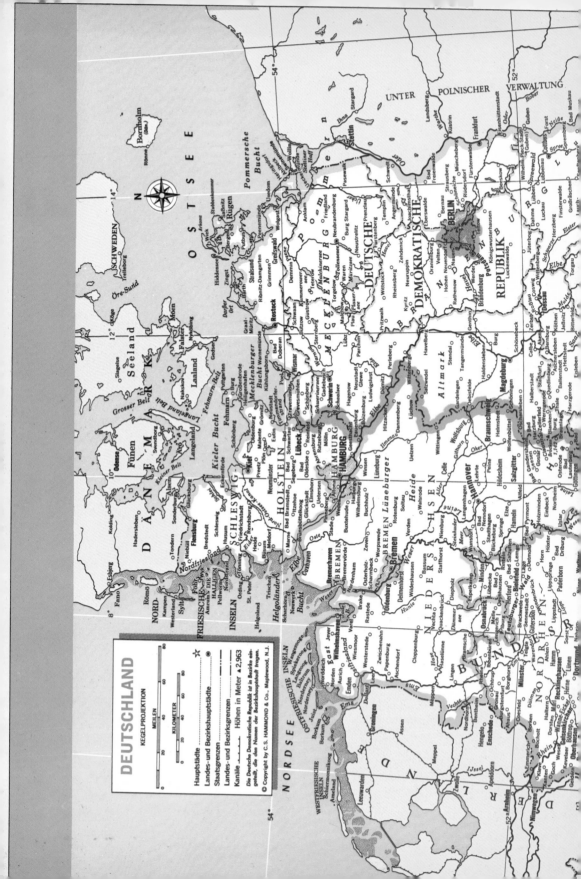